Reconciling Domestic Property Regimes and International Investment Protection

Nijhoff International Investment Law Series

VOLUME 30

The titles published in this series are listed at *brill.com/iils*

Reconciling Domestic Property Regimes and International Investment Protection

Origins, Comparisons and Contestations

By

Inga Martinkute

BRILL | NIJHOFF

ISSN 2351-9542
ISBN 978-90-04-76344-9
ISBN 978-90-04-76351-7 (PDF)
DOI https://doi.org/10.1163/9789004763517

Library of Congress Control Number: 2026906703

Brill Nijhoff and Koninklijke Brill BV are part of De Gruyter Brill.
www.degruyterbrill.com

Questions about General Product Safety Regulation: productsafety@degruyterbrill.com.

Contents

Acknowledgements

I would like to express gratitude to Professor M. Sornarajah and Professor Wang Jiangyu for their encouragement and guidance throughout the Ph D programme. I am also grateful to Associate Professor Jean Ho, Professor Joseph H H Weiler and Professor David Schneiderman for their generous engagement with my work and for their valuable comments.

I was fortunate to spend my time in Singapore among outstanding scholars and colleagues, including Professors James E Penner, Damian Chalmers and Michael G Bridge, and Associate Professors Gary Bell, N Jansen Calamita, J Christopher Thomas, Eliana Cusato and others, whose advice and support I greatly appreciated.

Through ESIL, I had the privilege of meeting many remarkable individuals, including Pierre d'Argent, Gleider Hernández and Christian J Tams, who have been a continual source of academic inspiration and practical support, particularly in navigating legal questions arising from Russia's unlawful attack on Ukraine.

I am grateful to Selma Hoedt from Brill, the series editors and the anonymous reviewer for beneficial feedback. I also thank my long-time friend Audra Durham for her careful proofreading of successive drafts and for her many helpful suggestions.

Finally, and most importantly, I thank my family – Andrius, Sofija, Teo, my parents and my father-in-law – for their steadfast love, patience and support. This book would not have been possible without them.

Abbreviations

AfCHPR	African Charter on Human and Peoples' Rights
ACHR	American Convention on Human Rights
BITs	Bilateral investment treaties
BGB	German Civil Code
CETA	EU–Canada Comprehensive Economic and Trade Agreement
DCFR	Draft Common Frame of Reference
EU	European Union
ECHR	European Convention on Human Rights
ECtHR	European Court of Human Rights
EU–Singapore FTA	EU–Singapore Free Trade Agreement
FCN	Friendship, Commerce and Navigation
FET	Fair and equitable treatment
ICC	International Chamber of Commerce
ICCPR	International Covenant on Civil and Political Rights
ICESCR	International Covenant on Economic, Social, and Cultural Rights
ICJ	International Court of Justice
ICSID	International Centre for the Settlement of Investment Disputes
ICSID Convention	Convention on the Settlement of Investment Disputes between States and Nationals of Other States
IIAs	International Investment Agreements
ILC	International Law Commission
ISDS	Investor–state dispute settlement
NIEO	New international economic order
OECD	Organisation for Economic Co-operation and Development
PCIJ	Permanent Court of International Justice
TPP	Trans-Pacific Partnership Agreement
UDHR	Universal Declaration of Human Rights
UN	United Nations
UNCITRAL	United Nations Commission on International Trade Law
UNCTAD	United Nations Conference on Trade and Development
USA	United States of America
USMCA	United States–Mexico–Canada Agreement
WWI	World War I
WWII	World War II

CHAPTER 1

Introduction

International investment law and arbitration under investment treaties protect the economic interests of foreigners and provide a mandatory dispute resolution mechanism for disagreements between investors and foreign states. They were the crown jewels of the post–Cold War era of globalisation and neoliberalism because they engrafted business interests and Western individualistic values into the international system. Recently, the number of international investment agreements has reached a staggering 3318, and the number of known investment arbitrations has exceeded 1368.[1] Not all amounts of investment claims are publicly available, but in two-thirds of investment cases where such data is available, the total amount of claims exceeds 667 billion USD only in the last twenty years.[2]

From its conception and throughout the peak of its popularity, international investment law and arbitration were lauded for their achievements[3] as well as criticised for shortcomings and failures.[4] Together with the increasing numbers of investment disputes, criticism of the investor–state dispute settlement (ISDS) has grown, both procedurally and substantively.[5] Non-transparency, parallel procedures, inconsistency, forum shopping, the double hatting of arbitrators, the lack of accountability, the broad interpretation of treaty standards, and the shrinking policy space for states were identified as some of

1 UNCTAD, 'International Investment Agreements Navigator' and 'Investment Dispute Settlement Navigator', available at <https://investmentpolicy.unctad.org/international-investment-agreements> and <https://investmentpolicy.unctad.org/investment-dispute-settlement> accessed on 12 February 2025.

2 UNCTAD, 'Investment Dispute Settlement Navigator', available at <https://investmentpolicy.unctad.org/investment-dispute-settlement> accessed on 9 May 2021. The author is grateful to Antanas Danys for the help with calculations.

3 Rudolf Dolzer and others, 'History, Sources, and Nature of International Investment Law' in *Principles of International Investment Law* (Oxford University Press 2022) 13; Stephan Schill, *The multilateralization of international investment law* (Cambridge University Press 2009) xiv.

4 Muthucumaraswamy Sornarajah, *The International Law on Foreign Investment* (5th edn, Cambridge University Press 2021) 46; Sundhya Pahuja, *Decolonising International Law: Development, Economic Growth and the Politics of Universality* (Cambridge University Press 2011) 95.

5 Susan D Franck, 'The Legitimacy Crisis in Investment Treaty Arbitration: Privatizing Public International Law Through Inconsistent Decisions' (2005) 73 *Fordham Law Review* 1524.

 | HTTPS://DOI.ORG/10.1163/9789004763517-002

the causes of tension within the ISDS system.[6] International investment law has been undergoing an existential rethink for the last decade.

Several upgraded investment treaties were negotiated, and many ISDS reform initiatives have focused on the procedural aspects of investment disputes, including the appeal mechanism, adjudicator appointment system, code of conduct, cost and length of procedure, third-party participation, counterclaims, and multiple proceedings.[7] Unfortunately, just like negotiating parties during the drafting of the Convention on the Settlement of Investment Disputes between States and Nationals of Other States (ICSID Convention) in 1965, the United Nations Commission on International Trade Law (UNCITRAL) Working Group III, focusing on reform, leave many substantive issues of international investment law aside as too controversial. This book suggests that procedural reform alone is insufficient to resolve the tensions between different stakeholders, including businesses, states, and civil society.

The real problem behind the legitimacy crisis and backlash against the ISDS is the lack of global consensus between different states and societies over substantive rules of investment.[8] Carried on the wave of globalisation, investment treaties set out to unify investment protection around the world by providing a neoliberal economic outlook, but the task proved to be too challenging. Even a limited impact of investment protection on the host state economies became a controversial issue: "[c]itizens no longer believed that free trade, open borders, and investment treaties were delivering for them."[9] This book is a timely reflection on the status of international investment law and its merits in the era when the globalisation agenda and universal liberal economic standards are questioned not only by civil society, academics, but by world leaders too.[10]

---

6 Michael Waibel, *The backlash Against Investment Arbitration: Perceptions and Reality* (Wolters Kluwer Law & Business 2010) xl.

7 Malcolm Langford and others, 'Special Issue: UNCITRAL and Investment Arbitration Reform: Matching Concerns and Solutions: An Introduction' (2020) 21 *The Journal of World Investment & Trade* 167, 171.

8 Sornarajah 463.

9 Apostolos Thomadakis, *The End of an Era: What's Next After Globalisation?* (2025) <https://www.socialeurope.eu/the-end-of-an-era-whats-next-after-globalisation> accessed on 7 November 2025.

10 Steve Schifferes, *The rise and fall of globalisation: why the world's next financial meltdown could be much worse with the US on the sidelines* (2025) <https://theconversation.com/the-rise-and-fall-of-globalisation-why-the-worlds-next-financial-meltdown-could-be-much-worse-with-the-us-on-the-sidelines-267920> accessed on 7 November 2025; Anthea Roberts and Martti Koskenniemi, *Is International Law International?* (Oxford Academic, Oxford University Press 2017) 322.

The efforts to reform procedural aspects of investment law and arbitration overlook a more fundamental issue: the problems within substantive rules of international investment protection and significant divergence from national property regimes. International investment law, often promoted as universal, imposes standards that clash with diverse domestic legal, cultural, and societal perspectives on property. This clash adds fuel to the anti-globalist, protectionist, and populist rhetoric. The legitimacy crisis in international investment law cannot be resolved without reexamining key questions about investment protection: what should be the optimal scope and level of investment protection to achieve its purpose? Is there a need for a universal standard? Is investment protection truly neutral, autonomous, and global? And to what extent can states interfere with investment? Drawing on historical debates about state responsibility for the injury to alien property, comparative analysis, and property theories, this book seeks to challenge the ostensible consensus on the universal investment protection standard, which ignores the plurality of domestic property regimes. Investment protection, designed under neoliberal and individualistic property paradigms,[11] has become detached from the communitarian property understandings that exist at the national level. This mismatch explains the current tensions in the ISDS.

1 The Parallel between Property and Investment

The vast network of investment treaties based on similar templates and investment arbitration practices produced by frequently appointed arbitrators created a very fragile *status quo* between states with very different histories, economies, views, interpretations, and practices of regulation. In order to understand and explain the current tensions surrounding ISDS, we have to go down to the core concepts of property and investment and how these concepts interplay in the national legal context and international investment law.

Although existing in separate legal systems[12] and bearing different names, property, and investment have multiple points of contact and interaction.

---

11 Stephan Schill, *International Investment Law and Comparative Public Law* (Oxford University Press, 2010) 17.

12 On the general interplay between international law and national law see Hersch Sir Lauterpacht, *Private Law Sources and Analogies of International Law: With Special Reference to International Arbitration* (Archon Books 1970) 1; Lambertus Erades, M Fitzmaurice, and C Flinterman, *Interactions Between International and Municipal Law: A Comparative Case Law Study* (TMC Asser Instituut 1993) 103; Benedetto Conforti, *International Law and The Role of Domestic Legal Systems* (Martinus Nijhoff 1993) 13; Janne Elisabeth

Furthermore, they evolve over time and crossbreed, producing some unexpected results.[13]

First, investment protection historically originated from the protection of alien property, and this continuity and transformation explain some of the inherited problems that ISDS is facing today.[14]

Second, legal concepts used to define investment and justify its protection originate from the national legal systems and economic policies. All subjects participating in ISDS, starting from drafters of investment treaties, applying institutions, adjudicators, and parties to disputes, consciously or unconsciously perceive and interpret investment protection through the prism of their domestic social consensus for property protection.[15]

Furthermore, investment and property often overlap – investment protection treaties were specifically drafted to include as many categories of assets as possible and some other rights, creating a much wider scope of interests that are granted the protection of property. However, this overlap between investment and property is more pronounced in the Western industrialised states, while other states usually have a narrower scope of interests that are protected as property.[16]

Ultimately, the philosophical and economic framework that explains and justifies investment protection relies heavily on neoliberal ideology, overlooking important aspects of property theory. Investment protection depends on the prestige and authority of property protection, but fails to accommodate other societal interests. The vague and abstract language of investment treaties glosses over the conceptual divides that exist at the national level. Still, tensions erupt during dispute resolution, especially when the arbitration award challenges local property law and requires changes in the domestic ordering of entitlements.[17]

Nijman and André Nollkaemper, *New Perspectives on the Divide Between National and International Law* (4th edn, Oxford University Press 2007) 130; Hege Elisabeth Kjos, *Applicable Law in Investor-State Arbitration the Interplay Between National and International Law* (Oxford University Press 2013) 302.

13 See below Chapter 6.

14 On alien property protection as a way to promote and maintain European interests, see Antony Anghie, *Imperialism, Sovereignty, and the Making of International Law*, vol 37 (Cambridge University Press 2005) 8, 239.

15 On a significant variation of interpretation and application of international law, see Anthea Roberts and others, 'Conceptualizing Comparative International Law' in *Comparative International Law* (Oxford University Press 2018) 4.

16 See below Chapter 3.

17 Amnon Lehavi, *Property Law in a Globalizing World* (Cambridge University Press 2019) 13.

At this point, some clarifications of definitions are due. In this book, 'property' generally refers to things and assets, but I am mindful of the great philosophical and economic debate about whether all assets can or should be treated as property. Different legal systems provide different answers to that question. For example, Continental legal systems may refuse to treat certain assets, such as contractual rights, as property.[18] Permits, licences, concessions, pensions, monetary claims, information, occupation or certain offices, and statutory rights reside within this grey zone between property and obligations. Investment treaties often include many of these rights in the definition of investment, thereby greatly expanding the scope of protected foreign interests.

The term 'property' is also used to denote ownership rights, which include some or all rights held by the owner, such as the rights to use, manage, benefit from, transfer, or destroy property (*ius utendi, fruendi et abutendi* (lat)), as well as certain proprietary rights, such as mortgages, pledges, charges, liens, servitudes, and usufructs.[19] The common law tradition tends to treat possession as a self-standing proprietary interest. States following the civil law tradition are usually more conservative, limiting the list of ownership rights by statute.[20]

Thus, the meaning of the term 'property' should always be construed in the context of legal relations, and 'property protection' refers to the general concept of how property is protected in a particular legal system, which includes both formal rules and their actual implementation.

The understanding of property, the scope of legal interests defined as property, and the weight the protection of property has in relation to other interests in society vary significantly from state to state, depending on the stage of development, historical and social circumstances, legal tradition, and even prevailing ideology. The idea of property in every society carries a heavy load not only of formal regulation and recognition but also cultural and ideological connotations:

18 Inga Martinkute, 'The delimitation of contractual rights and property in international investment law' (2016) 1 European Investment Law and Arbitration Review 3; Christian von Bar, Ulrich Drobnig and European Commission Directorate-General for Health and Consumer Protection, *The Interaction of Contract Law and Tort and Property Law in Europe: a Comparative Study* (Sellier 2004) 320–323. See also John G Sprankling, *The International Law of Property* (Oxford University Press 2014) 21.

19 Christian von Bar and others (eds), *Principles, Definitions and Model Rules of European Private Law: Draft Common Frame of Reference* (Sellier European Law Publishers 2009) 422–423.

20 Lehavi 16.

> The integration of law and equity in the conception of property is crucial to the way in which the right to property is approached because it suggests that regulation that goes beyond the prevention of nuisance-like activity need not be treated as a deprivation of property.[21]

The concept of property is so central to most legal systems because it serves as a basis for prosperity, the engine of the economy, and, in a way, a mirror image of the underlying values and priorities of a particular society. Property regimes are intrinsically linked to the economic policy choices of a society and also reflect the locally agreed-upon balance between individual and community or state interests. The scope of protected interests and how they are protected are among the most defining legal rules in the national legal systems and international law.

Since the emergence of investment treaties, significant efforts have been made to define investment and provide for its protection in a manner that would eliminate the problems and difficulties associated with the plurality of national property regimes. This tendency reflected broader societal trends of globalisation and liberalisation after the World War II (WWII), and was especially dominant after the collapse of the Soviet Union. Many scholars and practitioners argue that investment protection is a reincarnation of the international minimum standard and is completely separate from national concepts and levels of property protection.[22] For example, Sprankling, drawing mainly on Anglo-American experience, claimed the emergence of international property law as a general principle of law.[23] A variation of this idea is an argument by Alvarez that property protection is one of the universal human rights and should be extended to the protection of investments.[24]

However, these arguments that modern international law is based on natural law and universal virtues were criticised by Koskenniemi, who argued that universal claims about property protection are historically contingent and

---

21 Tom Allen, *The Right to Property in Commonwealth Constitutions* (Cambridge University Press 2000) 144.

22 Ibrahim F I Shihata and Antonio R Parra, 'Applicable Substantive Law in Disputes Between States and Private Foreign Parties: The Case of Arbitration under the ICSID Convention' (1994) 9 ICSID Review 183, 193–194; Schill, *The Multilateralization of International Investment Law* 8; Rudolf Dolzer and Christoph Schreuer, *Principles of International Investment Law*, vol Second edition (Oxford University Press 2012) 3.

23 Sprankling 23, 219. The assumptions about the link between individualism, capitalism and international law seem to be taken for granted, see Wilhelm Georg Grewe and Michael Byers, *The Epochs of International Law* (Walter de Gruyter 2000) 167.

24 José E Alvarez, 'The Human Right of Property' (2018) 72 University of Miami Law Review 581.

politically motivated.[25] Sornarajah also pointed out the contested nature and unsettled practice of property protection in international law.[26] Even Douglas criticised some investment cases where tribunals failed to characterise investment rights properly and argued that domestic law should be given more weight in investment disputes involving property.[27] Perrone goes even further than formal characterisation and applicable law problems, arguing that the international investment law and ISDS serve specific economic neoliberal goals, not universal values.[28] He further argued that international investment law and ISDS are not the result of spontaneous interpretations, but rather the normative project, aimed at strengthening foreign investor rights and minimising state economic interference, and realised by a coalition of business leaders, bankers, and their lawyers in the post-WWII period.[29] Slabodian concurred:

> [w]hat neoliberals seek is not a partial but a complete protection of private capital rights, and the ability of supranational judiciary bodies [...] to override national legislation that might disrupt the global rights of capital.[30]

Another strand of international economic law literature explained international investment protection and ISDS as a global constitutional review mechanism, providing a form of oversight that can constrain state sovereignty. Van

---

25 Martii Koskenniemi, *The Gentle Civilizer of Nations: The Rise and Fall of International Law 1870–1960* (Cambridge University Press 2002) 127; Martti Koskenniemi, 'Empire and International Law: The Real Spanish Contribution' (2011) 61 University of Toronto Law Journal University of Toronto Law Journal 1, 3, 16; Martti Koskenniemi, 'Sovereignty, Property and Empire: Early Modern English Contexts' (2017) 18 Theoretical Inquiries in Law 355; Martti Koskenniemi, *To the Uttermost Parts of the Earth: Legal Imagination and International Power 1300–1870* (Cambridge University Press 2021) 726.

26 M Sornarajah, *Resistance and Change in the International Law on Foreign Investment* (Cambridge University Press 2015) 191.

27 Zachary Douglas, *The International law of investment claims* (Cambridge University Press 2009) 207; Zachary Douglas, 'Property, Investment and the Scope of Investment Protection Obligations' in Zachary Douglas, Joost Pauwelyn, and Jorge E. Viñuales (eds), *The Foundations of International Investment Law: Bringing Theory Into Practice* (Oxford University Press 2014) 369.

28 Nicolás M Perrone, 'Neoliberalism and Economic Sovereignty: Property, Contracts, and Foreign Investment Relations' in Honor Brabazon (ed), *Neoliberal Legality Understanding the Role of Law in the Neoliberal Project* (Routledge 2016) 43.

29 Nicolás M Perrone, *Investment Treaties and the Legal Imagination: How Foreign Investors Play by Their Own Rules* (Oxford Academic, Oxford University Press 2021) 2.

30 Quinn Slobodian, *Globalists: The End of Empire and the Birth of Neoliberalism* (Harvard University Press 2018) 12–13.

Harten took a public law approach to international investment law, viewing it as a form of global public administrative law that grants investors significant power to challenge state regulatory actions.[31] Schneiderman also tried to bridge comparative constitutional law and international investment law, explaining that:

> the investment rules regime, aim to institutionalize a model of constitutional government intended primarily to facilitate the free flow of goods, services, capital, and persons unimpeded across the borders of national states.[32]

Montt further explored the relationship between property rights as investment and the public interest through the prism of constitutional restraint.[33] He proposed a comparative method to restrain arbitrators' discretion in reviewing state action, but he makes limited references to the jurisprudence of the USA, the UK, France, Germany, and the ECtHR.[34] Schill also turned to comparative constitutional property analysis for inspiration on how to integrate investment protection within broader national public and administrative systems, but again, for the reasons of convenience, limited the analysis to German, French, English, and the USA legal systems.[35] The selection of a limited number of Western industrialised states for the comparison, aiming to identify and explain the general principle of investment protection, will inevitably produce tilted results. The terms and legal concepts used to define investment and how it is protected from state interference inevitably reintroduce national property preferences and presumptions, as well as legal interpretations and questions of political economy, while ignoring other alternative solutions existing in the world. There is a great deal of biased selectivity in deter-

---

31 Gus Van Harten, *Investment Treaty Arbitration and Public Law* (Oxford University Press 2007) 90.

32 David Schneiderman, *Constitutionalizing Economic Globalization: Investment Rules and Democracy's promise* (Cambridge University Press 2008) 2.

33 Santiago Montt, *State Liability in Investment Treaty Arbitration: Global Constitutional and Administrative Law in the BIT Generation*, vol 26 (Hart Publishing 2009) 165; See also Jan Klabbers, Anne Peters, and Geir Ulfstein, *The Constitutionalization of International Law* (Oxford University Press 2009) 342.

34 Montt 170.

35 Schill, *The Multilateralization of International Investment Law* 30. See also Markus Perkams, 'The Concept of Indirect Expropriation in Comparative Public Law – Searching for Light in the Dark' in Stephan W Schill (ed), *International Investment Law and Comparative Public Law* (2010) 107; B Sabahi and N Birch, 'Comparative Compensation for Expropriation' in Stephan W Schill (ed), *International Investment Law and Comparative Public Law* (Oxford University Press 2010) 755.

mining which national preferences will be elevated to the international level and promoted as a universal standard. Most importantly, the tendency to have a universal investment protection standard fixed at a particular scope and level has significant social and economic implications for countries that operate within different frameworks.

2 Finding the Proper Applicable Law

While the classical international law was primarily directed at the states, national law regulated the characteristics and scope of private property as well as the behaviour of private parties.[36] The developments in international law saw an increasing overlap and co-regulation with national law.[37] Recent agreements and case law of international courts and tribunals attribute an increasing role to individuals and corporations in international law.[38] While these inroads by international law into the traditional sphere of national regulation are still relatively recent in the history of international law, they are not uncontested. At the heart of the ISDS crisis is the question which international norms can and should overrule national law on economic matters and to what extent the review function was delegated to the international adjudicators?[39] Not all branches of international law made equal advances on national law, but international investment law probably was the only one where international regulation was accompanied by a very efficient enforcement mechanism. Investment arbitration practice clearly prioritises international agreements over national law, and under investment treaties, interna-

36 *Payment of Various Serbian Loans Issued in France* (*France v Kingdom of the Serbs, Croats and Slovenes*), 1929 PCIJ (ser A) No 20 (July 12) para 68. See also *Payment in Gold of Brazilian Federal Loans Contracted in France* (*France v Brazil*), 1929 PCIJ (ser A) No 21 (July 12) para 71.

37 For the overview of normative flows between international treaties and domestic investment law see: Steven R Ratner, 'International Investment Law and Domestic Investment Rules: Tracing the Upstream and Downstream Flows' (2020) 21 The Journal of World Investment & Trade 7; Daniel Peat, *Comparative Reasoning in International Courts and Tribunals* (Cambridge University Press 2019) 3; Anne-Marie Slaughter and William W Burke-White, 'The Future of International Law is Domestic' in Andre Nolkaemper and Janne Nijman (eds), *New Perspectives on the Divide Between National and International Law* (Oxford University Press 2007) 111.

38 Christian J Tams, Conclusion, *The Sources of International Investment Law* (Brill 2012) 321.

39 Nicolás M Perrone, 'Expropriation' in David Schneiderman and Gus Van Harten (eds), *Rethinking Investment Law* (Oxford Academic, Oxford University Press 2023) 87–88.

tional adjudicators decide whether national law contravenes international rules.[40] Thanks to the network of investment treaties, the current reality for most of the globe is that any national law, decision or measure on economic matters can be challenged at least by some investors.

As international regulation mechanisms and the idea of global governance seep into more and more areas that traditionally were regulated by national law, what are the mechanisms through which international law influences national property laws and economic policies? What national property ideas does the international regime emulate? Investment tribunals were split between 'total disregard of municipal law' and certain recognition of interaction between municipal and international law.[41] Modern investment treaties do not mention property directly, but the interplay between property and investment is implied within a broader architecture of legal systems.

First, international law uses the basic legal concepts and terminology, such as assets, property, contracts, legal entities, intellectual property, permits, and licences, which were forged in the domestic law systems and then used by international instruments and processes with the occasional pretence to universality. While this borrowing of legal instruments might look innocent, it goes hand in hand with the interpretation and, to some degree, reinvention of those national concepts. For instance, while determining if certain statutory rights are assets in a host state legal system, the tribunals might apply a Common law liberal and flexible test, which stretches the definition of investment beyond initial Civil law understandings of property. Investment treaties and the practice of investment arbitration have collaboratively fostered the perception that these concepts possess a consistent and autonomous definition, simultaneously embedding them with neoliberal content,[42] while the latter aspect is missing in the national property regimes. For example, Civil law countries are reluctant to treat contractual rights as property and to grant them the level of property protection, while Common law countries are more flexible and liberal, admitting various rights and interests as property

40 Andreas Kulick, *Global Public Interest in International Investment Law* (Cambridge University Press 2012) 11; *Vigotop Limited v Hungary* (ICSID) para 313, 327; *Saint-Gobain Performance Plastics Europe v Bolivarian Republic of Venezuela* (ICSID) para 473–474; *Yukos Universal Limited (Isle of Man) v Russian Federation* (PCA) para 316.

41 Monique Sasson, *Substantive Law in Investment Treaty Arbitration: The Unsettled Relationship Between International Law and Municipal Law* (Kluwer Law International 2010) 77–80.

42 David Schneiderman, '"Writing the rules of the global economy": how America defines the contours of international investment law' (2018) 6 London Review of International Law 255, 257.

and subsequently as investment.[43] Divergent interpretation and content of domestic property rights are still relevant in investment arbitration, which is based on investment treaties. This is because the jurisdiction of the tribunal sometimes is limited to expropriation cases[44] requiring legal qualification of property rights under national law.[45] In principle, there is nothing wrong with the fact that domestic law is used to interpret international treaties or fill the gaps of international law.[46] Issues arise when international adjudicators overlook host state domestic property regimes or prioritise other interpretations and understandings of rights without adequate justification, simply because tribunal members happen to be educated in a legal system that has a more liberal and individualistic understanding of property regimes. This situation arises in investment disputes where both parties involved originate from Civil law jurisdictions upholding a traditional, narrower understanding of property, yet most members of the arbitral tribunal are representatives of Western industrialised Common law countries.

A similar problem was often observed in nineteenth and early twentieth-century cases involving property questions, where the general principle of property protection was attempted to be deduced from Western domestic legal systems without conducting a wide and representative comparative analysis of property laws worldwide.[47] The problem is aggravated by the fact that international adjudicators, when deciding investment disputes, cherry-pick different elements from a variety of domestic property systems (usually Western) to make a neoliberal investment protection regime.

The second area of friction between national and international law concerns the corrective function of international law.[48] Domestic law is still a

---

43 See below Chapter 3.

44 Expropriation, taking, mandatory or compulsory acquisition in this book are used as synonyms, bearing in mind that at the national level expropriation is more commonly used in civil law countries, taking in the USA, mandatory or compulsory acquisition in the Commonwealth.

45 *Les Laboratoires Servier, SAS, Biofarma, SAS and Arts et Techniques du Progres SAS v Republic of Poland* (UNCITRAL) para 676; Reza Eftekhar, *The Role of the Domestic Law of the Host State in Determining the Jurisdiction ratione materiae of Investment Treaty Tribunals: The Partial Revival of the Localisation Theory?* (Brill | Nijhoff 2021) 104.

46 Rudolf Dolzer, 'Indirect Expropriation of Alien Property' (1986) 1 ICSID Review 41, 60.

47 See below Chapter 4.

48 W Michael Reisman, 'The Regime for Lacunae in the ICSID Choice of Law Provision and the Question of Its Threshold' (2000) 15 ICSID Review 362; *AIG Capital Partners, Inc and CJSC Tema Real Estate Company v Republic of Kazakhstan* (ICSID) para 10.1.2; *Pac Rim Cayman LLC v Republic of El Salvador* (ICSID) Case No ARB/09/12, Award 14 October 2016 para 5.62.

proper applicable law for most aspects of the civil turnover and commercial transactions, which include foreign investments. The acquisition, existence and termination of property, rights or interests must be ascertained in accordance with the national law, including rules on illegality, requirements on validity, contract formation or title transfer. Attempts have been made to advocate for the internationalisation of contracts and property; however, this issue remains contentious. The controversy arises not only from the challenge of determining what elevates a commercial relationship to an international level, but also from the fact that, with limited exceptions such as certain provisions in investment treaties, international law lacks comprehensive regulation over civil and commercial matters. This includes issues related to legal personality, contract formation, validity, transfers, liability, remedies, and other fundamental aspects.[49]

The classical tenet still holds that international law does not create property and does not have substantive rules on property, but only provides protection for the rights that are created under domestic law.[50] Also, the illegality of investment is primarily established with reference to domestic law, and compliance with domestic law is a precondition for the establishment and operation of some investments.[51] In a simple and straightforward scenario where a state arbitrarily, without justification and without observing legal procedures, takes a specific foreigner's property, the corrective function of international law serves to restore justice to the victim. The controversy arises when international tribunals attempt to override certain aspects of mandatory national law, such as notarial execution or the registration of title at the public registry, arguing that these requirements breach international law because national law is too formalistic and does not adequately serve business needs. In a more extreme version, an investment tribunal might declare that national law or particular economic policy or law reform is in breach of international law.

49 Jean Ho, 'Internationalisation and State contracts: are State contracts the future or the past?' in C. L. Lim (ed), *Alternative Visions of the International Law on Foreign Investment: Essays in Honour of Muthucumaraswamy Sornarajah* (Cambridge University Press 2016) 377. Also Jean Ho, *New Property in International Law* (Oxford Academic, Oxford University Press 2024) 16.

50 *Panevezys-Saldutiškis Railway case* (*Estonia v Lithuania*) Ser A/B No 76 (PCIJ) [1939] 18; Zachary Douglas, 'The hybrid foundations of investment treaty arbitration' (2004) 74 British Yearbook of international Law 151, 198.

51 *Gambrinus Corporation v Bolivarian Republic of Venezuela* (ICSID) Case No ARB/11/31, Decision on Annulment 30 October 2017 para 202; *Grupo Francisco Hernando Contreras SL v Republic of Equatorial Guinea* (ICSID) Case No ARB(AF)/12/2, Award on Jurisdiction 5 December 2015 paras 231–234, 262.

When international law rules overlap national regulation, adjudicators under investment treaties have a wide discretion to decide whether national regulation violates an international rule. On the one hand, this power of adjudicators may correct faulty national regulation or arbitrary measures. On the other hand, an international overreach can easily redesign economic or social policies and redistribute burdens, profits and externalities within a foreign society or in the words of Schneiderman and Van Harten 'tribunals have been given the power to second-guess all variety of state measures, no matter how essential to social or economic well-being'.[52] The crux of the dilemma so far has been not only to determine what international law on investment protection is, but also how far the corrective function of international law can go without upsetting system users. Coupled with very little accountability to the affected society and disagreements over the value of the investment, it is no surprise that the ISDS system is experiencing a crisis.

The third area of interaction is domestic law's contribution towards the sources of international law, such as general principles and customs. It is widely claimed that the general principles of domestic legal systems are used as a source for the general principles of international law, despite all the problems associated with the identification of general principles.[53] However, the diversity of domestic property regimes makes it challenging to identify even the lowest common denominator besides a very general notion that most legal systems recognise private property as such.[54] Sasson concluded that it is impossible to 'extract a general principle regarding the relationship' between investment and property.[55] Nonetheless, states and adjudicators often assert or suggest that their domestic property regime represents the prevailing international standard.[56]

Comparable challenges are encountered when using domestic law to identify international customary norms. Early international practice of alien property protection, with its numerous national exceptions and unclear contours,

---

52 David Schneiderman and Gus Van Harten (eds), *Rethinking Investment Law* (Oxford Academic, Oxford University Press 2023) 1.

53 L Yves Fortier and Stephen L Drymer, 'Indirect Expropriation in the Law of International Investment: I Know It When I See It, or Caveat Investor' (2004) 19 ICSID Review 293, 294.

54 Andrea Leiter, 'Protecting concessionary rights: General principles and the making of international investment law' (2022) 35 Leiden Journal of International Law 55.

55 Sasson 69–70.

56 Sprankling 23, 219; Steven R Ratner, 'Regulatory Takings in Institutional Context: Beyond the Fear of Fragmented International Law' (2008) 102 The American Journal of International Law 475 475; Frederick Alexander Mann, 'Outlines of a History of Expropriation' (1959) 75 Law Quarterly Review 188, 203–208.

was highly contested.[57] National property regimes and practices exhibit considerable diversity, preventing the establishment of an international custom. This variation arises from the distinct local economic and social requirements addressed by each domestic system:

> As human conditions and needs change, so will the bases on which property regimes were constructed. What may have been an appropriate configuration of property rights in one era, may be an undesired burden or constraint in another.[58]

Like with the general principle of property protection, the international custom of property protection as emerging from the totality of national property regimes can be articulated only at such a general and vague level that it would be unworkable as a legal rule for any real dispute. The whole purpose of investment treaties was to overcome the difficulties associated with the variety of national property regimes and the absence of consensus on a single alien property protection standard. Thus, without neoliberal creativity, it is difficult to imagine that an international custom could be distilled from national property regimes.[59]

Throughout the book, various modes of interaction between national and international legal regimes are assessed to identify and expose the different national influences on the scope and content of investment protection and *vice versa*, how the international investment regime tries to control domestic economic policies related to property.

---

57 Nicholas R Doman, 'Postwar Nationalization of Foreign Property in Europe' (1948) 48 Columbia Law Review 1125; Chittharanjan Felix Amerasinghe, *State Responsibility for Injuries to Aliens* (Clarendon P 1967) 127–128; Ian Brownlie, *Principles of Public International Law* (6th edn, Oxford University Press 2003) (6th edn, Oxford University Press 2003) 509–512; Jean d' Aspremont, 'International Customary Investment Law: Story of a Paradox' in *International Investment Law* (Brill 2012) 14; Kate Miles, *The Origins of International Investment Law: Empire, Environment, and the Safeguarding of Capital* (Cambridge University Press 2013) 63; Andrea Leiter, *Making the World Safe for Investment: The Protection of Foreign Property 1922–1959* (Cambridge University Press 2023) 1.

58 Laura S Underkuffler-Freund, 'Takings and the Nature of Property' (1996) 9 Canadian Journal of Law and Jurisprudence 179.

59 See below Chapter 4.

3 Comparative Approach and Scope

The conventional wisdom sought solutions to the ISDS crisis within the system, advocating for gradual evolution and adaptation.[60] However, many problems in international investment law stem from its leaning towards neoliberal goals and its disconnection from a broader philosophical, social, and economic framework of national property regimes.

According to Mann, international law on 'expropriation, confiscation or nationalisation' has not been adequately compared with the national laws.[61] Before the influx of investment arbitrations, some comparative work was conducted by Dolzer and Higgins, but primarily limited to Western industrialised states.[62] The gap in the legal literature was noted by Van Harten and Schneiderman, who compared international investment law and arbitration to domestic administrative and constitutional law.[63] Montt explored state liability for interference with property rights, observing that the comparative method could be used to restrain arbitrators' discretion, but again he made references to the jurisprudence of the USA, France, Germany, Spain, and the ECtHR only.[64] The comparative work between the systems was further advanced under the editorial supervision of Schill, but mostly focused on the comparison of administrative law, while explaining the merits of the comparative lens.[65] Yet again, for the reasons of convenience, this work is limited to the Western industrialised states.[66] Aside from a handful of attempts to integrate invest-

60 S W B Schill, 'The Sixth Path: Reforming Investment Law from Within' in J E Kalicki and A Joubin-Bret (eds), *Reshaping The Investor-State Dispute Settlement System: Journeys for the 21st Century* (Brill 2015); Freya Baetens, 'Judicial Review of International Adjudicatory Decisions: A Cross-Regime Comparison of Annulment and Appellate Mechanisms' (2016) 8 *Journal of International Dispute Settlement* 432; Federico Ortino, 'Investment Treaties, Sustainable Development and Reasonableness Review: A Case Against Strict Proportionality Balancing' (2017) 30 Leiden Journal of International Law 71. Also see critical works: M Sornarajah, 'The past, present and future of the international law on foreign investment' in Shan Wenhua and Su Jinyuan (eds), *China and International Investment Law: Twenty Years of ICSID Membership* (2014) 23; Sornarajah, *Resistance and Change in the International Law on Foreign Investment* 347; Roberts and others 27.

61 Frederick Alexander Mann, 'State Contracts and State Responsibility' in *Studies in International Law* (Oxford University Press 1973) 316.

62 Dolzer 47, 61; Rosalyn Higgins, *The Taking of Property by the State: Recent Developments in International Law* (the Hague Academy of International Law 1982) 259.

63 Van Harten 4; Schneiderman, *Constitutionalizing Economic Globalization: Investment Rules and Democracy's Promise* 3.

64 Montt 172.

65 Schill, *International Investment Law and Comparative Public Law* 26.

66 Ibid 30; Perkams 107.

ment protection with general interests[67] as well as human rights laws,[68] comparative studies have been sporadic[69] and mainly focused on developed Western states.[70] Vadi warned that even though the comparative approach in investment arbitration seemed promising for the purpose of legitimising the system, judicial borrowing was fraught with risks and limitations.[71]

The first problem is already apparent from the brief overview of comparative work in the field – the jurisdictions selected for comparisons were heavily tilted towards the side of Western industrialised states and their property regimes. The selection bias was also replicated in the reasoning of the arbitral tribunals.[72] Schill noted how comparative reasoning was used by investment tribunals for the interpretation of investment treaties.[73] This interpretation was based on the biased selection of jurisdictions used for the comparison, mainly Western industrialised states, producing an extremely individualistic investment protection regime.

Thus, this book offers a much broader comparative inquiry evaluating the main legal traditions of the world, major geographical regions and states in different stages of development. Legal systems based on common law are represented by the USA, the UK, Canada, Australia, India, and Singapore. Civil law tradition is represented by German, French, and Dutch legal systems, which share certain liberal attitudes towards property. Poland, the Baltic States and Russia represent former communist civil law countries that comparatively recently experienced substantial transformations in their private property regimes. The comparison also includes a limited sample of property regimes in Asia, Africa, and Latin America. Islamic legal tradition was excluded due to space limitation, but it would fall under the category of developing states with the communitarian understanding of property. The abovementioned coverage of national legal systems was necessary to map, at least roughly, the variety of existing domestic property regimes.

---

67 Kulick 11; Sabahi and Birch 755.

68 Alvarez 580.

69 Tom Allen, 'The Right to Property' in Tom Ginsburg and Rosalind Dixon (eds), *Comparative Constitutional Law* (Elgar 2011) 515.

70 Ratner, 'Regulatory Takings in Institutional Context: Beyond the Fear of Fragmented International Law' 475.

71 Valentina S Vadi, 'Through the Looking-Glass: International Investment Law through the Lens of a Property Theory' (2011) 8 Manchester Journal of International Economic Law 22.

72 Valentina Vadi, *Analogies in International Investment Law and Arbitration* (Cambridge University Press 2015) 109.

73 Schill, *International Investment Law and Comparative Public Law* 27, 32.

The second problem associated with the comparative approach is the popularity of *praesumptio similitudinis* as a comparative method.[74] This has led, among other reasons, to the emphasis on the similarities between some property regimes and investment protection,[75] creating an illusion of universal property right. However, more detailed comparative work revealed that an effort to find the common trends for property protection around the world led to oversimplification for the sake of uniformity.[76] The differential comparison in the context of international investment law exposes that concepts bearing the same name, such as property or contractual rights, have different meanings and practical application in other legal systems.

With these approaches in mind, the book attempts to map different property regimes and their relationships among themselves as well as towards international investment law. The comparative nature of the project dictates that a big part of it is expository scholarship. The scope of the research is undeniably vast geographically and chronologically, but this is necessary in order to catch at least the most general understandings of such complicated phenomena as property. The breadth of the study comes at the price of depth. The book cannot accommodate the exhaustive and comprehensive comparative survey of a dozen national property regimes with significant differences and various exceptions.[77] Thus, it should be read as a starting point for further dialogue on the interaction between property regimes and international investment law.

In such a multifaceted topic, involving aspects of legal theory, human rights law, constitutional and private law, the list of what is excluded from the analysis is probably longer than what is included.

First, although certain philosophical discussions and examples are drawn from the Middle Ages and ancient times, they are used solely to explain the current understanding and expose certain myths about property protection. Since some claims about the universality of property protection are based on historical arguments, the book revisits those historical circumstances to debunk these myths or, at the very least, to highlight their limitations. There is considerable emphasis on the Enlightenment era, as the historical, economic, and sociological factors of that period were paramount to our current under-

74 Konrad Zweigert and Hein Kötz, *Introduction to Comparative Law*, vol 3 (Clarendon Press 1998) 40.

75 Investment tribunals too easily presume that domestic legal concepts are similar to the international or their own understanding of it: *Caratube International Oil Company LLP and Devincci Salah Hourani v Republic of Kazakhstan* (ICSID) Case No ARB/13/13, Award 27 September 2017 para 941.

76 Vadi 108.

77 Allen, 'The Right to Property' 505–512.

standing of property and the economic setup within which investment operates. Still, the main focus of the analysis is the current state of affairs, and historical context is provided only to help better understand the current situation.

Second, in broad terms, the book is about the individual's stance *vis-à-vis* a state, as a representative of a broader community, with respect to property.[78] More specifically, the book analyses the interplay between national property regimes and investment protection through the matrix of four elements: (i) the scope of protected rights and interests asking how broad the understanding of property in different legal traditions is, and how it relates to the typical definitions of investment; (ii) the distinction between permissible regulation and indirect expropriation questioning what restrictions private or constitutional laws impose on private property and what interferences of rights are tolerated without compensation; (iii) the conditions and requirements for expropriation, how they are defined, understood, interpreted, and applied in national law and investment arbitration; and (iv) the procedures and standards of compensation in national and international expropriation cases.[79] To maintain the focus of the book on property and investment, other standards, such as fair and equitable treatment or national treatment, are sidelined because they relate to property only indirectly. Although, in principle, it would be possible to find national functional equivalents for fair and equitable treatment, non-discrimination, or national treatment, a separate study would be required for it.

Finally, the book excludes separate international investment laws within national legal systems for several reasons. Very often, national investment laws bear similarities to investment treaties, and their widespread adoption in the 1990s coincided with the peak of the popularity of investment treaties. National investment laws rarely form the basis of investment claims and do not appear at the forefront of tensions that need to be addressed, although they are a weaker version of the investment treaties. As an extension of the programme to 'attract foreign investment', those national laws do not represent the underlying thinking about property and its place in the host society. Thus, this book chooses more embedded national property regimes for comparison with international law.

78 The question to what extent communities are represented by states is complicated and is better addressed by other sociological and political studies, see Max Weber, *From Max Weber: Essays in Sociology* (Routledge 2009) 112.

79 The specific typology of property rights in each national jurisdiction is excluded from the scope of the work because, for this study, it is more important to ascertain more general features of property and the levels of its protection.

4 The West and the Rest through Property Prism

Using the comparative methodology, the book identifies and discusses a significant difference between national legal property regimes. The property regimes of Western industrialised and developed societies are a starting point of the enquiry. The scope and level of domestic property protection regimes in various other parts of the world greatly depend on their integration into Western socio-economic structures. Developed Western states were the main driving force behind early international cases on the protection of alien property and BIT templates; thus, early investment treaties reflected and, to some extent, aligned with the national property regimes of Western industrialised states. However, during the last two decades of the twentieth century, the interpretation of those treaties in the arbitral awards acquired strong neoliberal overtones, pushing the globalisation agenda as a golden standard for economic development to the rest of the world.[80] At this point, investment protection exceeded the property protection as understood and practised by Western industrialised states.

Developing states and states in transition often have a narrower and more traditional understanding of property, lower levels of property protection, and tend to tolerate interference with private property rights, as they prioritise community interests over those of an individual. During its heyday, international investment law and its decision-makers were either ignoring that different balance or antagonistic to the communitarian understanding of property. Only recently, new-generation investment treaties reintroduced the notion of the balance between individual and community interests through the right to regulate.[81]

The comparison of various property regimes worldwide reveals that no single standard for property protection exists to guide investment protection in its quest for universality, as property protection is inherently rooted in the local needs and values of a society.

The identified gap between property and investment protection is not just an empirical difference but a useful lens that allows for grasping what is wrong with the conceptual foundations of investment arbitration. For example, at the national level, property is a significantly narrower concept than investment.

80 T C Boas and J Gans-Morse, 'Neoliberalism: From New Liberal Philosophy to Anti-Liberal Slogan' (2009) 44 *Studies in Comparative International Development* 144; Slobodian 6; Chios Carmody, *A Communitarian Theory of WTO Law* (Cambridge University Press 2023) 427.

81 Aikaterini Titi, *The Right to Regulate in International Investment Law*, vol 10 (Nomos 2014) 28.

Even this narrower national concept of property often clashes with local *bona fide* legislative reforms and executive initiatives. That means investment protection, which is considerably broader and more individualistic than property, is even more likely to conflict with state measures, making it very complicated for host states to achieve fundamental social and economic reforms. This is evident in recent cases involving tobacco control, nuclear phase-out, renewable energy, and climate change, where incumbent property or investment interests clash with society's need to introduce changes to the existing regime.

Furthermore, property, unlike investment, entails obligations, and in many jurisdictions, property has social functions. At the national level, property protection is never absolute and is balanced against other societal values and interests. Investment, on the other hand, operates under the presumption that a state must justify any interference with investment; a state bears the burden of proving the proportionality and reasonableness of a measure affecting the profitability of an investment.

The mismatch between the dominant interpretation of investment protection and the principles of property protection as they function under national laws creates tensions worldwide, as the elevated investment protection differs from the national consensus on the place and value of property in society. Where investment protection diverges significantly from a national property regime, the local community views the investment protection as lacking legitimacy. Despite arbitral awards ruling in favour of investors, in such societies, investment protection fails to be internalised and is passively resisted.

National property regimes are fertile grounds for jurisprudence on the proper boundaries of private property rights and state interference, and could be instructive in finding the right balance between individual and communitarian interests at the international level, provided that all legal traditions and geographical regions are represented. Finally, the reasoning and legitimacy of investment awards could be considerably enhanced if the variety of national property protection practices were taken into account.

5 One-Size Investment Does Not Fit All States

This book challenges the ostensible international consensus on a single, universal idea of investment protection, based on an extremely individualistic understanding of property.[82] Despite the cynicism, naivete, or idealism of

82 Pahuja noted how liberal capitalist view of property was posited as universal and international: Pahuja 158.

globalists or universalists, several problems are associated with the 'one size fits all' approach. Those problems become apparent when different property regimes are compared among themselves and with the investment protection regime.

Different legal property regime configurations have different economic implications. These property regimes are the result of historical circumstances, the values, and the needs of a particular society. It is quite impossible to export a property regime without negative externalities because it is impossible to replicate the historical experiences, social structures, needs, and values of a particular population. 'The Western size fits all' approach is problematic for developing states because the Western property regimes are oriented towards wealth preservation and the corrective function of law, which is not ideal for the change-oriented needs of developing countries.

The extreme individualistic understanding of property exported through BITs and investment arbitration practice presumes and relies on the values of Western societies. Different societies do not attribute the same value to individualism, and this is reflected in the property regimes around the world. Even if the values of a particular Western society could be successfully exported globally, it is questionable if such a venture is justified.

Another problem becomes apparent when considering investment and property in parallel. The national debates about property protection have accepted a long time ago that property protection is not absolute but limited. For example, in some Western countries, even heavy regulatory burdens are considered to be part of property rather than deprivation.[83] In other European states, property rights, administrative permissions, and licences are perceived as arising from state authority and recognition. Thus, those rights are inherently subject to state adaptation or withdrawal. Meanwhile, international investment protection, for a long time, operated in a fragmented environment as an absolute right and ignored the balancing of interests performed by national courts. Although recently, the debate on the contours of permissible state regulation and non-compensable interference with an investment is gaining attention in new-generation treaties,[84] there is still a remarkable dis-

---

83 Allen, *The Right to Property in Commonwealth Constitutions* 144; Michael R. Antinori, 'Does Lochner Live in Luxembourg? An Analysis of the Property Rights Jurisprudence of the European Court of Justice' (1995) 18 *Fordham International Law Journal* 1778, 1781–1782; Joseph H H Weiler, 'Eurocracy and distrust: some questions concerning the role of the European Court of Justice in the protection of fundamental human rights within the legal order of the European Communities' (1986) 61 *Washington Law Review* 1103, 1127–1128.

84 Van Harten 90; Titi 76.

connect between the general theory of property and international investment law. It might be that the investment protection under BITs exceeded even the highest national property protection standards found in the USA.[85] It could be that investment protection was elevated to some mythical levels of absolute property protection, which is unworkable in practice and does not exist anywhere in the world.

Such neoliberal investment protection creates tension and controversy not only for developing states, tying their hands in implement reforms involving some redistribution of wealth. Even stable and economically advanced nations wishing to implement new policies in order to address ecological problems, technological, social, and economic shifts have to defend their policy changes in investment disputes.[86] This clash between investment protection and competing values and interests of local society is visible at least in some investment awards.[87] The local consensus and balance of competing values and interests are reflected in a variety of national property regimes, but investment protection imposes a much more individualistic and neoliberal balance on host societies. The awareness of those differences and their implications should guide the substantive ISDS reform.

BITs and investment protection were invented as a panacea for the problems and difficulties associated with national property regimes, where sovereign control in the public interest is an inherent feature. But the new international terminology did not resolve the underlying tensions: how to find the right and universal balance between communal and individual interests? What is the role of a state in economic life, and what are the limits society wants to draw for the state's actions? It seems that the current crisis of ISDS is at least partially a *déjà-vu* of the debate on 'the international minimum standard v national standard' and the failure to harmonise property protection at

---

85 Schneiderman, *Constitutionalizing economic globalization: investment rules and democracy's promise* 48; Vicki Been and Joel C Beauvais, 'The Global Fifth Amendment? NAFTA's Investment Protections and the Misguided Quest for an International "Regulatory Takings" Doctrine' (2003) 78 *New York University Law Review* 30.

86 *Vattenfall AB, Vattenfall Europe AG, Vattenfall Europe Generation AG & Co KG v The Federal Republic of Germany* (ICSID) (settled); *Philip Morris Asia Limited v Commonwealth of Australia* (PCA) para 567.

87 In *Southern Pacific Properties (Middle East) Limited v Arab Republic of Egypt* (ICSID) the tribunals considered the importance of cultural heritage, but prioritized proprietary interest. In the following cases tribunals also prioritised proprietary interest over environmental: *SD Myers Inc v Canada (UNCITRAL NAFTA Chapter 11 Arbitration Tribunal)*; *Compañía del Desarrollo de Santa Elena v Republic of Costa Rica (ICSID)* para 12.

the international level some 70 years ago.[88] Thus, in order to understand the current tensions in the ISDS, property protection at the national and international level has to be revisited.

Investment protection is a derivative of property protection. Very often, investment protection is justified by the same arguments that are conceived for property protection.[89] Although economically, investment protection on an international level performs similar functions to constitutional property protection in national systems,[90] there are important differences in where and how those systems operate. While property is situated among other protected values and interests of society, international law does not have mandatory mechanisms that integrate the interests of others. Investment protection is ensured by result-oriented obligations and mandatory dispute resolution mechanisms, but the protection of other interests of the international community, such as the environment, human rights, and the prohibition of the use of force, only have rudimentary protection on the international level.[91] The equalisation of international investment law with some kind of global constitution restraining sovereign states has been criticised for prioritising markets, existing wealth distribution, and inhibiting reforms necessary for development.[92] This asymmetry and fragmentation also contribute to dissatisfaction with how the ISDS operates.

---

88 FV García-Amador, Louis B Sohn and RR Baxter, *Recent Codification of the Law of State Responsibility for Injuries to Aliens* (A. Sijthoff 1974) viii; M Sornarajah, *The Pursuit of Nationalized Property* (1986) 32; Tzvika Alan Nissel, 'A History of State Responsibility: The Struggle for International Standards (1870–1960)' (Doctoral Dissertation, University of Helsinki 2016) 320–344.

89 Harold Demsetz, 'Toward a Theory of Property Rights' (1967) 57 The American Economic Review 347; Douglass C North, *Institutions, Institutional Change, and Economic Performance* (Cambridge University Press 1990) 139.

90 Riddhi Dasgupta, *International Interplay: The Future of Expropriation Across International Dispute Settlement* (2013) 30–34.

91 Federico Ortino, 'The Social Dimension of International Investment Agreements: Drafting a New BIT/MIT Model?' (2005) 7 *International Law Forum du droit international* 243; Anne van Aaken, 'Fragmentation of International Law: The Case of International Investment Protection' (2006) 17 Finnish Yearbook of International Law 91; Suzanne A Spears, 'The Quest for Policy Space in a New Generation of International Investment Agreements' (2010) 13 Journal of International Economic Law 1037; Rainer Hofmann and Christian Tams, *International Investment Law and Its Others* (Nomos 2012) 9.

92 Stephen Gill and Claire A Cutler, *New Constitutionalism and World Order* (Cambridge University Press 2014) 1; Jean D'Aspremont, 'International Legal Constitutionalism, Legal Forms, and the Need for Villains' in Anthony F Lang and Antje Wiener (eds), *Handbook on Global Constitutionalism* (Edward Elgar 2017) 155; Slobodian 12–13; Perrone, *Investment Treaties and the Legal Imagination: How Foreign Investors Play By Their Own Rules* 2–3.

6 Structure of the Book

Below this Introduction, Chapter 2 explains the origins of different philosophical approaches to property and how they play out in the competing narratives of international law and interpretations of investment treaties. For the purposes of this analysis, the thinking about property is categorised into two broad ideologies. On the one hand, communitarian ideology, which prioritises community interest, and on the other hand – individualistic ideology, which prioritises individual interest or at least claims that the common interest of society can be served better through the satisfaction of individual interests. Some states and communities have historical tendencies to favour one ideology over the other, but none of them has it in pure form. For good or for bad, international investment law was based on a very individualistic understanding of property, although this was masked under abstract and general language. The problem with one-dimensional international investment law was that neither the international community nor separate host states could widely support it, as it was too individualistic and clashed with local communitarian values and interests.

Chapter 3 shows how different societies have drawn different boundaries of property protection *vis-à-vis* a state, depending on their particular needs and historical experience. For this purpose, a public, private, and constitutional law overview of different legal systems and how they perceive property protection is provided. Common law jurisdictions, such as the USA, the UK, Australia, Singapore, and India, are compared with mixed legal systems (Canada, South Africa) and civil law countries (France, Germany, the Netherlands, Poland, Baltic states and Russia, China, South Korea, Japan, and Brazil).

Chapter 4 ties into the previous chapters by showing the transformation from the national concept of property protection to investment protection under investment treaties. The chapter explores the historical origins of property protection in customary international law and how property protection was redefined by international law instruments and practice. Through the Iran–US claims tribunals practice, BITs, and investment arbitration, the chapter tries to capture the general scope and level of investment protection and analyses how it compares to property protection under national legal systems.

The interplay between national property regimes, investment protection, and human rights law is discussed in Chapter 5. The scope and level of protection of possessions under the European human rights practice could be situated somewhere between national property regimes and international investment protection. However, it is difficult or even impossible to identify a universal practice with regard to the human right to property. Social and economic rights have regional understandings, and any interpretation should be applied with caution outside the region where it originated. This especially concerns the practice of the European Court of Human Rights (ECtHR) on the protection of possessions.

Chapter 6 argues that property and investment protection have embarked on two divergent trajectories, and this mismatch creates tensions on various levels. In principle, international investment law adheres to the individualistic property paradigm of stable and developed states, which are oriented towards wealth preservation. Investment arbitration practice is antagonistic towards development and change-oriented legal systems, which prioritise community interests over individual interest.

The primary implication of this divergence is that the tensions created by the gap between the dominant interpretation of investment protection and the principles of property protection under national laws can seriously undermine the ISDS system. For the system to survive, property protection and investment protection should be more compatible. The book explores the possible reconciliation of property and investment protection strategies. Redistributive aspects of property regimes, which are present in most of the developing states, should be recognised as valid considerations in investment arbitration, thus lowering the tensions in the system and enhancing the perceived legitimacy of investment awards, acceptance, and internalisation of international investment law.

CHAPTER 2

Philosophical Framework for Property Protection

Historically originating from property protection, investment protection is often justified in the name of the 'sacred' right to property. Despite the close intersections between the two, conversations within international investment law have routinely excluded the theory of property, which offers a broader perspective on the place and value of property in society. Having a better understanding of the different ideologies behind property should help to appreciate and explain the tensions in the ISDS. These insights might provide a useful normative framework for the ISDS reform.

1 Property Law: Relative or Universal?

Various societies, at different times and for numerous historical, geopolitical, and social reasons, have developed diverse understandings of property and expectations regarding its protection.[1] A spectrum of distinct national notions of property exists, outlining varying boundaries of property protection according to the specific needs and historical experiences of each society. These conceptual differences are significant, even if discourse in international investment law does not articulate them, or merely simplifies them as North *versus* South or developed *versus* developing states' divide. International investment law conceals much deeper ideological and philosophical divisions than may be apparent at first glance.

International investment law originated from national concepts of property, but it has also evolved towards some neoliberal ideal. The current mismatch between national property regimes and investment protection has been downplayed in the investment arbitration practice for several decades by promoting investment protection as a completely separate standard, divorced from the national problems of property protection. Nevertheless, the present challenges in international investment law and arbitration may necessitate a thorough reassessment of the origins, extent, and underlying assumptions about investment protection.

1 Crawford Brough Macpherson, *Property: Mainstream and Critical Positions* (University of Toronto Press 1978) 1.

 | HTTPS://DOI.ORG/10.1163/9789004763517-003

Against the backdrop of diverse national concepts of property, economic and social contexts, as well as philosophical justifications for them, this chapter examines two divergent ideologies regarding property: communitarian and individualistic.[2] The communitarian understanding of property suggests that disputes regarding the boundaries and substance of property rights are typically resolved with a focus on the interests of society as a whole. In contrast, the individualistic understanding of property indicates a propensity to resolve conflicts in favour of the owner.

National property regimes are more communitarian than international investment law, as property in national law exists alongside and amidst various societal interests and considerations. In contrast, international investment law, as it is constructed and interpreted, tends to favour the concept of individualistic and neoliberal investment protection detached from wider societal concerns.[3] The design of the ISDS leaves other interests of society outside of the system. For instance, the possibility of counterclaims was not envisaged in early BITs, and investment arbitration practice is sceptical about such a possibility unless specifically allowed by the agreement.[4] Furthermore, concerns regarding the environment, health and safety, and proper market functioning do not inherently belong to the investment protection regime under investment treaties.[5] These concerns are only considered as defences for a state in investment arbitration, and even then, they enjoy varying degrees of success.

Orthodox international investment law interpretation and practice mostly reflect the individualistic understanding of property that, at a certain historical moment, suited the foreign policy objectives of the most powerful countries, ideological schools, or even some influential individuals and compa-

---

2 This taxonomy and terminology are inspired by the debate between liberals and communitarians. However, the divide is relative and adopted only with the purpose of facilitating the comparison of different attitudes and practices: Daniel A Bell, *East Meets West: Human Rights and Democracy in East Asia* (Princeton University Press 2000) 7.

3 Slobodian 272.

4 Yaraslau Kryvoi, 'Counterclaims in Investor-State Arbitration' (2012) Minnesota Journal of International Law 216; See also arguments allowing tribunals to hear a wider range of counterclaims in Mees Brenninkmeijer and Fabien Gélinas, 'Counterclaims in Investment Arbitration: Towards an Integrated Approach' (2023) 38 ICSID Review – Foreign Investment Law Journal 567.

5 There are modest developments towards integration in the new treaties: Crina Baltag, Riddhi Joshi, and Kabir Duggal, 'Recent Trends in Investment Arbitration on the Right to Regulate, Environment, Health and Corporate Social Responsibility: Too Much or Too Little?' (2023) 38 ICSID Review – Foreign Investment Law Journal 381.

nies.[6] The one-sidedness of the ISDS system becomes apparent when comparing it with national legal systems and how they operate.

The debates over the dualistic nature of property started in the ancient world. Ever since then, people have been fascinated with the idea of property, its place in society, and its interaction with power and authority.[7] Depending on different organising principles and values – freedom, happiness, justice, wealth – different societies provide slightly different answers to the basic questions of property theory: What could be owned? What are the limits of property, if any? What does it mean to own? Why do we have property systems? What are the benefits and costs of property regimes? What purposes should the property serve, if any? Is property a natural institution or a social construct? Do ownership rights trump all other considerations? How are conflicting interests resolved? Are obligations towards the society part of property?

While some argue that '[p]rivate property has always enjoyed a unique sanctity under modern international law' and 'modern international law developed for the express purpose of protecting private property rights from state interference',[8] others maintained that law, in general, is not natural and universally discoverable by faith or reason, but a social construct depending on social circumstances.[9] For example, Underkuffler argued that property cannot be defined by a theory of rights only, that individual rights are 'fluid in time, established and re-established' as new circumstances justify, and that values that property claims assert are socially construed, changeable, and often contentious.[10] Alexander reiterated that property can serve multiple historically assigned purposes:

> Property rights are epiphenomenal. They are not ends in themselves but rather an instrument designed to instantiate and serve deeper substantive values, such as wealth maximisation, personal privacy, and individual self-realisation. In this

---

6 Slobodian 8, 11; Perrone, *Investment Treaties and the Legal Imagination: How Foreign Investors Play By Their Own Rules* 2, 170.

7 The academic debate whether property is a natural or conventional right is intensive and extensive. See for example: Bret Boyce, 'Property as a Natural Right and as a Conventional Right in Constitutional Law' (2007) 29 Loyola of Los Angeles International and Comparative Law Review 202.

8 L Benjamin Ederington, 'Property as a Natural Institution: The Separation of Property from Sovereignty in International Law' (1997) 13 American University International Law Review 263, 264–265.

9 Martti Koskenniemi, 'The politics of international law' (1990) 112 European Journal of International Law 4, 7.

10 Laura S Underkuffler, *The Idea of Property: Its Meaning and Power* (Oxford University Press 2003) 51.

> sense property rights are never 'fundamental'. Only the substantive interests they serve can be.[11]

Even though different societies and languages use the same term – 'property', it means different things to them, because '[i]n different periods, different perceptions produce more or less subtly different treatments of what is widely regarded as a central issue in social and moral life: property – its origins, legitimacy and status'.[12] Thus, regional human rights instruments and national constitutions recognise the right to property to varying degrees.[13]

The following brief and predominantly Eurocentric historical overview of the philosophical discourse on property is essential to critically re-evaluate widely held stereotypes and assumptions concerning property in investment arbitration. The philosophical discussion on property starts in antiquity, and this chapter traces the major ideas and conversations among philosophers, theologians, scholars, advocates, and politicians. This chapter challenges the selective use of historical arguments for the benefit of the individualistic interpretation of property in the international context:

> those who defend the existing property order (whatever that happens to be) maintain that something has happened in the past (often, in the very distant past) which makes the present arrangements legitimate – and inviolable.[14]

2 Two Opposing Views of Property

Written discussions on the nature of property and its content have reached us from Ancient Greece, where only male citizens were allowed to own property. At that time, two dominant attitudes towards property were established. Plato argued that the best system for the ideal *Republic* was when its governing class was denied the ability to own property and had to share resources communally.[15] According to Plato, such a system prevented the selfishness of those

---

11 Gregory S Alexander, 'Property as a fundamental constitutional right?: the German example' (2003) 88 Cornell law review 733, 738.

12 Peter Garnsey, *Thinking about property: from antiquity to the age of revolution* (Cambridge University Press 2007) 2.

13 National property regimes will be addressed in Chapter 3 and human rights in Chapter 5.

14 Christopher Pierson, *Just Property: A History in the Latin West. Volume One: Wealth, Virtue, and the Law* (Oxford University Press 2013) 10.

15 Plato, *The Republic* (Benjamin Jowett tr, 360 BCE) <http://classics.mit.edu/Plato/republic.6.v.html> accessed on 27 April 2021.

who had been granted the power to rule the lives of others. However, Plato did not deny that other classes of the society could own property.

Aristotle criticised Plato's ideas about property, claiming that without private property, individuals had no incentive to either work or manage resources effectively.[16] According to Aristotle, 'democracy should not confiscate the wealth of rich people, virtuous or otherwise, and divide it up', because 'there will be endless quarrels'.[17]

This Plato–Aristotle dichotomy had such a profound influence on property theory development that all subsequent writings on the topic could be viewed as merely footnotes to the Plato–Aristotle discussions.[18]

However, historical arguments are prone to abuse. Some commentators claimed that the principle of protection of alien property was known since the Roman times. For example, Escarcena, relying on Roman law, implied that foreign property should be protected from state interference.[19] Similar claims, were based on the earliest main Roman law source – the Twelve Tables. The Sixth Table allegedly stated that the '[r]ight of ownership is inalienable for ever in dealings with a stranger' (*hostis*).[20] However, this 'argument' was not accurate, since it was constructed from an inadequate translation of rule 6 of the Sixth Tablet. The rule should be translated as '[a]gainst a foreigner the right to property shall be valid forever'.[21] This means completely the opposite than the protection of alien property: the foreigner cannot benefit from limitation periods or other restrictions on vindication. This example only illustrates the myth about the absolute property protection:

> In the nineteenth century, legal theory created the myth of absolute, exclusive, and unbounded individual ownership, which seemingly had its roots in classical Roman law. [However] ownership was never an abstract, unlimited right in

16 Garnsey 6, 24.

17 James Gordley, *Foundations of Private Law: Property, Tort, Contract, Unjust Enrichment* (Oxford University Press 2006) 9.

18 Alfred North Whitehead, *Process and Reality: An Essay in Cosmology* (The Free Press 1979) 39.

19 Sebastian Lopez Escarcena, *Indirect Expropriation in International Law* (Edward Elgar Publishing Limited 2014) 2.

20 Marcus Tullius Cicero, *De Officiis*, Book I, para 37, Translated by Walter Miller Loeb edn. (Cambridge: Harvard University Press) 1913, <http://www.constitution.org/rom/ de_officiis.htm> accessed on 25 January 2017.

21 Oliver J Thatcher, ed, *The Library of Original Sources* (Milwaukee: University Research Extension Co, 1901) Vol. III: *The Roman World* 9–11; Coleman-Norton, PR, *The Twelve Tables* (Princeton: Princeton University 1960) <http://www.gutenberg.org/cache/epub/14783/pg14783-images.html> accessed on 18 April 2019.

> ancient Rome. Ownership was rather a dynamic category with changing legal content according to its social, political, and economic environment.[22]

There were many reasons why the myth of absolute Roman property rights was useful at the time of interpretation.[23] In reality, random or almost random expropriations, redistributions, and regulations of the use of property without compensation were frequent in Roman times. For example:

> a corpus naviculariorum – was instituted, consisting of landowners who had to invest in the building and maintenance of ships which, with the ships of other landowners, were organised into a fleet. This fleet, managed by the corpus, would transport grain for the public distributions from Africa to Ostia, where it was unloaded.[24]

Landowners were obliged to provide certain services to the public: 'the maintenance of roads and the public postal system came to be a charge, this time imposed on adjoining landowners'.[25] Ownership of property entailed obligations for the common good and in this way resembled communitarian understanding of property rather than individualistic because '[t]he Roman law of property ... had a strong component of social obligation'.[26] Despite providing the early definitions of property and exposing the content of ownership rights, Roman property law was not giving preference to the interests of the owner. On the contrary, very often, the property was subjugated to the interests of the state, monarch, or wider society. Thus, the reliance on Roman law to explain and justify an individualistic understanding of investment protection is misplaced.

---

22 Eva Jakab, 'Property Rights in Ancient Rome' in Paul Erdkamp, Koenraad Verboven, and Arjan Zuiderhoek (eds), *Ownership and Exploitation of Land and Natural Resources in the Roman World* (Oxford University Press 2015) 107–130; Anna di Robilant, *The Making of Modern Property: Reinventing Roman Law in Europe and its Peripheries 1789–1950* (Cambridge University Press 2023) 39.

23 Boyce 211.

24 Boudewijn Sirks, 'Public Law' in David Johnston (ed), *The Cambridge Companion to Roman Law* (Cambridge University Press 2015) 340.

25 Ibid 341.

26 Boyce 211.

3 The Rise of Individualistic Approach to Property

The polemic on property and its nature was evolving throughout Medieval Europe. During the early Middle Ages, the rejection of property and wealth was a Christian ideal.[27] Similar to Plato's communitarian argument, Saint Ambrose and Saint Augustine argued that 'by nature all things are held in common' and 'private property is the result of sin', thus 'relative and conditional'.[28] Later, the Christian Church changed this opinion to the more pragmatic Aristotle's line of argument.[29] Saint Thomas Aquinas, discussing the nature of justice, refined Aristotle's ideas that to prevent chaos, property is necessary;[30] however, in 'Aquinas's view, private ownership is not a part of the natural law, but it is not against natural law'.[31]

It was only later that the Franciscan Order and William of Ockham started crafting individualistic theories of property rights, which were useful for the struggle against the pope and absolute monarchs.[32]

The Dominican monks Francisco de Vitoria and Domingo de Soto from the School of Salamanca discussed property and *dominium* in the context of the American conquest. Salamancans attempted to justify the war against Amerindians arguing, not on the basis of faith and religion, but on natural law, that allegedly self-preservation required and entitled individuals to engage in trade, craft, and travel, as well as to send ambassadors and missionaries.[33] While in Europe, property was emerging as a concept separate from religious and sovereign powers, outside Europe, it was projected as an outcome of power relations, encouraging travellers to seize uncultivated land.[34] *Jus gentium*, originating from the natural divine order, allegedly allowed Europeans 'to travel into the lands [of Indians] and to sojourn there', 'carry on trade among the native Indians' and spread the religion.[35] Francisco de Vitoria argued that '[t]

27 Peter Garnsey, *Thinking About Property From Antiquity to the Age of Revolution* (Cambridge University Press, 2008) 62–63, 86, 106.

28 Richard Schlatter, *Private Property: The History of an Idea* (Allen & Unwin 1951) 35–38.

29 Koskenniemi, *To the Uttermost Parts of the Earth: Legal Imagination and International Power 1300–1870* 92.

30 Garnsey, *Thinking About Property From Antiquity to the Age of Revolution* 43.

31 Pierson 91.

32 Boyce 215.

33 Andrew Fitzmaurice, *Sovereignty, Property and Empire, 1500–2000* (Cambridge University Press 2014) 48.

34 Koskenniemi, *To the Uttermost Parts of the Earth: Legal Imagination and International Power 1300–1870* 113, 338; Anghie 13.

35 Franciscus Victoria, *De Indis et de Ivre Belli Relectiones* (John Pawley tr, The Carnegie Institution of Washington 1917) First Relectio s 3, 151, 152.

he Spaniards have a right' under the law of nations (*jus gentium*), which either is natural law or derived from God.[36] If the natives 'wish to prevent' it, the Spaniards could 'make war on the Indians'[37] with all subsequent effects, such as the loss of property, territory, and sovereignty.

The ideology behind property rights, shaping their scope and content, became a tool for geopolitics and political economy. This potential to bend the concept of property for self-serving ends was evident in the works of Hugo Grotius. On the one hand, among European sovereign states, he was claiming that foreigners 'owe obedience to the sovereign, for the time during which they reside in his territories'[38] and should 'submit to the established laws of the place, and avoid every occasion of exciting tumult and sedition'.[39] But, on the other hand, he argued that property might be acquired by occupation, especially if the territory is outside Europe, which suited the United East India Company's (VOC's) interests in Southeast Asia, denying the natives any sovereignty and legitimacy of their property.[40]

Notwithstanding the exclusion of other races, civilisations and continents, the European natural law school, subject to some limitations, agreed 'that by nature, or originally, or in principle, all things belong to everyone' and 'private ownership is instituted to overcome the disadvantages of common ownership'.[41] Thus, 'one person could not deprive another of his property' and '[t]he owner may have more than he ideally should since an incentive has to be given to work and to manage'.[42]

Locke developed the idea of property as a natural right further arguing that labour turns common goods of nature into private property. The labour theory of property justified American discovery, conquest, and colonisation.[43] Amer-

36 Ibid 154.

37 Ibid 155.

38 Hugo Grotius, *The Rights of War and Peace, including the Law of Nature and of Nations* (trans AC Campbell, New York, M Walter Dunne, 1901) Book II, Chapter II, 'The General Right of Things' s V.

39 Ibid XVI.

40 Benjamin Straumann, 'Natural rights and just wars' in *Roman Law in the State of Nature: The Classical Foundations of Hugo Grotius' Natural Law* (Cambridge University Press 2015) 32, 180; Martti Koskenniemi, 'International Law and the Emergence of Mercantile Capitalism: Grotius to Smith' in *The Roots of International Law: Liber Amicorum Peter Haggenmacher* (Martinus Nijhoff Publishers 2014) 6.

41 Gordley 10.

42 Ibid. Pufendorf echoed ideas of Aristotle and Thomas Aquinas that property is a social construct beneficial for the society adding the idea that all citizens should bear equal burden before governmental duties: Boyce 221.

43 Gregory S Alexander and Eduardo M Peñalver, *An Introduction to Property Theory* (Cambridge University Press 2012) 39.

ican land was conveniently presumed to be uncultivated and unoccupied, while native populations were presumed to be 'uncivilised' to have sovereignty:

> As much land as a man tills, plants, improves, cultivates, and can use the product of, so much is his property. He by his labour does, as it were, inclose it from the common.[44]

The labour theory of property forms the basis of the current individualistic understanding of property and is the backbone of investment protection. In very broad terms, Locke's theory of property emphasised an individual's contribution to the creation of property, and subsequently excluded the broader society from the enjoyment of that property. In moral terms, the isolation of property from the general needs of society was justified by labour, but Locke could not explain why slaves did not own the fruits of their labour. Also, his theory undermines the redistributive aspect of colonial appropriation and to what extent occupation was backed by force. Locke's ideas suited the times of the Glorious Revolution and later inspired Blackstone and the USA Constitution. '[T]he rise of private property as an objective, historical process' was braided into the natural law reasoning, where kings had limited powers to tamper with commerce.[45] Despite internal contradictions, Locke's theory had a profound influence on the USA understanding of property[46] and later had many followers.[47]

While general law was liberating from the theologian embrace, private property received individualistic endorsement from the Scottish and German Enlightenments.

Adam Smith argued that by 'general principles, which ought to be the foundation of the law of all nations' the government is subordinated to the idea of property: 'the very end of [government] is to secure wealth, and to defend the rich from the poor'.[48] In line with mercantile and pragmatic interests, he

---

44 John Locke, *Two Treatises of Government* (Cambridge University Press 1988) The Second Treatise of Civil Government Ch V sec 32, 290.

45 Koskenniemi, *To the Uttermost Parts of the Earth: Legal Imagination and International Power (1300–1870)* 336, 340.

46 Boyce 233.

47 Alexander and Peñalver 44.

48 Adam Smith, *Lectures on Jurisprudence (Lectures on Justice, Police, Revenue and Arms, delivered in the University of Glasgow)* (Clarendon Press 1869) 1, 15 <https://oll.libertyfund.org/title/smith-lectures-on-justice-police-revenue-and-arms-1763#lf1647_head_006>accessed on 22 October2021.

explained the occurrence of property and the initial distribution of wealth as a natural historical process from '"the common sense" of the impartial spectator'.[49] Hume went even further, ignoring the dilemma of the first distribution and focusing on the justification of the current property system – the social utility that it brings to society.[50]

In addition, the German Enlightenment fostered global perspectives based on the principles of individual freedom and will.[51] According to Kant, individual freedom was a central organising principle from which duties and property could be explained: 'it is a duty of right to act towards others so that what is external (usable) could also become someone's'.[52] Hegel was explaining that property, the economy, and the state were necessary for realising the free will of a person: 'when I as a free will am in possession of something, I get a tangible existence, and in this way first became an actual will. This is the true and legal nature of property'.[53] For Hegel, property was not a goal in itself, but only a canvas for the free will of a person.

As Europe was abolishing feudalism and absolutism, as well as in the context of the American Revolution, philosophical theories of individual rights and private property were useful tools of persuasion in a struggle against the ancient regime.[54] The success of the private property argument in the struggle against the absolutist monarchies contributed a lot towards the mythologisation of private property in later centuries.[55]

Post-revolutionary Europe and America were fertile grounds for divergent discussions on the nature and limits of the right to property. Although some general trends could be observed, the understanding of property was always contested. For example, in England, some radical proposals were formulated concerning property at the time of the Revolution, arguing for a wider redis-

---

49 Christopher Pierson, *Just property: Enlightenment, revolution, and history Volume two* (First edn, Oxford University Press 2016) 30.

50 David Hume, *A Treatise of Human Nature* (Oxford University Press 2000) 314, 3.2.2; Koskenniemi, *To the Uttermost Parts of the Earth: Legal Imagination and International Power 1300–1870* 656.

51 Pierson, *Just property: Enlightenment, Revolution, and History, Volume two* 70.

52 Immanuel Kant, *The Metaphysics of Morals* (Mary J. Gregor tr, Cambridge University Press 1996) [6:252] 42–43.

53 Georg Wilhelm Friedrich Hegel, *Philosophy of Right* (S.W Dyde tr, Batoche Books Kitchener 2001) note 45, 58.

54 Koskenniemi, *To the Uttermost Parts of the Earth: Legal Imagination and International Power 1300–1870* 958.

55 di Robilant 131.

tribution of wealth, advancing a social cause.[56] In France, Rousseau, continuing Plato's communitarian tradition, argued that property is a social construct and should be redefined and redistributed to correct the error of the first occupancy when humanity was not ready for the property system. Rousseau continued that transformation with an element of coercion might be necessary to bend individual will to the general will.[57] To that effect, the French Revolution nationalised the property of the Roman Catholic Church and the Crown. The French Declaration of the Rights of Man and of the Citizen of 1789 cemented this major redistribution of wealth after the Revolution by recognising individual property rights. Across the Atlantic, the original USA Constitution failed to include the protection of property, although the right to property quickly found its way into the Fifth Amendment of the USA Constitution.[58]

As evident from this brief overview, the emergence of the notion of property as a natural and universal right, in contrast to the social construct that could be adapted to the needs of society, was gaining traction in the Western European states on the path to industrialisation. However, consensus, even within Western Europe, was lacking, and despite occasional declarations of absolute and sacred private property, numerous initiatives were undertaken to redefine property and redistribute wealth.

4 The Myth of Sacred Private Property

In nineteenth-century Western Europe, liberalism captivated the imagination of lawyers and became a dominant ideology:

> [b]oth civil and common lawyers tried to preserve a systematic legal doctrine, while purging it of concepts of commutative and distributive justice which they had inherited from an earlier era and which no longer made sense to them. The key concept around which they tried to build private law was will.[59]

---

56 Myriam-Isabelle Ducrocq, 'The Debate on Property during the First English Revolution 1647–1659: A Historical Perspective' Miranda OpenEdition (2016) 1.

57 John James Rousseau, *Discourse upon the Origin and Foundation of the Inequality among Mankind* (R and J Dodsley 1761) 97.

58 Michael W McConnell, 'Contract Rights and Property Rights: A Case Study in the Relationship between Individual Liberties and Constitutional Structure' (1988) 76 California Law Review 267.

59 Gordley 14.

The 'free will', 'freedom', 'individual's self-interest' became cornerstone values and organising principles for most Western societies. The liberal order emphasised individual interests, passions, and subjective preferences which are limited only by the prohibition to cause harm to others.[60] This was especially noticeable in economic matters related to property.[61]

Other parts of the world during the nineteenth and twentieth centuries had much more communitarian attitudes towards property and state-individual relations. For example, in Russia, national interest was put above individual interests, and the sovereign had much more power against individuals than what was acceptable in the Anglo-Saxon world.[62] Malksoo, citing Taube, argued that one of the main differences from Western Europe in the context of private law was a weak notion of property rights in Russia, as well as anti-liberal anti-democratic attitudes.[63] No wonder that Russia in 1917 challenged the individualistic concept of property with Marxist ideology.[64] Private property, as it was and is understood in the Western world, did not exist in the Soviet Union at all.[65] While the Soviet school of conceptualising the relationship between the state and the individual did not survive after the collapse of the Soviet Union, the communitarian understanding of property thrives in many places around the world. It does so not because the rest of the world follows the Soviet school of international law, but because it resonates with that alternative vision for property and the relationship between the individual and the community.

The oscillation between individual and communitarian understandings of property is far from settled, even now in Western Europe. Depending on the economic cycle, the laws, public attitudes governing politics lean either

60 Martti Koskenniemi, *From Apology to Utopia: The Structure of International Legal Argument* (Cambridge University Press 2006) 76.

61 Carol M Rose, 'Property as the Keystone Right?' (1995) 71 Notre Dame Law Review 329, 333; di Robilant 167.

62 Lauri Mälksoo, *Russian approaches to international law* (Oxford University Press 2015) 40–41, 47–48; Lauri Mälksoo, 'The History of International Legal Theory in Russia: a Civilizational Dialogue with Europe' (2008) 19 European Journal of International Law 218, 223.

63 Mälksoo, *Russian approaches to international law* 68; Michail A Taube and Walther Schücking, *Russland und Westeuropa* (*Russlands histor. Sonderentwicklg in d. europäischen Völkergemeinschaft*) (G Stilke 1928) 51; D W Treadgold, The West in Russia and China, vol 1 Russia, 1472–1917 (Cambridge: CUP, 1973) XXII.

64 Kate Miles, '1917: Property, Revolution and Rejection in International Law' in K. Greenman and others (eds), *Revolutions in International Law The Legacies of 1917* (Cambridge University Press 2021) 271.

65 Grzybowski Kazimierz, 'Reform of Civil Law in Hungary, Poland, and the Soviet Union' (1961) 10 The American Journal of Comparative Law 253, 260–261.

towards more active or more passive state participation in the economy, with accompanying redefinition of private rights. Thus, the twentieth century saw two conflicting tendencies and narratives about the nature of property.[66]

On the one hand, during times of economic crisis and depression, an increase in the welfare and regulatory state, as well as the extensive limitation of individual private rights in the interest of society, was observed even in Western societies.[67] Active state participation in economic affairs with ensuing redefinition of property rights was evident in Theodore Roosevelt's progressive reforms, in state-led reforms and projects addressing the Great Depression, as well as the rebuilding of Europe with economy-wide nationalisations after WWII. In fact, the current regulation of all features of modern life has been so pervasive that almost all aspects of property and its rights are positively regulated in some form, and most regulatory changes will result in a changing scope of property rights.[68] Singer also argued for a systemic rather than individualistic view of property, explaining that property regimes coordinate competing entitlements and claims within a society; thus, regulation is an integral part of defining and allocating the entitlements.[69]

On the other hand, the economic reality of the Western world was still dominated by the rhetoric of 'free will' and 'individual autonomy' accompanied by the myth of sacred property protection.[70] The industrialised world enjoyed wealth and economic advances, attributing success to private property, but ignored the demise of philosophical 'free will' as an organising principle of society.[71] However, the narrative of individualistic private property dominated the revival of classical liberalism oriented towards export – the rest of the world. For example, the Washington Consensus was based on 'the work of Ronald Coase, Harold Demsetz, and Douglass North and their emphasis on' the superiority of private property as the main organising principle of

66 Diane A Desierto, *Public Policy in International Economic Law: the ICESCR in trade, finance, and investment* (First edn, Oxford University Press 2015) 52.

67 John Maynard Keynes, *The Collected Writings of John Maynard Keynes: The General Theory of Employment, Interest and Money*, vol 7 (Cambridge University Press 2013) 373; Morris Raphael Cohen, 'Property and sovereignty' (1927) 13 Cornell Law Review 21–22.

68 Carol M Rose, 'Property and Exporpriation: Themes and Variations in American Law' (2000) 1 Utah Law Review 4, 38.

69 Joseph William Singer, *Introduction to Property* (2 edn, Aspen Publishers 2005) 4.

70 Friedrich A von Hayek and Bruce Caldwell, *The Road to Serfdom: Text and Documents*, vol 2 (Definitive edn, University of Chicago Press 2007) 49; Ederington, 264; John Linarelli, Law, Rights and Development, in John Linarelli (ed), *Research Handbook on Global Justice and International Economic Law* (Edward Elgar Publishing, 2013) 318.

71 Gordley 16; di Robilant 204.

society.[72] Clear and strong property rights protected from any wealth redistribution, combined with other neo-liberal economic policies, were treated by the World Bank as the key component of good governance and economic development.[73] Sprankling, drawing mainly on Anglo-American experience and understanding of property, also claimed the emergence of international property law as a general principle of law accepted by the majority of states.[74] Furthermore, the neoliberal attitudes to property so popular in the USA – the dominating superpower – received an unexpected endorsement from the collapse of the Soviet Union and the reorientation of the economies and societies of its former satellites. The successful export of neoliberal attitudes to property was riding the wave of increasing globalisation and economic growth.[75]

Besides the aforementioned two general tendencies, one more development in recent discussions on property has to be mentioned – the property claims by the First Nations in previously colonised lands.[76] Recognising legal and moral complications created by the colonisation, there has been growing recognition of 'land claims by the autochthonous population in countries such as Australia, Canada, South Africa and the United States', which 'used their land before Western property law was brought to them'.[77] These claims by the First Nations question the Western type of ownership law, but curiously enough combine communitarian and the individualistic understandings of property to achieve their goals.[78]

72 Frank K Upham, *The Great Property Fallacy: Theory, Reality, and Growth in Developing Countries* (Cambridge University Press 2018) 1–2.

73 World Bank, *From Plan to Market: World Development Report* (1996), 48–49; Ibrahim F I Shihata, *The World Bank legal papers* (Martinus Nijhoff 2000) 272–273, 277; Taylor St John, *The Rise of Investor-State Arbitration: Politics, Law, and Unintended Consequences* (Oxford Academic, Oxford University Press 2018) 138.

74 Sprankling 23, 219.

75 Successful strategies for development are still debated. See for example, Daron Acemoglu and James A. Robinson, *Why Nations Fail: The Origins of Power, Prosperity, and Poverty* (Profile Books 2013) 428.

76 Roger Merino, 'The Land of Nations: Indigenous Struggles for Property and Territory in International Law' (2021) 115 AJIL Unbound 129; Perrone, *Investment Treaties and the Legal Imagination: How Foreign Investors Play By Their Own Rules* 203.

77 Nils Jansen and Sjef Van Erp, 'Comparative Property Law' in (Oxford University Press 2006) 1045.

78 David Schneiderman, *Investment Law's Alibis: Colonialism, Imperialism, Debt and Development* (Cambridge University Press 2022) 129; John Borrows, 'Indigenous Diversities in International Investment and Trade' in John Borrows and Risa Schwartz (eds), *Indigenous Peoples and International Trade: Building Equitable and Inclusive International Trade and Investment Agreements* (Cambridge University Press 2020) 11.

Summarising the philosophical discussions about property, it could be observed that both communitarian and individualistic ideologies, to a greater or lesser extent, have existed in almost all societies at different points in time. All philosophical schools, doctrines, and theories, despite their differences, agree on one thing – property was never an aim *per se,* but just an instrument for achieving other underlying goals of individuals or society in general.[79] Property was only a tool to realise some other virtues. What those underlying ideals are and how to achieve them was often subject to disagreement. Despite the collapse of the main proponent of the communitarian understanding of property, many thinkers and communities are sceptical about the fundamental nature of the right to property and agree to a substantial reconfiguration of property rights through the legislative process.[80]

5 Investment Protection Ignores Communitarian Aspirations for Property

Property in the national legal systems is situated among and balanced by other societal interests and considerations. National private and public laws maintain historical mechanisms balancing individual and general interests. Consequently, the countries that favour higher levels of property protection for historical reasons have other ways to satisfy the common interests, be they cultural, economic, social, or military. In very crude terms, we could theorise that a rather individualistic approach to property in the UK is balanced by a well-functioning healthcare, education, social security system, and environmental protection. Meanwhile, the social consensus to prioritise owner's interests in the USA[81] is balanced by the promise of constant economic growth and the possibility of realising the American dream.

Other nations rely on the ability to adapt property rights or impose obligations on property to meet the needs of the community. For instance, many Northern, Central, and Eastern European countries, along with others, have upheld the right to free-roaming, meaning that the owner of land or forest cannot exclude others from enjoying nature.[82] It means the limits of property

---

79 Alexander 738.

80 Jeremy Waldron, *The Rule of Law and the Measure of Property* (Cambridge University Press 2012) 111.

81 Although Chapter 3 discusses many examples when the US legal system prioritises general interest of the society.

82 Gregory S Alexander, 'The Sporting Life: Democratic Culture and the Historical Origins of the Scottish Right to Roam' (2016) 2016 University of Illinois Law Review 321.

rights are set up, taking into account the general interest of society – to access and enjoy nature by way of camping, swimming, picking herbs, mushrooms, and berries.

The conceptual tensions in international investment law arise from the attempt to impose an individualistic understanding of property on societies that favour a communitarian perspective of property, which takes into account other societal interests, such as the protection of the environment or historical heritage, rational urban planning, or market functioning. The investment protection regime prioritises individual interests to operate the property abroad in a way that is the most profitable for the owner, excluding the interests of others. The ISDS system has mandatory dispute resolution and very efficient enforcement mechanisms remedying the interests of investors, while the presumed benefits for the host society are neither guaranteed nor have any realistic remedies. In other words, international investment law relies heavily on the individualistic understanding of property, ignoring other accounts of property and the interests of the local community, which supports the property regime.

In some situations, ISDS protects investors from outright theft, gross abuse of power, and discriminatory measures, and in that regard, ISDS is an achievement for efficiency, predictability, and stability in economic matters. However, investment disputes have sometimes been about value conflicts and how individual interests are protected from the competing interests of the general society. In that sense, the tensions that exist in international investment law are very similar to the conceptual problem of property – is it a social construct and thus relative depending on the consensus and cooperation within a particular society? This fundamental problem is further complicated by the fact that, in international investment law, the interests and values of two or more societies clash. In many Western societies, the individualistic concept of property is geared towards the maximisation and preservation of wealth. A high level of property protection fits the policy objectives of those countries that are interested in preserving the acquired wealth and which, due to their size and wealth, are able to project their ideology and power outside of their territories.[83] Thus, international investment law, as a neoliberal project, emphasises the absolute notion of property protection.

83 Slobodian 12–13; Perrone, *Investment Treaties and the Legal Imagination: How Foreign Investors Play By Their Own Rules* 2–3; Filip Batselé, 'Foreign Investors of the World, Unite! The International Association for the Promotion and Protection of Private Foreign Investments (APPI) 1958–1968' (2023) 34 European Journal of International Law 415; Fuad Zarbiyev, ''These are my principles. If you don't like them I have others.' On

The lack of interest in the communitarian approach to property in investment treaties and investment arbitration could be explained by several factors. First, comparative studies of property are limited and have not been readily available to the drafters of investment treaties and scholars because of the difficulties involved in the comparison of different property regimes. Second, international investment law was primarily oriented abroad and perceived by states and their negotiating officials as a zero-sum game. That is, the rules advocated by developed countries and crystallised in investment treaties are primarily concerned with extracting profit from foreign operations and maximising the benefits of the home country's enterprises. Any developmental benefits to the host country were perceived as externalities and not mandatory.

Furthermore, the Western notion of property, heavily influenced by the Anglo-Saxon legal tradition, can only exist without broad opposition in relatively wealthy countries that do not suffer from acute poverty, famine, healthcare problems, frequent natural disasters, or wars. Only a relatively stable Western social, economic, and geopolitical environment can persistently secure a high level of property protection. Countries that have to deal with natural or human-made calamities have a very different priority – the survival of the people or the state. Even Western philosophers and most legal systems admit that if a choice has to be made between life and property, life takes priority.

The neoliberal protection of property enshrined in IIAs elicits adverse reactions and resistance in host countries that confront different circumstances and choices than those of Western countries. Hybrid property systems, created by plugging in neo-liberal notions of property into foreign legal systems, have created discontent in capital-importing and developing states. This discontent sometimes is regarded as an unwillingness to pay debts or a wish to avoid contractual obligations or interference with 'sacred' property rights. However, the point that BITs export completely alien concepts of property is often overlooked.

As a practice and scholarly discipline, international investment law adopted the neoliberal understanding of property theory in international law without questioning its soundness and initial assumptions. The spread of the individualistic and neoliberal notion of property to non-Western, non-industrialised countries through investment treaties and arbitration was done on the promise that it would contribute to the prosperity of the host state. This underlying premise of international investment law was not tested and supported by

justifications of foreign investment protection under international law' (2023) 26 Journal of International Economic Law 525.

developmental studies. Recent Nobel Prize laureates argue that the inclusivity of institutions and social structures is the main factor explaining the differences in prosperity that we see today.[84] Acemoglu and Robinson do not deny that secure property rights are important, but they also emphasise that creative destruction of old forms and entitlements may be necessary to move the society from extractive to inclusive.[85] Other studies also indicate that creative destruction of old property rights that protect extractive structures may be vital to the reforms enabling fast industrialisation and prosperity of host states.[86]

It is impossible to resolve the current crisis in the system and to reform ISDS without admitting the other half in the property theory, that is, communitarian approaches to property in many developing host states. The discourse on property theory might help to put international investment protection into its proper context – among other means for achieving communal and even global goals.

In conclusion, international investment law, as evidenced in investment treaties, is predominantly built on neoliberal ideologies, based on 'freedom' and 'free will' philosophies of the Enlightenment. However, even back then, property was not perceived as a goal in itself. To a greater or lesser extent, it was subjugated to the interests of the community that supported a particular property regime. International investment law borrowed only a peculiar aspect from national property theories – the individual nature of property protection. It overemphasised the high level of property protection and ignored the variety of different understandings of property that existed in theory and worldwide. Despite some criticism, for several decades, the international investment law literature was unable to reflect on the broader implications of the individualistic understanding of property developed and best suited for the Western societies. For many years, IIAs were interpreted and applied in line with the neoliberal understanding of property, ignoring the communitarian aspirations and the balance between private, public, and global interests.[87]

84 Acemoglu and Robinson 75.

85 Ibid 84–85.

86 Daniel Behn, Tarald Laudal Berge, and Malcolm Langford, 'Poor states or poor governance? Testing claims of systemic bias in investment treaty arbitration' University of Oslo Faculty of Law Research Paper No 2016-08, 37 <https://ssrn.com/abstract=2956295> accessed on 17 May 2017; Upham 1–2; Brian Tamanaha, 'The Dark Side of the Relationship between the Rule of Law and Liberalism' (2008) 3 New York University Journal of Law & Liberty 516; Tom Allen, 'Comparative Constitutional Law in Asia' in *The Right to Property in Asia* (2014) 265.

87 See Chapter 4.

At a different developmental stage, host states might need more flexibility to implement reforms affecting property rights and individual interests. International investment law practitioners and academics should not distance themselves from the national legal traditions and complex questions of property theory, since such oversight can deprive the field of the possibility to create a sustainable global solution.[88]

88 The trend of new generation investment treaties is addressed in the Chapter 6.

CHAPTER 3

National Property Regimes

The previous chapter identified the two broad ways of thinking about property protection and, by extension, investment. The present chapter analyses how those communitarian and individualistic understandings of property are reflected in national legal systems.[1] The chapter illustrates the spectrum of national solutions, ranging from individualistic to communitarian. The binary allows us to grasp the broad diversity of legal systems and to analyse them in a meaningful way without losing perspective.

Despite the use of similar language to describe property and its protection, national legal systems have developed very different content. The understanding, interpretation, and application of property rules depend significantly on the stage of economic development, the underlying values of the society, and historical circumstances. Those understandings about property and its place in a society are among the most deeply ingrained and difficult to change, although not impossible. The similarities in national property regimes are relatively superficial and more apparent in countries that share a common historical path or stage of economic development. The mere fact that all legal systems have private property and the concept of expropriation does not warrant a conclusion that there is a universally recognised and accepted property protection standard, because the ways it is understood and applied differ substantially. For example, there is considerable variation in the understanding of indirect expropriation and regulatory takings. In other words, the universality of property protection is possible only at such a level of generalisation that it renders the principle unworkable in contemporary disputes.

Commonwealth countries tend to lean towards a liberal understanding of property, which is seen as 'an area of individual choice in the face of govern-

1 An early and shorter version of this chapter was published in Inga Martinkute, 'State interference with private property' in Rainer Grote, Frauke Lachenmann and Rüdiger Wolfrum (eds), *Max Planck Encyclopedia of Comparative Constitutional Law* (Oxford University Press 2020) §157, reproduced with permission of the OUP through PLS clear. See also: Nils Jansen and Sjef Van Erp, 'Comparative Property Law' in, Mathias Reimann and Reinhard Zimmermann (eds), *The Oxford Handbook of Comparative Law* vol 1 (Oxford University Press 2006) 1045–1046; Gregory S Alexander, *The Global Debate Over Constitutional Property: Lessons for American Takings Jurisprudence* (University of Chicago Press 2006); Andre van der Walt, *Constitutional Property Clauses: A Comparative Analysis* (Juta 1999).

HTTPS://DOI.ORG/10.1163/9789004763517-004

mental coercion'.[2] Perhaps, due to its orientation towards an individualistic understanding of property, the Anglo-American legal systems, as well as arbitrators and practitioners, are the preferred choice for claimants in investment disputes. However, some countries within that group, such as Canada, Australia, and Singapore, while still very respectful of property, have found a way to balance individualistic notions of private property with state activism.

The civil law tradition is even more diverse than the common law tradition in its approaches to property and its protection. The German, French, and Dutch legal systems, which operate in developed economies, share more similarities with the Anglo-American legal systems in terms of scope and level of property protection than with other developing civil law countries. Eastern Europe, Asia, Africa, and Latin America have a much stronger communitarian vision for property 'as an essential element in the construction and maintenance of the social order'.[3]

Any national property law is an immensely vast and complex area of law, encompassing both private and public law aspects. While the primary legal sources are frequently surprisingly similar, the real difference appears at the stage of interpretation and application. Thus, this chapter relies significantly on case law and scholarly commentaries. Furthermore, the chapter focuses on select aspects of national property regimes that best illustrate an individual's relationship with the state. This relationship is explored through several points of comparison, such as the scope of rights and interests that are granted the status of property and the limits of interference with private property that a given society tolerates as legitimate and permissible. Additionally, the analysis in this chapter includes a comparison of the definitions and practices of expropriation, as well as an investigation into the standards and procedures for compensation in cases of expropriation.

The jurisdictions are arranged from the most individualistic to the most communitarian.[4] The relative standing of jurisdictions is tentative and based on the author's general evaluation of a multitude of conflicting ideas and opinions about property within a particular jurisdiction. Quantitative measurement in this area is challenging because not all jurisdictions have recorded cases that illustrate national solutions for disputes involving similar factual

---

2 Allen, *The Right to Property in Commonwealth Constitutions* 143.

3 Ibid 143.

4 The classification of lower and higher levels of protection is quite relative, because it depends from a perspective. Looking from the perspective of an owner or investor a more individualistic understanding of property and investment will be more desirable. On the contrary, a lower level of property protection means that such a system is better geared to respond to communitarian interests.

settings.[5] An effort is made to identify and situate jurisdictions in relation to each other, but like all taxonomies, it requires certain simplification in order to facilitate an overview.[6]

Before proceeding to the particular jurisdictions, a few general observations about common and civil law traditions are offered that should help readers put specific property regimes into the context of their respective legal traditions.

Certain common law attitudes to property can be explained and better understood with reference to historical circumstances. The common law terminology on property 'is still rooted in the feudal system'[7] and the existence of dual legal systems – common law and equity. This has resulted in a fluid and 'relational approach to property law'[8] seeking to establish the priority of entitlement, not an absolute entitlement.[9] In contrast to civil law tradition, which was 'focused on substantive law', common law 'was organized procedurally, in terms of writs or forms of actions'.[10] The ideology of property protection in common law countries was and still is primarily based on liberal theories[11] and property is viewed in terms of rights, rather than obligations. Moreover, common law was not very bothered with the systemic distinction of property from other legal institutions and approached each case from a very pragmatic perspective.[12] The discourse on the constitutional protection of property from the interference of the state or other communal interests is hopelessly mingled within the private law paradigm. Thus, a balance of individual and communal interests is usually perceived as a private dispute, lacking the public law element characteristic of civil law traditions.

---

5 Various governance indexes try to catch the level of property protection, however they are criticised for methodological shortcomings: Tom Ginsburg, 'Pitfalls of Measuring the Rule of Law' (2011) 3 Hague Journal on the Rule of Law 269; Stephan Haggard, Andrew MacIntyre and Lydia Tiede, 'The Rule of Law and Economic Development' (2008) 11 Annual Review of Political Science 205; Svend-Erik Skaaning, 'Measuring the Rule of Law' (2010) 63 Political Research Quarterly 449.

6 The evidence from some legal systems are very contradictory. For example Philippines legal system has many communitarian traits, but the constitutional property protection practice is very individualistic. Similar situation exist in Malaysia.

7 Jansen and Van Erp, 'Comparative Property Law' 1057.

8 Ibid 1059–1060.

9 *Waverley Borough v Flether QB 334, 345 (CA) [1996]*.

10 Gordley 43 (footnote omitted).

11 Allen, *The Right to Property in Commonwealth Constitutions* 133, 161.

12 F H Lawson and Bernard Rudden, *The Law of Property* (3rd rev edn, Oxford University Press 2002) 21.

Despite the similarities, there are substantial differences in the treatment of property among the common law countries, which prevent the unification or appearance of a common standard for property protection.[13] However, it is impossible to ignore the influence of the Anglo-American understanding of property on international investment law and investment arbitration practice. Investment protection, taking individualistic property protection as inspiration, became an extreme version of a neo-liberal order, which is not supported by any domestic legal system. Even if property protection in common law countries enjoys a relatively high level of protection, it is balanced by other considerations protected by statutory measures, in contrast to international law, which does not have mandatory protection mechanisms for different values or interests, such as human rights, the environment, social and economic rights, etc.

The civil law tradition, based on the doctrinal analysis of Roman law, has a clearly defined structure, which makes it easier to approach and study. But despite the common origin, the civilian law tradition covers a wider geography, which means there are more extreme variations of it – from very individualistic Dutch law to communist Chinese law.

There are some general features of the civil law tradition that should help in understanding its basic approaches to property and its protection *vis-à-vis* a state. First, the civil law operates under the framework of *numerus clausus* and has a clear separation between real (*in rem*) and personal (*in personam*) rights. Those two characteristics mean that civil law countries have a limited number of types of interests in property,[14] such as 'ownership, mortgage (hypothec), pledge, servitude, usufruct, *superficies*, *emphyteusis*', and any other property rights have to be clearly authorised by the statute.[15] Second, civil law perceives ownership as unitary, 'it cannot be divided among several persons and new real rights cannot be created'.[16]

In the context of expropriation, those differences mean that in civil law countries, usually real rights (*in rem*) within the *numerus clausus* list are considered as being capable of being expropriated, while in common law countries, personal rights (*in personam*) are more readily accepted as objects of expropriation. In the context of indirect expropriation, civil law countries do not recognise the bundle of rights doctrine that is popular in common law

13 M Sornarajah, 'Starting anew in international investment law' *Columbia FDI Perspectives*, No 74, 16 July 2012.

14 Gordley 49.

15 Jansen and Van Erp, 'Comparative Property Law' 1053.

16 Ibid 1055–1056.

tradition. The resulting difference is that the extinguishment of one of the rights within a bundle is more readily treated as indirect expropriation in common law countries, while the bar in civil law countries is much higher – nearly all real rights need to be extinguished before expropriation is acknowledged.

The general observation that emerges is that even within the civil law tradition, developed and stable states adopt a more individualistic understanding of property, granting higher levels of property protection to their citizens. A higher level of private property protection is balanced by well-functioning state institutions and mechanisms that recognise and protect communitarian interests and values, such as environmental protection, human rights, healthcare, and social security systems. In some civil law countries, the social obligation is viewed as a constituent part of property.[17] In contrast, developing states that undergo legal reforms or social transformations tend to prioritise public and communitarian interests over individual ones.

The survey begins with Anglo-American legal systems that have the broadest scope for property protection and individualistic property protection, as well as the highest interest in the retention of the current *status quo* in wealth distribution. The analysis then turns to mature and stable Western European legal systems that do accept the high level of property protection, but which entertain certain communitarian aspects of property. The Eastern European and Asian jurisdictions are torn between the legacy of communitarian understanding of property and more recent reforms introducing individualistic property regimes. The chapter ends with an analysis of Latin American and African legal ethos that harbours strong communitarian notions of property. Under each jurisdiction, the concept of property, the boundaries of property *vis-à-vis* regulation, expropriation, and compensation standards are analysed.

1 The UK

In comparison to other legal systems, English law has an expansive and liberal interpretation of property: debts, business goodwill, leasehold interests, and restrictive covenants over land are treated as property and protected as such from the interference of the state.[18] Furthermore, it lacks a clear line of sepa-

17 Sjef Van Erp, *Can European Property Law be Codified?* (Brill) 155.

18 Allen, *The Right to Property in Commonwealth Constitutions* 122–123; Kevin J Gray and Susan Francis Gray, *Elements of land law* (5th edn, Oxford University Press 2009); Robert Megarry and H W R Wade, *The Law of Real Property* (6th edn, rev by Charles Harpum 2000).

ration between property and personal rights,[19] as well as a clear justification for why some interests deserve the same level of protection as property.[20] The practical solution adopted by courts appears to be what Allen refers to as the distinction between 'legal property' as it is understood in private relations, on the one hand, and 'constitutional property' on the other. The latter is interpreted more narrowly for protection *vis-à-vis* the state.[21] This separation allows for a comprehensive definition of property, which includes various interests that, under other legal systems, would not be treated as property.[22]

As a general rule, interests and rights have to 'be definable, identifiable' to be treated as property and to gain the protection of property,[23] but sometimes this requirement is treated lightly as in the case of money in a bank account.[24] Possession was sometimes used as a criterion, although with conflicting success.[25] Excludability justifies the treatment of intellectual property as constitutional property, but it is a weak guiding principle in complicated cases, such as confidential information[26] and reputation.[27] Transferability of interest is widely used as a criterion of 'constitutional property',[28] but it is not the single and sufficient factor to treat interest as constitutionally protected property.[29] The economic value of interest is usually a reliable indicator of property in

---

19 Michael G Bridge, *Personal Property Law* (4 edn, Oxford University Press 2015) 4.

20 Allen, *The Right to Property in Commonwealth Constitutions* 122.

21 Ibid 127–128.

22 Of course, such taxonomy is only theoretical and based on general observations, while courts give only vague and sometimes contradicting guidelines when certain borderline interests should be treated as constitutional property deserving protection from state interference.

23 Bridge 3, citing *National Provincial Bank v Ainsworth* AC 1175 (HL) [1965] 1247–1248; the Sale of Goods Act 1979, s 16, 20A; *Knight v Knight* 3 Beav 148 [1840] 173.

24 Michael J Milo, 'Property and real rights' in J M Smits (ed), *Elgar Encyclopedia of Comparative Law* (2 edn, Edward Elgar 2012) 732; Lawson and Rudden 88–89; Robert Goff Baron Goff of Chieveley and Gareth H Jones, *The Law of Restitution* (6th edn, Sweet & Maxwell 2002) 80–82, 97–104.

25 Land Compensation Act (1973)c 26 part I s 2; *D'Aguiar v Attorney-General* 4 WIR 481 (SC British Guiana) [1962]; *Alleyne-Forte v Att-Gen and Another* LRC 338 (PC TT) [1997], but see *Commonwealth v Tasmania* 158 CLR 1 [1983].

26 Norman E Palmer and Ewan McKendrick, *Interests in Goods* (Lloyd's of London Press 1993) 187–206.

27 Allen, *The Right to Property in Commonwealth Constitutions* 131; Kevin Gray, 'Property in Thin Air' (1991) 50 The Cambridge Law Journal 281.

28 *Dwarkadas Shrinivas v Sholapur Spinning and Weaving Co Ltd* AIR 1954 SC 119, 136; *Government of Mauritius v Union Flacq Sugar Estates Co Ltd* 1 WLR 903 (PC Mauritius) [1992]; *Ackerman v Nova Scotia* 47 DLR (4th) [1988] 681.

29 Allen, *The Right to Property in Commonwealth Constitutions* 135; Bridge 3–4; *Sanders v British Columbia (Milk Board)* 77 DLR (4th) 603 [1991] 609.

both private and commercial contexts, but for constitutional protection, it poses problems. Usually, the economic value of interest is asserted in the context of regulatory taking. If a regulation reduces the value of an interest or a right, expropriation is claimed, presuming the existence of property. However, this does not indicate whether there was 'constitutional property' in the first place, especially since the protection is guaranteed only for property, and there is no guarantee against a pure loss. The problem is illustrated by a market share,[30] access rights to the market,[31] offices, and occupations,[32] all of which have a particular value to the holder, but compliance with legal requirements might reduce this value or profit. Those instances do not constitute property for constitutional protection; however, NAFTA jurisprudence protected them as property.[33] In other words, just because something has an economic value, it does not become a property with all its constitutional safeguards.

This distinction is frequently ignored in investment arbitration in favour of a broader concept of investment.[34] The conceptual blur creates problems further down the line when it becomes complicated to justify permissible regulations that affect the economic value of rights and interests. The perception of property as economic value often interferes with legitimate regulation where compensation should not usually be required.

The equivalent of American rule on 'police powers' is found in *Belfast Corporation v OD Cars* where the House of Lords held that restrictions on land use were not compensable when the purpose of the limitation is public amenity and health.[35] Similarly, 'compensation is not paid for the forfeiture of property, the execution of civil judgments and court orders, or the limitation of

30 *British Medical Association v The Commonwealth* 79 CLR 201 [1949] 270–271.

31 *Saghir Ahmad v The State of Uttar Pradesh* SCR 707 [1955].

32 However, there have been a number of Indian cases where it was recognized as property: *Kakinada Annadana Samajam v Commissioner of Hindu Religious & Charitable Endowments, Hyderabad and Others* AIR 1971 SC 891; *Tilkayat Shri Govindlalji v Rajasthan* 1 SCR 561, AIR 1963 SC 1638 [1964].

33 Some investment tribunals found access to the market to be a protected right under Article 1110 of NAFTA: *Pope & Talbot Inc v Government of Canada* (UNCITRAL) [2000] Interim Award, 26 June 2000; *Merrill & Ring Forestry LP v Government of Canada* (UNCITRAL, ICSID Administered) Award 31 March 2010.

34 Priority, statutory and contractual rights having economic value were found to be capable of being expropriated: *Emmis International Holding, BV, Emmis Radio Operating, BV and MEM Magyar Electronic Media Kereskedelmi és Szolgáltató Kft v Hungary* (ICSID) para 109; *Magyar Farming and others v Hungary* (ICSID) Case No ARB/17/27 [2019] para 359.

35 *Belfast Corporation v OD Cars* AC 490 [1960]; *R (Mott) v Environment Agency* UKSC 10 [2018].

actions and acquisition of title by adverse possession' as well as for wartime destruction, the abatement of nuisance by a public authority.[36] However, it is widely believed that if a 'regulation gives state authorities powers' of an owner, courts will treat it as expropriation.[37]

In general, the dominant view in the UK is that property is individual and private.[38] Whatever is required for the social order is perceived as external to property, something that a state or others have to take care of, and those duties are entirely separated from property. That means charity and other measures for the good of society are separate from property and legally voluntary. From this perspective, any measure, even for the common good, is an interference with property and individual will for that property.[39] This might be a paradigmatic difference from other societies with more communitarian approaches to property, where constraints on the use of property are more readily accepted for common needs or objectives, and where the obligations towards a society that sustains a property regime are perceived as an integral part of that property.

In this context of widely interpreted property understanding, English law *per se* does not have a written constitutional right to property. The protection of property against the interference of a state is performed by two fundamental principles of English law. First, only the parliament may authorise the compulsory acquisition of property (expropriation), and second, it can be done only when it is in the public interest and only upon payment of compensation.[40] These fundamental rules of English law were entrenched 'into the written constitutions of most Commonwealth states'.[41]

---

36 Allen, *The Right to Property in Commonwealth Constitutions* 163.

37 Ibid 125; *Belfast Corporation v OD Cars Limited* AC 490 [1960]; *Government of Mauritius v Union Flacq Sugar Estates Co Ltd* 911, but see *Attorney-General v Lawrence* LRC (Const) 921 (the Court of Appeal of St Christopher and Nevis) [1985] 930.

38 Alan Macfarlane, *The Origins of English Individualism: The Family, Property and Social Transition* (Blackwell 1978) 5.

39 This notion is reflected in the sole effects doctrine, meaning that the reasons for the interference with private property rights are irrelevant when deciding whether expropriation occurred: *Tecnicas Medioambientales Tecmed SA v The United Mexican States* (ICSID) para 116; *Siemens AG v Argentine Republic* ((ICSID) Case No ARB/02/8) [2007] para 270; *National Grid PLC v Argentina Republic* (UNCITRAL) Award 3 November 2008 para 147; *SAUR International SA v Argentine Republic* (ICSID) paras 366, 441; *Burlington Resources Inc v Republic of Ecuador* (ICSID) Case No ARB/08/5, Decision on Liability 14 December 2012 paras 396–397.

40 William D McNulty, 'The Power of "Compulsory Purchase" under the Law of England' (1912) 21 The Yale Law Journal 639, 644, 649.

41 Allen, *The Right to Property in Commonwealth Constitutions* 36. See also Koskenniemi, 'Sovereignty, Property and Empire: Early Modern English Contexts' 356.

The question of compulsory acquisition is discussed in detail by the literature[42] and regulated extensively by the Lands Clauses Consolidation Act;[43] the Land Compensation Act;[44] the Compulsory Purchase Act;[45] the Land Compensation Act;[46] the Housing Act;[47] the Town and Country Planning Act;[48] the Planning and Compensation Act;[49] and the Planning and Compulsory Purchase Act 2004 (UK).[50] Theses statutes provide detailed descriptions of compulsory purchase powers, time limits, notices, and the calculation of compensation. Moreover, they provide certain valuation assumptions and take into account various development possibilities, dispute resolutions, and other relevant factors. The statutes also regulate the right to compensation for depreciation of interest caused by public works, the special functions of local housing authorities in acquiring housing or land for housing purposes, and compensation for prohibition or demolition orders.

The Land Clauses Consolidation Act of 1845 c 18 s 63 requires consideration not only of 'the value of the land to be purchased or taken', but also 'the damage, if any, to be sustained by the owner of the lands by reason of the severing of the lands taken from the other lands of such owner, or otherwise injuriously affecting such other lands'. This statute itself does not specify a compensation standard – whether it is 'just', 'fair', or 'full market value' compensation. The Land Compensation Act 1973 c 26 p I s 4–7 provides that compensation shall be assessed on the first day of the claim, excluding any benefits associated with public works, any possible change of use of a land plot, and a

42 Frederick Vernon Sir Corfield, Robert Carnwath and DA Richards, *Compulsory Acquisition and Compensation* (Butterworths 1978); Michael Barnes, *The Law of Compulsory Purchase and Compensation* (Hart Publishing 2014); Barry Denyer-Green, *Compulsory Purchase and Compensation* (12th edn, Routledge 2025).

43 S 16–68 of the Lands Clauses Consolidation Act (1845) <https://www.legislation.gov.uk/ukpga/Vict/8-9/18/contents> accessed on 26 March 2025.

44 Land Compensation Act (1961) c 33 <https://www.legislation.gov.uk/ukpga/Eliz2/9-10/33/contents> accessed 26 March 2025.

45 Compulsory Purchase Act (1965) c 56 <https://www.legislation.gov.uk/ukpga/1965/56/contents> accessed on 26 March 2025.

46 Land Compensation Act c 26 <https://www.legislation.gov.uk/ukpga/1973/26/contents> accessed on 26 March 2025.

47 Part 17 Housing Act (1985) c 68 <https://www.legislation.gov.uk/ukpga/1985/68/part/XVII> accessed on 26 March 2025.

48 Town and Country Planning Act (1990) c 8 <https://www.legislation.gov.uk/ukpga/1990/8/contents> accessed on 26 March 2025.

49 Planning and Compensation Act (1991) c 34 <https://www.legislation.gov.uk/ukpga/1991/34/contents> accessed on 26 March 2025.

50 Planning and Compulsory Purchase Act (2004) c 5 <https://www.legislation.gov.uk/ukpga /2004/5/contents> accessed on 26 March 2025.

certain minimal amount. The decisions of the authorities may be challenged before the High Court.[51] Also, some new laws strengthening the compulsory purchase regime are being discussed in Parliament.[52]

As a consequence, under English law, relatively few individuals receive compensation for indirect expropriation, because, in a wide variety of instances, the regulation affecting property rights would be regarded as permissible without compensation. In those rare cases when a state, through statute acquires the powers of an owner, the expropriation would be compensated at the market value.[53]

Despite the legal mechanisms designed to give effect to communitarian interests, the UK is among the jurisdictions with the widest scope and highest level of property protection. Even though English public administration would be perceived by many as an optimal standard for investment protection anywhere in the world, it is far from clear if all legislative initiatives or administrative practices in the UK would survive investment arbitration scrutiny.[54]

2 The USA

It is often argued that the most individualistic version of the property regime can be found in the USA,[55] where the taking of property without compensation is prohibited by the constitution:[56]

---

51 Chester Brown and Audley Sheppard, 'United Kingdom' in Chester Brown (ed), *Commentaries on Selected Model Investment Treaties* (Oxford University Press 2013) 702.

52 Research Briefing: Planning and Infrastructure Bill 2024–2025, House of Commons Library <https://commonslibrary.parliament.uk/research-briefingscbp-10216/> accessed on 26 March 2025.

53 Allen, *The Right to Property in Commonwealth Constitutions* 195.

54 The takeover of struggling bank by authorities would be a major issue in investment arbitration: Dominic O'Connell, 'The collapse of Northern Rock: Ten years on' BBC <https://www.bbc.com/news/business-41229513> accessed on 26 October 2018; Forced sales to the tenants would likely violate majority of investment treaties, but was not a violation of the ECHR: *James and others v The United Kingdom* (ECtHR).

55 Richard A Epstein, *Takings: Private Property and the Power of Eminent Domain* (Harvard University Press 1985); William B Stoebuck, 'A General Theory of Eminent Domain' (1971) 47 Washington Law Review 553; Philip Nichols and others, *Nichols on Eminent Domain* (3 edn, LexisNexis 2012).

56 The Fifth Amendment of the United States Constitution (1791). S 3113 of Title 40, Ss 1358 and 1403 of Title 28 of the United States Code regulate the jurisdiction and the procedure of takings for public use. Also, separate federal states have their own statutes and regulations governing the exercise of eminent domain.

> The traditional rights of property ownership – the rights to possess, use, exclude, and dispose of property – are among the most foundational individual rights in the American legal system [and they have been] part of the Anglo-American legal system since feudal times.[57]

In the mainstream mind, the USA property regime has been defined as 'free-market, minimalist-state libertarianism' and mostly 'insulated (by constitutional guarantee) from otherwise legitimate public demands'.[58] Without any doubt, such a choice is based on the values of society:

> Because our political and legal tradition places the burden of persuasion squarely on the shoulders of government to justify regulation, owners are often not called upon to justify themselves even when they act in a manner that adversely affects others.[59]

State legislative initiatives were often challenged in the courts as interfering with private property rights enshrined in the Fifth Amendment of the Constitution. The *Lochner* jurisprudence became an illustration of the conflict between private property and legislation 'for social and economic change'.[60]

However, the situation is much more contradictory than initial perceptions and even the USA legal system harbours certain elements of a communitarian understanding of property.[61] Besides the plurality of opinions in the USA about what interests (individual or community's) and to what extent property should serve, those opinions also change over time.[62]

Having inherited a broad concept of property from the common law, the USA law generally recognises its non-physical aspects.[63] But in the context of

---

57 Underkuffler 69.

58 Ibid 159.

59 Joseph William Singer, *Entitlement: the Paradoxes of Property* (Yale University Press 2000) 16.

60 Tom Allen, 'Constitutional Law, Social Justice and the Redistribution of Land' in Ting Xu and Jean Allain (eds), *Property and Human Rights in a Global Context*, vol 20 (Hart Publishing Ltd 2015) 69.

61 William A Fischel, *Regulatory Takings: Law, Economics, and Politics* (Harvard University Press 1995); Singer, *Introduction to Property*; Stoebuck 553.

62 Gregory S Alexander, *Commodity and Propriety: Competing Visions of Property in American Legal Thought, 1776–1970* (University of Chicago Press 1997) 7.

63 *Gardner v Trustees of Village of Newburgh et al* 2 Johns Ch 162 (NY) [1816]; *Proprietors of Piscataqua Bridge v New-Hampshire Bridge* 7 NH 35 [1834].

eminent domain, the USA courts[64] for a long time refused compensation for certain intangible interests associated with property, such as access to a land plot[65] or environmental degradation.[66] This resulted in a belief for a long time that takings required interference with actual possession.[67] At the beginning of the twentieth-century property was mostly appreciated for its use value, thus the physical taking of property or interference with possession was emphasised.[68] With economic structures becoming more sophisticated and the advance of a commodified understanding of property, the idea that property has an exchange value, diverging from its direct characteristics, became more popular. Since *United States v Welch*, the USA Supreme Court recognised easements as requiring compensation.[69] The economic value of something became recognised as one of the main indicia of property.[70] That resulted in a conclusion that depreciation of value by regulation could amount to a taking too – 'while property may be regulated to a certain extent, if regulation goes too far it will be recognized as a taking'.[71] Japan and South Korea, influenced by the USA, developed similar regulatory taking theories.[72] However, in the USA, the requirement of physical deprivation is still strong, as well as the condition that the owner must lose nearly 'all economically beneficial uses' of his property before the measure is declared as a taking.[73] Similar language

64 The term of eminent domain or condemnation is usually used for expropriation in the USA jurisprudence.

65 *Callender v Marsh* 18 Mass (I Pick) 418 [1823]; *Monongahela Navigation Co v Coons 6 Watts&S 101, 114 (Pa)* [1843]; *O'Connor v Pittsburgh* 18 Pa (6 Harris) 187 [1851]; *Randall v City of Milwaukee* 212 Wis 374, 249 NW 73 [1933].

66 *Batten v United States* 306 F2d 580 (10th Cir) [1962]; *Nunnally v United States* 239 F2d 521 (4th Cir) [1956].

67 *Richards v Washington Terminal Company* 233 US 546 [1914].

68 The permanent physical presence test was more recently confirmed in *Loretto v Teleprompter Manhattan CATV Corp* 458 US 419 [1982]. In contrast, French courts refused to treat administrative easements as regulatory takings: *Eiffel tower case*, CC decision No 85-198 DC, 13 December 1985, Rec 78.

69 217 US 333 (1910).

70 Allen, *The Right to Property in Commonwealth Constitutions* 139. Also see Fischel 64; Lawrence M Friedman, 'A Search for Seizure: Pennsylvania Coal Co. v. Mahon in Context' (1986) 4 Law and History Review 1; Carol Rose, 'Mahon Reconstructed: Why the Takings Issue is still a Muddle' (1984) 57 Southern California Law Review 561.

71 *Pennsylvania Coal Company v Mahon* 260 US 393 [1922] followed in *Lucas v South Carolina Coastal Council* 505 US 1003 [1992] 1014.

72 Tsuyoshi Kotaka, 'Japan's Land Use Law' in Tsuyoshi Kotaka and David L Callies (eds), *Taking Land: Compulsory Purchase and Regulation in Asian-Pacific Countries* (University of Hawai'i Press 2002) 4.

73 *Tahoe-Sierra Preservation Council, Inc v Tahoe Regional Planning Agency* 122 S Ct 1465, 1483 [2002] (quoting *Lucas v South Carolina Coastal Council* para 1019).

defining the indirect expropriation could be observed in investment arbitration practice.[74]

American courts had difficulties in separating permissible regulations from takings and abandoned the effort by adopting a case-by-case approach.[75] It is claimed that the *Penn Central* case established the criteria for differentiation: the economic impact of the regulation on the claimant, the extent to which the regulation interfered with distinct investment-backed expectations, and the character of the governmental action.[76] These criteria are surprisingly similar to the language of investment tribunals in investment awards.[77]

The schizophrenic nature of property protection within USA jurisprudence resembles the UK taxonomy of 'legal' and 'constitutional' property, i.e., where property is interpreted very widely for commercial purposes, but only a narrower 'constitutional' property is protected from regulatory state interference and may require compensation. Underkuffler calls it 'common' and 'operative' conceptions of property, where a common or popular belief has more features of the individualistic understanding of property, while 'operative' property resembles communitarian understanding of property.[78] Alexander also notes the dual nature of property: first, as a commodity satisfying individual preferences, and second, as a basis for social order and public good. He vividly illustrates how communitarian and individualistic attitudes towards property alternated in USA history.[79] The founders had a rather communitarian conception of property, but during the *laissez-faire* era, property was undergoing

---

74 *Southern Pacific Properties (Middle East) Limited v Arab Republic of Egypt* para 158; *Compañía del Desarrollo de Santa Elena v Republic of Costa Rica* 12; *Cargill Inc v United Mexican States* (ICSID) para 356–358, 370–377.

75 Allen, *The Right to Property in Commonwealth Constitutions* 14; Andrea K Bjorklund, 'NAFTA Chapter 11' in Chester Brown (ed), *Commentaries on selected model investment treaties* (First edn, Oxford University Press 2013) 469.

76 *Penn Central Transportation Company v New York City* 438 US 104, 127 [1978].

77 *MCI Power Group, LC and New Turbine Inc v Republic of Ecuador* (ICSID) para 300; *AES Summit Generation Limited and AES-Tisza Erömü Kft v Republic of Hungary* (ICSID) Case No ARB/07/22, Award 23 September 2010 para 14.3.1; *Total SA v Argentine Republic* (ICSID) [2010] para 196; *RosInvestCo UK Ltd v Russian Federation* (SCC) para 624; *Tza Yap Shum v Republic of Peru* (ICSID) para 163; *Ulysseas, Inc v Ecuador* (UNCITRAL) Final Award 12 June 2012 para 173; *Marion Unglaube v Republic of Costa Rica* (ICSID) para 226; *Reinhard Hans Unglaube v Republic of Costa Rica* (ICSID) para 226; *Bernhard von Pezold and others v Republic of Zimbabwe* (ICSID) para 516; *Telenor Mobile Communications AS v Republic of Hungary* (ICSID) para 70; *Spyridon Roussalis v Romania* (ICSID) Case No ARB/06/1, Award 1 December 2011 para 330.

78 Underkuffler 46, 70.

79 Alexander, *Commodity and propriety: competing visions of property in American legal thought, 1776–1970* 1, 17.

commodification.[80] A swing to an individualistic understanding of property was counter-balanced by the Supreme Court's interference as a reaction to 'the massive changes in the nature of American business enterprise' and imbalance 'of power in the market place'.[81] Throughout the nineteenth century:

> [g]overnment had a pervasive regulatory presence ... throughout all sectors of society, including the world of market. ... Responding in part to pressure from groups that were adversely affected by new dominant industries, such as the railroad, state legislatures adopted a more restrictive attitude toward the freedom of enterprises to conduct their affairs as they saw fit. ... [s]tate legislatures increasingly asserted their power to impose limits on the freedom of enterprises to use their property in whatever way they wished.[82]

After the death in 1888 of Justice Waite who harboured communitarian visions of property, the more individualistic views of Justice Field became dominant in the USA Supreme Court. Justice Field tried to limit the 'social role' of property and propagated the profit-making dimension of property only for its owners.[83] Thus, by the end of the nineteenth century, the jurisprudence of the USA Supreme Court was leaning towards the individualistic understanding of property.[84] The liberal doctrines were again reversed after the Great Depression in *West Coast Hotel Co v Parrish* (1937)[85] and *United States v Carolene Products* (1938).[86]

The tensions between the individualistic understanding of property and communitarian aspects of it continued to persist throughout the twentieth century, with increasing recognition that 'there is no scientific or politically neutral basis upon which to decide how far regulation may legally interfere with property'.[87] There are several cases where the use of property and its

80 Ibid 27.

81 Ibid 259, 262 citing *Slaughterhouse Cases* 83 US (16 Wall)36 [1873]; *Munn v Illinois* 94 US 113 [1877].

82 Alexander, *Commodity and Propriety: Competing Visions of Property in American Legal Thought, 1776–1970* 252–253.

83 Ibid 266–267, 269, 271 citing *Chicago, Milwaukee & St Paul Ry v Minnesota* 134 US 418 [1890] and *Smyth v Ames* 169 US 466 [1898].

84 Alexander, *Commodity and Propriety: Competing Visions of Property in American Legal Thought, 1776–1970* 275.

85 (1939) 300 US 379.

86 (1938) 304 US 144.

87 Alexander, *Commodity and Propriety: Competing Visions of Property in American Legal Thought, 1776–1970* 331.

economic profitability were severely curtailed by legislation in the interests of public health, safety, morals, urban planning, environmental, historic-preservation, monopoly regulation, and other without compensation.[88] In the context of general public interest, it was often ruled that the general diminution in value is not a compensable taking.[89] The USA practice also indicates that a property owner 'necessarily expects the uses of his property to be restricted, from time to time' by legislative changes[90] and that the owner could not expect continuous use of its property when it is needed for the 'greater value to the public'.[91] The USA Supreme Court repeatedly accepted the government's judgment that the disputed action was for 'public use', except in the most outrageous cases.[92]

The communitarian thinking about property could be recognised in *Hawaii Housing Authority v Midkiff*, where the owner was forced to sell its property to tenants because it was required for the common good of the local society.[93] The general interest of a community also played a role in *Kelo v City of New London,* where private land was taken for commercial redevelopment that arguably could have benefited the local community.[94]

Underkuffler argued that 'the protection of property [in the USA] has been honoured ... more in the breach than in the practice'.[95] However, this fanciful notion of individualistic property associated with a very high level of protection was quite successfully exported to the international realm.

After comparing the USA domestic law and international treaties on state liability for regulatory changes, several scholars concluded that arbitral tribu-

88 *Hadacheck v Sebastian* 239 US 394 [1915]; *Reinman v Little Rock* 237 US 171 [1915]; *Mugler v Kansas 123 US 623 [1887]*; *Bowditch v Boston* 101 US 16, 18–19 [1879]; *Goldblatt v Hempstead* 369 US 590 [1962]; *Calhoun v Massie* 253 US 170, 175 [1920]; *Corn Products Refining Company v Eddy* 249 US 427 431–432 [1919]; *Walls v Midland Carbon Company,* 254 US 300 (1920); *Miller v Schoene,* 276 US 272 (1928).

89 Underkuffler 47; Joseph Sax, 'Takings and the Police Power' (1964) 74 Yale Law Journal 155.

90 *Lucas v South Carolina Coastal Council* para 1027; *Block v Hirsh* 256 US 135, 155 [1921].

91 Underkuffler 48 citing *Penn Central Transportation Company v New York City,* 438 US 104, 127 (1978) 125–126.

92 *Hawaii Housing Authority v Midkiff* 467 US [1984] 240; *Old Dominion Company v United States,* 269 US 55, 66 (1925); *United States v Gettysburg Electric Railway Company,* 160 US 668, 680 (1896); *Nollan v California Coastal Commission* 483 US 825 [1987] 837; *Dolan v City of Tigard,* 512 US 374 (1994) 391; *City of Monterey v Del Monte Dunes,* 526 US 687 (1999), 702–703.

93 *Hawaii Housing Authority v Midkiff* 240; See also *People v Pullman's Palace-Car Co* 51 NE 664, 674 (Ill) [1898].

94 545 US 469 (2005).

95 Underkuffler 159.

nals had interpreted investment treaty rules in the manner far more favourable to the interest of investors than the approaches adopted in the USA courts.[96]

3 The Netherlands

Dutch private laws have been influenced by both the French Civil Code and German BGB.[97] Having undergone a recent reform, the Dutch Civil Code (*Burgerlijk Wetboek*) benefited from a comparative approach with business and trade needs in mind.[98] The Netherlands follow a civil law tradition with personal and real rights distinctions and *numerus clausus* principles.[99] The basic definition of property provided in Article 3:1 includes all corporeal (tangible) things, proprietary rights and interests.[100] Similar to German law, it does not recognise ownership of claims[101] but has a functional equivalent allowing the transfer and pledge of claims.[102] There is also a limited possibility for contractual parties to create real rights by the deed of establishment of *emphyteusis* or servitude.[103] The provisions defining and regulating property had a considerable influence on countries in economic transition.

96 Been and Beauvais 30; Lise Johnson and Oleksandr Volkov, 'Investor-state contracts, host-state "commitments" and the myth of stability in international law' (2013) 24 American Review of International Arbitration 361. Cf Parvanov and Kantor claim that at least some aspects of investment protection do not exceed the USA domestic protection: Parvan P Parvanov and Mark Kantor, 'Comparing U.S. law and recent U.S. investment agreements: Much more similar than you might expect' (2011) 2010–2011 Yearbook on International Investment Law and Policy 836.

97 G A Meijer and S Y T Meijer, 'Influence of the Code Civil in the Netherlands' (2002) 14 European Journal of Law and Economics 227, 229–230; J A M A Sluysmans, Stijn Verbist and Emma Waring, *Expropriation Law in Europe* (Wolters Kluwer 2015) 3.

98 The Dutch Civil code (1992) <http://www.dutchcivillaw.com/civilcodegeneral.htm> accessed on 15 May 2019.

99 JMJ Chorus, PHM Gerver and EH Hondius, *Introduction to Dutch Law* (4th rev edn, Kluwer Law International 2006) 103.

100 HCS Warendorf, RLMA Thomas and Ian Sumner, *The Civil Code of the Netherlands* (Kluwer Law International 2009) 433; Milo 732; Wouter Snijders, 'Ongeregeldheden in het vermogensrecht', (2005) *Weekblad voor Privaatrecht, Notariaat en Registratie* 6607, 79 and *Weekblad voor Privaatrecht, Notariaat en Registratie* 6608, 94.

101 Sabrina Praduroux, 'Objects of property rights: old and new' in Michele Graziadei and Lionel D Smith (eds), *Comparative property law: global perspectives* (Edward Elgar Pub 2017) 61.

102 Van Erp 166.

103 Jansen and Van Erp, 'Comparative Property Law' 1054.

In 1983 the Bill of Rights was reformulated in the Dutch Constitution with Article 14 providing property protection clause with a special provision for regulatory takings:

> (1) Expropriation may take place only in the public interest and on prior assurance of full compensation, in accordance with regulations laid down by or pursuant to Act of Parliament.
> (2) Prior assurance of full compensation shall not be required if in an emergency immediate expropriation is called for.
> (3) In the cases laid down by or pursuant to Act of Parliament there shall be a right to full or partial compensation if in the public interest the competent authority destroys property or renders it unusable or restricts the exercise of the owner's rights to it.[104]

The issue has a long history in Dutch law, and recently, the rules on expropriation were revised.[105] The high level of property protection, similar to the French property protection clause, is accompanied by the requirement to prove 'public interest'. Exceptions are allowed only in cases of 'dams and military works, infrastructure, water supply, and removal of waste, fire and flooding, spatial planning and public housing, and land use and nature protection'.[106] However, as there is no constitutional review, there is no constitutional practice on the question of private property protection.[107]

Generally, the dominating attitudes are liberal, but considerable economic sectors are reserved for 'public monopolies (these include the Netherlands Central Bank, the Schiphol airport, the Netherlands railways, and the public broadcasting network)'.[108] Although the government has been reluctant to interfere with private property rights, it has done so in a number of situations: the nationalisation of mining industries in 1945 or the nationalisation of the ABN AMRO bank in 2008.[109] The Dutch property protection laws were tested

---

104 The Constitution of the Kingdom of the Netherlands (1983) <https://www.government.nl/binaries/government/documenten/reports/2019/02/28/the-constitution-of-the-kingdom-of-the-netherlands/WEB_119406_Grondwet_Koninkrijk_ENG.pdf> accessed on 27 March 2025.

105 Expropriation Act (1851) was recently amended by the Environment and Planning Act (Omgevingswet) (2016), Netherlands, <https://wetten.overheid.nl/BWBR0037885/2024-01-01> accessed on 27 March 2025.

106 Nico Schrijver and Vid Prislan, 'The Netherlands' in Chester Brown (ed), *Commentaries on Selected Model Investment Treaties* (First edn, Oxford University Press 2013) 537 fn 7.

107 Chorus, Gerver and Hondius 307.

108 Schrijver and Prislan (footnote omitted) 538.

109 Ibid 538.

during the government's push for the ownership unbundling in the energy sector.[110] The Court of Hague pronounced that the requirement for ownership unbundling is not a regulatory taking, mainly because the effect on the ownership rights is proportional to the general public interest in gas supply security.[111] In a similar vein, the new law introduced a national security screening mechanism for investments in sensitive industries, *de facto* limiting disposal and potentially the value of company shares.[112]

Expropriation of immovable property in the general interest now occurs through an 'expropriation order' issued by designated administrative bodies, such as municipal councils, the general water board, provincial councils, or responsible ministers, rather than by royal decree.[113] An expropriation must meet certain criteria, such as necessity, urgency, and alignment with public interest. The process follows administrative law, requiring public notification, a review period for interested parties to submit objections, and ratification by an administrative judge.[114] The compensation for expropriation is determined by the civil court.[115] Compensation is based on the actual market value, determined as if the property were sold freely between a willing buyer and seller but special cases may require different valuation methods.[116] Benefits or losses arising from government projects related to expropriation are not factored into compensation.[117] There is only cassation and finalising expropriation requires a notarial deed, ensuring legal compliance and registration before ownership transfers to the expropriating institution.[118]

110 Iñigo del Guayo, Gunther Kühne and Martha Roggenkamp, 'Ownership Unbundling and Property Rights in the EU Energy Sector' in Aileen McHarg and others (eds), *Property and the Law in Energy and Natural Resources* (Oxford University Press 2010) 350, 354.

111 *Cases Nos 293142/HA ZA 07-2538, 296094/HA ZA 07-3089 and 306147/HA ZA 08-756* (Rechtbank's Gravenhage) [2009]. Investment arbitration case *OAO Gazprom v The Republic of Lithuania* (PCA) Case No 2011-2016, discontinued on 31 March 2015 had factual similarities.

112 The Act on Security Screening of Investments, Mergers and Acquisitions (Wet veiligheidstoets investeringen, fusies en overnames) (2023), Official Gazette of the Kingdom of the Netherlands, <https://www.eerstekamer.nl/behandeling/20220610/publicatie_wet/document3/f=/vltnd0546kvp.pdf> accessed on 27 March 2025.

113 Articles 11.1–11.3 of Environment and Planning Act (Omgevingswet).

114 Ibid Article 16.1.

115 Ibid Article 15.36.

116 Ibid Article 15.22.

117 Ibid Article 15.23.

118 Ibid Article 11.16 – 20.

Overall, the Netherlands, like Israel, offers generous compensation levels for any state interference with private property rights.[119]

4 France

The Revolution is central to the French understanding of property and its place in society. The medieval tenure system divided property, mainly land, between nobility, which formally owned it, and users, who used the opportunity to acquire it under their names.[120] The Revolution caused a massive redistribution of property, and the beneficiaries of the new regime were interested in securing their new status. This culminated in 1789 with the Declaration of the Rights of Man and of the Citizen, which declares that property is 'an inviolable and sacred' right.[121] The principles of the Declaration have a constitutional value even now through the preamble of the current constitution.[122] The Revolution led to the Napoleonic Civil Code adopted in 1804, which is based on the philosophy of individual liberalism,[123] and Article 544 of the Civil Code celebrates absolute property rights:

> Ownership is the right to enjoy and dispose of things in the most absolute manner, provided they are not used in a way prohibited by statutes or regulations.[124]

Over the past two hundred years, French property law saw two conceptual developments.

---

119 Rachelle Alterman and Evangelia Balla, *Takings International: A Comparative Perspective on Land Use Regulations and Compensation Rights* (American Bar Association, Section of State and Local Government Law 2011) 36.

120 George A Bermann and Etienne Picard, *Introduction to French law* (Kluwer Law International 2008) 147.

121 Article 17 of the Declaration of the Rights of Man and of the Citizen (1789) <http://avalon.law.yale.edu/18th_century/rightsof.asp> accessed on 1 February 2018.

122 The Constitution of France (1958) <http://www.conseil-constitutionnel.fr/conseil-constitutionnel/english/constitution/constitution-of-4-october-1958.25742.html> accessed on 1 February 2018.

123 Walter Cairns and Robert McKeon, *Introduction to French law* (Cavendish Publishing Ltd 1995) 52–53.

124 Civil Code (1804) <https://www.legifrance.gouv.fr/Media/ Traductions/English -en/code _civil_20130701_EN> accessed on 23 October 2018.

First, the concept of property was expanding. The code uses the term '*chose*' for 'a thing', but '*bien*' to signal that not all things can be owned.[125] The civil code was written with tangible property in mind, but with the approach of the modern world '*bien*' was interpreted to include intangible things, such as debts, securities, and intellectual property.[126] Even though French law has a separation between personal rights (*droits personnels*) and real rights (*droits réels*), claims to money, shares, or other interests in commercial or financial companies, as well as pensions and other welfare benefits, are also understood as property.[127] This may be because, for some time, French law recognised long-term lease, construction lease, and a right of ownership of a volume in space as real rights, and like common law, it allows the creation of real rights by contract.[128] But the expectation that a concession will be renewed, the authorisation to operate public transport services, or hydroelectric concessions have not been recognised as property rights[129] in contrast to international investment law, which includes the concessions under the definition of investment and sometimes even protects the right to the renewal of permits.[130]

Second, the property was socialised admitting the community's interest in it. French law harbours strong communitarian features in the understanding of property: some things cannot be privately owned due to the public interest in them. For example, roads, rivers, beaches, ports, harbours, gates, walls, ditches, and fortresses have a special 'public domain' regime.[131]

In France, the expropriation is directly regulated by the statute[132] and property was subject to an increasing number of regulations and socialisation in the general interest. In the modern world, restrictions on property for the good of the community became unavoidable, either in the form of electricity and tele-

---

125 Articles 516 and 544 of the French Civil Code <https://www.legifrance.gouv.fr/Media / Traductions/English-en/code_civil_20130701_ EN> accessed on 23 October 2018; See also John Bell, Sophie Boyron and Simon Whittaker, *Principles of French law* (Oxford University Press 2008) 270.

126 Bermann and Picard 152.

127 Bell, Boyron and Whittaker 273; Praduroux 63.

128 *Caquelard v Lemoine* S 34 I 205 [1834] (Cour de Cassation Chambre des Requetes); Bermann and Picard 149.

129 *Transport Law case* [1982] (French Constitutional Council). All decisions of the French Constitutional Council can be found here <https://www.conseil-constitutionnel.fr/decisions> accessed on 24 October 2018; Praduroux 64.

130 *Metalclad Corporation v United Mexican States* (ICSID) para 107, 111; *Tecnicas Medioambientales Tecmed SA v The United Mexican States* para 113–114.

131 Bell, Boyron and Whittaker 274.

132 Expropriation for Public Interest Code (1977), France, <https://www.legifrance.gouv.fr/loda/id/LEGISCTA000025089265> accessed on 27 March 2025.

phones cables, gas and water pipes, or planning and environmental regulations. Thus, Bell and others argued that while the conceptual structure of French property law remained the same, 'its operational context has changed radically and concepts often serve new policy objectives'.[133] The social welfare reforms of 1930, nationalisations after WWII, state-run 'public services such as the railways and television',[134] Article 9 of the Preamble to the 1946 Constitution requiring to transfer some property to community, regulations on lease, agriculture and planning made 'restrictions on the use of property in the public interest' not just more acceptable, but even a part of modern French property law.[135]

Although Article 17 of the 1789 Declaration and Article 544 of the Civil Code protect private property in absolute terms, the latter has always been qualified, and the Constitutional Council provided only a 'cautious endorsement of property rights'.[136] The constitutional jurisprudence more often reflected the evolution of property rights and limitations in the name of public interest.[137] *Nationalizations*[138] and *Privatizations*[139] are two defining constitutional cases. The Constitutional Council has declared that the question of public necessity is for the legislature to decide and that it will intervene only in a case of a manifest error in evaluation.[140] Since nationalisations were initiated in order to address the economic crisis, the Constitutional Council refused to pronounce breach of property rights, but after the change of governing party, a right-wing coalition tried to reverse the nationalisation by privatisation programme. The Constitutional Council did not object either, only insisted that the transfer should be made at market value.[141] The Constitutional Council was reluctant to pronounce that any interference with property rights arising

---

133 Bell, Boyron and Whittaker 270.

134 Ibid 274.

135 Ibid 269; Loic Philip 'La Valeur juridique de la Declaration des droits de l'homme et du citoyen du 26 aout 1789 selon la jurisprudence de Conseil constitutionnel' in Etudes offertes a P.Kayser (Aix 1979) II 332–333; Roger Errera, 'The right of property and freedom of enterprise in French Constitutional law', XII International Forum on Constitutional Review, Saint – Petersburg, 2009 13 <http://www.rogererrera.fr/libertes_publiques/docs/ Droit_de_propriete_St_Petersbourg_09.pdf> accessed on 23 October 2018.

136 John Bell, *French Constitutional Law* (Clarendon Press 1992) 176.

137 *TGV Nord* [1989] (French Constitutional Council).

138 *Nationalizations* [1982] (French Constitutional Council).

139 *Privatizations* [1986] (French Constitutional Council).

140 Bell 178.

141 Ibid 180.

from regulations amounts to the 'taking' under Article 17 of the Declaration.[142] The practice in civil law cases was also to refuse compensation 'for the rights of passage for public services', such as telegraph wires, electricity cables, etc.[143] The concept of administrative easement without compensation is illustrated by the *Eiffel Tower Amendment* decision of 13 December 1985, which allowed to install and use the equipment for radio and television transmission on other buildings.[144] The city of Paris as an owner of the Eiffel Tower challenged it, arguing that there was no public utility in such a state measure and no safeguards to minimise the interference with private property. The Constitutional Council argued that administrative easement was not a deprivation of property rights since it did not deprive the use of the property totally and absolutely, i.e., leaving principal use intact.[145] Other planning and zoning regulations did not amount to a deprivation of property rights.[146] Even permanent and temporary restrictions on disposal were not recognised as takings.[147] Only the power of the minister to appoint representatives for private shareholders 'if necessary' was considered as significant interference with private rights.[148]

A considerable public authority to limit private property rights is counterbalanced by the principles of good administrative behaviour, which require a government to prepare decisions carefully, give clear reasons for its decisions, and treat all of its citizens equally. It also includes the requirement to take proportionate measures and not to abuse its powers (*détournement de pouvoir*).[149] Someone affected by state measures may be able to obtain compensation even without establishing the breach of property rights, i.e., on the basis of the administrative principle – equality before public burdens.[150]

---

142 Emma Guernaoui, 'Procedural Requirements for Administrative Limits to Property Rights in France' in Martina Conticelli and Thomas Perroud (eds), *Procedural Requirements for Administrative Limits to Property Rights* (Oxford Academic, Oxford University Press 2022) 22.

143 Bell 182; F Colly, 'Le Conseil constitutionnel et le droit de propriete' (1988) Revue du droit public et de la science politique en France et à l'étranger 135, 174, 180.

144 *Eiffel Tower Amendment case* [1985] (French Constitutional Council).

145 Bell 183.

146 *Adapting Agriculture to the Environment* [1990] (French Constitutional Council); *Town Planning* [1985] (French Constitutional Council); Alterman and Balla 30.

147 *Application of Privatization* [1989] (French Constitutional Council); *Structure of Agricultural Law* [1984] (French Constitutional Council).

148 *Democratization of the Public Sector* [1983] (French Constitutional Council); *Tobacco and Alcohol Advertising* [1991] (French Constitutional Council). Similar approach was taken in Indian cases and in the case law of the Iran-US Claims Tribunal.

149 Van Erp 162.

150 Bell 184.

Both Article 17 of the 1789 Declaration[151] and Article 545 of the Civil Code[152] imply that expropriation of private property is possible upon compensation. While the question of public purpose or necessity was left for the legislature to decide, the real battles were fought only about compensation.

While taking of property rights is compensated at full value, other interferences are compensated only to the extent that they cause losses that 'had a direct, certain, serious, and special character, different from those suffered by other members of the community'.[153] In the case of land planning and restrictions on the use of land and developmental rights, no compensation was available at all until 1998 when it was recognised after the ECHR decision that in the most extreme cases some compensation might be due.[154]

The *Nationalizations* and *Privatizations* decisions scrutinised the valuation methods, compensation procedures, and criteria in considerable detail, requiring to evaluate average share value, the value of assets, profits, subsidiaries, and dividends. However, the Constitutional Council took a more elusive approach in *TGV Nord*, stating that 'to be just, the compensation should cover the totality of the direct, material, and certain harm caused by the expropriation'.[155] Overall, interferences with property rights offer a shallow level of compensation in France, and a number of other countries, such as Greece, Sweden, and Belgium, were significantly influenced by French tradition.[156]

5 Germany

In Germany, Article 14 of the Basic Law of 1949 provides a constitutional property protection clause:

> (1) Property and the right of inheritance shall be guaranteed. Their content and limits shall be defined by the laws.
>
> (2) Property entails obligations. Its use shall also serve the public good.

---

151 'no one shall be deprived thereof except where public necessity, legally determined, shall clearly demand it, and then only on condition that the owner shall have been previously and equitably indemnified.'

152 'No one may be compelled to yield his ownership, unless for public purposes and for a fair and previous indemnity.'

153 Bell 184.

154 Alterman and Balla 30–31.

155 Bell 186.

156 Alterman and Balla 26, 31, 41; Sluysmans, Verbist and Waring 3.

> (3) Expropriation shall only be permissible for the public good. It may only be ordered by or pursuant to a law that determines the nature and extent of compensation. Such compensation shall be determined by establishing an equitable balance between the public interest and the interests of those affected...[157]

Historically, in German private law, ownership dealt primarily with tangible things and only reluctantly accepted intangible things.[158] For example, in German law, the buyer with a delayed payment and retention of title clause was given an '*Anwartschaftsrecht*, or expectation right over the purchase, which was something less than ownership, but similar to the beneficial ownership under English Equity'.[159]

Starting from the limited scope of ownership of objects in private law, the German Constitutional Court developed a much broader understanding of property, which includes:

> all rights that have economic value, and which the legal order has attributed to the individual in such a way that he is allowed to exercise them according to his autonomous decision and for his private benefit.[160]

Gradually, this included company shares,[161] intellectual property,[162] personal claims[163] and even certain aspects of social security systems based on personal contributions.[164] But a licence is not a protected property right:

---

157 Basic Law for the Federal Republic of Germany (1949) with amendments as of 2014 <https://www.gesetze-im-internet.de/englisch_gg/englisch_gg.html#p0090> accessed on 31 March 2025.

158 s 903–1011 of the BGB (1900); Norbert Horn and others, *German Private and Commercial Law: An Introduction* (Clarendon Press 1982); E J Cohn and O C Giles, *Manual of German Law*, vol 2 (2 edn, The British Institute of international and comparative law 1968–1971); Milo 731; Howard D Fisher, *The German legal system and legal language: a general survey together with notes and German vocabulary* (4 edn, Routledge-Cavendish 2009) 108.

159 Jansen and Van Erp, 'Comparative Property Law', 1054; Baur Fritz Baur, Rolf Stürmer and Fritz Baur, *Sachenrecht* (Beck 2009) s 57–58.

160 *The Right of Pre-Emption case* BVerfGE 83, 201 [1991] as translated in Sabine Michalowski and Lorna Woods, *German constitutional law: the protection of civil liberties* (Ashgate/Dartmouth 1999) 320.

161 BVerfGE 14, 263 (1962).

162 BVerfGE 31, 229 (1971).

163 BVerfGE 83, 201 (1991).

164 *Egualisation of Pensions upon Dissolution of Marriage Decision* BVerfGE 53, 257 [1980].

> Such licences to operate dangerous plants are state permits which, depending on their configuration, overcome either repressive or preventive prohibitions that reserve the option of granting the permission to carry out the activity sought. Thus they are not comparable with those subjective public rights on which established constitutional case-law confers protection of the type provided to property. According to this case-law, such property-type protection is granted due to the fact that those rights provide individuals with a legal interest which is tantamount to that of an owner and strong enough to assume that depriving it without compensation would contradict the Basic Law in terms of its rule-of-law content (BVerfGE 40, 65 <83>).[165]

In Germany, EON Kernkraft GmbH, RWE Power AG, Kernkraftwerk Krümmel GmbH & Co oHG, and Vattenfall Europe Nuclear Energy GmbH challenged a democratic decision to phase-out nuclear power plants.[166] In this national case, the German Constitutional Court emphasised that a licence to operate nuclear power plants did not constitute property and found no expropriation, which presupposes the loss of title.[167] The Court found no breach of the German constitution when some output allowances were revoked. But the revocation of other allowances based on a specific compensatory mechanism was found to be unequal, disproportionate, and in breach of legitimate expectation.[168] Therefore, the new German regulation requiring faster nuclear phase-out was found to be in breach of national law.

Although constitutional property is interpreted quite broadly, the constitutional protection of that property is interpreted narrowly.[169] The German legal system is not fuelled by the drive to maximise the profit-bearing features of the

165 BVerfG, Judgment of the First Senate of 6 December 2016–1 BvR 2821/11 para 231. In investment arbitration it is not unheard that the cancelation of licence is treated as indirect expropriation: *Casinos Austria International GmbH and Casinos Austria Aktiengesellschaft v. Argentine Republic* (ICSID) Case No ARB/14/32, Decision on Jurisdiction 29 June 2018 [2018] para 229.

166 BVerfG, Judgment of the First Senate of 6 December 2016–1 BvR 2821/11.

167 Ibid paras 231, 242 and 252.

168 Ibid paras 262, 312 and 344. German administrative law principle of the protection of trust made a significant influence on the interpretation of the fair and equitable treatment standard in investment arbitration: Michele Potestà, 'Legitimate Expectations in Investment Treaty Law: Understanding the Roots and the Limits of a Controversial Concept' (2013) 28 ICSID Review – Foreign Investment Law Journal 88, 94.

169 Foroud Shirvani, 'Procedural Requirements for Administrative Limits to Property Rights in Germany' in Martina Conticelli and Thomas Perroud (eds), *Procedural Requirements for Administrative Limits to Property Rights* (Oxford Academic, Oxford University Press 2022) 29.

property like in the USA constitutional jurisprudence, but rather to provide the minimum basis for subsistence for individuals. This relatively broad understanding of constitutional property protection is substantially qualified by values of the Basic Law, namely the freedom of self-determination and social obligation.[170] Arguably, the German Constitutional Court will resolve differently the dispute involving the proprietary rights of a widowed pensioner, whose livelihood depends on a single source of income and the controversy over the level of profitability of commercially used assets. Furthermore, German constitutional jurisprudence continuously develops the meaning of constitutional property to address the changing circumstances and values of society,[171] and recent solutions might differ from early decisions.

In general, the regulation is not perceived as external to property rights, but rather internal, providing the content and limits of those property rights, as long as the regulation complies with the principles of proportionality and non-discrimination.[172] The 'Groundwater' cases (*Naßausskiesungsentscheidungen* (Ger)) provide an example of balancing individual property rights and communitarian interests in the context of regulatory takings.[173] The crux of the case was new legislation that introduced permits to operate gravel pits. The owner, who was denied the permit, claimed that his property was expropriated. The Constitutional Court appreciated the importance of communal water resources, because 'an orderly water management scheme was vital for the population as well as for the overall economy'.[174] Thus, the claim was rejected,[175] even though it was based on the express provision of the German Civil Code (BGB s 905) that '[t]he right of the owner of a parcel of land extends to the space above the surface and to the resources below the surface'. The Constitutional Court 'concluded that the constitutional meaning of property is not determined solely by the private-law meaning, but by the constitution itself',[176] including its provisions on the social aspect of property. The Groundwater cases are a perfect example in the German constitutional jurisprudence where it is openly admitted that property rights are not absolute, even when they are spelt out by the civil code, but limited by other German constitutional

170 *Co-Determination decision 50 BVerfGE 339* [*1979*]; *Trademark decision 51 BVerfGE 193* [*1979*]; Alexander, *The Global Debate Over Constitutional Property: Lessons for American Takings Jurisprudence* 97.

171 Alexander, 'Property as a fundamental constitutional right?: the German example' 30.

172 Michalowski and Woods 322.

173 *Groundwater cases* 58 BVerfGE 300 [1981].

174 Ibid 341, citing 10 BVerfGE 113.

175 58 BVerfGE 300 (1981) 345.

176 Alexander, 'Property as a fundamental constitutional right?: the German example' 33.

values, such as well-functioning society, individual self-realisation, and dignity.

In contrast to American jurisprudence, the German Constitutional Court does not prioritise a wealth-creating function of property or property as a commodity.[177] It means that 'the constitutional right to property does not guarantee the right to exploit the resource for its highest economic value'.[178] The reasoning of the *Groundwater* cases was later reaffirmed in the *Right of Pre-Emption* case.[179]

Another essential aspect transpiring from the *Groundwater* cases is the Court's conclusion that the legislation in question did not deprive the owner of its property completely, but only limited its use.[180] In doing this, the German constitutional jurisprudence rejected the doctrine of 'conceptual severance', meaning that the taking of a separate right did not amount to the expropriation of the whole property.[181] This differs from investment arbitration practice, where deprivation of a separate right out of a bundle could be treated as expropriation in itself.[182]

The community's interests in property are balanced by the principle of justified expectations and protection of trust:

> to restructure individual legal positions by issuing an appropriate and reasonable transition rule whenever the public interest merits precedence over some justified expectation, based on continuity of practice, in the continuance of a vested right.[183]

State liability based on the civilian principle of individual sacrifice and the principle of proportionality also plays an important role in German expropriation cases.[184] The obligation to submit a copy of every published book to the public library was considered proportional in case of massive production, but

177 Ibid 50.

178 Ibid 42.

179 BVerfGE 83, 201 (1991).

180 58 BVerfGE, 345.

181 Alexander, 'Property as a fundamental constitutional right?: the German example' 41–42.

182 *Saar Papier Vertriebs GmbH v Republic of Poland* (UNCITRAL) para 87; *Pope & Talbot Inc v Government of Canada*, para 96; *SwemBalt AB v Republic of Latvia* (UNCITRAL) para 38; *Merrill & Ring Forestry LP v Government of Canada* para 143; *Les Laboratoires Servier, SAS, Biofarma, SAS and Arts et Techniques du Progres SAS v Republic of Poland* para 674.

183 58 BVerfGE paras 350–351.

184 Rudolf Dolzer and Yun-I Kim, 'Germany' in Chester Brown (ed), *Commentaries on Selected Model Investment Treaties* (First edn, Oxford University Press 2013) 191–192.

a disproportionate burden for publishers of a small number and exquisite books:

> Responsibilities following from property must always be proportionate. Measured against the social context and the social significance of the property, as well as in the light of the purpose of the regulation, [these regulations] may not create a disproportionate burden and may not unreasonably affect the owners in the economic area.[185]

However, the rent regulations preventing the termination of tenancy, except in some very limited cases, were considerate proportionate.[186] Here again, it was confirmed that the common good in having stable tenancy agreements takes priority over the interest of the owner to earn higher profit from her property. Under German constitutional law, even expropriation for the benefit of a private party might be considered as a public good if it creates jobs.[187]

When considering the regulation of property, the Constitutional Court explicitly acknowledged the individual and communitarian aspect:

> When fulfilling its responsibility … of determining the content and limits of property, the legislator has the task of realising the social model the normative elements of which follow partly from the constitutional recognition of private property … and partly from the social command of At. 12(2): the use of property shall at the same time promote the common good.[188]

Compensation can be an important element in the process of balancing individual and community interests:

> The compensation for expropriation should be the result of a balancing of interests and not of the one-sided recognition of the interests of the person concerned, or of those of the community.[189]

185 *Deposit Copy case* BVerfGE 58, 147–148.
186 *First Termination for Personal Use Decision* BVerfGE 68, 361 (1985).
187 *Boxberg decision* BVerfGE 74, 264 [1987].
188 *Allotment decision* BVerfGE 52, 1 [1979].
189 *Hamburg Dyke Order Act case* BVerfGE 24, 421 [1968].

Thus, under German law, the balancing of interests might require 'less than full market value of the property' even in the cases of expropriation[190] and is unlikely to be awarded at all in the case of a general regulation affecting property rights unless specifically provided by the law itself.[191]

Schill argued that investment arbitration practice does not exceed property protection under the German Constitution.[192] However, without a communitarian aspect balancing individualistic attitudes to investment, the outcomes in investment disputes would be different from German constitutional jurisprudence.[193]

The German tradition is followed in Austria, which has a similar legal system. Historically, Article 365 of the Austrian general Civil Code emphasised the communitarian aspect of property: '[i]f the common good so requires, a citizen of the state must cede even the complete ownership of property for a suitable compensation'.[194] However, the property protection clause is interpreted narrowly.[195] The Austrian Supreme Court and the Constitutional Court have developed concepts of public interest, proportionality, and compensation similar to the German legal system.[196] The German approach to property and expropriation is also observed in other countries, which were influenced by the German legal system.[197]

6 Canada

Canada does not have an explicit constitutional property protection clause. The Canadian Bill of Rights, enacted in 1960, in section 1 acknowledges that the enjoyment of property cannot be deprived without due process of law.[198]

190 Michalowski and Woods 332; Hans-Bernd Schäfer, 'Taking Law from an Economic Perspective with Reference to German Law' in Iljoong Kim, Hojun Lee and Ilya Somin (eds), *Eminent Domain: A Comparative Perspective* (Cambridge University Press 2017) 13.

191 A rezoning preventing any construction was not compensated in BVerfGE 23, 30; Alterman and Balla 34.

192 Schill 621.

193 Christian Riffel, 'International Investment Law, Rule of Law, and Democracy: When the Solution Is Part of the Problem' (2025) 26 German Law Journal 613, 623.

194 The Austrian Civil Code (1811).

195 Alterman and Balla 32.

196 August Reinisch, 'Austria' in Chester Brown (ed), *Commentaries on Selected Model Investment Treaties* (First edn, Oxford University Press 2013) 16.

197 Alterman and Balla 48.

198 The Bill of Rights (1960) <http://laws-lois.justice.gc.ca/eng/acts/C-12.3/page-1.html> accessed on 31 March 2025.

The language is very general and 'there is some doubt that it provides anything more than procedural rights'.[199] Such brevity could probably be explained by the fact that the property clause was abandoned when the Privy Council tried to invalidate Canadian legislation addressing the effects of the Great Depression.[200]

Despite strong communitarian sympathies[201] and recognising the fiduciary duties towards indigenous people[202] on a practical level, Canadian courts are respectful of property.[203] Following a common law tradition, the mandatory acquisition has to be expressly regulated by the law. At the federal level, the Expropriation Act provides for the general definitions, requirements, notices and procedures, as well as the possibility to challenge and compensation levels.[204] The provinces have their own expropriation acts with local specifics.[205]

The Canadian judiciary has ambivalent attitudes towards regulatory takings or indirect expropriations. In general, Article 2(1) of the Canadian Expropriation Act protects 'any estate, interest or right that has been lost, in whole or in part', which theoretically allows claims for severance of rights and indirect expropriation. However, a regulation that affects the economic value of a right or interest is not compensable unless specifically provided by the statute.[206]

The interpretations of statutes vary, and the intent of the legislature plays a significant role in courts' reasoning. In *Manitoba Fisheries v The Queen* the claimant was put out of business due to the state monopoly to export fish, i.e., his goodwill was taken by legislation, and the Canadian court ruled the owner was entitled to compensation because the intangible property was not excluded in the list.[207] In *The Queen v Tener*[208] and *Casamiro Resource Corp v*

199 Allen, *The Right to Property in Commonwealth Constitutions* 70.

200 Ibid 145–146.

201 David Schneiderman, 'Property rights and regulatory innovation: Comparing constitutional cultures' (2006) 4 International Journal of Constitutional Law 371.

202 *Guerin v The Queen* 13 DLR (4th) 321 [1984]; *R v Sparrow* 70 DLR (4th) 385 [1990]; *Delmaguukw v British Columbia* 153 DLR (4th) 193 [1997].

203 Richard W Bauman, 'Property Rights in the Canadian Constitutional Context' (1992) 8 South African Journal on Human Rights 344; Eric C E Todd, *The Law of Expropriation and Compensation in Canada* (Carswell 1992) 35.

204 Expropriation Act (RSC, c E-21) (1985) <https://laws-lois.justice.gc.ca/eng/acts/e-21/index.html> accessed on 31 March 2025.

205 For example, Ontario Expropriations Act (RSO 1990, c. E.26), British Columbia Expropriation Act (RSBC 1996, c. 125), Alberta Expropriation Act (RSA 2000, c. E-13), Quebec Expropriation Act, (CQLR c. E-24).

206 Celine Levesque and Andrew Newcombe, 'Canada' in Chester Brown (ed), *Commentaries on Selected Model Investment Treaties* (Oxford University Press 2013) 56.

207 *Manitoba Fisheries v The Queen* 88 DLR (3d) 462 [1978].

208 *The Queen v Tener* 1 SCR 533 [1985].

British Columbia,[209] the natural resources situated in parks could not be excavated due to a rezoning decision. Canadian courts ordered compensation to the claimants because rezoning made the claims to minerals unusable.

In contrast, in *Cream Silver Mines Ltd v British Columbia*, the British Columbia Court of Appeal refused compensation for a statutory claim to minerals in the park, arguing that no compensation was provided by the statutes and therefore the requirement of compensation should not be implied.[210] In *Canadian Pacific Railway Co v Vancouver (City)* the Supreme Court of Canada refused compensation for the city planning decision prohibiting redevelopment of a land plot under a disused railway line, arguing that compensation for an owner must be paid only if the state acquires a beneficial interest in a property and the property is deprived of any reasonable use.[211]

Articles 25–26 of the Canadian Expropriation Act provide that the compensation for expropriated interest or right has to be calculated at the market value 'being the amount that would have been paid for the interest or right if, at the time of its taking, it had been sold in the open market by a willing seller to a willing buyer'.[212] The law also provides certain valuation presumptions, additional factors, and exceptions, such as in the case of the loss of occupation, residence, specially designed buildings, etc.[213]

The Canadian Supreme Court also adopted the proportionality test requiring a rational balance between public needs and state measures that affect private property,[214] but that balance is coloured by the common law individualistic presumptions.

7 Australia

The Australian Constitution does not contain a constitutional right to property. Instead, Section 51(xxxi) of the Australian Constitution of 1900 only provides the Parliament with the power to acquire property:

> The Parliament shall, subject to this Constitution, have power to make laws for the peace, order and good government of the Commonwealth with respect to: …

209 *Casamiro Resource Corp v British Columbia (Attorney-General)* 80 DLR (4th) 1 (BCCA) [1991].

210 *Cream Silver Mines Ltd v British Columbia* 99 DLR (4th) 199, 208 [1993].

211 *Canadian Pacific Railway Co v Vancouver (City)* SCC 5, 1 SCR 227 [2006].

212 Expropriation Act (RSC, c E-21).

213 Ibid Article 26.

214 *The Queen v Oakes* 26 DLR (4th) 200, 227 [1986].

(xxxi) the acquisition of property on just terms from any State or person for any purpose in respect of which Parliament has power to make laws.[215]

Following a common law tradition in Australia, expropriation is framed in terms of acquisition of property, i.e., compensation is due only if the state acquires the property, not when a citizen is deprived of property or loses a certain value of it. Australian courts broadly interpret acquisition to include any form that in substance constitutes a transfer of property,[216] but acknowledge that certain limitations on property rights derive from the concept of property itself.[217]

In *Commonwealth v WMC Resource,* a mining company lost an interest in an exploration permit due to legislation, but the High Court held that no acquisition of property had occurred, meaning that no compensation was due.[218]

Australian practice concerning regulations is quite similar to the general common law tradition: sovereign powers akin to 'police powers' are permissible and not compensable. Although constitutional norms on the protection of free trade and commerce between states, including section 51(xxxi), were successfully used to invalidate an attempt to nationalise private banks.[219]

Like everywhere else, the balance between environmental interests and regulation, on one hand, and property rights, on the other hand, raises many controversies and disputes in Australia. The licence holder's right to receive the highest possible profitability was addressed in a case concerning the exploitation of a sand mine near the Great Coral Reef: *Murphyores Inc Pty Ltd v Commonwealth.*[220] Although set in the context of export and trade, the

215 The Commonwealth of Australia Constitution Act (1900), including amendments up to Act No. 84, 1977, <https://www.legislation.gov.au/C2004Q00685/latest/text> accessed 9 April 2025.

216 *Georgiadis v Australian and Overseas Telecommunications Corporation* 179 CLR 297 [1994]; Australian Law Reform Commission, *Traditional Rights and Freedoms – Encroachments by Commonwealth Laws* (2015), <https://www.alrc.gov.au/publication/traditional-rights-and-freedoms-encroachments-by-commonwealth-laws-alrc-report-129/18-property-rights/summary-221/> accessed 10 April 2025.

217 *British Medical Association v The Commonwealth* 270 and *Commonwealth v Tasmania 1.*

218 *Commonwealth v WMC Resources* 194 CLR 1 [1998]. In similar investment arbitration cases investors have been prevailing: *Copper Mesa Mining Corporation v Republic of Ecuador*, PCA Case No 2012-2, Award (Redacted), 15 March 2016 6.677, 6.123; *Abengoa, SA y COFIDES, SA v United Mexican States* (ICSID) para 610; *Metalclad Corporation v United Mexican States* para 107, 111; *Casinos Austria International GmbH and Casinos Austria Aktiengesellschaft v. Argentine Republic* para 229.

219 *Bank of New South Wales v Commonwealth* 76 CLR 1 [1948].

220 *Murphyores Inc Pty Ltd v Commonwealth* HCA 20, 136 CLR 1 (14 April 1976) (High Court) [1976].

Australian High Court concluded that the prohibition to export mineral sand was valid and within the regulatory power of a state.[221] More recently, the High Court of Australia reached a conclusion in the special case regarding the replacement of a groundwater bore licence with an aquifer access licence entailing a smaller groundwater entitlement, which was similar to the German case.[222] It was determined that reducing entitlements does not equate to property acquisition, as water is a natural resource, and the state has always possessed the authority to regulate the amount of water taken.[223]

The Lands Acquisition Act of 1989 regulates in detail the modes of acquisition of land (including for exploration and mining activities) for a public purpose, including institutions authorised in the process, notifications, calculation of compensation, etc.[224] The goal is to ensure the person receives fair compensation for their loss or disadvantage resulting from the acquisition. In particular, the compensation should take into account the market value of the interest at the acquisition date, any added financial benefit linked to ownership, loss in value of other land interests due to severance, change in value of retained land caused by the acquisition, as well as other consequential loss.[225] Section 56 of the Lands Acquisition Act explains that the market value is understood as 'the amount that would have been paid for the interest if it had been sold at that time by a willing but not anxious seller to a willing but not anxious buyer'.[226] Also, the law instructs to exclude certain factors from the calculation of the compensation, such as some planning restrictions and special enumerated circumstances that unusually affect the value of the interest.[227]

Similar trends and considerations favouring the balanced approach to property could be observed in New Zealand too.[228]

This pattern of Australian case law on the issue of indirect expropriation could be contrasted with the decision in *Revere Copper v OPIC*, where an

---

221 Ibid.

222 *Groundwater cases* 58 BVerfGE 300 (1981).

223 *ICM Agriculture Pty Ltd & Ors v The Commonwealth of Australia* 240 CLR 140 [2009].

224 Lands Acquisition Act (1989) with amendments up to 14 October 2024, Australia <https://www.legislation.gov.au/C2004A03763/latest/text> accessed 10 April 2025.

225 S 55 of ibid.

226 Ibid.

227 S 59–60 of ibid.

228 Richard P Boast and Susy Frankel, 'Defining the Ambit of Regulatory Takings' in Susy Frankel and Deborah Ryder (eds), *Recalibrating Behaviour: Smarter Regulation in a Global World* (LexisNexis NZ 2013); Richard P Boast and Neil C Quigley, 'Regulatory Reform and Property Rights in New Zealand' in Susy Frankel (ed), *Learning from the Past, Adapting for the Future: Regulatory Reform in New Zealand* (LexisNexis NZ 2011) 130.

increase in tax rate by Jamaica was deemed expropriatory.[229] The stabilisation agreement present in the *Revere Copper v OPIC* and absent in the Australian cases might partially explain the difference in outcomes. However, the essence of the disputes is somewhat similar, as it relates to the governmental change of conditions under which the natural resources are extracted and used. The different outcomes from similar factual settings illustrate that ISDS practice embarked on a different trajectory than national property protection jurisprudence.

8 Singapore

The Singaporean Constitution does not contain a right-to-property clause and manages to combine common law attitudes to commerce with a rather communitarian understanding of property, where community developmental interests are prioritised over individual rights. Scarcity of land is frequently mentioned as a reason for a government to promote the most efficient development of it for the general benefit of society.[230] In 1966, the Land Acquisition Act was enacted[231] to regulate the compulsory acquisition of land for public purposes without placing a heavy financial burden on Singapore.

In common law tradition, the Singaporean Land Acquisition Act speaks about the acquisition of land, not the taking or diminution of value.[232] The law allows acquisition of land for any public, residential, commercial, or industrial purposes. Land could be acquired by any person if a minister deems it necessary for the public interest, benefit, or utility. In light of such broad public powers, any challenges to the public purpose seem futile.[233] There are also other statutes that authorise the taking of property if it is needed for the devel-

229 *Revere Copper v OPIC* 56 ILR 258, 292. Also similar *Compañía del Desarrollo de Santa Elena v Republic of Costa Rica*.

230 Bryan Chew and others, 'Compulsory Acquisition of Land in Singapore: A Fair Regime?' (2010) 22 Singapore Academy of Law Journal 166.

231 Land Acquisition Act No 41 (1966), 2020 revised edition <https://sso.agc.gov.sg/Act/LAA1966> accessed 11 April 2025.

232 Ibid.

233 *Basco Enterprises Pte Ltd v Soh Siang Wai* 1 MLJ 193 [1990]; Jean Ho, 'Singapore' in Chester Brown (ed), *Commentaries on selected model investment treaties* (First edn, Oxford University Press 2013) 626 citing *Eng Foong Ho & Ors v Attorney-General* 2 SLR 542 [2009]; *Teng Fuh Holdings Pte Ltd v Collector of Land Revenue 2 SLR 568* [2007].

opment or public interest, for example, by the Port of Singapore Authority, the Housing and Development Board, or the Land Transport Authority.[234]

Since there is no constitutional guarantee of the right to property, the question of diminution of private property value due to regulations, such as land planning or environmental protection, is also nonexistent.

The compensation for the mandatory acquisition was the most controversial issue for years in Singapore, since the Land Acquisition Act of 1966 initially did not calculate the market value at the moment of expropriation. For many years, compensations were fixed to the values of the land in 1973. The reason for this was that:

> [t]he appreciation in land value which resulted, *inter alia*, from good land planning and infrastructure development by the Government ought to accrue to the infrastructure provider, *ie* Government, and not to individual landowners. The Government may in turn re-distribute the wealth gained from the appreciation in land value to the population through infrastructure and other public developments.[235]

Some more controversial valuation disputes were settled out of court, involving the question as to how the calculation of the compensation of land is affected by zoning decisions. In one case, car parking lost all its value because it was zoned for a road extension. In another case, the compensation was nominal because the acquisition was made for the metro station, substantially increasing the value of the remaining land plot.[236]

Once major developments and zoning were completed, and social as well as economic structures were settled, the Land Acquisition Act was amended to provide for the market value. Compensation is calculated taking various interests into account, and the review is carried out by a quasi-judicial body, but the appeal is possible only on questions of law.[237]

Singapore's example confirms that substantial development projects might require flexibility on the part of property rights. After the improvement of living standards is reached and wealth accumulated, the local social consensus shifts towards more stable and fixed property rights.

---

234 William J M Ricquier, 'Compulsory Purchase in Singapore' in Tsuyoshi Kotaka and David L Callies (eds), *Taking land: compulsory purchase and regulation in Asian-Pacific countries* (University of Hawai'i Press 2002) 271–272.

235 Chew and others 169–170.

236 Singapore Parliamentary Debates, Official Report (15 August 2003) vol 76, cols 2459–2462 (Assoc Prof Ho Peng Kee, Senior Minister of State for Law).

237 Section 29 of the Land Acquisition Act.

9 Developed Asian States

Almost all pre-modern Asian societies relied heavily on social harmony, hierarchy, consensus, and communal property, remnants of which are still evident today.[238] In feudal Japan, the right of the members of a village community to a common land has been called *iriai* or *iriaiken,* but modern codifications ignored it, leading to clashes between official owners and 'the farmers who depended upon their common lands in customary practices'.[239]

In terms of individual property protection *vis-à-vis* a state, the defining experience was probably the close alliance of Japan, South Korea, and Taiwan with Western powers after WWII. Despite national variations, on a conceptual level, the liberal influence explains the existing attitudes to property there. Immediately after WWII, Japan, South Korea, and Taiwan benefited from land reforms that redistributed farmland to peasants, usually for less than market value,[240] despite constitutions resembling American and German constitutional jurisprudence on property.[241] Article 29 of the Japanese Constitution of 1946 guarantees:

> The right to own or to hold property is inviolable.
> Property rights shall be defined by law, in conformity with the public welfare.
> Private property may be taken for public use upon just compensation therefor.[242]

Due process is also implied, and discrimination is prohibited in Japan.[243] Similarly, in South Korea, the Constitution of 1948 provides:

> (1) The right to property of all citizens shall be guaranteed. The contents and limitations thereof shall be determined by an Act.
> (2) The exercise of property rights shall conform to the public welfare.

---

238 Tom Ginsburg, 'Confucian Constitutionalism? The Emergence of Constitutional Review in Korea and Taiwan' (2002) 27 Law & Social Inquiry 763.

239 Masaji Chiba, Asian Indigenous Law in Interaction with Received Law, (1986 KPI London, New York) 329–330.

240 Allen 265; Upham 77.

241 Walt 256–257.

242 The Constitution of Japan (1946) <https://japan.kantei.go.jp/constitution_and _government_of_japan/constitution_e.html> accessed on 11 April 2025.

243 Articles 13, 14, and 31 of the Constitution of Japan.

(3) Expropriation, use, or restriction of private property from public necessity and compensation therefor shall be governed by Act: provided that in such a case, just compensation shall be paid.[244]

In South Korea, specifically land, goods, and rights (ownership and other rights such as mining, fishing, and use of natural resources) are protected from expropriation.[245] As Japan and South Korea have a more limited understanding of property than common law countries,[246] constitutional 'protection does not extend to economic opportunity or mere expectation'.[247]

Special acts usually regulate the expropriation procedure and provide guidance on public interest.[248] Article 3 of the Japanese Land Expropriation Law provides that roads, railways, river improvements, water and waste disposal facilities carry public interest, and Japanese case law interprets 'public use' widely, even including redistribution of land to private users.[249] The public interest in South Korea is defined more broadly by national defence and military affairs, as well as innumerable instances of private and public infrastructure, such as railroads, roads, airports, harbours, parking lots, cargo terminals, water and sewerage systems, erosion control, windbreak, fire prevention, reservoirs, oil and gas supply, waste treatment, electricity, telecommunications, broadcasting, meteorological observations, schools, libraries, museums, and art galleries.[250]

In South Korea, even takings by private corporations that were necessary for the development of industrial complexes or housing projects were not treated as breaches of the right to property.[251] However, in Japan, several public infrastructure projects were burdened by violent owners' protests, and

244 Article 23 of the Constitution of the Republic of Korea (1948) <https://elaw.klri.re.kr/eng_service/lawView.do?lang=ENG&hseq=1> accessed on 11 April 2025.

245 Article 3 of the Act Concerning the Acquisition of Land, etc for Public Interest Projects and the Compensation Therefor No 6656 (2002) (Korean Act on Expropriation).

246 Walt 258.

247 Hi-Taek Shin, 'Republic of Korea' in Chester Brown (ed), *Commentaries on selected model investment treaties* (First edition. edn, Oxford University Press 2013) 396.

248 Korean Act on Expropriation (2002) with the amendments up until 2022, <https://elaw.klri.re.kr/eng_mobile/viewer.do?hseq=60423&type=part&key=35> accessed on 11 April 2025; the Japanese Land Expropriation Law No 219 (1951); the Japanese Law of Special Measure for Land Acquisition No 150 (1961), English translations of Japanese laws could be found here <http://www.japaneselawtranslation.go.jp> accessed on 11 April 2025.

249 Walt 261.

250 Article 4 of the Korean Act on Expropriation (2022).

251 *Private Taking decision of 24 September 2009* case No 2007Hun-Ba114 (Korean Constitutional Court) [2009] <https://isearch.ccourt.go.kr/view.do> and *Granting a Private Developer to Claim Transfer of Land from Private Owner Case* Decision of 26 Novem-

since then, the preferred method of the government has been negotiation instead of expropriation.[252]

Other sectoral laws usually regulate property and state's interference with it, such as the Korean National Land Planning and Utilization Act, Road Act, River Act, Mining Industry Act, Electricity Business Act, and the Patent Act.[253] In the context of the regulation of property, an obligation to bear the expenses of the excavation of cultural heritage was not treated as a breach of the constitutional property guarantee.[254] Although 'indirect expropriation' is not generally recognised in South Korea,[255] and land use rights are defined primarily by the ban on the development, unless specifically permitted,[256] land planning solutions limiting the owners' rights for an extended period of time were at least in some cases treated as a breach of the constitutional property clause.[257]

The same controversy exists in Japan.[258] Judge Takatsuji argued for a balanced approach in answering the question of whether compensation is due for the regulation affecting property.[259] He argued that the following three categories of regulations do not entail compensation, even though they interfere with property rights: (i) regulation and limitation of property rights is caused by the owner's actions; (ii) when the interference is within the social obligation of the property; (iii) regulation is necessary for the preservation and

ber 2009, No 2008Hun-Ba133 (Korean Constitutional Court) <https://isearch.ccourt.go.kr/view.do> both accessed on 11 April 2025.

252 Kenneth L Port, *Comparative law: law and the legal process in Japan* (Gerald Paul McAlinn ed, Carolina Academic Press 2003) 608–609.

253 Most of the Korean legislation in English can be accessed here <https://elaw.klri.re.kr/eng_mobile/part.do> 11 April 2025.

254 *Imposition of Expenses for the Excavation of Cultural Heritage case* Decision of 28 October 2010, No 2008Hun-Ba74 (Korean Constitutional Court) <https://isearch.ccourt.go.kr/view.do> accessed on 11 April 2025.

255 Shin 396.

256 Won Woo Suh, 'Land Use Planning and Compensation in Korea' in Tsuyoshi Kotaka and David L. Callies (eds), *Taking land: compulsory purchase and regulation in Asian-Pacific countries* (University of Hawai'i Press 2002) 170.

257 *Urban Planning Long-term Non-performance case* Decision of 21 October 1999, No 97Hun-Ba26 (Korean Constitutional Court) <https://isearch.ccourt.go.kr/view.do> accessed on 11 April 2025.

258 Shotaro Hamamoto and Luke Nottage, 'Japan' in Chester Brown (ed), *Commentaries on selected model investment treaties* (First edn, Oxford University Press 2013) 349. But certain safety regulations limiting the owner's rights were not treated as breaches of property right: Japanese Supreme Court, 18 February 1983, 37 Minshu 1, 59 [1983]. See also Kenneth Port 617.

259 Masami Takatsuji, 'Study on Property Right' (1962) 38 Jichi-Kenkyu3 as translated in Kotaka 152.

enhancement of public welfare.[260] The non-compensable regulation was illustrated by the case in the Japanese Supreme Court relating to the ban on planting trees or constructing buildings on the embankments of irrigation ponds:

> This regulation is necessary in social life in order to prevent disaster and promote public welfare, and any person with property rights on the embankment has to take this burden.[261]

Those and similar land planning and zoning regulations aim to prevent the abuse of property rights and harm to others, and thus do not require compensation, but the welfare of society is usually also mentioned as the reason for the regulations.[262] As a way of exception in cases related to the regulation of historical heritage, compensation is typically paid in nature reserves that freeze the current use of property.[263]

In Japan, compensation can be claimed on the basis of the constitutional norm, even in cases when the relevant expropriation law does not mention it.[264] All actual and economic losses caused by expropriation and calculated by fair market value should be compensated, but the loss of profit is excluded.[265] In Japan, the price of property is calculated for the purposes of compensation at the moment the decision on expropriation becomes known.[266] Although full compensation should be paid in straightforward expropriation cases, in cases of legal reforms or restrictions aimed at public welfare, something less than full market value could be compensated.[267]

In South Korea, the Constitutional Court held that 'just compensation' refers to the full market price, or in other words reasonable sale price.[268] As a general rule, Article 63(1)(2) of the Korean Act on Expropriation indicates the general sale price as a basis for compensation unless other acts provide other-

---

260 Ibid.

261 Decision of 6 June 1963 17 Keisyu 521 (Japanese Supreme Court) [1963]. See also Decision of 18 February 1983 37 Minshu 1, 59 (Japanese Supreme Court) [1983].

262 Kotaka 158–159; Walt 257, 259.

263 Decision of 6 June 1963, 17 Keisyu 521 [1963]; Decision of 27 November 1968 22 Keishu 12, 1402 (Japanese Supreme Court) [1968].

264 Decision of 13 March 1975 771 Hanrei-Jiho 37 (Japanese Supreme Court) [1975].

265 Cabinet decisions on the Guideline of Standard for Compensation for Loss Caused by Acquisition of Land for Public Use of 1962 and the Guideline of Standard for Compensation for Public Loss Caused by Execution of Public Project of 1967; Walt 263.

266 Article 26, para 1 of the Land Expropriation Law (Japan).

267 Decision 18 October 1973 27 Minshu 9, 1210 (Japanese Supreme Court) [1973]; Walt 263; Upham 77.

268 Shin 396.

wise. The abovementioned article also mentions the possibility that compensation may be made by bonds issued by the relevant project operator under certain circumstances.[269]

The compensation adjudicated by the competent land tribunal has to be paid in cash or at least deposited no later than the date of expropriation.[270] The moment of calculation of property value in Korea is the date of the agreement or adjudication, when the value of the property is usually already lower. Also, the offsetting of owners' losses with gains accrued due to the public interest works is prohibited in Korea.[271]

Overall, and not even mentioning developing and socialist states, it could be said that even in economically developed Asian states, the content and scope of property clauses are geared towards public welfare, and the balance of jurisprudence is tilted towards community interests rather than individual interests, in contrast to what is observed in Anglo-American legal systems. Although Kim, Lee, and Somin observed 'a clear relationship between a nation's level of economic development and the degree of protection for property rights'[272] the causality of this relation remains unclear, and it is hard to deny strong state-induced industrialisation efforts in those Asian states that managed to achieve GDP per capita comparable to Western economies.

10 India

Customary law in India had strong communitarian principles, where common pastures were a usual component of village life.[273] Hindu law emphasised the social and ethical function of private property,[274] the purpose of which was to conduct religious rituals.[275] The Hindu legal view of property, besides being pluralistic, was also inherently fragmented: ownership meant rights and obli-

---

269 Article 63(7–8) of the Korean Act on Expropriation.

270 Article 40 of ibid.

271 Article 66 of ibid.

272 Iljoong Kim, Hojun Lee and Ilya Somin (eds), *Eminent Domain: A Comparative Perspective* (Cambridge University Press 2017) 297.

273 WH Rattigan, 'Customary Law in India' (1884) 10 Law Magazine and Law Review 1, 9.

274 Priyanath Sen, *Tagore Law Lectures, 1909. The General Principles of Hindu Jurisprudence* (1918) 6–7, 24, 51–52.

275 Jr Donald R Davis, *The Spirit of Hindu Law* (Cambridge University Press 2010) 100.

gations and could belong to different persons simultaneously.[276] Different castes had different ownership claims to the same land:

> Brahmins in Kerala always held the *janmam* / *attipēr* dominion rights to land and Pulaya Untouchables always held *kutima* / *atima* occupancy (or slavery) rights. In between, other castes held rights as mortgagees (*veppu*, etc.), renters (*pāttam*), or cultivators (*kānam*).[277]

The traditional understanding of property was changed by the British.[278] Since 1864 Hindu pandits and Muslim maulvis were no longer consulted, and *Dharmaśāstra* was gradually replaced by common law and statutes,[279] but the old beliefs coloured the practice. British colonial rule imposed on India a very individualistic property protection clause,[280] which differed even from the concept of property acquisition applicable in England. Article 299 of the Government of India Act of 1935 provided:

> (1) No person shall be deprived of his property in British India save by authority of law.
> (2) Neither the Federal nor a Provincial Legislature shall have power to make any law authorising the compulsory acquisition for public purposes of any land, or any commercial or industrial undertaking, or any interest in, or any company owning, any commercial or industrial undertaking, unless the law provides for the compensation for the property acquired and either fixes the amount of compensation, or specifies the principles on which, and the manner in which, it is to be determined.
> (3) No Bill or amendment making provision for the transference of public ownership of any land or for the extinguishment of modification of rights

---

276 John Duncan Martin Derrett, 'The Development of the Concept of Property in India c. A. D. 800–1800' in John Duncan Martin Derrett (ed), *Essays in classical and modern Hindu law* (Brill 1976) 86.

277 Donald R Davis, *The boundaries of Hindu law: tradition, custom and politics in medieval Kerala* (CESMEO 2004) 41–78.

278 Jr Donald R Davis, 'A historical overview of Hindu law' in Donald R Davis Jr, Jayanth K Krishnan and Timothy Lubin (eds), *Hinduism and Law: An Introduction* (Cambridge University Press 2010) 26.

279 P K Menon, 'The Traditional Hindu Law in India – Transformation from Customary to Codified Law' (1988) 16 Korean Journal of Comparative Law 105; P K Irani, *India* (Mohr Siebeck 1973) I-14.

280 Madhumita Datta Mitra, 'Evolution of Property Rights in India' in Sony Pellissery, Benjamin Davy and Harvey M Jacobs (eds), *Land Policies in India: Promises, Practices and Challenges* (Springer Singapore 2017) 37.

> therein, including rights or privileges in respect of land revenue, shall be introduced or moved in either Chamber of the Federal Legislature without the previous sanction of the Governor-General in his discretion, or in a Chamber of a Provincial Legislature without the previous sanction of the Governor in his discretion.[281]

Arguably, at that time, there was very little interest in 'the state's capacity to govern effectively', but considerable interest in protecting what was already appropriated.[282] It is surprising that when the Constituent Assembly was convened in 1946 for the drafting of the independent Constitution, the constitutional property protection clause was kept almost identical to the abovementioned Article 299.[283] It became one of the most disputed provisions and a centre stage for the clash of different interests. The government initiated land reforms hoping to redistribute large landholdings formed by the colonial administration, but the judiciary objected to it, ruling that the reform was discriminatory to previous owners and tax collectors – the zamindari.[284] The common law concept of the acquisition of property by the state was substantially extended by the judiciary to include abstract deprivation of property or loss. The combined effect of *Dwarkadas Shrinivas v Sholapur Spinning and Weaving Co Ltd,*[285] *State of West Bengal v Subodh Gopal Bose,*[286] *Saghir Ahmad v The State of Uttar Pradesh,*[287] and *Vajravelu v Special Deputy Collector, West Madras*[288] was that the property protection clause provided in Article 31(2) of the Constitution became applicable to regulations affecting property rights and required just compensation. The parliament passed several amendments of the Constitution to reverse such practice and to save the reforms,[289] but in *Golak Nath v State of Punjab*, the Supreme Court declared that the right to property was unamendable.[290] In 1967, the parliament managed to change that and, to avoid doubt, added that certain directive princi-

281 The Government of India Act (1935) <http://www.legislation.gov.uk/ukpga/ 1935/2/pdfs /ukpga_19350002_en.pdf> accessed 14 April 2025.

282 Allen, *The Right to Property in Commonwealth Constitutions* 5.

283 The Constitution of India (1949) <https://legislative.gov.in/constitution-of-india/> accessed on 15 May 2019.

284 *Kameshwar Singh v State of Bihar* AIR 1951 Patna 91; *State of West Bengal v Bela Banerjee* AIR 1954 SC 170.

285 *Dwarkadas Shrinivas v Sholapur Spinning and Weaving Co Ltd.*

286 *State of West Bengal v Subodh Gopal Bose* SCR 587 [1954].

287 *Saghir Ahmad v The State of Uttar Pradesh.*

288 *Vajravelu v Special Deputy Collector, West Madras* AIR 1965 SC 1017.

289 *Kunhikoman v Kerala* AIR 1962 SC 723.

290 *Golak Nath v State of Punjab* AIR 1643 [1967].

ples are beyond the reach of judicial review, which, of course, was challenged in *Kesavananda v State of Kerala*.[291] After that, Article 31 was repealed,[292] and now only Article 300A provides that 'No person shall be deprived of his property save by authority of law'.[293]

The scope of property is also problematic. Like in other common law countries, in India, transferability is generally an important indication of property; for example, occupations are not treated as property because they are not transferable.[294] But in certain cases, when the issue related to the main source of income for a person, it was held that 'certain governmental obligations to make payments to individuals' were property, even though it could not be alienated.[295] Furthermore, Indian jurisprudence sympathises with the bundle of rights theory of property, which means that the taking of a single right from a bundle might be sufficient to qualify the taking as an expropriation.[296]

Overall, it seems that the relatively wide scope of property and common law approach to its protection conflicted with the local traditions, needs, and 'constitutional provisions on social justice, egalitarianism, and land reform'.[297] This resulted in a clash between the legislative powers and the judiciary. The requirement for 'market value' compensation made land reforms, large-scale government-induced industrialisation and building of infrastructure more costly and challenging to implement. Instead of encouraging the development, the clash between individualistic and communitarian understandings of property sapped the limited administrative and human capacity resources of a young state at a critical moment. In this conflict, it seems that the legal culture won over formal legal texts. Currently, the issue is regulated by the Right to Fair Compensation and Transparency in Land Acquisition, Rehabilitation and Resettlement Act (2013), which ensures transparency, adherence to the procedure on notification, acquisition, and resettlement as well as requires social impact assessment and fair compensation.[298]

291 *Kesavananda v State of Kerala* 4 SCC 225 [1973].

292 Allen, *The Right to Property in Commonwealth Constitutions* 37.

293 The Constitution of India.

294 *Rajasthan v Union of India* AIR 1977 SC 1361.

295 *Madhav Rao Scindia v Union of India* AIR 1971 SC 530.

296 *West Bengal v Subodh Gopal Bose* [1954] SCR 587, 672–673.

297 Allen, 'Constitutional Law, Social Justice and the Redistribution of Land' 65.

298 The Right to Fair Compensation and Transparency in Land Acquisition, Rehabilitation and Resettlement Act (2013) India <https://www.indiacode.nic.in/bitstream/123456789/2121/1/A2013-30.pdf> accessed on 14 April 2025.

11 Poland

While Eastern Europe firmly belonged to the civil law tradition and was exposed to German influence, decades of communist ideology and rule left some deep scars in its social fabric. A swift reintroduction of private property institution accompanied by the constitutionalisation of private property rights, swung the pendulum to the other extreme, leaving most of the population not only perplexed but also in deep economic crisis. Economic transition policies advocated by the Western countries and international financial institutions were adopted, espousing 'a mythological version of eighteen-century laissez-faire'.[299] Any remnants of the socialist past were brushed aside, together with a peculiar welfare system, while investments in the region were following domestic growth rather than leading it.[300] The region is haunted by several contradictions associated with private property and state intervention. Formally, property rights are at the pinnacle of the legal systems, but this only hides a popular belief that individual interests should yield to community interests. Recent studies fail to find a correlation between stronger property protection rights and long-run economic gains or better economic performance.[301] For example, Estonia, Moldova, and Ukraine provide very strong constitutional protection of property, but only Estonia can claim economic success with economic indicators resembling Western Europe. In contrast, the Czech Constitution barely mentions private property rights, but it is 'one of the economically most successful countries in the region'.[302]

In most of the transition states, the public institutions had to be created anew. Due to a variety of reasons, many state institutions in the region are weak and inept for the functions that statutes assign to them, as well as underfinanced. But the welfare expectations in the region that was used to full employment are still very high. The divergent realities and expectations are easily exploited by the populist governments that tend to be elected in the region from time to time.

In the context of such contradictions, disputes over privatisation, 'good governance', and economic and legal reforms are inevitable. More than a quar-

299 Alice H Amsden, Jacek Kochanowicz and Lance Taylor, *The Market Meets its Match: Restructuring the Economies of Eastern Europe* (Harvard University Press 1994) VIII.

300 Ibid 11.

301 Christian Bjørnskov, 'Constitutional property rights protection and economic growth: evidence from the post-communist transition' (2015) 26 Constitutional Political Economy 247, 276–277.

302 Ibid 256–257.

ter of a century has passed since the collapse of communism, but the balance between private property rights and community interest is far from settled.

Poland has a long constitutional history, and now Article 20 of the Polish Constitution states that the economic system in Poland is based on the freedom of economic activity, private ownership, solidarity, and cooperation between social partners,[303] which to some extent resembles the German notion of social obligation of property. In 2005, the Constitutional Court held that 'the social aspect of ownership is now unanimously recognized'.[304] There is no further case law explaining to what extent property has to be socialised.[305] But the conflation of rights and duties of citizens, as well as policies of the state, may suggest that individual rights are not seen as ultimate 'restraints upon the exercise of state power'[306] and that a certain level of state intervention aiming to secure social rights is perceived positively in society.

Article 21(1) of the Constitution reads: '[t]he Republic of Poland shall protect ownership ...'. The scope of '*własność*' mentioned in this Article has sparked internal debates and contradictory constitutional jurisprudence.[307] Like in German law, only material things may be the object of *in rem* rights, including ownership, and have to be sufficiently separate from the environment.[308] Unless expressly allowed by law, contractual rights, permits, licences, awards or judgments are not property and consequently are not protected as such.[309] Following the civil law tradition, ownership is the most extensive of the property rights specifically listed by the Civil Code[310] and ownership cannot be fragmented in Poland. The pre-emption right is not recognised as a

---

303 Constitution of Poland (1997) <https://www.sejm.gov.pl/prawo/konst/angielski/kon1.htm> accessed on 15 April 2025.

304 Decision K 9/04 OTK ZU 3A/2005, poz 24 (Polish Constitutional Tribunal) [2005], all decisions of the Polish Constitutional Tribunal can be accessed here <https://otkzu.trybunal.gov.pl/Katalog> accessed on 14 April 2025.

305 Alterman and Balla 33–34.

306 Martin Krygier and Adam W Czarnota, *The Rule of Law After Communism: Problems and Prospects in East-Central Europe* (Ashgate 1998) 183.

307 The official translation translates the term as 'ownership'.

308 Stanislawa Kalus and Magdalena Habdas, 'The notion of real estate and rights in selected legal systems' in Elizabeth Cooke, Martin M A Dixon and Nicholas Hopkins (eds), *Modern studies in property law*, vol 3 (Hart Pub 2001) 252, 254.

309 Magdalena Habdas, *Property and trust law in Poland* (Kluwer Law International 2015) 205; Kamil Zaradkiewicz, Property Law – Introduction, <http://polishprivatelaw.pl/property-law-introduction/> accessed on 22 February 2018.

310 Article 140 of the Polish Civil Code (1964) <https://isap.sejm.gov.pl/isap.nsf/download.xsp/WDU19640160093/U/D19640093Lj.pdf> accessed on 15 April 2025.

proprietary right under Polish law,[311] which is in contrast to the ruling of the arbitral tribunal in *Eureko v Poland* case that certain contractual rights concerning the future IPO were expropriated.[312]

On one occasion, the Constitutional Tribunal interpreted that Article 21(1) protects only ownership, but not other *in rem* rights.[313] But on another occasion, the Constitutional Tribunal interpreted that the same term '*własność*' in constitutional jurisprudence should be understood as 'closer to economic understanding of property, thus being a synonym of the entirety of proprietary rights' and that it exceeds the civil law understanding of property.[314] Further constitutional jurisprudence was leaning towards a broader interpretation of '*własność*', including all kinds of private ownership entitlements.[315]

During the past decades, Poland, like other Eastern European countries, experienced extreme ideological swings from total control by a communist state to the abolition of any business restraints and back to the reintroduction of certain administrative authority over business.[316] Currently, like in the rest of the EU, the regulation of property in all aspects of life is pervasive. From zoning laws to environmental, cultural and historical protection, regulations are inescapable and inseparable from any activity. The Polish Constitution tries to strike a balance between the liberal values prevalent during the 1990s and historical state activism. In the Polish understanding of property, like in Germany, very often, extensive regulations are not seen as a limitation but as an integral part of property, beyond which the right to ownership does not exist.[317] Constitutional provisions reiterate that 'expropriation may be allowed solely for public purposes and for just compensation'[318] and that 'property may

311 Piotr Szafarz, Real Property Law – Poland Report, 5 <https://www.eui.eu/Documents/ DepartmentsCentres/Law/ResearchTeaching/ResearchThemes/EuropeanPrivateLaw/RealPropertyProject/Poland.PDF> accessed on 12 May 2025.

312 *Eureko BV v Republic of Poland* (Ad Hoc) para 241–243.

313 Decision No P 2/98 OTK ZU No 1/1999 (Polish Constitutional Tribunal) [1999] s 2.

314 Decision No K 14/99 OTK ZU 2/2000, poz 61 (Polish Constitutional Tribunal) [2000].

315 Inga Kawka and Łukasz Kozera, 'Procedural Requirements for Administrative Limits to Property Rights in Poland' in Martina Conticelli and Thomas Perroud (eds), *Procedural Requirements for Administrative Limits to Property Rights* (Oxford Academic, Oxford University Press 2022) 45.

316 Stanisław Frankowski and Paul B Stephan, *Legal reform in post-communist Europe: the view from within* (M Nijhoff 1995) 187; Balázs Szabolcs Gerencsér, 'The Value of Property in Central and Eastern Europe: Comparative Expropriation in Poland, Ukraine, and Hungary' in Martina Conticelli and Thomas Perroud (eds), *Procedural Requirements for Administrative Limits to Property Rights* (Oxford Academic, Oxford University Press 2022) 300.

317 Kalus and Habdas 262.

318 Article 21(2) of the Constitution of the Republic of Poland.

be forfeited only in cases specified by statute, and only by virtue of a final judgment of a court'.[319] The constitutional jurisprudence reiterates that limitations of ownership have to be at the level of statute and cannot be delegated to the lower levels of legislation.[320] The Land Administration Act of 1997 defined expropriation as physical taking[321] initially, but the constitutional clause was interpreted broadly to allow complaints about indirect expropriation.[322] Later, the Constitutional Tribunal limited the interpretation of expropriation to the situations expressly provided by the Land Administration Act.[323] For example, 'if the use of a property ... has become impossible or is limited in an essential manner',[324] the owner may claim compensation due to the changes in zoning, building, or developmental regulations.[325] However, the possibility of compensation for indirect expropriation in other situations is quite unlikely.

Polish laws oblige a state to buy land designated for public use, but certain exemptions allow authorities to postpone compensations, for which Poland was found in breach of the ECHR.[326] The litigation over state measures affecting the value of private property is relatively low, arguably because the owners do not consider state measures as an encroachment on their individual rights. Scholars agree that in the Constitution, public purpose is interpreted quite broadly.[327]

---

319 Article 46 of the Constitution of the Republic of Poland.

320 Kawka and Kozera 47.

321 Article 112-135 of Land Administration Act of 1997, Dz U of 2004, No 261 (Poland).

322 Decision No K 1/90 OTK ZU 1990, poz 2 (Polish Constitutional Tribunal) [1990]; Decision No K 8/98 OTK ZU 3/2000, poz 87 (Polish Constitutional Tribunal) [2000]; Boguslaw Banaszak, *Prawo Konstytucyjne* (2001) 244 (Pol); Jerzy Oniszczuk, *Konstytucja Rzeczypospolitej Polskiej W Orzecznictwie Trybunału Konstytucyjnego Na PocząTku Xxi W* (2004) 196 (Pol); Fryderyk Zoll, 'Prawo własności w Europejskiej Konwencji Praw Człowieka z perspektywy polskiej' 5 Przegląd Sądowy (1998) 24, 31 (Pol).

323 Decision No P 25/02 OTK ZU No 6/A/2005 (Polish Constitutional Tribunal) [2005] para 65, followed in the Decision No P 12/11 OTK ZU No 135/11/A/2012 (Polish Constitutional Tribunal) [2012] para 1472.

324 Article 36(1) of Land Planning Act (2003) Dz U 2003, No 80 item 717 (Poland).

325 Alterman and Balla 46.

326 *Czajkowska and Others v Poland* (ECtHR) Application No 16651/05, Judgment 13 July 2010.

327 M Szewczyk, 'Ingerencja publicznoprawna w prawo własności jednostki w demokratycznym państwie prawa' in: J Filipek (ed), *Jednostka W Demokratycznym Państwie Prawa* (Bielsko Biała 2003) 655; L Garlicki, 'Artykuł 21' in *Konstytucja Rzeczypospolitej Polskiej. Komentarz,* (vol 3, Warsaw 2003) note 18; T Dybowski, 'Własność w przepisach konstytucyjnych wedle stanu obowiązywania w 1996' in J Trzciński, A Jankiewicz (eds) *Konstytucja i Gwarancje Jej Przestrzegania. Księga pamiątkowa ku czci prof. Janiny Zakrzewskiej* (Warsaw 1996) 326; Magdalena Habdas, 'Expropriation Law in Poland' in J A M A

Article 64 of the Polish Constitution indicates the limits of ownership rights – 'the right of ownership may only be limited by means of a statute and only to the extent that it does not violate the substance of such right'.[328] Although theoretically possible, there is no case law litigating the limits of property, except the planning decisions mentioned above and the Environmental Protection Law, which allows compensation for 'limited use zone' with significant impacts on the environment.[329]

Attitudes towards compensation for expropriated property resemble the unsettled character of the issue in Poland. Poland had to deal with the legal consequences of Soviet nationalisation. Very often, those restitutionary claims were satisfied with partial lump-sum compensations, while restoration in-kind was allowed only in exceptional circumstances.[330] Nowadays, Article 21(2) of the Constitution speaks about *'za słusznym'* compensation, which could be translated as 'deserved' or 'just'. Linguistically, there is no indication of 'full' compensation, and the Constitutional Tribunal admitted that it does not imply the requirement to compensate for every kind of loss.[331] This leaves out any other costs associated with the expropriation and other interests that do not qualify as *in rem* rights.[332] The Constitutional Tribunal ruled that compensation has to be made in such amount as 'not [to] harm nationals',[333] 'not [to] violate the core idea of compensation for taken rights' and should put an owner on an equal economic footing.[334] Only the Land Administration Act requires the payment of market value compensation for the expropriation of real property, determined by the independent evaluator.[335] The decisions of the public institutions related to the expropriation can be challenged before administrative courts.[336]

Sluysmans, Stijn Verbist and Emma Waring (eds), *Expropriation Law in Europe* (Wolters Kluwer 2015) 412.

328 Article 64(3) of the Constitution of the Republic of Poland.

329 Alterman and Balla 69.

330 Frankowski and Stephan 176–177.

331 Decision No K20/02 OTK ZU 7A/2003 poz 76 (Polish Constitution Tribunal) [2003]. Also in *Decision in case No K 4/10* OTK ZU 9A/ 2012 poz 106 (Polish Constitutional Tribunal) [2012].

332 Habdas, 'Expropriation Law in Poland' 420.

333 Decision No K2/90 OTK ZU 1/1990 poz 3 (Polish Constitutional Tribunal) [1990].

334 *Decision No K 1/90*.

335 Zdzisław Brodecki, *Polish Business Law* (Kluwer Law International 2003) 187.

336 Kawka and Kozera 52.

12 Baltic States

The Baltic states will be reviewed together, despite slight differences among them. The primary variance being that Latvia and Estonia were protestant countries influenced by German attitudes to property. Estonia was also more exposed to Finnish influence due to language similarity and geographical proximity. Meanwhile, Lithuania was Catholic with the Polish–Lithuanian Commonwealth heritage. However, similar experiences of these states during the last hundred years allow for analysing them together as a group.

Similar to Poland, the Baltic states experienced a swing between extreme collectivism during the Soviet era and the liberalism of the 1990s. Article 23 of the Lithuanian Constitution formulates a property clause in an absolutist manner similar to the French Declaration of the Rights of Man and of the Citizen:

> Property shall be inviolable.
> The rights of ownership shall be protected by laws.
> Property may only be seized for the needs of society in accordance with the procedure established by law and shall be justly compensated.[337]

But Article 46 of the Lithuanian Constitution, similar to the German tradition, states that 'the State shall regulate economic activity so that it serves the general welfare of the Nation'. Constitutional jurisprudence also reinforces the notion that property protection is not absolute and is qualified by its social function.[338]

Article 105 of the Latvian Constitution is influenced by the German approach and hints at the inherent limits of individual property rights:

> Everyone has the right to own property. Property shall not be used contrary to the interests of the public. Property rights may be restricted only in accordance with the law. Expropriation of property for public purposes shall be allowed

---

337 The Constitution of the Republic of Lithuania (1992) <http://www.lrkt.lt/en/about-the-court/legal-information/the-constitution/192> accessed on 15 April 2025.

338 *Decision on the restoration of the ownership rights of citizens to land and residential houses, case No 15/97* (Lithuanian Constitutional Court) [1998]. All decisions of the Lithuanian Constitutional Court are available on the internet: <https://lrkt.lt/en/court-acts/rulings-conclusions-decisions/171/y2025> accessed on 15 April 2025; Laurynas Didžiulis, Algirdas Taminskas, and Marius Matiukas, *Daiktinė teisė* (Vilniaus universiteto leidykla 2025) 230–231.

> only in exceptional cases on the basis of a specific law and in return for fair compensation.[339]

Likewise, Article 32 of the Estonian Constitution provides:

> The property of every person is inviolable and equally protected. Property may be taken from the owner without his or her consent only in the public interest, in the cases and pursuant to a procedure provided by law, and for fair and immediate compensation… Limitations of this right are provided by law. Property may not be used in a manner that contravenes the public interest…[340]

Estonian property law resembles German *Sachenrecht* (law of things).[341] Latvian property understanding is also very similar to German with accompanying problems related to intangible things.[342] The Latvian Civil Law Act Article 1050 implies that only tangible things can be owned,[343] leaving the status of intellectual property and claims in question. The Latvian Constitutional Court initially supported a narrow understanding of property,[344] holding that social security payments and pensions are not property rights,[345] which was at odds with the ECtHR practice in the cases concerning Article 1 of the First Protocol of the ECHR.[346] For the purpose of constitutional pro-

339 Constitution of the Republic of Latvia (1922) <http://saeima.lv/en/legislative-process/constitution> accessed on 16 April 2025.

340 Constitution of the Republic of Estonia (1992) <https://www.riigiteataja.ee/en/eli/521052015001/consolide> accessed on 15 April 2025.

341 Paul Varul, 'Legal Policy Decisions and Choices in the Creation of New Private Law in Estonia' (2000) 5 Juridica International 104,107–108.

342 Janis Rozenfelds, 'Latvian Property and Collateral Law and Protection of Foreign Investments' (2001) 6 Juridica International 108–109.

343 The Latvian Civil Law Act (1937) Valdības Vēstnesis 41, 20 February 1937, <https://likumi.lv/ta/en/en/id/225418> accessed on 15 April 2025.

344 *Decision on the Procedure for the Repayment in Cash to Persons who were Granted Vouchers for the Former Landed Property in Rural Areas in case No 04-01 (99)* (Latvian Constitutional Court) [1999]. All Latvian Constitutional jurisprudence could be found at < http://www.satv.tiesa.gov.lv/en/cases/> accessed 15 April 2025.

345 *Decision on Compulsory Social Insurance in Respect of Accidents at Work and Occupational Diseases in case No 2010-17-01* (Latvian Constitutional Court) [2010]; *Decision on State Funded Pensions in case No 2010-21-01* (Latvian Constitutional Court) [2010]; *Decision on Transitional Provisions of the Law 'On State Pensions' in case No 2016-03-01* (Latvian Constitutional Court) [2016].

346 *Decision on the Saeima Election Law and the Law on Electing City Council and County Council in case No 2000-03-01* (Latvian Constitutional Court) [2000]; *Decision on Amendments to the Cabinet of Ministers Regulation 'On Keeping Dogs and Cats' in case No 2002-*

tection, the understanding of property was eventually broadened to include all property rights that a person can exercise on his own behalf and which a person may use according to his own will.[347] This now comprises contractual rights with economic value[348] and other claims for future income, if a clear legal basis exists for it.[349]

Due to the Dutch and Quebec influence on the new Lithuanian Civil Code, its property concept was much broader from the beginning than in other Baltic states.[350] Article 1.97 of the Lithuanian Civil Code provides that the objects of civil rights can be 'things, money and securities, other property and property rights, results of intellectual activities, information, actions and results thereof, as well as any other material and non-material values', while Article 4.38 of the Lithuanian Civil Code defines the object of ownership right as 'things and other assets.[351] Intellectual property enjoys constitutional protection,[352] as well as social security payments, which, like in Germany, are recognised as property.[353] As a consequence, rights theoretically could be treated and transferred as property,[354] but in practice, the Lithuanian Supreme Court refused to recognise the sale of the lease rights of the state-owned land.[355]

Facing an extensive understanding of property and the neo-liberal property protection clause, the Lithuanian Constitutional Court realised that the invio-

---

01-03 (Latvian Constitutional Court) [2002]; *Decision on Amendments to Law 'On Coercive Expropriation of Real Estate for State or Public Needs' in case No 2005-12-0103* (Latvian Constitutional Court) [2005].

347 *Decision on Regulations on Financial Assistance Quotas for Biofuel in case No 2010-12-03* (Latvian Constitutional Court) [2010]; *Decision on Public Procurement Law in case No 2011-05-01* (Latvian Constitutional Court) [2011].

348 *Decision on termination of proceedings in case No 2009-100-03* (Latvian Constitutional Court) [2010].

349 *Decision on Public Procurement Law in case No 2011-05-01*; *Decision on Regulations on Financial Assistance Quotas for Biofuel in case No 2010-12-03*.

350 Andrius Smaliukas, *Property and trust law in Lithuania* (2017) 145; R Juzikienė, V Mizaras, A Smaliukas, 'Civilinės teisės objektai', in *Civilinė teisė. Bendroji dalis* (Justitia, 2009) 466.

351 The Lithuanian Civil Code (2000), <https://e-seimas.lrs.lt/portal/legalAct/lt/TAD/512506f2684411eea182def3ac5c11d6?jfwid=-ynvzjy81> accessed 15 April 2025.

352 *Decision on the restoration of the ownership rights of citizens to land in case No 18-99* (Lithuanian Constitutional Court) [2001].

353 *Decision on the state pensions of officials and servicemen in a cases No 46/2001–48/2001–50/2001–2/2002–6/2002–18/2002* (Lithuanian Constitutional Court) [2003].

354 Articles 6.425–6.427 of the Lithuanian Civil Code.

355 *UAB DMD Investment v BVI Visagino statybininkai and UAB Sėlių investicijos in case No e3K-3-399-219/2018* (Lithuanian Supreme Court) [2018]. All Lithuanian court decisions are available here <https://liteko.teismai.lt/viesasprendimupaieska/detalipaieska.aspx?detali=2&tid=23> accessed on 15 April 2025.

lability of property is an illusion rather than a reality.[356] Article 4:39(1) of the Lithuanian Civil Code provides that property rights may be limited by law or a court decision. Like in other Western European countries, the use and disposal of land are heavily regulated. The Land Law imposes statutory obligations and restrictions on landowners.[357] The Law on Zoning and Planning of Territories[358] and Law on Construction[359] define the limits of land use. The Law on Forests limits the use and enjoyment of forest land and does not allow any other development.[360] Laws on protection of cultural heritage[361] and Law on Protected Territories[362] and Environmental Protection[363] protect other communal interests that collide with private property rights. The restrictions and limitations of property rights imposed by those laws are not compensated, and most of them are not even challenged as takings,[364] arguably because such regulations are seen as an integral part of property right.[365] In several cases, the Lithuanian Constitutional Court confirmed that:

> the right of ownership is not absolute, it can be limited by means of a law due to the character of the object of ownership, due to committed deeds, which are contrary to law, and/or due to the need which is necessary to the society and constitutionally grounded.[366]

---

356 Egle Svilpaite, 'Constitution and the possibilities of limiting property rights' (2002) 30 Jurisprudencija 68 citing the decision of the Lithuanian Constitutional Court of 13 December 1993 in case No 7 regarding the Criminal Code and Criminal Procedure Code.

357 The Land Law No XIV-1311 (2022). All Lituanian statutes are available here <https://e-seimas.lrs.lt/portal/documentSearch/lt> accessed 15 April 2025.

358 The Law on Zoning and Planning of Territories No XII-407 (2013).

359 The Law on Construction No XII-2573 (2016).

360 The Law on Forests No IX-240 (2001).

361 The Law on Protection of Immovable Cultural Heritage No IX-2452 (2004) and the Law on Protection of Movable Cultural Valuables No X-1682 (2008).

362 The Law on Protected Territories No XIV-2350 (2023).

363 The Law on Environmental Protection No I-2223 (1992).

364 Kristina Ambrazevičiūtė, *Problems of applying right to property, right to economic activities and initiative, consumer rights* (2012) 14–17 <http://teise.org/wp-content/uploads/2016/07/Teises_i_nuosavybe_uztikrinimo_problemos.pdf > accessed 15 April 2025.

365 *Decision on the repayment of a loan contract in case 4/94* (Lithuanian Constitutional Court) [1994]; *Decision on the manufacture, storage, transporting, sale and realisation of alcohol in case No 10/97-3/98-10/98* (Lithuanian Constitutional Court) [1998]; *Decision on the reorganisation of the joint-stock companies 'Būtingės nafta', 'Mažeikių nafta', and 'Naftotiekis' in case No 29/98-16/99-3/2000* (Lithuanian Constitutional Court) [2000].

366 *Decision on membership in the associations of apartment house owners in case No 8/99* (Lithuanian Constitutional Court) [2000]; followed in other decisions: *Decision on territorial planning in case No 16/07-17/07-20/08*(Lithuanian Constitutional Court) [2009]; *Decision on certain provisions of the Criminal Code regulating criminal liability of*

Furthermore, the Lithuanian Constitutional Court captures the essence of the constitutional property protection clause, which could be representative of the general property understanding in the region on broad terms:

> Article 23 of the Constitution means that property relations are the matter of legal regulation. ... Bearing in mind the fact that a legal system is constantly evolving, coordination of its elements is a permanent task the solution of which is not always unequivocal.[367]

A similar story could be observed in Latvia, where several state laws affecting property rights were not treated as breaches of Article 105 of the Latvian Constitution.[368] For example, the prohibition of interest payments from a company that experienced financial difficulties and was benefiting from state aid was not considered to be a breach of property rights.[369] Furthermore, regulations promoting a healthy environment were not considered as a breach of private property rights in Latvia. Such cases included complaints about noise from a racing track in a residential area[370] and disputes over spatial planning.[371] The case involving a tax on renewable energy subsidies deserves special attention because it is similar to a dozen investment arbitration cases that

---

legal persons in cases No 34/2008–36/2008–40/2008–1/2009–4/2009–5/2009–6/2009–7/2009–9/2009–12/2009–13/2009–14/2009–17/2009–18/2009–19/2009–20/2009–22/2009(Lithuanian Constitutional Court) [2009].

367 *Decision on the administrative penalty of property confiscation in case No 12/96-5/97* (Lithuanian Constitutional Court) [1997].

368 *Decision regarding changes to territorial planning in case No 2008-38-03* (Latvian Constitutional Court) [2009]; *Decision regarding the requirements for companies to re-register in case No 2009-113-0106* (Latvian Constitutional Court) [2009]; *Decision regarding forced leased agreements in case No 2008-34-01* (Latvian Constitutional Court) [2009]; *Decision regarding bio-fuel subsidies and others in case No 2010-12-03* (Latvian Constitutional Court) [2010]; *Decision regarding the taxation of dividends in case No 2010-25-01* (Latvian Constitutional Court) [2010]; *Decision on land use rights in case No 2022-02-01* (Latvian Constitutional Court) [2023]; *Decision on confiscation of property obtained through criminal means in case No 2022-32-01* (Latvian Constitutional Court) [2025].

369 *Decision on Control of Aid for Commercial Activity in case No 2014-36-01* (Latvian Constitutional Court) [2015]; in another case arising from the aftermath of 2008 financial crisis the Latvian Constitutional Court ruled that protection of financial market is a legitimate aim to restrict property rights: *Decision on Credit Institutions Law in case No 2012-07-01* (Latvian Constitutional Court) [2013].

370 Press release of the Latvian Constitutional Court of 17 January 2017 <http://www.satv.tiesa.gov.lv/en/press-release/a-case-initiated-regarding-regulation-on-noise-in-the-vicinity-of-auto-racing-tracks/> accessed 15 April 2025.

371 *Decision regarding changes to territorial planning in case No 2008-38-03*; *Decision on Compliance of the Binding Regulation 'On Spatial Plans of Rucava County' in the Part of*

are being adjudicated against the Czech Republic, Italy, and Spain. In Latvia, like in the rest of Europe, subsidised feed-in tariffs were introduced to encourage the development of renewable energy. Due to the advances in technology, the huge popularity of the scheme, and maybe the methodology of the calculations, the feed-in tariffs became costly for the state. However, they were profitable for businesses engaged in it. Instead of reducing the feed-in tariffs, the Latvian government decided to manage the situation by imposing a special tax on subsidised energy producers. This tax was challenged as a breach of property rights.[372] The Latvian Constitutional Court ruled that 'the aim of the restriction of property rights'[373] was legitimate and measures proportionate,[374] taking into account the discretion of the legislator to choose economic means. The standard of review adopted by the Court was to check whether the tax had not been introduced arbitrarily and whether objective and rational considerations had been provided.[375]

In cases concerning legal reforms, the Estonian Supreme Court is also very cautious and deferential to the legislative and executive powers,[376] but it was more active when the Parliament repeatedly failed to address the question of the return of property to people who emigrated from Estonia to Germany in

---

Establishing Wind Energy Zone in the Territory of Dunika Parish in case No 2010-48-03 (Latvian Constitutional Court) [2011].

372 *Decision on Subsidized Electricity Tax Law in case No 2014-12-01* (Latvian Constitutional Court) [2015].

373 Taxation is treated as a restriction of the property right and not as an expropriation of property: *Decision on the Tax on Pensions in case No 2007-01-01* (Latvian Constitutional Court) [2007]; *Decision on the Natural Resources Tax for Small Hydroelectric Power Stations in case No 2014-11-0103* (Latvian Constitutional Court) [2015].

374 *Decision on the Spatial Plan of Limbaži in case No 2006-38-03* (Latvian Constitutional Court) [2007]; *Decision on Binding Regulation on the Use of and Construction in the Territory of Culture and Recreation Park 'Mežaparks' in case No 2014-04-03* (Latvian Constitutional Court) [2014].

375 *Decision on Subsidized Electricity Tax Law in case No 2014-12-01* (Latvian Constitutional Court). Similar *Decision on the Natural Resources Tax for Small Hydroelectric Power Stations in case No 2014-11-0103* (Latvian Constitutional Court). *Contra Decision on Increasing the State's Participation in a Credit Institution in case No 2010-71-01* (Latvian Constitutional Court) [2011].

376 *Decision on Privatisation of Dwellings Act and etc in case No 3-4-1-2-96* (Estonian Supreme Court) [1996]; *Decision on Principles of Ownership Reform Act in case No 3-4-1-5-02* (Estonian Supreme Court) [2002]; *Decision on the invalidation of the Tallinn City decision for Return of and Compensation for Unlawfully Expropriated Property in case No 3-3-1-63-05* (Estonian Supreme Court) [2006]. Estonian constitutional jurispridence is available here <https://www.riigikohus.ee/en/judgements/constitutional-judgments> accessed 15 April 2025.

1941.[377] Similarly, in Lithuania, the Constitutional Court refused to interfere in the process of reinstatement of property rights that were nationalised by the Soviets.[378]

All Baltic states require expropriation acts to be embodied in the laws, to the extent that the Constitutional Court in Lithuania has invalidated some laws that delegate powers to the government to establish certain conditions on the restoration of the ownership of land.[379] Furthermore, the Latvian Constitution requires the state to adopt a specific law on each expropriation and emphasises the due process during the procedure.[380] For example, the provision of the municipality regulations on the retention of the infrastructure fee paid upon the issuance of a development permit was declared invalid, because it restricted the owner's rights and was not expressly provided in the regulations.[381] The emphasis on the formal requirement to embody the expropriation act in the law is very strong throughout Eastern Europe. Paradoxically, instead of strengthening property rights, it excludes the possibility of claiming indirect expropriation. There is a wide belief in the region that compensation for the interference with private property rights could be obtained only if expressly provided by the law. That means all other instances that sit in the grey area between regulation and property rights are not even brought to courtrooms because individual claimants do not feel they have a right to complain about general regulation interfering with private property.

The general rules on expropriation in Lithuania are codified in Article 4:100 of the Lithuanian Civil Code, which provides that property may be expropriated only in exclusive cases. It is further detailed in Chapter 8 of the Land Law.[382] The prioritisation of general interest over individual rights is reflected

377 Berit Aaviksoo, 'Judicial Activism in Constitutional Review Decisions of the Supreme Court of Estonia' (2007) XIII Juridica International 68.

378 *Decision on the methods for establishing the nominal price of land purchased by the state in cases No 11/96, 27/01–5/02-01/03* (Lithuanian Constitutional Court) [1998]; *Decision on the restoration of ownership rights to leased land case No 28/2010* (Lithuanian Constitutional Court) [2013]; *Decision on compensation for urban land subject to purchase by the state in case No 5/2012* (Lithuanian Constitutional Court) [2013].

379 *Decision on the restoration of the ownership rights of citizens to land in case No 2/95* (Lithuanian Constitutional Court) [1995].

380 *Decision on Amendments to Law 'On Coercive Expropriation of Real Estate for State or Public Needs' in case No 2005-12-0103*; *Decision on the Expropriation of Immoveable Property (The Border Checkpoint Terehova) in case No 2009-01-01* (Latvian Constitutional Court) [2009].

381 *Decision on the Municipal Fee for the Maintenance and Development of the Municipality Infrastructure in Riga in case No 2015-13-03* (Latvian Constitutional Court) [2016].

382 Lithuanian Land Law No XIV-1311 (2022).

in the Law on taking land in the interest of society for special projects of state importance, which provides simplified and faster procedures for the state initiatives that have tremendous public interest.[383] Article 45 of the Land Law provides an exemplary list how the public interest is understood: economic projects of state importance, national defence, international airports, railways, roads, pipelines, electricity lines, ports, waste landfills and their facilities, social, educational, scientific, cultural, and health care projects, environmental protection, public order, natural and cultural heritage, etc.

In Latvia, the Law on the Expropriation of Real Estate Necessary for Public Purposes[384] codifies procedure, compensation for the expropriation of real estate as well as avenues for complaint. Article 2 of the Law provides that public purposes would include the development of cultural, educational, and sports facilities, other infrastructure necessary for public needs and defence, as well as environmental protection, health, and social security needs. The peculiarity of this statute is that it allows litigation regarding the necessity of the property for a public purpose.[385] Although it is declared that '[i]f disputes between the private property rights and immediate interests of the state arise, then the private ones shall retreat before the state interests'[386] at least in some cases arising out of the 2008 financial crisis, state measures designed to save money were declared unconstitutional.[387] Overall the impression in Latvia is that the majority of contested state measures were found compatible with the property protection clause, despite several rulings where the opposite was concluded.[388]

Estonia also has an Immovables Expropriation Act,[389] which besides expropriation procedures and deadlines provides an extensive list of public interest similar to that of Lithuania and Latvia. In Estonia, the existence of the public

---

383 Law on Taking a Land in the Interest of Society for Special Projects of State Importance No XI-1307 (2011).

384 Law on the Expropriation of Real Estate Necessary for Public Purposes (2010) <https://likumi.lv/doc.php?id=220517> accessed on 15 April 2025.

385 Article 6(2) ibid.

386 *Decision on Amendments to Law 'On Coercive Expropriation of Real Estate for State or Public Needs' in case No 2005-12-0103.*

387 *Decision on Compensation for Damages Caused by Animals under Special Protection in case No 2013-13-01* (Latvian Constitutional Court) [2014]; *Decision on Increasing the State's Participation in a Credit Institution in case No 2010-71-01.*

388 Decision of 8 March 2006 in case No 2005-16-01 (Latvian Constitutional Court) [2006]; other decisions of 19 June 2010 in case No 2010-02-01; of 21 December 2009 in case No 2009-43-01 (Latvian Constitutional Court).

389 Estonian Immovables Expropriation Act No 274 (2018) <https://www.riigiteataja.ee/akt/129062018001> accessed on 28 July 2025.

purpose is the question for the legislature, not the reviewing court,[390] but unlike in France, failure to provide compensation for the statutory obligation to tolerate utility networks on the property in the public interest was declared unconstitutional.[391]

Like in Poland, the general standard of compensation guaranteed by the constitutions in all Baltic states is 'just', not 'full market', value. Thus, the Latvian Constitutional Court argued that:

> there are cases, when the state, expropriating a property, belonging to a person with an aim of reaching greater social justice, does not have the duty to pay the market price, for example, during the process of property reform.[392]

Furthermore, in at least one Latvian case, the applicant's request to receive equivalent property in kind was not entertained.[393] In Estonia also the legislator is entitled to decide on necessary expropriations and to establish means of compensation, which should be:

> fair from the aspect of transformation of relationships, [and] which do not need to guarantee total compensation of market value to the owner of property.[394]

In Lithuania, restrictions on property rights of forest owners and land plots in protected areas remained uncompensated.[395] However, in the case of direct expropriation, special legal acts very often provide for the full compensation standard. For example, Article 4:100(2) of the Lithuanian Civil Code requires market value compensation for expropriated property. Article 47 of the Lithuanian Land Law requires 'a fair compensation in cash amounting to the market price', as well as compensating other losses, but the value is calculated in accordance with the principal purpose of the land use, not the most beneficial use. A similar provision is found in Article 13 of the Law on Taking Land in the Interest of Society for Special Projects of State Importance.

---

390 Decision of 8 November 1996 in case No 3-4-1-2-96 (Estonian Supreme Court).

391 Decision of 17 April 2012 in case No 3-4-1-25-11 (Estonian Supreme Court) [2012]; Decision of 30 April 2004 in case No 3-4-1-3-04 (Estonian Supreme Court) [2004]. The most important Estonian constitutional jurisprudence could be found at <https://www.riigikohus.ee/en/judgements/constitutional-judgments> accessed on 26 February 2018.

392 Decision of 16 December 2005 in case No 2005-12-0103 (Latvian Constitutional Court).

393 Decision of 9 December 2016 in case No 2016-08-01 (Latvian Constitutional Court) [2016].

394 Decision of 18 March 2005 in case No 3-2-1-59-04 (Estonian Supreme Court) [2005].

395 Ambrazevičiūtė, 14–17.

Section 22 of the Latvian Law on the Expropriation of Real Estate Necessary for Public Purposes also requires to compensate the market value or residual replacement value of the expropriated property, whichever is higher.

In Estonia, at the constitutional level it is required that compensation be paid without delay, and overall the Estonian legislative framework defines a wider circle of protected interests.[396] Article 1 of the Estonian Immovables Expropriation Act emphasises that it applies not only to immovable property but also to certain proprietary rights and movable property. Interference with other rights and interests that fall outside the scope of this article, as in the other Baltic States, will not be compensated. Also, Estonian law requires the owner to be compensated for the value of the taken property and for pecuniary damage and loss of income that arise directly from the expropriation.[397] The assessment of the value of the taken property or rights, and of the damage is carried out restoring the owner to the position they would have been in had the expropriation not occurred.[398] The Articles 13–20 specifically address compensations for the inability to use a building or other improvements, the loss of development potential of the land plot, destruction of greenery, and deterioration of access, the loss of residential housing, administrative expenses, servitudes, usufruct or rights of first refusal, as well as for the costs incurred by a tenant or user due to the expropriation.[399]

13 Russia

A few historical observations regarding the Russian understanding of property may help to comprehend the current situation better. Although based on Byzantine Roman law, Muscovy did not experience the development of individual ownership rights as an essential instrument limiting the absolutist powers of the tsar.[400] The term 'ownership' was first used in the Treaty of 29 September 1710 regarding the granting of previous privileges and priorities to the inhabitants of the conquered Estonian duchy.[401] The remnants of communal property and land repartitions were continuing practice until the nineteenth

396 Estonian Immovables Expropriation Act No 274 (2018).

397 Ibid Article 11.

398 Ibid Article 12.

399 Ibid.

400 William G Wagner, *Marriage, Property, and Law in Late Imperial Russia* (Clarendon 1994) 264–265.

401 A B Babaev, *Sistema Veshchnykh Prav* (Wolters Kluwer, Moscow, 2006) 50; Vladislav Starzhenetskiy, 'Property rights in Russia: reconsidering the socialist legal tradition' in

century in Russia.[402] This raised the question whether the absence of strong property rights explained Russia's political history[403] or *vice versa*. Even the Enlightenment ideas were filtered through specific Russian values and legal concepts[404] entrenching the state as a coercive power, but not as an authority based on a social contract of different groups.[405] Russian private property rights were severely curtailed, almost to the brink of extinction, after the Bolshevik revolution.[406] The social function of property is widely acknowledged[407] and 'the disdain for individual rights' in legal culture borders on hostility.[408] The chaotic transition in the 1990s from a planned economy to a market economy was particularly painful and the distribution of property questionable. Since then maybe 'the physical violence and outright criminality' has been reduced, but risks to property rights associated with the state remain in the form of seizure of assets, raids, extortion, and illicit fines.[409]

Formally, Article 35 of the Russian Constitution of 1993 provides that:

> (1) The right to private property shall be protected by law.
> (2) Everyone shall have the right to have property and to possess, use and dispose of it both individually and jointly with other persons.
> (3) Nobody may be deprived of property except under a court order. Forced alienation of property for State requirements may take place only subject to prior and fair compensation.[410]

Lauri Mälksoo and Wolfgang Benedek (eds), *Russia and the European Court of Human Rights: The Strasbourg Effect* (Cambridge University Press 2017) 295.

402 Steven Nafziger, 'Communal property rights and land redistributions in Late Tsarist Russia' (2016) 69 The Economic History Review 773; Murray Raff and Anna Taitslin, 'A Comparative Perspective on the Concept of Ownership in Russian Law: From the Svod Zakonov to the 1994 Civil Code' (2016) 41 Review of Central and East European Law 312.

403 Richard Pipes, *Property and freedom* (1st edn, Vintage Books 2000) 159.

404 Ekaterina Pravilova, *A Public Empire: Property and the Quest for the Common Good in Imperial Russia* (Princeton University Press 2014) 21.

405 Frankowski and Stephan 7; Starzhenetskiy 299.

406 Veronika Bílková, 'Sovereignty, Property and the Russian Revolution' (2017) 19 Journal of the History of International Law 147, 158.

407 Kamyshanskij VP, *Pravo Sobstvenosti: Predely I Ograničenija* (Zakon i pravo, Moskva, 2000) 28.

408 Frankowski and Stephan 17.

409 Jordan Gans-Morse, 'Threats to Property Rights in Russia: From Private Coercion to State Aggression' (2012) 28 Post-Soviet Affairs 263, 265.

410 Constitution of the Russian Federation (1993) <https://mid.ru/upload/medialibrary/fa3/xwhwumdwunawy9iprvhcxdqds1lzxqdx/CONSTITUTION-Eng.pdf> accessed on 1 March 2025.

Even intellectual property is expressly protected by Article 44 of the Constitution, and the 1999 Foreign Investments Law provides basic guarantees to foreign investors, although curtailed by moral, health, human rights, socio-economic development, and national security considerations.[411] The problem with the formal protection of property in Russia is that it does not accurately reflect the practice. For example, critical property protection disputes do not even reach the Constitutional Court and are resolved by other means.[412] Russian lawyers claim that the new civil legislation provides a high level of property protection[413] and maybe that is true in comparison with the Soviet legal system, but not in comparison with Western legal systems. The description of Russian property protection as adequate is highly internalised and very different from the Western paradigm of property protection.

The Russian concept of property is torn between traditional narrow and modern broad approaches. On the one hand, it was inspired by a traditional German legal system of things[414] and like other civil law countries emphasises the owner's relationship with a specific thing instead of the exclusion of all others.[415] The traditional *in rem / in personam* distinction is still widely observed,[416] resulting in the conclusion that:

> a commodity in the economic sense does not always constitute an object of the right of ownership in the law. Only individually determined things form the objects of ownership.[417]

Sukhanov explains that tangible 'things' together with money, negotiable papers, and proprietary rights constitute property. Meanwhile, intangible things resulting from intellectual activity (works of science, literature, and art, inventions, industrial designs) or granted similar status by the legal regime (trademarks, places of origin) should be called intangible objects of commer-

---

411 Russian Foreign Investment Law (1999) <https://mid.ru/ru/foreign_policy/economic_diplomacy/1726314/> accessed on 5 March 2025.

412 Terry Macalister, Tom Parfitt, '$20bn gas project seized by Russia' Guardian <https://www.theguardian.com/world/2006/dec/12/business.oil> accessed on 7 March 2018.

413 Yevgeny Sukhanov, 'The Concept of Ownership in Current Russian Law' (2001) 6 Juridica International 102, 106.

414 Ibid 104; Raff and Taitslin 305.

415 Sukhanov; David Lametti, 'Objects of Private Property in the Civil Code of the Russian Federation and in the Civil Code of Quebec' (2005) 30 Review of Central & East European Law 19.

416 Raff and Taitslin 268; Starzhenetskiy 298.

417 Sukhanov 103.

cial character.[418] Thus, intellectual property, which is protected by Article 44 of the Russian Constitution, was excluded from the scope of protection of Article 35 of the Constitution.[419] Even though Article 128 of the Russian Civil Code provides that almost all patrimonial rights, including intangibles, could be objects of civil rights, it does not translate that all rights could be objects of property. The object of property could only be things capable of being identified, and ownership of rights is totally excluded.[420]

On the other hand, certain aspects of the lease of immovable property became protected as property rights and may continue even after the transfer of ownership.[421] In line with the practice of the ECHR, the Russian Constitutional Court was expanding the understanding of constitutional property, which should be characterised by the economic value and should be capable of identification in the material or immaterial sense.[422] In practice, property includes proprietary rights such as the right of lifelong unlimited use,[423] shares and other interests in business ventures,[424] claims to money in bank accounts,[425] and money held by third parties for the reconstruction of apartment blocks collected in a mandatory way.[426] The Constitutional Court recognised that a constitutional understanding of property might be wider than private law understanding.[427]

The abovementioned examples attest to the departure from a traditional understanding based on Roman law and an expansion of the understanding of

418 Yevgeny Sukhanov, *Russian civil law* (Statut 2011) 121.

419 Decision of 13 December 2016 in case No 28-P (Russian Constitutional Court) [2016]. Russian Constitutional jurisprudence could be found at <http://www.ksrf.ru/ru/Decision/Pages/default.aspx> accessed 8 March 2018.

420 Sukhanov, *Russian civil law* 492, 494, 496–7.

421 Hiroshi Oda, 'Property and Land Law' in *Russian Commercial Law* (Brill 2007) 310–311.

422 VD Zorkin, *Russia and Constitution in 21st Century* (2 edn, Norma 2008) 190. However, the Russian Constitutional Court refused to recognise the ECtHR decision in a dispute of high stakes: Decision of 19 January 2017 in case No 1-P (Russian Constitutional Court) [2017]; Starzhenetskiy 323.

423 Decision of 13 December 2001 in case No 16-P (Russian Constitutional Court) [2001]; Decision of 16 May 2000 in case No 8-P (Russian Constitutional Court) [2000]; Decision of 3 July 2001 in case No 10-P (Russian Constitutional Court) [2001].

424 Decision of 10 April 2003 in case No 5-P (Russian Constitutional Court) [2003].

425 Decision of 16 May 2000 in case No 8-P; Decision of 10 December 2014 No 31-P (Russian Constitutional Court) [2014]; Decision of 17 December 1996 No 20-P (Russian Constitutional Court) [1996].

426 Decision of 12 April 2016 in case No 10-P (Russian Constitutional Court) [2016].

427 Decision of 20 May 1997 in case No 4-P (Russian Constitutional Court) [1997].

property in Russia.[428] Thus, it is hard to reconcile this trend with the exclusion of intellectual property from constitutional protection. It may be that the Russian Constitution and Civil Code try to introduce more liberal and individualistic values into the legal system,[429] but face antagonistic legal traditions in practice.

Although the Russian Constitutional Court ruled that owners have a right to demand state institutions do not interfere with property rights,[430] rights in Russia are viewed as arising primarily from a statute, which means they can also be limited by a statute.[431] Even constitutional law books rarely mention protection of property as a constitutional guarantee and avoid analysing the content of this right, while extensively investigating the limitations of rights and duties of the citizen.[432] Article 1(2) of the Russian Civil Code provides that all civil rights may be limited by law insofar as much as it is necessary to safeguard constitutional order, morals, health, rights and interests of others, and defence and security of the state. Article 10 of the Civil Code prohibits the abuse of rights and usage of rights in such a way that limits competition or allows abuse of a dominant market position. Article 209(2) of the Russian Civil Code expressly provides that property rights are restricted by law and 'the interests of other persons protected by law',[433] including the right to free-

428 L R Buhonova 'Tendencii i perspektivy razvitija konstitucionnogo prava chastnoj sobstvennosti v sovremennom mire' (2016) 1 Aktualnye Problemy Rossijskogo Prava 55; M B Corgaeva 'Transformacija otnochenij sobstvennosti v informacionnoj ekonomike' (dissertation St Petersburg 2015) 9, 10, 14.

429 David Lametti, 'General Concepts of Private Law Relating to Private Property in the Civil Code of the Russian Federation and in the Civil Code of Quebec' (2005) 30 Review of Central and East European Law 7, 9.

430 Decisions of 10 November 2016 in case No 23-P (Russian Constitutional Court) [2016]; Decision of 4 June 2015 No 13-P (Russian Constitutional Court) [2015].

431 M Raff and A Taitslin, 'Private Law in the Shadow of Public Law: A Legacy of 20th Century Marxism and the Soviet Legal Model' in Thomas Bustamante and Oche Onazi (eds), *Human Rights, Language and Law* (Franz Steiner Verlag 2012) 157; Avakjan SA, Konstitucionnoe Pravo Rossii: Uchebnyi Kurs, 4 ed vol 1 (2010) 756; Vasiljanskaja AI, 'K voprosu o soderzhatelnom napolnenii konstitucionnogo prava chastnoj sobstvennosti' 9 Konstitucionnoe i Municipalnoe Pravo (2010) 27; Olnev DA, Konstitucionnoe regulirovanie prava chastnoj sobstvennosti na zemlju, dissertation (Cheliabinsk, 2012) 44–78; Chicherin BN, Sobstvennost i Gosudarstvo (SPb.RHGA 2005) 82.

432 DT Karamanukian, AV Minzhurenko and others, *Human rights in Russia: history, theory and practice* (2015); AV Bezrukov, *Constitutional Law of Russia* (Justicinform 2015); SI Nosov, Alzheev IA and others, *Constitutional Law of Russian Federation* (Statut 2014); RM Valeeva, AH Abashidze and others, *International and Internal Protection of Human Rights* (Statut 2011).

433 Russian Civil Code (1994) <http://www.pravo.gov.ru/proxy/ips/?compare_vert&nd=102033239&rdkleft=85&rdkright=0> accessed on 5 March 2018.

roaming for other non-owners.[434] The Russian Constitutional Court held that rights might be limited by federal law if it is necessary for the protection of other constitutional values, including rights and lawful interests of other people, if its fair, reasonable, proportionate, general and abstract, applicable only to the future and does not violate the essence of the respective constitutional right.[435]

Furthermore, land is not treated as usual property and is very heavily regulated. Article 36 of the Russian Constitution provides that only 'citizens and their associations shall have the right to possess land as private property', and Article 15(3) of the Land Code of 2001 specifies that foreigners cannot acquire land in the border regions and other areas provided by the law.[436] Landowners must follow 'environmental prescriptions and prohibitions' as well as planning and zoning designations.[437] One case, where the claimant was refused the permit for construction of a residential home on a land plot that was designated for a cultural centre, could have illuminated the nature of the restrictions on land use, but the Constitutional Court refused even to investigate the complaint.[438]

Ownership, use, enjoyment, and disposal of land and natural resources are subject to several restrictions imposed by law[439] and ownership entails an obligation to maintain it.[440] Limitations upon rights in Russia are understood not as external, but 'rather as an implicit part of the [ownership] institution'.[441] Moreover, temporary restrictions on property, when the title is not seized, are not considered as takings.[442] Article 306 of the Russian Civil Code provides that the state is obliged to compensate owners if a statute removes

434 Article 262 of the Russian Civil Code.

435 Decision of 12 May 2011 in case No 7-P (Russian Constitutional Court) [2011].

436 The Russian Land Code No 136-F3 (2001) with amendments <http://www.consultant. ru/cons/cgi/online.cgi?base=LAW&n=301443&dst=4294967295&cacheid=B00F16736F0ED6DC308250F1B1E001C2&mode=rubr&req=doc&rnd=4C9421FF2F30F2E905C4852D936BB423#01487954610618506> accessed on 24 October 2018.

437 Sukhanov, 'The Concept of Ownership in Current Russian Law' 105.

438 Decision of 6 November 2003 in case No 387-O (Russian Constitutional Court) [2003].

439 Article 9 (2) of the Constitution of the Russian Federation and Article 129 (3) of the Russian Civil Code.

440 Article 310 of Russian Civil Code; Decision of 31 May 2005 in case No 6-P (Russian Constitutional Court) [2005]; Decision of 16 April 2009 in case No 495-O-O (Russian Constitutional Court) [2009]; Decision of 22 April 2011 in case No 5-P (Russian Constitutional Court) [2011]; Decision of 24 December 2012 in case No 2353-O (Russian Constitutional Court) [2012].

441 David Lametti, 'Rights of Private Property in the Civil Code of the Russian Federation and in the Civil Code of Quebec' (2005) 30 Review of Central and East European Law 29, 31.

442 Decision of 20 May 1997 in case No 8-P (Russian Constitutional Court) [1997]; Decision of 11 March 1998 in case No 8-P (Russian Constitutional Court) [1998].

ownership rights, but in a separate case, it was interpreted that taking is understood as only direct expropriation of ownership right.[443] The Constitutional Court is reluctant to unravel the material content of property protection, and the constitutional jurisprudence could be defined by regular refusals to investigate complicated cases of indirect expropriation where private and communal interests clash.[444]

The exceptional nature of expropriation is noted by Article 235 of the Russian Civil Code, which provides some general grounds for the loss of ownership: immovable property taken due to inappropriate use; a land plot taken for the state or municipal needs; a property being requisitioned or confiscated, etc. Nationalisation in Russia should be declared by law and be compensated.[445] Articles 279–287 of the Russian Civil Code regulate the expropriation of land in more detail. For example, the decision on taking property for the needs of the state or municipality is made by the federal executive organs, organs of executive power of subjects of the Federation or the local municipality.[446] State and municipality needs are understood very broadly, but at least in one case, the taking of a land plot was deemed illegal because the municipality decided to take it for commercial redevelopment and did not sufficiently establish public interest and needs.[447] The owner has to be notified about the taking and may agree on deadlines, compensation and other circumstances of the expropriation. In case he fails to agree, the conditions of expropriation are determined by the court.[448]

The Russian Constitutional Court emphasises the procedural aspect of the property protection clause – the decision on expropriation and the amount of compensation must be reviewed by a court.[449] The Russian Constitutional

443 Decision of 24 February 2002 in case No 3-P (Russian Constitutional Court) [2002].

444 Decisions of 29 September 2016 in case No 1984-O (Russian Constitutional Court) [2016]; Decision of 7 October 2014 in case No 2026-O (Russian Constitutional Court) [2014]; Decision of 15 February 2005 in case No 59-O (Russian Constitutional Court) [2005]; Decision of 25 September 2014 in case No 2295-O (Russian Constitutional Court) [2014]; Decision of 23 June 2009 in case No 662-O-O (Russian Constitutional Court) [2009].

445 Article 306 of the Russian Civil Code.

446 Article 279(3) of the Russian Civil Code.

447 Decision of 14 August 2015 in case No 303-es15-5520 (Russian Supreme Court) [2015]. Russian case law could be found at <https://vsrf.ru/lk/practice/cases> accessed on 8 March 2018.

448 Article 279(5–6), 282 of the Russian Civil Code.

449 Decision of the of 16 July 2008 in case No 9-P (Russian Constitutional Court) [2008]; Decision of 24 February 2004 in case No 3-P (Russian Constitutional Court) [2004]; Decision of 11 May 2012 in case No 758-O (Russian Constitutional Court) [2012]; Decision of 3 July 2007 in case No 714-O-P (Russian Constitutional Court) [2007].

Court held that if public legal relations permanently affect the legal title of a property, as opposed to temporary restrictions, *ex-ante* court review is obligatory.[450]

Article 284 of the Russian Civil Code also allows the taking of land due to a different use than indicated in the land planning and zoning documents. For example, if the land plot is designated as agricultural and the owner fails to use it as such for three years, the land could be taken away, but longer deadlines can be provided by other laws. Furthermore, Article 285 of the Russian Civil Code allows the taking of land if it is used in violation of Russian laws, in particular, if it is used in breach of land planning and zoning decisions or its use essentially worsens the fertility of agricultural land or damages the environment.

Lametti notes that such instances illustrate 'the heightened role of the state' in property relations and the importance of the state's role in land planning and zoning.[451] The issue of compensation for the restrictions of property rights due to land planning decisions is not even discussed.

Article 35 of the Russian Constitution of 1993 allows expropriation only subject to prior and fair compensation.[452] Article 281 of the Russian Civil Code further specifies the standard of compensation for land plots. For the taking of land, another immovable property and other real rights market value has to be paid, and other losses, including lost chance, have to be compensated in accordance with the law. The same Article of the Russian Civil Code allows compensation in kind if such an option is provided by other laws.

The overview of case law provided by the Russian Supreme Court argued that compensation amounting to a lower value than market value breaches the constitutional guarantee of property protection.[453] In another case, the Russian Constitutional Court found a breach of Article 35 of the Constitution by the law on bankruptcy as far as it allowed transferring to municipal institutions social housing, kindergartens, and social infrastructure necessary for the region without paying compensation to owners, which secures the balance between public and private interests.[454] But this decision somehow lowered the compensation standard – there was no requirement for market value,

450 Decision of 10 March 2005 in case No 97-O (Russian Constitutional Court) [2005].

451 Lametti, 'Rights of Private Property in the Civil Code of the Russian Federation and in the Civil Code of Quebec' 33.

452 The Constitution of the Russian Federation.

453 Overview of the case law of the Russian Supreme Court of 17 July 2002.

454 Decision of 16 May 2000 in case No 8-P.

only that the amount must be fair, reasonable, and proportionate with the public interest.[455]

The real difficulty in ascertaining the dominant understanding of property and the level of its protection lies is that formal law in Russia differs from its application in practice. Although the texts of the constitution and civil code adopted in the early 1990s were drafted in an individualistic spirit, in reality, the state retained a paternalistic role and resolved the major clashes of interests out of court.

14 China

Asia is immensely vast and diverse, ranging from highly developed states with saturated markets to mega-developing countries with evolving social and economic standards. There are legal systems in Asia with advanced economies that favour an individualistic understanding of property and its protection *vis-à-vis* the state. However, China, due to its size, economic volume and political clout, not only exerts influence on other smaller states in the region, but also to some degree represents prevailing cultural and legal attitudes towards property of a broader region, not limited to the exact territory of China. Like Eastern Europe, China also underwent a remarkable transformation in its formal treatment of property.

As with any laws, the habits and mindset of people are more challenging to change than statutes, so a few comments will be made about the legal culture and social context in China. Confucian values and principles influenced some egalitarian tendencies, but overall, the interests of a centralised, hierarchical, stable, harmonious and orderly society are prioritised over individual rights.[456] In pre-modern times, no individual rights existed that could be exercised against an emperor or a state.[457] On the contrary, property was redistributed

455 Alexei Trochev, 'Russia's Constitutional Spirit: Judge-made Principles in Theory and Practice' in Gordon B Smith and Robert S Sharlet (eds), *Russia and its Constitution: Promise and Political Reality* (Nijhoff 2008) 58.

456 Taisu Zhang, 'Social Hierarchies and the Formation of Customary Property Law in Pre-Industrial China and England' (2014) 62 American Journal of Comparative Law 171; Norman P Ho, 'A Confucian Theory of Property' (2016) 9 Tsinghua China Law Review 1, 7, 13; John C H Wu, 'Chinese Legal Philosophy – A Brief Historical Survey,' Chinese Culture 1 (1958) 39.

457 Lei Chen, '100 Years of Chinese Property Law: Looking back and Thinking forward' (2012) Towards a Chinese civil code: comparative and historical perspectives 87, 88–89.

every time the ruling dynasties changed.[458] During the early twentieth century, Japanese and German influence was absorbed.[459] The first Civil Code was adopted in 1931 but was quickly repealed, this was followed by the massive nationalisations and redistributions of 1949.[460] Communist China was influenced by the socialist legal school and ideology, which was antagonistic to individual rights and private ownership.[461] Its main premise was that people through the state are true owners of all property, allowing only minimal personal belongings. On a conceptual level, rights were not protected against interference by the state, mainly because they were perceived as granted by the state and thus could be modified or taken away.

Faced with practical difficulties and an urgent need for fast industrialisation, certain types of rights were developed within socialist legal theories, which in all practical aspects resembled ownership. This fragmentation of property rights, characteristic to the Soviet legal system, occurred in China too:

> Property rights are called forth to set up the process of national modernization. Privatizing property serves the end of national wealth maximization, while its function for increasing individual liberty falls away.[462]

Even further fragmentation within the legal system occurred in parallel between property owned by Chinese nationals and foreign businesses.[463] During the Deng Xiaoping era, a series of laws and amendments were adopted, creating a separate legal regime for foreign investment that was more liberal than the national property regime. The Regulation on the Exploration of Offshore Petroleum Resources in Cooperation with Foreign Enterprises of 1982 already

---

458 John P Powelson, 'Property in Chinese Development: Some Historical Comparisons', in James A Dom, Wang XI (eds.), *Economic Reform in China: Problems and Prospects*, (the University of Chicago Press 1990) 165–179.

459 Chen 89.

460 Extensive coverage of this era is provided by Chuanhui Wang, *The Constitutional Protection of Private Property in China: Historical Evolution and Comparative Research* (Cambridge University Press 2016) 45.

461 Mo Zhang, 'From public to private: The newly enacted Chinese property law and the protection of property rights in China' (2008) 5 Berkeley Business Law Journal 317, 326.

462 Qinglan Long, 'Reinterpreting Chinese Property Law' (2009) 19 The Southern California Interdisciplinary Law Journal 5570 (footnote excluded).

463 Wenhua Shan, 'China And International Investment Law' in Leon E Trakman and Nicola W Ranieri (eds), *Regionalism in International Investment Law* (Oxford University Press 2014) 225. Since the separate legal regime for foreign investment within Chinese national legislation was more of an exception and does not represent the dominant national understanding of property, for the comparative purposes the domestic Chinese property regime is used.

acknowledges possible expropriation.[464] The Wholly Foreign-Owned Enterprises Law of 1986 went even further and admitted that in special circumstances appropriate compensation might be due. Aiming for rapid industriaisation, China was willing to experiment with the legal regime for foreign investments, while maintaining a rather 'weak protection of individual rights'.[465] Though slowly, the national property regime was eventually developing towards a more individualistic understanding of property. In 1986 the General Principles of the Civil Law recognised that the law protects all kinds of civil law rights, including ownership, right of use, right to manage land under contract, the right of operation, etc.[466] In abstract terms, the General Principles of the Civil Law admitted that '[a] citizen's lawful property shall be protected by law'.[467] Only in 2004, the constitutional amendments awarded protection to private property rights,[468] but it is still very far from the liberal and individualistic understanding of property.[469] In China property is still perceived as 'means, not the end' and the ultimate aim of the economic and property reform is 'the wealth and power of the nation-state, which must also carry on the struggle for survival on the international stage'.[470]

This phenomenon of purely defined and protected property rights accompanied by rapid economic growth contravenes the Washington consensus and neo-liberal development model, which proclaims that secure property rights are necessary for high rates of economic growth and prosperity of a society.[471] The conceptual differences between the Western and Chinese understanding of property may explain this phenomenon. In Asia, the institution of private property did not develop in a Western sense as a tool for limiting the absolute power of monarchs. On the contrary, 'the specific Chinese cultural and historical' context indicates that the limits and content of property will be shaped to

---

464 Norah Gallagher and Wenhua Shan, 'China' in Chester Brown (ed), *Commentaries on Selected Model Investment Treaties* (Oxford University Press 2013) 139.

465 Long 69; Zhang Xiaobo, *Asymmetric Property Rights in China's Economic Growth,* 33 WM Mitchell Law Review 567 (2007).

466 Article 47 of General Principles of the Civil Law (1986), <http://www.npc.gov.cn/zgrdw/englishnpc/Law/2007-12/12/content_1383941.htm> accessed on 9 May 2025.

467 Article 75 of the General Principles of the Civil Law (1986).

468 Article 13 of the Constitution of the People's Republic of China (1982) with amendments <https://english.www.gov.cn/archive/lawsregulations/201911/20/content_WS5ed8856ec6d0b3f0e9499913.html> accessed on 9 May 2025.

469 Wang 81.

470 Long 64.

471 Randall Peerenboom, 'Law and development in China and India' in Jiangyu Wang and Muthucumaraswamy Sornarajah (eds), *China, India and the International Economic Order* (Cambridge University Press 2010) 492.

serve the national interest,[472] so, it belongs to the group of states with a strong communitarian understanding of property. Upham has suggested that relative success of Chinese development should be attributed not to the scope or strength of property and investment protection but to the ability of the system to adapt and reinvent property through occasional creative destruction of certain property rights.[473]

The taxonomy of different types of property (state, collective, and private) helps to manage and avoid the clash of individual and government interests.[474] Only the state can own urban land and natural resources,[475] but private enterprise is a significant part of the Chinese economy. Thus separate 'use rights' akin to Soviet 'operative management' developed that allow the private use and enjoyment of land plots.[476] Instead of full land ownership, 'land-use rights' (similar to *superficies*) developed in China. They can be transferable, they entitle the holder to build on it and in many ways resemble true ownership, except that formally 'use rights' are only one of several proprietary rights and the remainder of the rights' rest with the state. The 'use rights' are limited by duration and have to be renewed.[477] Such an arrangement with a narrower scope of protected interests is more flexible for the state, which may modify the content of 'use right' without breaching the property protection clause. But in all material economic parameters, 'use rights' are equivalent to the ownership right since Article 10(4) of the Constitution added in 1988 provides that '[l]and use rights may be transferred pursuant to the legal provisions'.

The Property Law of 2007 regulates in more detail such 'use rights' (contractual management of land, land use for construction, land use for housing, and easements), which are extensively used because land ownership is limited to state and agricultural collectives.[478]

The Property Law of 2007 also regulates collective ownership of agricultural land. After 1980, almost all agricultural land that was formally collectively owned was distributed for individual use, granting villagers 'right to occupy land, cultivate crops and receive interest on production' in exchange for a

---

472 Long 67.

473 Upham 2, 83.

474 Article 4 of the Property Laws (2007) <http://www.npc.gov.cn/zgrdw/englishnpc/Law/2009-02/20/content_1471118.htm> accessed on 9 May 2025.

475 Article 10 of the Constitution of the People's Republic of China.

476 Gebhard M Rehm and Hinrich Julius, 'The New Chinese Property Rights Law: An Evaluation from a Continental Perspective' (2008) 22 Columbia Journal of Asian Law 177, 193.

477 Zhang 356.

478 Rehm and Julius 208.

certain proportion of their harvest.[479] The most contentious disputes arise from the taking of those rights by local authorities and transforming it into the urban land for commercial development.

Other proprietary rights such as security rights (mortgages, pledges, liens) and possession are recognised and regulated by the Property Law of 2007.

By accepting German influence on its property law China inherited the controversy whether only *'res'* (things) can be owned.[480] There are opinions that 'creditor rights would not be regarded as a 'thing' or *'res,'* but such rights may be deemed a kind of 'property.'[481]

The administrative tradition of state planning in China is still powerful despite conceding certain areas to a market economy. Considering the paternalistic state tradition and the fact that private property rights only recently were granted constitutional protection it would be safe to say that almost any regulation would be perceived either as a legitimate limitation of individual interests or would not even be considered as any limitation at all. Article 3(2) of the Property Law still mentions the socialist market economy, while Article 5 emphasises that types and content of property right are stipulated by law. Furthermore, Article 7 of the Property Law provides that property rights should be exercised in compliance with laws and social morality, and not harm public interests and the legitimate rights and interests of others.[482]

Due to the fragmentation land is heavily regulated: the 'right to contractual management of land' is regulated by Articles 124–134, the 'right to use land for construction' – by Articles 135–151, and the 'right to use domestic land plots' – by Article 152–155 of the Property Law. Those rights have a limited varying duration with different renewal procedures.[483] The rights to the use of land for residential construction in towns are valid for 70 years, for industrial construction 50 years, for education, natural sciences, culture, hygiene and sports facilities 50 years, for trade, travel and entertainment facilities 40 years, and for other purposes 50 years.[484]

479 Wang 51.

480 Article 2(2) of Property Law (China).

481 Zhang 322.

482 Rehm and Julius 196.

483 Article 126, 149, 153 of the Property Law.

484 Article 12 of the Provisional Regulation on Transfer and Surrender of Rights of Use to Urban State-owned Land in China No 55 (1990) <https://www.lehmanlaw.com/resource-centre/laws-and-regulations/real-estate/provisional-regulations-of-the-peoples-republic-of-china-on-assigning-and-transferring-the-urban-state-owned-land-use-right-1990.html> accessed on 9 May 2025.

Even after the 2004 constitutional amendment, the individual inviolable sphere is minimal. A few examples illustrate the extent of the state's interference with private rights. Firstly, in the Xuhui district of Shanghai, a certain residential area was designated for redevelopment and the relevant rights sold to an urban development company. Soon the purpose of the land was changed to the nature reserve, and the development company refused to relocate the inhabitants or pay sufficient compensations. The removal company was held responsible for setting the houses of the inhabitants who refused to move on fire, and for their death.[485] Secondly, in Jiahe County, the local government also resorted to violent means to evict residents from an area designated for redevelopment.[486]

Even earlier, specialised legislation retained the state's right to expropriate property for the public interest, but the Property Law regulates it explicitly and in a more orderly manner. It applies to all types of property:

> For public interests, land owned by the collectives, and the houses and other immovables of units and individuals may be expropriated within the limits of power and in compliance with the procedures provided for by law.[487]

The initial draft law prohibited expropriation for commercial development purposes, because of wide-spread conflicts between residential homeowners and local governments granting land use rights for construction.[488] However, the final text left it to the courts to develop the criteria for public interest, and scholars suggested the following factors: '(a) scope of beneficiaries, (b) burdens on the general public, (c) priority of interests involved, and (d) availability of alternatives'.[489] The main problem related to the takings of land in urban areas was the local government's abuse of the 'public interest'. It is argued that 'Beijing and Shanghai alone have evicted about four million residents for urban redevelopment'.[490] The Administrative Regulations on Urban Housing Demolition and Relocation and the Regulations on Expropriation and Compensation of Housing on State-owned Land of 2011 tried to manage the ten-

485 Wang 95.
486 Ibid.
487 Article 42(1) of the Property Law.
488 Zhang 358.
489 Ibid 361.
490 Long 67.

sions[491] by defining the public interest as national security, economic and social development needs and other public interests. It also provides an exemplary list of those needs: national defence and diplomacy, energy infrastructure projects, communication, science and technology, education, culture, sports, protection of environment and resources, prevention and reduction of disasters, protection of cultural relics, social welfare and municipal administration, construction of affordable housing, and the renewal and reconstruction of the old city areas, etc.[492] This regulation prohibited the expropriation of urban houses for non-public purposes.[493]

The 2019 amendments to the Chinese Land Administration Law regulate in more detail compensation not only to the owners but also the land use right holders if the land use right is terminated due to public interests and renovation of old towns, as well as provide certain procedural requirements.[494] These amendments further liberalise the system and allow the transfer of collective land use rights. Article 47 of the Land Administration Law provides the standards of compensation for expropriated land.

The problem in rural areas is that land is formally owned by agricultural collectives and not individuals. Not only is the allocation of land plots for individual use problematic, but peasants cannot sell, mortgage or change the designation of those slots from agricultural to the commercial designation. This allows local governments to reap the benefits of converting the farm land for commercial redevelopment.[495]

For many years China resisted the full market compensation standard and argued for 'liquidation' value.[496] But in its quest for rapid industrialisation and seeking to attract foreign investments, China was amenable to include the appropriate[497] or reasonable[498] standard of compensation in its legislation. However, domestic individual rights are still limited in that regard. For exam-

491 'China issues new regulations on house expropriation' China Daily, 22 January 2011 <http://www.chinadaily.com.cn/china/2011-01/22/content_11900647.htm>accessed on 15 March 2018.

492 Wang 127.

493 Ibid 129.

494 Law on the Administration of Land (1986) with 2019 amendments, link to the original and summary in English can be found here <https://www.fao.org/faolex/results/details/en/c/LEX-FAOC193250> accessed on 9 May 2025.

495 Long 66.

496 Lianlian Lin and John R Allison, 'An Analysis of Expropriation and Nationalization Risk in China' (1994) 19 Yale Journal of International Law 135, 182.

497 Article 2 of the Joint Venture Law of 1990.

498 Article 5 of the Wholly Foreign-Owned Enterprise Law of the Peoples Republic of China.

ple, the Constitution required making at least some compensation, without any mention of reasonableness.[499]

Throughout the drafting of the Property Law, four compensation standards were discussed: reasonable, proper, adequate, and market price.[500] But legislators chose to exclude the compensation standard, thus leaving it for local governments and other central agencies because they can evaluate local needs.[501] But at the same time, local governments have an incentive 'to keep the compensation as low as possible'.[502]

As a consequence, Article 42 of the Property Law does not provide the universal standard of compensation. Instead, several other articles or regulations offer some guidance on it. For example, Article 121 of the Property Law requires to make corresponding or relevant compensation for a usufructuary right, or movable and immovable property. Article 132 of the Property Law requires making similar relevant compensation for the taking of contractual right to manage land. The standard of compensation for the use of minerals, natural resources, or sea are regulated by other laws. Article 148 of the Property Law for the withdrawal of construction rights over land is vaguer because compensation only refers to the house and real estate that is built and does not mention the standard of compensation. Agrarian land should be compensated at a rate equivalent to 6–10 times the average annual productive value for the preceding three years.[503] In the case of expropriations, certain social security measures are also offered to farmers.[504]

A sufficient amount of compensation would allow nearly all the inhabitants of 'nail houses' or peasants to acquire economically equivalent housing or arable land, but two factors make this solution elusive. First, the institution or developer interested in acquiring the land typically seeks to minimise expenses and reduce the costs associated with land clearing. Secondly, private owners and users, for psychological and practical reasons, nearly always overappreciate things that belong to them. Thus, an effective agreement on this issue is somewhat rare, and a political decision must be made. Such a decision is better made in the statute rather than left to local administrations on a case-

499 Article 13 of the Constitution of Peoples Republic of China (as amended in 2004).

500 Hu Kangsheng, Explanations to the Property Law of the People's Republic of China 7–9, 103.

501 Hu Kangsheng, Explanations to the Property Law of the People's Republic of China 7–9, 102–103.

502 Wang Liming, Study On Crucial and Difficult Problems of Chinese Civil Code 258, 259 (2006) 427.

503 Article 47 Law on the Administration of Land.

504 Rehm and Julius 221.

by-case basis, despite the difficulties in articulating such a standard. The alternative of leaving the question of valuation to the local administration is fraught with increased risk of corruption and abuse unless an efficient court review system could be established.

The struggle in assessing the actual level of property protection in China is similar to the Russian problem – the actual state of affairs differs from the formal language of legal statutes, as real lives are more guided by the policies of the Chinese Communist Party's Central Committee than by the Constitution.

15 Brazil and Other South American States

Latin American states were significantly influenced by the civil law tradition and only later by the Anglo-American tradition.[505] Initially, Latin American civil codes adopted the liberal idea of property contained in the 1804 French Napoleonic Code.[506] Later, most of them introduced stronger communitarian notions emphasising shared models of governance through the use of such language as 'public', 'publica', and 'social' in their respective constitutions.[507] Regular public unrest accompanied by expropriation and nationalisation, recognition of rural collective property and the social function of ownership hint at a specific Latin American legal ethos,[508] which *inter alia* includes the principles of non-discrimination, national treatment, the exhaustion of national remedies, and sovereign equality of states. Despite the introduction of socio-economic rights in various constitutions, Latin America is still one of the most economically unequal regions in the world. Disputes rage, whether it is due to economic policy with its focus on individual rights that hinders the necessary reforms,[509] or due to the gap between law and reality, or insufficient commit-

---

505 Jan Kleinheisterkamp, 'Development of Comparative Law in Latin America' in Mathias Reimann and Reinhard Zimmermann (eds), *The Oxford Handbook of Comparative Law* (2006) 286.

506 Jorge L Esquirol, 'Formalizing property in Latin America' in Michele Graziadei and Lionel D Smith (eds), *Comparative Property Law: Global Perspectives* (Edward Elgar Publishing 2017) 336; Matthew C Mirow, 'Borrowing private law in Latin American: Andrés Bello's use of the Code Napoléon in drafting the Chilean civil code' (2001) 61 Louisiana Law Review291; Diego Mendoza Perez, *Evolucion de la Propiedad en Colombia 1897* (Bogota 1983) 47–51.

507 Rosalind Dixon and Tom Ginsburg, *Comparative Constitutional Law in Latin America* (1 edn, Edward Elgar MUA 2017) 7, 15.

508 Almut Schilling-Vacaflor and Detlef Nolte, *New Constitutionalism in Latin America: Promises and Practices* (Routledge Ltd 2016) 5.

509 Dixon and Ginsburg 14.

ment to the social cause.[510] Alviar Garcia argued that even left-leaning understandings of property are unable to accomplish the economic redistribution and reforms necessary for Latin America,[511] while de Soto advises formalising property rights to bring more prosperity to the region.[512]

The Latin American region is huge and diverse, making it impractical to provide comprehensive details on every state in a book that attempts to cover the world. Instead, Brazil is used as a representative example of regional attitudes towards property due to its status as a major developing country and investment destination with a large economy.

Article 5 of the Constitution of the Federal Republic of Brazil of 1988 provides:

> All persons are equal before the law, without any distinction whatsoever, Brazilians and foreigners residing in the country being ensured of inviolability of the right … to property … on the following terms: …
> XXII – the right of property is guaranteed;
> XXIII – property shall observe its social function;
> XXIV – the law shall establish the procedure for expropriation for public necessity or use, or for social interest, with fair and previous pecuniary compensation, except for the cases provided in this constitution;[513]

Before colonisation, indigenous Latin American communities relied heavily on communal land and collective tilling for their subsistence. Thus, there is a strong and old element of communal interest in the understanding of property. The Spanish law influence in Latin Civil Codes is manifested through the reception of Roman law and understanding of property as inherently limited by law, rights and interests of others as well as the prohibition against using property in a way that harms others.[514] Many independent Latin American codes were influenced by Andre Bello's civil codification, which defined own-

---

510 Antonio Azuela, *Property in the Post-post-revolution: Notes on the Crisis of the Constitutional Idea of Property in Contemporary Mexico*, vol 89 (2011) 1915.

511 Helena Alviar Garcia, 'Looking beyond the Constitution: the social and ecological function of property' in Rosalind Dixon and Tom Ginsburg (eds), *Comparative Constitutional Law in Latin America* (1 edn, Edward Elgar MUA 2017) 154.

512 Hernando de Soto, *The Mystery of Capital: Why Capitalism Triumphs in the West and Fails Everywhere Else* (Basic Books 2000).

513 The Constitution of the Federal Republic of Brazil (1988) with amendments available at <https://www.stf.jus.br/arquivo/cms/legislacaoConstituicao/anexo/brazil_federal_constitution.pdf> accessed on 12 May 2025.

514 Carlos Felipe Amunategui Perello, 'The Definition of Property in Andrés Bello's Code and the Limits of Use against the Rights of Others' (2010) 57 Osaka University Law Review 113.

ership through power over tangible things.[515] This poses the question of whether intangible things or rights could amount to property and be protected as such. The problem is especially acute in Latin America when international arbitration under the influence of common laws recognises contractual or concession rights as property.[516]

The drafting of civil codes at the dawn of independence in the region was influenced by the individualistic notions of Enlightenment and French absolutism of property rights. This tendency exacerbated the economic inequality inherited from colonial times. The *latifundio* system made land and property, in general, an object of constant reforms, in the hope that state intervention may alleviate chronic underdevelopment.[517] It was argued that property should serve a social function, in contrast to the liberal understanding of property where it is supposed to serve only the individual interests of the owner.[518] Thus, almost all constitutions of Latin America refer to the social function of property.[519] The drafters of the first Brazilian Civil Code of 1916 also expressed the need to balance individual and societal interests.[520] The new Brazilian Civil Code of 2002 similarly mentions the social function of property,[521] but scholars still debate whether it is an external or internal feature of property rights.[522] The drafters of this code opined that 'sociality has, and collective values must prevail over individual ones'.[523]

Probably under the influence of communitarian values, the property rights of indigenous communities are also safeguarded by the Brazilian Federal Con-

515 Ibid 108.

516 *Shufeldt Claim* (*USA v Guatemala*) 2 UN RIAA 1079 [1930] 1098.

517 Jessica A Clark, 'Eminent Domain and Expropriation: A Comparison between Fifth Amendment Precedent and Latin American Land Redistribution' (2015) 28 Regent University Law Review 326.

518 Sheila R Foster and Daniel Bonilla, 'Introduction' (2011) 80 Fordham Law Review 1003; Robert Jackson Alexander, *Agrarian reform in Latin America* (Collier Macmillan Publishers 1974) 191.

519 All Latin American Constitutions can be found at the CODICES database of the Venice Commission: <https://codices.coe.int/codices/documents/welcome> accessed 12 May 2025.

520 Clóvis Bevilaqua, *Direito das Coisas* (Freitas Bastos 1941) 134.

521 Brazilian Civil Code (2002) available at <http://www.wipo.int/wipolex/en/text.jsp?file_id =226199#LinkTarget_4802 =226199#LinkTarget_4802> accessed on 1 May 2025.

522 Cunha Alexandre dos Santos, 'The Social Function of Property in Brazilian Law' (2011) 80 Fordham Law Review 1171, 1180.

523 Miguel Reale, *O Projeto do novo Código civil: situação após a aprovação pelo Senado Federal* (Saraiva 1999) 7.

stitution and the Indian National Foundation.[524] Although the exact balance between the interests of indigenous communities to land and modern title holders is frequently contested both in the courts and Senate.[525]

In Brazil, like in all states, regulatory measures affecting property range from an agrarian, conservation, territorial planning, environmental protection to protection of indigenous communities and management of risk areas. The Supreme Federal Court is responsible for constitutional review in Brazil. The Court practice balances between regulations in the public interest and individual property rights, leaning towards a communitarian understanding of property. For example, in *the Brazilian electricity crisis* case, the water level in the hydroelectric reservoirs dropped below the minimum due to the lack of rainfall, causing power shortages. The federal government introduced measures rationing electric power. The Supreme Federal Court held that the electricity quotas and associated fees for exceeding these quotas were not violating property rights, and even if they were, the property should meet its social function and be subject to the conditions defined by law.[526] In another case, the statute establishing the National System of Arms, which requires registration of guns and regulates the possession and trade of firearms, was challenged based on constitutional property rights.[527] The Supreme Federal Court rejected the claim that the mandatory periodical renewal of the registration of firearms with a fee breached property rights since the bearer can surrender his firearm for compensation.[528]

In other words, when assessing cases of urban development or progressive taxation, or the rights of occupants of a land plot, the Supreme Federal Court tends to interpret property rights narrower and limit them in favour of various other interests that are thought to ensure social stability of the community and sustainable economic development.[529] In Brazil, there is very little space

---

524 Social Development Unit Latin America and the Caribbean Region Sustainable Development Department of World Bank, *Involuntary Resettlement in Brazil: A Review of Policies and Practices* (2011) 14.

525 Constance Malleret, 'Controversial Brazil law curbing Indigenous rights comes into force' *The Guardian* (28 December 2023) <https://www.theguardian.com/world/2023/dec/28/brazil-law-indigenous-land-rights-claim-time-marker> accessed on 12 May 2025.

526 *The Brazilian electricity crisis case* 13 December 2001, ADC 09, Official Gazette 23 April 2004 (Brazil Supreme Federal Tribunal) <https://redir.stf.jus.br/paginadorpub/paginador.jsp?docTP=AC&docID=883> accessed on 13 May 2025.

527 Brazilian Law on Disarmament Statute No 10.826 (2003).

528 *Disarmament Statute case* No ADI 3112, Official Gazette 26 October 2007 (Brazil Supreme Federal Tribunal) <https://redir.stf.jus.br/paginadorpub/paginador.jsp?docTP=AC&docID=491806> accessed on 13 May 2025.

529 Alexandre dos Santos 1176.

for indirect expropriation, as illustrated by the *Serra do Mar State Park* case where the courts refused to treat environmental limitations on property rights as indirect expropriation and refused compensation.[530] In a similar investment arbitration case involving the Santa Elena nature reserve, Costa Rica was held liable for the breach of investors' rights and ordered to pay the full value of the land.[531]

However, some compensation may sometimes be granted by courts due to the objective state liability arising under Article 37 para 6 of the Brazilian Constitution:

> Public legal entities and private legal entities rendering public services shall be liable for damages that any of their agents, acting as such, cause to third parties, ensuring the right of recourse against the liable agent in cases of malice or fault.

In general, Latin American states have been expropriating property for economic development for years.[532] The Brazilian Decree-Law No 3.365 of 1941 with 2023 amendments regulate expropriation for public purposes,[533] and a special federal law regulates expropriation in the social interest.[534] The qualification of expropriation requires the total loss of ownership rights or the impossibility of using property; partial loss of some property rights does not amount to expropriation.[535] The Law on Expropriation provides procedures for expropriation and allows expropriation upon the declaration of public utility or social interest.[536] The wide variety of entities providing public services or carrying out functions delegated by the government, and even contractors and permit holders, may also initiate expropriation.[537] Article 5 of the Law on Expropriation explains public interest as national security and defence,

---

530 *Serra do Mar State Park case* case No 9 842765/1-00-Paraibuna (Braz) (São Paulo Court of Appeal) 147.

531 *Compañía del Desarrollo de Santa Elena v Republic of Costa Rica* para 64.

532 Clark 328.

533 Federal Decree-law on Expropriation for Public Purposes No 3.365 (1941) with law No 14.620/2023 amandments (Brazil) <https://www.planalto.gov.br/ccivil_03/decreto-lei/del3365.htm#:~:text=DECRETO%2DLEI%20N%C2%BA%203.365%2C%20DE%2021%20DE%20JUNHO%20DE%201941.&text=Disp%C3%B5e%20sobre%20desapropria%C3%A7%C3%B5es%20por%20utilidade%20p%C3%BAblica.> accessed on 12 May 2025.

534 Federal Law on Expropriation for Social Interest No 4.132 (1962) (Brazil).

535 Leonardo Munhoz, 'The environmental limitations to property rights in Brazil and the United States of America' (Pace University 2014) 93 <http://digitalcommons.pace.edu/lawdissertations/15/> accessed on 15 May 2025.

536 Article 2 of the Law on Expropriation for Public Purposes (Brazil).

537 Article 3 of the Law on Expropriation for Public Purposes (Brazil).

government assistance in case of emergencies, public health, public services, preservation of cultural and historic monuments, urban or industrial redevelopment, etc.[538] Social interest is defined as of somewhat lesser importance: (i) agricultural zoning corrections, (ii) the maintenance of favelas in urban areas, (iii) construction of public housing, (iv) public infrastructure and services, such as sanitation, ports, transportation, electrification, water storage, and irrigation, (v) the protection of soil, water and forest resources.[539] Expropriations for social interest are subject to the same rules as expropriation for a public purpose. A declaration of social interest is valid for two years,[540] while a declaration of public interest is valid for five years.[541] Courts are deferential to the legislative or executive power on the question of public purpose or interest.[542]

In terms of land reform, the Brazilian Constitution specifically allows expropriation of the unproductive rural property upon the issuing of agrarian bonds:

> It is within the power of the Union to expropriate on account of social interest, for purposes of agrarian reform, the rural property which is not performing its social function, against prior and fair compensation in agrarian debt bonds with a clause providing for maintenance of the real value, redeemable within a period of up to twenty years computed as from the second year of issue, and the use of which shall be defined in the law.[543]

Even rural land owned by a condominium was condemned for expropriation, even though each member's share constituted a small or medium-size property.[544]

Clark claims that at least some land reforms in Latin America were adequate, and would withstand the scrutiny of the US Supreme Court for the exercise of eminent domain despite fierce diplomatic opposition from the USA.[545]

538 World Bank 14.

539 Federal Law on Expropriation for Social Interest No 4.132 (1962) (Brazil).

540 World Bank 15.

541 Article 10 of the Law on Expropriation for Public Purposes (Brazil).

542 Luís Daniel Tavela and Luis Antonio Gonçalves de Andrade, 'Expropriation in Brazilian Law: an International Standard?' in Daniel de Andrade Levy, Ana Gerdau de Borja and Adriana Noemi Pucci (eds), *Investment Protection in Brazil* (Wolters Kluwer, Law & Business 2014) 120.

543 Article 184 of the Constitution of the Federal Republic of Brazil.

544 Alexandre dos Santos 1178.

545 Clark 348.

However, almost any legal reform affecting property rights would most likely be condemned by the arbitral tribunals as expropriation.[546]

Article 32 of the Brazilian Constitution requires paying fair compensation in advance, but the Constitution also allows exceptions, as in the case of land reforms. The compensation is usually based on market value, which is calculated on the basis of value submitted for calculation of real estate tax but could be adjusted looking at similar transactions.[547] The *Serra do Mar State Park* cases brought about a discussion on the methods for the calculation of compensation for the limitation of property rights in a nature reserve.[548] The Brazilian courts had to take previous limitations to land use and prices of similar properties into account when calculating damages.[549]

Customary compensation standards in other Latin American states also tend to favour fair compensation[550] and consider various factors, including the purpose of the state measure, previous use, and income from the property, but almost never full market value or lost profit.

In comparison with other regions of the world, Latin America's property regime is clearly leaning towards the communitarian understanding of property, where individuals accept interferences with private property rights for the general interest. It also means that there is a significant gap here between national property protection and investment protection under the BITs.

16 Property Rights across Africa

People in Africa also tend to have a more pronounced communitarian understanding of property.[551] Glenn theorises that this is deeply connected with the way of life:

---

546 *ADC Affiliate Limited and ADC & ADMC Management Limited v Republic of Hungary* (ICSID) para 424; *Total SA v Argentine Republic* para 117–122; *SAUR International SA v Argentine Republic* para 396–402; *Eiser Infrastructure Limited and Energía Solar Luxembourg Sàrl v Kingdom of Spain* (ICSID) Case No ARB/13/36, Award 4 May 2017 para 382.

547 Marçal Justen Filho, *Curso de direito administrativo* (Saraiva 2006) 54; *Serra do Mar State Park case* 147.

548 Tavela and Andrade 122.

549 Raimundo Alves Campos, *O conflito entre o direito de propriedade e o meio ambiente e a questão da indenização das áreas de preservação florestal* (Juruá 2007); *Serra do Mar State Park case* 147.

550 *Davis & Co v Mexican Eagle Co [1938–40] Annual Digest and Reports of Public International Law Cases 25 (No 12) (Court of Rotterdam).*

551 Kwamena Bentsi-Enchill, 'The Traditional Legal Systems of Africa' in Frederick H Lawson and others (eds), *International Encyclopedia of Comparative Law: Property and Trust,*

> Living close to the land and in harmony with it means … there is no reason to accumulate land, or map it (other than to show trails); there is nothing to be done to it or with it, except enjoy its natural fruits. Chthonic notions of property are therefore thus of a chthonic life, and the human person is generally not elevated to a position of domination, or dominium, over the natural world.[552]

Normative rules in such communities seek 'to protect shared values and communal peace rather than individual rights'.[553] Thus, Africa has a much higher proportion of communal land, and the development of private property rights has been restrained. Western-style private property regimes introduced in colonial times were in conflict with local traditional understandings of property.[554] The controversy and confusion continued well into the twentieth century when liberal concepts of property were used to argue for the reclamation of communal landholding.

New constitutions of independent African states try to balance the Western-style property rights with indigenous rights and development aims.[555] The South African interim Constitution was a result of complicated conciliation politics.[556] Now the constitutional property protection clause is found in Article 25, which prohibits arbitrary deprivation of property and allows deprivation of property only by the law of general application (a) for a public purpose or in the public interest, and (b) subject to compensation, which has to be either agreed or approved by a court.[557] However, the constitutional property clause in South Africa is not aimed at the preservation of the *status quo*, but instead at the creation of a balance between individual and public interest – solving the tension between the preservation of current private property rights and the elimination of the consequences of apartheid policies.[558] These socio-

---

vol 6 (JCB Mohr (Paul Siebeck) 1973) 74–77; Alexander, *The Global Debate Over Constitutional Property: Lessons for American Takings Jurisprudence* 149.

552 HP Glenn, Legal Traditions of the World: Sustainable Diversity in Law (2004) 66.

553 Robert Home, '"Culturally Unsuited to Property Rights?": Colonial Land Laws and African Societies' (2013) 40 Journal of Law and Society 403, 406.

554 Alison Clarke, 'Land titling and communal property' in Warren Barr (ed), *Modern Studies in Property Law – Volume 8* (Bloomsbury Publishing PLC 2015) 221.

555 Allen, *The Right to Property in Commonwealth Constitutions* 37–38.

556 Walt 322; CC van der Merwe, Juanita M Pienaar and Marius J de Waal, *South Africa* (Kluwer Law International 2015) 30.

557 Constitution of the Republic of South Africa (1996) <https://www.gov.za/documents/constitution/constitution-republic-south-africa-1996-04-feb-1997> accessed 14 May 2025.

558 CC van der Merwe, Marius J de Waal and David L Carey Miller, 'South Africa' in R. Blanpain and others (eds), *International Encyclopaedia of Laws: Property and Trust*

economic reforms envisioned by the Constitution would most likely contravene investment protection clauses provided by the South African BITs.[559]

Most of the African legal systems support a rather wide definition of property. Article 16 of the Constitution of Namibia refers to all movable and immovable property,[560] and in *Cultura 2000 and Another v Government of the Republic of Namibia and others,* the High Court confirmed that it also applies to intangible property.[561] The Zimbabwean Constitution also covers a wide array of property rights and interests.[562] South African law belongs to the mixed legal tradition, but its property law is based on civil law tradition.[563] Article 25(4) of the South African Constitution expressly notes that property is not limited to land, but the question remains to what extent it includes contractual rights or interests. While drafting this Constitution there were efforts to broaden the definition, which could encompass the interests of rural Africans in land, but it was later realised that 'rights in property' would limit the state's power to regulate property.[564] The Constitutional Court hinted that at least mineral rights or the intellectual property might be within the meaning of 'property' anyway.[565] Legal scholars also argued that property includes *in rem* rights and rights that constitute ownership, i.e., right to use, enjoy, dispose of, exclude, etc.[566] South African private law also leans towards a wide definition of property, which includes usufructs in respect of mineral rights or an entire estate, security over leases, personal servitudes, etc.[567]

Law (Kluwer Law International 2000) 164; Bernadette Atuahene, 'Property Rights & the Demands of Transformation' (2009) 31 Michigan Journal of International Law 765, 771.

559 Schneiderman, *Constitutionalizing Economic Globalization: Investment Rules and Democracy's Promise* 144.

560 Constitution of the Republic of Namibia (1990) <https://www.un.int/namibia/namibia/chapter-3-fundamental-human-rights-and-freedoms> accessed on 12 May 2025.

561 *Cultura 2000 and another v Government of the Republic of Namibia and others* 1993 (2) SA 12 (NHC).

562 Section 71 of the Constitution of Zimbabwe Amendment (No 20) Act (2013) with amendments, however the previous version of the Constitution failed to protect white farmers from 'fast track land reform': <https://faolex.fao.org/docs/pdf/zim127325.pdf/> accessed on 12 May 2025.

563 TB Smith, 'Mixed jurisdictions' in Frederick H Lawson and others (eds), *International Encyclopedia of Comparative Law: Property and Trust / Volume 6* (JCB Mohr (Paul Siebeck) 1973) 121.

564 Allen, *The Right to Property in Commonwealth Constitutions* 124–125.

565 *Re (First) Certification of the Constitution of the Republic of South Africa case* (10) BLCR 1253 (South African Constitutional Court) [1996] 27.

566 J de Waal, I Currie & G Erasmus, The Bill of Rights Handbook (Juta Cape Town 4th ed 2001) 412–417.

567 Merwe, Waal and Miller 52; Schneiderman, *Constitutionalizing economic globalization: investment rules and democracy's promise* 144–145.

Earlier land reforms in other African countries were substantially influenced by foreign aid programmes,[568] and strong property rights were presented by some authors as a necessary condition for development and economic prosperity.[569] Scholars only recently voiced public interest concerns and more communal versions of property understanding,[570] but the South African Constitution tried already in Article 25(4) to carve out legal reforms from property protection by acknowledging the public interest. Other provisions of Article 25 also hint at the communitarian values and desired redistribution of property, especially of land:

> (5) The state must take reasonable legislative and other measures, within its available resources, to foster conditions which enable citizens to gain access to land on an equitable basis.
>
> (6) A person or community whose tenure of land is legally insecure as a result of past racially discriminatory laws or practices is entitled, to the extent provided by an Act of Parliament, either to tenure which is legally secure or to comparable redress.
>
> (7) A person or community dispossessed of property ... as a result of past racially discriminatory laws or practices is entitled, to the extent provided by an Act of Parliament, either to restitution of that property or to equitable redress.
>
> (8) No provision of this section may impede the state from taking legislative and other measures to achieve land, water and related reform, in order to redress the results of past racial discrimination.[571]

It is widely recognised that absolute ownership was hollowed out by public regulations, starting from motor vehicle use, to disease, arms, marketing and broadcasting control, not to mention zoning, planning and nature reserves.[572] The regulation is not considered a deprivation of property rights as long as it is authorised by law, general, non-arbitrary, and follows clear as well as fair pro-

---

568 Ambreena Manji, 'Land reform in the shadow of the state: The implementation of new land laws in Sub-Saharan Africa' (2001) 22 Third World Quarterly 327.

569 Soto 55.

570 E Fernandes, 'The Influence of de Soto's The Mystery of Capital' (2002) 14 Land Lines 5; A Gilbert, 'On the Mystery of Capital and the Myth of Hernando de Soto' (2002) 24 International Development Planning Rev 1; C Lemmen, The Social Tenure Domain Model (2000); Also two UN initiatives – the Global Campaign for Secure Tenure and the Global Land Tools Network (GLTN).

571 The Constitution of the Republic of South Africa (1996).

572 Merwe, Waal and Miller 168–170.

cedures.[573] Legislative initiatives and reforms are primarily viewed as allowing 'the concept of ownership to fulfil its social function by *inter alia* eradicating fundamental inequalities that exist in contemporary society'.[574] The conceptual changes of the institution of property were illustrated by the *Diepsloot* case, where landowners tried to prevent the settlement of homeless persons, arguing the diminution of value to their land, but the courts rejected their claims, arguing for the changing contours of ownership.[575] Recent constitutional jurisprudence also tends to exclude the possibility of indirect expropriation.[576] In *Du Toit v Minister of Transport,* it was held that expropriation is a crucial power of a state and a tool for the redistribution of land.[577] Thus, property protection at the national level is lower than the investment protection standard provided by the South African BITs.[578]

Article 22 of the Namibian Constitution also allows the limitation of property rights, provided the law affecting it is 'of general application, shall not negate the essential content thereof, and shall not be aimed at a particular individual' and 'specify the ascertainable extent of such limitation'.[579] A similar limitation of rights provision is found in the South African Constitution Article 36, and in Section 86(2) of the Zimbabwean Constitution of 2013:

> The fundamental rights and freedoms … may be limited only in terms of a law of general application and to the extent that the limitation is fair, reasonable, necessary and justifiable in a democratic society based on openness, justice, human dignity, equality and freedom, taking into account all relevant factors…[580]

573 Ibid 167–168.

574 AJ van der Walt, 'Towards the Development of Post-apartheid Land Law: An Exploratory Survey' 1990 *De Jure* 1.

575 *Diepsloot Resident's and Landowners's Association v Administrator, Transvaal* 3 SA 336 (A) [1994].

576 Andre van der Walt and Rachael Walsh, 'Comparative Constitutional Property Law' in Michele Graziadei and Lionel D Smith (eds), *Comparative property law: global perspectives* (Edward Elgar Publishing 2017) 212 citing *Agri South Africa v Minister for Minerals and Energy* ZACC 9 [2013] 33; Fola Adeleke, 'Human rights and international investment arbitration' (2016) 32 South African Journal on Human Rights 48, 59.

577 *Du Toit v Minister of Transport* 1 SA 297 (Constitutional Court of South Africa) [2006] para 25–26.

578 Schneiderman, *Constitutionalizing Economic Globalization: Investment Rules and Democracy's Promise* 145; Adeleke, 58.

579 Constitution of the Republic of Namibia; Walt 317.

580 Constitution of Zimbabwe Amendment (No 20) Act <https://www.zimlii.org/zw/legislation/num-act/2013/Amendment%20No.%2020%20of%20The%20Constitution%20of%

Article 44(2) of the Nigerian Constitution also includes a long list of subject matters, where state measures affecting property rights will not be treated as expropriation.[581] The extent of police powers is discussed in *the Union of Campement Sites Owners and Lessees v The Government of Mauritius* where it was held that a tax is a liability, not expropriation.[582] However, in *Commissioner of Taxes v CW (Pvt) Ltd*[583] and *Nyambirai v National Social Security Authority and Another,* the Zimbabwean courts presumed that taxation could be assessed from the perspective of property protection.[584] In *Harksen v Lane* it was held that temporarily assigning of property to a bankruptcy administrator does not amount to expropriation.[585] *Davies and others v the Minister of Land, Agriculture and Water Development* was an important precedent confirming that regulatory deprivations were not compensated in Zimbabwe,[586] but after the expulsion of white farmers without any compensation any distinction between expropriation and deprivation probably became meaningless.

It can be said that most African states are still developing their stance *vis-à-vis* property, and despite common law influences are leaning towards the communitarian version of property with sometimes quite extreme enthusiasm.[587] For example, during the certification of the Constitution, the South African Constitutional Court not only stated that there is 'no universally recognized formulation of the right to property', but also that there is no universal standard for compensation.[588] Thus Article 25 (3) of the Constitution allows compensation at less than full market value:

> The amount of the compensation and the time and manner of payment must be just and equitable, reflecting an equitable balance between the public inter-

---

20Zimbabwe/Constitution%20of%20Zimbabwe%20-%2020th%20Amendment%2022 %20May%202013.pdf> accessed on 5April2018.

581 Constitution of the Federal Republic of Nigeria (1999) <http://www.nigeria-law.org/ConstitutionOfTheFederalRepublicOfNigeria.htm > accessed on 12 May 2025.

582 *The Union of Campement Sites Owners and Lessees v The Government of Mauritius* MR 100 [1984].

583 *Commissioner of Taxes v CW (Pvt) Ltd* 3 ZLR 361 (Zimbabwean Supreme Court) [1989], affirming [1988] 2 ZLR 27 (HC).

584 *Nyambirai v National Social Security Authority and another* 1 LRC 64 (Zimbabwean Supreme Court) [1996].

585 *Harksen v Lane* CCT 9/97, 2 LRC 171 (CC SA) [1998].

586 *Davies and others v the Minister of Land, Agriculture and Water Development* (1) BCLR 83 (Zimbabwean High Cout) [1995].

587 Elsabé van der Sijde, 'Reconsidering the relationship between property and regulation: A systemic constitutional approach' (Doctor of Laws, Stellenbosch University 2015) 281–282.

588 Allen, *The Right to Property in Commonwealth Constitutions* 80.

est and the interests of those affected, having regard to all relevant circumstances, including

(a) the current use of the property;
(b) the history of the acquisition and use of the property;
(c) the market value of the property;
(d) the extent of direct state investment and subsidy in the acquisition and beneficial capital improvement of the property; and
(e) the purpose of the expropriation.

In 2025 the Expropriation Bill was enacted, aligning it with the Constitution,[589] allowing expropriation for just compensation and allowing expropriation in exceptional cases without compensation, such as when the land is not being used or its market value is lower than state investment or subsidy.[590] Other African constitutions include similar limitations on the compensation guarantee and rarely provide for a full market value compensation standard.[591]

17 Diversity of National Property Regimes

Traditionally, Western European constitutions were designed to protect against arbitrary sovereign decisions, but they also have deeply embedded communitarian ideas about social order. An individualistic understanding of property is accompanied by a well-functioning social structure with adequate protection of general interests, such as environment and heritage protection, public administration, health, education and social welfare. Relatively strong property protection is balanced by communitarian interests that are protected by law and by state institutions in other ways.

The Anglo-American societies lean towards the individualistic understanding of property. Very often, property is perceived as a tool for satisfying personal preferences, but at the same time, property is not an absolute right either: extensive public regulation permeates all aspects of societal life, which is not considered an interference with private and individual rights. Due to the effects of equity in common law, many personal rights are treated as property for the purpose of private and commercial law if they satisfy certain criteria,

---

589 Expropriation Act No 13 (2024) (South Africa) <https://www.parliament.gov.za/storage/app/media/Acts/2024/Act_13_of_2024_Expropriation_Act_2024.pdf> accessed 12 May 2025.

590 Ibid section 12(3).

591 Walt 489.

but for the purpose of constitutional protection against interference of the state, a separate concept and criteria have been developed that are more restrictive. Typically, tangible property and certain traditional forms of intangible property fall within the category of protected 'constitutional property', while there is no guarantee against the interference with other rights or interests.[592]

Changing notions of wealth also influenced the legally recognised scope of property. More advanced and stable economies are more likely to provide constitutional protection to intangible wealth, including contractual rights, claims to money, franchises, goodwill, licences, permits, and quotas, whereas developing states tend to have more traditional, narrower views on the objects of property.

In Eastern Europe, Asia, Africa and Latin America, despite the liberal language of constitutions, societies still maintain hopes for distributive justice, where common interests prevail over individual interests. Thus, in comparison to the Western tradition, state interventionism there is usually not perceived as an encroachment on individual rights.

All reviewed national legal systems have an equivalents to the expropriation (taking, eminent domain or compulsory acquisition), which requires compensation, and the state's regulatory or police power, which is not compensable. However, there is an infinite variety of conditions attached to each of them. Some national courts tend to be more, some less deferential to the legislature or executive powers when interpreting a public purpose or interest,[593] but very often the statutes are very permissive and allow expropriation even for the benefit of another private party.[594] Many developed states adhere to the proportionality test, requiring a nexus between the purpose of legislation and burden on the individual; however, there is no uniform answer to what happens if regulations fail the proportionality test.

There are inevitable variations with regard to indirect expropriation. For example, American jurisprudence will be more tolerant of the limitations on rights imposed by urban planning, while European practice will more fre-

592 Allen, *The Right to Property in Commonwealth Constitutions* 10.

593 Cheng-Yi Huang, 'Judicial Deference to Legislative Delegation and Administrative Discretion in New Democracies: Recent Evidence from Poland, Taiwan, and South Africa' in Susan Rose Ackerman and Peter L. Lindseth (eds), *Comparative Administrative Law* (2010) 466.

594 Vincent Martenet, 'Comparative Perspectives on Expropriation and Other Takings: England, France, Germany, and the United States' in Martina Conticelli and Thomas Perroud (eds), *Procedural Requirements for Administrative Limits to Property Rights* (Oxford Academic, Oxford University Press 2022) 273.

quently require compensation for urban planning decisions that prohibit certain development of the land. Constitutional jurisprudence of a few developed economies maintains that especially harsh and unequal interference with private property should amount to indirect expropriation,[595] while a number of developing states do not recognise the doctrine of indirect expropriation or regulatory takings.

Most states recognise that expropriation has to be properly authorised, preferably by a statute, and in the public interest, and that the state has to provide some form of compensation. However, the standard of compensation varies, ranging from the full market value favoured in developed countries to the discretion to determine compensation principles, to minimal compensation in developing countries, considering some wide legal reforms involving the redistribution of wealth.[596]

This chapter has tried to map the broad range of national solutions available to the question of how to balance individual and society's interests. Hopefully, it will dispel the myth of a single international property protection standard or the conviction that a global compact exists over it.

Although it was initially assumed that legal traditions might play a significant role in shaping the national understanding of property, it became apparent that integration with Western structures and the stage of development have more correlations with attitudes towards property and investment. The level of protection afforded to individuals or the level of permissible state interference is a result of historical compromises among different social groups within each particular society. Economic, social, and other circumstances contribute to this delicate balance, which can be easily disrupted by revolutions or changing conditions. Land reforms were contentious issues everywhere, as the reforms trying to remedy historic inequality represent a substantial interference with incumbent property rights. Almost all states that managed to reform their land laws are doing overall better than those that failed to do so, meaning that absolute property rights, which prevent necessary economic reforms, are actually detrimental to a society's prosperity.

Property regime is an integral part of the societal fabric and cannot be easily exported to other societies without the accompanying social order. Thus, efforts to transplant the individualistic property protection regime of developed states into developing countries will most likely not only result in resentment but also fail to improve the living standards for the people of the recipient state. A high level of property protection is primarily geared and best suited

595 Ibid 273.

596 Allen, *The Right to Property in Commonwealth Constitutions* 12.

for the safeguarding of the *status quo* and current distribution of wealth, which is not an adequate strategy for most developing states.

The next chapter will demonstrate how certain selective elements of domestic property regimes, primarily individualistic and representing the neoliberal order, were incorporated into international practice.

CHAPTER 4

Protection of Property under International Law

Some national concepts and assumptions about property influenced the development of international law more than others. To expose the root cause of the current controversies surrounding the ISDS, Chapter 4 provides a closer examination of how certain individualistic assumptions about property have been incorporated into international law. The chapter walks through the most important stages of international law development and shows how communitarian notions of property were sidelined and left at the margins of international law.

To claim the customary nature of foreign property protection, many authors argued that property protection had existed since ancient times.[1] However, this general fact of the existence of private property is used to support a particular version of the property regime, namely individualistic, which is observed only in modern times.

The historical and empirical record of property protection throughout the last two millennia has been very controversial: it ranges from slavery and colonial occupation to massive nationalisations. At the same time, most societies had some form of private property system of their own, which differs from the version of property protection projected internationally. While domestic property regimes undergo creative destruction together with the evolution of society, international claims concerning property for a long time were a reflection of power relations, trying to impose a more individualistic understanding of property. The dominant claims and discussions on property in international law, wilfully or ignorantly, tried to ignore the philosophical complexity and diversity of property regimes.[2] For example, to impose their own understanding of property and world order upon the rest of the world, powerful states and international actors have creatively taken advantage of Kant, Locke, and Adam Smith's legacy.[3] The writings and teachings that could be generalised as the natural law school contain substantive reservations and represent very particular reactions to the historical circumstances of seventeenth and

1 Anderson 1927; International Law Association 1926; Roth 1949; Mann 1959. For the overview of custom as an international investment law source see: Aspremont 10.

2 di Robilant 280.

3 Koskenniemi, *To the Uttermost Parts of the Earth: Legal Imagination and International Power 1300–1870* 622, 957.

 | HTTPS://DOI.ORG/10.1163/9789004763517-005

eighteenth-century Europe. Regardless, in the nineteenth-century, these natural law ideas about individualistic property and minimal state interference found their way into international case law, but were used in completely different settings and without any caveats attached to the initial philosophical writings. The melange of these ideas about property forms a dominant narrative in European international law.

The grip of this conventional wisdom on property in international law is so strong that it requires a conscious effort to dispel it. The simplified views on property, ignoring its communitarian underpinnings, deprive the international community not only of a more holistic understanding of property, but also of a language to articulate alternatives and a possibility to communicate meaningfully with other societies holding different views.

1 The Contested Custom of Alien Property Protection

Despite Plato and Aristotle's different stances regarding private property, both would have likely agreed that, in ancient Greece, foreigners had no rights at all.[4] For example, 'in ancient Greek and Latin, the terms for "barbarian," "stranger," and "enemy" were originally synonymous'.[5] In a similar vein, the Roman law system, despite providing strong foundations for private laws, also had no regard for aliens, treating them as outlaws.[6] Although budding concepts of individual rights were used in European struggles against the popes and monarchs,[7] private foreigners were completely helpless throughout the Middle Ages.[8] Later, during the Renaissance, in the context of the Great Discoveries and subsequent colonisation, the legal position of an alien and that of an alien's property greatly depended on whether the alien was European and Christian, as well as whether the alien could rely on the military might of his home country.[9]

---

4 Edwin Borchard, 'Minimum Standard of the Treatment of Aliens' Faculty Scholarship Series <http://digitalcommons.law.yale.edu/fss_papers/3469> 445, accessed 15 May 2025.

5 David J Bederman, *International Law in Antiquity* (Cambridge University Press 2001) 120, 122.

6 Oliver J Thatcher, ed, *The Library of Original Sources*, vol 3, *The Roman World* (Milwaukee: University Research Extension Co 1901) 9–11; Edwin Borchard, *The diplomatic protection of citizens abroad* (1914) 47–48.

7 Garnsey, *Thinking about property from antiquity to the age of revolution* 43; Boyce 215.

8 Probably with the exception of diplomatic envoys, which later developed into diplomatic immunity: Borchard, 'Minimum Standard of the Treatment of Aliens' 445.

9 Victoria First Relectio, s 3, 151, 152; Fitzmaurice 60.

After the Westphalian peace, territorial sovereignty was one of the main organising principles of international law in Europe.[10] Aliens were typically 'prohibited from owning, inheriting or bequeathing real property, or from engaging in legal disputes about property'.[11] Emmerich de Vattel argued that foreigners were subject to the local law and any disputes should be 'settled by the local judge and according to the local laws', but a sovereign should protect foreigners 'as his own subjects and to see that they enjoy, as far as depends on him, perfect security'.[12] Emmerich de Vattel also developed the idea of diplomatic protection by claiming that a sovereign 'cannot claim any rights over the person of a foreigner who by his mere entrance into its territory does not become its subject', nor over his property.[13] However, the claims about the protection of alien property were almost always shaded by self-interest and no more than an allegation.[14]

The natural law theories challenged the idea of territoriality and contributed to the development of individual rights, which were also used in the context of property relations as a weapon 'against feudalism and absolutism'.[15] At the same time, natural law ideas justified war against indigenous communities if they refused to engage in trade and commerce with European powers.[16] Natural law ideas also justified European settlements outside Europe because those lands were allegedly unoccupied and uncultivated.[17] In the process, indigenous proprietary regimes for resource and risk allocation were of no interest to European powers. At the beginning of the nineteenth century, in the absence of clear international property protection rules, the use of force

10 Brownlie 500.

11 Raingard Esser, 'Citizenship and Immigration in 16th and Early 17th-Century England' in Ellis, Hálfdanarson and Isaacs (eds), *Citizenship in Historical Perspective* (Pisa University Press 2006) 240.

12 Emmerich de Vattel, *Law of Nations or the Principles of Natural Law* (Charles D Fenwick tr, Carnegie Institution of Washington 1916) s 103–104, 145.

13 Ibid s 108–109, 146.

14 Miles, *The origins of international investment law: empire, environment, and the safeguarding of capital* 22–24, 29; Lauren A Benton, *Law and colonial cultures: legal regimes in World history, 1400–1900* (Cambridge University Press 2002) 11.

15 Stephen C Neff, 'Peace and prosperity: commercial aspects of peacemaking' in Randall Lesaffer (ed), *Peace Treaties and International Law in European History: From the Late Middle Ages to World War One* (Cambridge University Press 2004) 365; See also Martti Koskenniemi, 'The Advantage of Treaties: International Law in the Enlightenment' (2009) 13 The Edinburgh Law Review 27, 45.

16 Koskenniemi 4, 113.

17 Koskenniemi, *To the Uttermost Parts of the Earth: Legal Imagination and International Power 1300–1870* 699.

'was seen as a tool for the pursuit of national interest'.[18] Nissel conceptualises this era as pre-legalism defined by unilaterally asserted breaches, violent reprisals and diplomatic protection.[19]

The end of the nineteenth century witnessed a transition to *ad hoc* legalism defined by messy *ad hoc* arbitrations usually imposed by force on new and vulnerable Latin American states in exchange for their international recognition.[20] Around this time, a liberal understanding of property was firmly established, although not uncontested, in Western societies. Claims regarding the universality of property protection gradually began to emerge in the international settings of Western governments and their scholars, despite the fact that, just a few decades ago, indigenous societies were deprived of the possibility to benefit from precisely the same right.[21] Since '[d]omestically Anglo-American lawyers canonised "property rights" within the common law during the late nineteenth century',[22] internationally '[t]he U.S. and other governments presented alien [property] rights as a matter of settled international practice'.[23] For example, one of the mixed United States–Mexico Claims Commissions echoed an extremely individualistic version of John Locke's and Immanuel Kant's theories stripped of their communitarian underpinnings by stating:

> Man must produce, appropriate and exchange, and he is destined, obliged and commanded to create and own individual property; the more distinctly so the further he succeeds in removing from the communistic state of the savage.[24]

The intra-American arbitrations chaired by Western-trained arbitrators helped to repackage the individualistic concept of property protection and present it as solid international law. Despite the grand rhetoric, those *ad hoc* arbitrations rarely provided legal sources for their reasoning or motivation.[25] Dumberry agrees that, often, tribunals asserting a customary rule of property

18 Neff 365; Jochen von Bernstorff, 'The Use of Force in International Law before World War I: On Imperial Ordering and the Ontology of the Nation-State' (2018) 29 European Journal of International Law 233.

19 Nissel 356–357.

20 Ibid 77.

21 Koskenniemi 113–114, 256.

22 Nissel 181 (footnotes omitted).

23 Ibid 145.

24 *FW Stückle v Mexico No 901*, 19 July 1871 in John Bassett Moore, *History and Digest of the International Arbitrations to Which the United States has been a Party*, vol 3 (Hein, Online 1898) 2936.

25 Nissel 144–145; Fabian Cardenas and Jean d'Aspremont, 'International investment law in Latin America: universalizing resistance' in Sufyan Droubi and Cecilia Juliana Flores

protection 'have not conducted their *own* analysis regarding the existence of customary rules'.[26] The awards were incoherent, and outcomes depended 'on the identities of litigating parties and arbitrators'.[27] Based on this assemblage of philosophical theories, limited nineteenth and early twentieth century predominantly intra-American arbitration practice, some states, authors and tribunals claim that a customary international norm on the protection of property emerged.[28] Western countries supported these claims not only with force but also with the philosophical, social, economic, and political frameworks developed in Western societies,[29] where individual rights were contrasted with and limited the state's (sovereign's) authority. Meanwhile, newly emerging and developing, as well as politically and economically unstable states, were trying to defend their newly found sovereignty from any external interferences by clinging to the old concept of territoriality.[30]

During that same nineteenth century, other parts of the world had different understandings of property and corresponding practices. The property question became one of the most disputed issues when visions of capitalist and communist world orders clashed.[31] Initially, the Russian Empire, but later Soviet Russia, prioritised national interests over the individual.[32] Also, Hindu law in India had a predominantly communitarian understanding of prop-

---

Elizondo (eds), *Latin America and International Investment Law* (Manchester University Press 2022) 403.

26 Patrick Dumberry, *The Formation and Identification of Rules of Customary International Law in International Investment Law* (Cambridge University Press 2016) 411.

27 Nissel 363–364.

28 Rudolf Dolzer, 'New Foundations of the Law of Expropriation of Alien Property' (1981) 75 American Journal of International Law 553, 557–572; Elihu Lauterpacht, 'International Law and Private Foreign Investment' (1997) 4 Indiana Journal of Global Legal Studies 259, 263–267; Kenneth J Vandevelde, 'Sustainable liberalism and the international investment regime' (1998) 19 Michigan Journal of International Law 373, 379–381, 384–390; OECD, 'Indirect Expropriation and the Right to Regulate in International Investment Law' 2004, 3; Campbell McLachlan, Laurence Shore and Matthew Weiniger, *International Investment Arbitration: Substantive Principles* (Oxford University Press 2007) 16; Dumberry 407; *Generation Ukraine v Ukraine (ICSID)* para 11.3; *Elettronica Sicula SpA (ELSI) case (United States v Italy)* ICJ Rep (ICJ) [1989] 15, paras 120–130; *M Meerapfel Sohne AG v Central African Republic* (ICSID) para 300.

29 Liberal attitudes to the property were influential even in the nineteenth century Latin America: Montt 41.

30 International Court of Justice, *Barcelona Traction, Light and Power Company Case: Separate Opinion of Judge Padilla Nervo* (1970) 246–248.

31 Kathryn Greenman and others, 'International Law and Revolution: 1917 and Beyond' in Anna Saunders and others (eds), *Revolutions in International Law: The Legacies of 1917* (Cambridge University Press 2021) 3.

32 Mälksoo, *Russian Approaches to International Law* 51.

erty.[33] In Asia, Confucian values and principles contributed to the widely held understanding that the interests of a centralised, hierarchical, stable, harmonious, and orderly society are more important than individual rights or private property.[34] Similarly, Africa and Latin America leaned towards a more communitarian approach to property than Western legal traditions.[35]

Whether individualistic or communitarian, in the nineteenth century, the international practice of protecting alien private property, with its numerous national exceptions and unclear contours, was highly contested. Cohen provided a list of examples when 'valuable property privileges [were] abolished without any compensation'.[36] D'Aspremont also argued that international property protection 'fail[ed] to meet the minimum threshold in terms of normative content that is necessary for such norms possibly to constitute (or give rise to) a customary rule'.[37] The concept of customary international law is wrought with its own controversies, which contribute to the difficulty of establishing a customary international scope of property and rules on property protection. The controversy of the customary nature of alien property protection is evident in the discussions over the international minimum standard.[38] If property was a relative concept, then sovereign states should be entitled to regulate property relations, including those affecting foreigners, within their territory, and non-discrimination principle should be sufficient for property protection. However, if property was a universal concept, as most Western states claimed, a universal minimum property protection standard that all states should adhere to should exist.

Unfortunately, even different versions of the same treatise presented conflicting views, indicating the shifting and varied attitudes. Oppenheim claimed

---

33 Sen 6–7, 24, 51–52.

34 John C H Wu, 'Chinese Legal Philosophy – A Brief Historical Survey, Chinese Culture 1 (1958) 39; Ho, 7, 13.

35 H Patrick Glenn, *Legal Traditions of the World: Sustainable Diversity in Law* (5th edn, Oxford University Press 2014) (2004) 69.

36 Cohen 23–26.

37 Aspremont 34.

38 Elihu Root, 'The Basis of Protection to Citizens Residing Abroad' (1910) 4 The American Journal of International Law 521; Borchard, *The Diplomatic Protection of Citizens Abroad* 516–518; Lionel Morgan Summers, 'The Calvo Clause' (1932) 19 Virginia law review 459; Andreas Hans Roth, 'The minimum standard of international law applied to aliens' (Leiden AW Sijthoff 1949) 117; S N Guha Roy, 'Is the Law of Responsibility of States for Injuries to Aliens a Part of Universal International Law?' (1961) 55 American Journal of International Law 889–890; Amerasinghe 125; García-Amador, Sohn and Baxter 53, 206–207; Richard B Lillich, *International Law of State Responsibility for Injuries to Aliens* (University Press of Virginia 1993) 3–6; M. Sornarajah, *The International Law on Foreign Investment* (Cambridge University Press, 2010) 122–128; Montt 36–48.

that 'foreigners fall at once under the territorial supremacy of the State they enter' and that the host states should only treat a foreigner with consideration, usually understood as non-discrimination, accompanied by some form of the national judicial system where the complaints could be heard:

> every State is by the Law of Nations compelled to grant to foreigners equality before the law with its citizens as far as safety of person and property is concerned.[39]

Later versions of that treatise, edited by Jennings and Watts, argued that the international minimum standard applies to alien property.[40] Numerous other twentieth-century scholars claimed that the protection of alien property constituted a minimum standard of treatment of foreigners, which was obligatory because of its customary nature.[41] Paparinskis echoes such claims, although admitting that it might be based on erroneous grounds.[42]

This claim of the customary status of property protection, its repetition and associated power dynamics represent remarkable and unexplored episodes of international law that deserve critical analysis.[43] The claims regarding the customary nature of property protection are usually based on *Norwegian Shipowners' Claims*,[44] the *Case Concerning Certain German Interests in Polish Upper Silesia*,[45] and the *Neer* case.[46] However, these cases have nearly no

39 Lassa Oppenheim, *International Law: A Treatise* (8th edn, Longmans, Green 1905) 376.

40 Lassa Oppenheim, Robert Jennings and Arthur Watts, *Oppenheim's international law: Peace*, vol 1 (9th edn, Longman Group UK Ltd 1992) 912.

41 Nicholas R Doman, 'Compensation for Nationalised Property in Post-War Europe' (1950) 3 International Law Quarterly 323; García-Amador, Sohn and Baxter 53, 212–213; Escarcena 2, 23; Sprankling 8; Andrew Paul Newcombe and Lluís Paradell, *Law and practice of investment treaties: standards of treatment* (Wolters Kluwer Law & Business 2009) 321.

42 Martins Paparinskis, 'The international minimum standard and fair and equitable treatment' (2013) 18.

43 Fitzmaurice explained how similar and related idea of occupation was manipulated to achieve European political goals: Fitzmaurice 332; Koskenniemi showed how sovereign power and property intertwined to build European empires: Koskenniemi, *To the Uttermost Parts of the Earth: Legal Imagination and International Power 1300–1870* 699.

44 *Norwegian shipowners claims* (*Norway v USA*) Reports of International Arbitral Awards [1922] (Anderson, Vogt, Valloton) 13 October 1922, 307–346.

45 *Certain German Interests in Polish Upper Silesia* (*Germany v Poland*) Series A No 7 (PCIJ) [1926].

46 US-Mexican General Claims Commission's award in *VLFH Neer and PE Neer* (*United States v Mexico*) UNRIAA 4 (US-Mexico General Claims Commission) [1926] Opinion, 15 October 1926, 61–62.

evidence of an established customary international law rule on property protection.

For example, in *Norwegian Shipowners' Claims*, 'the United States declared its willingness and desire to make just compensation for the property taken and recognized its liability to make compensation'[47] relying mostly on its own domestic law.[48] Because the USA accepted the liability, the award could not be said to represent the customary international law, and no analysis has been made to establish the general practice of states and *opinio juris* on the question. However, most of the later scholars and tribunals conveniently ignored that fact, misrepresenting that the award upheld a customary international law rule.[49]

The *Case Concerning Certain German Interests in Polish Upper Silesia* was based on the Geneva Convention regarding Upper Silesia of 1922, not customary international law.[50] The PCIJ did not examine whether customary international law protected the property of aliens; any remarks about it were only *obiter dictum*.[51] The President of the Arbitral Tribunal for Upper Silesia later argued:

> Of bilateral conventions limiting legislative power there are some examples. The most far-reaching is probably the German–Polish Convention of May 15, 1922, relative to Upper Silesia, which stipulates certain limitations to legislation for a period of fifteen years, combined with a system of compensation for the suppression or diminution of certain vested rights. This, however, constitutes exceptional law. It is neither declaratory nor even illustrative of general international law. For no general customary rule limiting the legislative power of states ... has ever been shown to exist. Nor has it ever been accepted in a multilateral law-making document.[52]

---

47 *Norwegian shipowners claims* (*Norway v USA*) 313.

48 Ibid 332; For other arguments see John Fischer Williams, 'International Law and the Property of Aliens' (1928) 9 British Yearbook of International Law 10; *Contra* Alexander P Fachiri, 'International Law and the Property of Aliens' (1929) 10 British Yearbook of International Law 41.

49 See for example Sprankling 8; *Mondev International Ltd v USA* (ICSID) para 98; Crawford gives an example of *Norwegian shipowners claims* as an instance of the application of equity: Ian Brownlie, *Principles of public international law* (7th edn, Oxford University Press 2008) 45.

50 *Certain German Interests in Polish Upper Silesia* (*Germany v Poland*) 20.

51 Ibid 21, 22.

52 G Kaeckenbeeck, 'The Protection of Vested Rights in International Law' (1936) 17 British Year Book of International Law 14. See also G Kaeckenbeeck, 'The Character and Work of the Arbitral Tribunal of Upper Silesia' (1935) 21 Transactions of the Grotius Society 27,

On the basis of the treaty protection afforded to the *Chorzów Factory*, some authors imply the existence of customary international law rules on property based on some universal standard:

> [t]he PCIJ also held, … that an illegal seizure of property requires reparation. These judgments reflected the view that states owe a duty to other states to treat foreign nationals and their property according to a minimum standard of treatment.[53]

The *Neer* case[54] is also credited with the creation of the customary rule. However, many authors agree that the *Neer* standard applies to 'claims predicated on the denial of justice',[55] but not for the protection of private property.[56] Bray notes that in a decision of 'less than three pages', the author provided no authority for its main conclusions: that 'the international, not domestic standard' applied to the treatment of aliens'.[57] The *Neer* neither analysed the international customary law nor confirmed the existence of the protection of property.

This yields a paradoxical situation in which the popular myth about the 'universal and customary' protection of property is baseless. As noted by D'Aspremont, there is very little customary in international customary law.[58]

36–37; Georges Kaeckenbeeck, 'La protection internationale des droits acquis (Volume 59)' in The Hague Academy of International Law, *Collected Courses of the Hague Academy of International Law* (Brill 1937) 412.

53 Newcombe and Paradell 14–15 (footnotes omitted). See also Dumberry 67–68; Dolzer, 'New Foundations of the Law of Expropriation of Alien Property' 558–559; Thomas Walde and Borzu Sabahi, 'Compensation for Expropriation and Action Tantamount to Expropriation' in Peter Muchlinski, Federico Ortino and Christoph Schreuer (eds), *The Oxford Handbook of International Investment Law* (Oxford University Press 2008) 1068; Jeswald W Salacuse, *The Law of Investment Treaties* (2th edn, Oxford University Press 2015) 64–65; even UNCTAD publication implies that *Chorzow factory* judgment constitutes international law without specifying that it is based on treaty, not custom: *UNCTAD series on issues in international investment agreements II* (2012) 7. For the contrary view see Sornarajah, *The International Law on Foreign Investment* 85.

54 *VLFH Neer and PE Neer* (*United States v Mexico*) 61.

55 Jan Paulsson and Georgios Petrochilos, 'Neer-ly Misled?' (2007) 22 ICSID Review 247. See also Heather L Bray, 'The Neer Rumour' (2012) 25 Hague Yearbook of International Law 211; Paparinskis 18.

56 M Sornarajah, *The International Law on Foreign Investment* (3rd edn, Cambridge University Press 2010) 122.

57 Bray 205.

58 Jean D'Aspremont, *The Discourse on Customary International Law* (Oxford University Press 2021) 3, 5; Cardenas and d'Aspremont 386.

Paparinskis explanation that '[s]tate practice based on an arguably erroneous premise is just as capable of contributing to customary law as well-informed practice' relied on Byers' argument that a mistaken belief about the existence of custom can prevent the new customary law rule from establishing itself.[59] Paparinskis analogy with Byers' argument was a stretch. Byers analysed the reverse situation: not how a false belief can create a new customary law, but rather how a false belief can prevent the formation of customary law. For the sake of clarity and predictability, the threshold of evidence for the formation of custom should be higher than for the argument that there is no custom.

Byers was analysing two instances from the history of international law. First, in the case of state immunity, he was arguing that a false belief about the absolute nature of state immunity was preventing the formation of the limited state immunity rule. Second, in the case of the breadth of the territorial sea, Byers claimed that disagreements regarding the extent of the territorial sea delayed the establishment of a 12-mile rule.[60] Byers does not provide a positive case for property protection in customary international law. Any innuendos that erroneous interpretations of some early cases by a few states, however influential, could create an international custom should be treated with scepticism.

Contrary to popular belief,[61] the three cases mentioned above, as well as a number of other nineteenth-century cases *per se*, did not prove the customary nature of the property protection rule. On the contrary, many of them illustrate political settlements achieved through some form of pressure. For example, Sicilians' acquiescence was achieved under the threat of the use of force *in*

59 Paparinskis 18 (footnote omitted); Byers M, *Custom, Power and the Power of Rules* (Cambridge University Press 1999) 111–118.

60 Ibid.

61 Borchard, 'Minimum Standard of the Treatment of Aliens' 453; M. A. B, 'Expropriation of Alien Property' (1960) 109 University of Pennsylvania Law Review 245; G Christie, 'What Constitutes a Taking of Property under International Law?' (1962) British Yearbook of International Law 307, 309; Dolzer, 'New Foundations of the Law of Expropriation of Alien Property' 558; Newcombe and Paradell 14; Escarcena 2, 20, 23; R Doak Bishop, James Crawford and William Michael Reisman, *Foreign Investment Disputes Cases, Materials, and Commentary* (Kluwer Law International 2005) 1063; Sprankling 8; Catherine Redgwell, 'Property Law Sources and Analogies in International Law' in McHarg Aileen and others (eds), *Property and the Law in Energy and Natural Resources* (Oxford University Press 2010) 102–103; *Glamis Gold Ltd v The United States of America* (UNCITRAL) para 22; *Pope & Talbot Inc v Government of Canada* 57; *Genin v Estonia* 6 ICSID Rep 241 [2001] para 367; *Mondev International Ltd v USA* para 115.

Sicilian Sulphur Monopoly case.[62] No judicial decision was rendered, and indemnity was achieved mostly due to the US negotiating efforts in *Rev Jonas King case.*[63] Tribunal was not addressing customary international law, but only the quantum of compensation in *Delagoa Bay Railway case.*[64] Similarly, in the *Portuguese Religious Properties case,* the arbitral tribunal reached a compromise without addressing the content of customary international law.[65] Furthermore, in the *Italian Insurance Monopoly* controversy, Italians agreed to postpone the entry into force of the insurance monopoly law. Consequently, the question of property protection under customary international law was never addressed by adjudicators.[66]

These cases and their settlements are susceptible to divergent interpretations. Kate Miles argues that through the assertion of foreign property protection rules as existing international law, together with the use of force, capital-exporting states directed the evolution of international investment law.[67] Leiter also summarised how concession arbitrations involving Western governments and companies in the first half of the twentieth century tried to promote the individualistic understanding of property through the separation of political and economic life.[68]

States' practices around the world were very different. After the revolutions, Russia and Mexico nationalised their entire economies without compensation.[69] Land reforms were widely implemented in Europe after the WWI. Redistributive elements of property are especially evident in peace trea-

62 *Great Britain v Sicily*, 1831–1832, British State Papers, (1839–1840) vol XXVIII, 1168–1242, vol XXIX, 175–204, vol XXX, 111–120; David Urquhart, The sulphur monopoly (T Brettell 1840) 1.

63 *The United States v Greece* (1853) Moore's Digest, vol VI, 262–264; Whiteman, Damages (1937), vol 2, 1387–1391.

64 *The United States and great Britain v Portugal* (1889–1891) 2 Moore, History and Digest of the International Arbitrations, 1865 (1898).

65 *Great Britain, France, Spain v Portugal* (1913), (1920) I RIAA 7.

66 The opinion of Edouard Clunet published in Bulletin des Assurances (1912) part 3, 51; C Audinet, 'Le monopole des assurances sur la vie en Italie et le droit des etrangers', 20 *Revue Generale De Droit International Public* (1913) 5; The Rumano-Hungarian dispute over the Transylvania expropriations (Budapest, 1924) 152; G H Hackworth, Digest of International Law (1940–1944), vol 5, Government Printing Office, Washington DC 588.

67 Miles, *The Origins of International Investment Law: Empire, Environment, and the Safeguarding of Capital* 69–70.

68 Leiter, *Making the World Safe for Investment: The Protection of Foreign Property (1922–1959)* 21.

69 Miles, '1917: Property, Revolution and Rejection in International Law' 272.

ties.[70] The unsettled nature of the property protection rule was confirmed by Mexico in 1938 when it expropriated American oil interests: '[f]or over two years following expropriation, the oil companies made extravagant demands for compensation, which the Mexicans repeatedly rejected'.[71] Finally, Mexico agreed to pay a fraction of the requested sums by signing the settlement agreement, and the United States agreed to it, ignoring the requirements of the Hull formula sent at the beginning of the dispute,[72] which was only a starting point of the negotiating position, not customary law. The same could have been said about other states' pleadings and public statements – their value as customary law evidence was notably low because they often represented rhetoric and self-interested claims, not the law itself.

Overall, in the middle of the twentieth century, the claim that customary international rule of property protection existed was problematic because '[t]he controversy concerning the national and international standards' prevented the formation of customary law.[73] In addition to the difficulties with universal recognition and acceptance, the content of the property protection rule was not clear:

> the content of the protection so offered to aliens remained in limbo and the object of incommensurable controversy, thereby putting into question the customary status commonly attributed to that rule.[74]

2 Post-WWII Developments and Consolidation Efforts

In the immediate aftermath of the WWII, several factors influenced the legal development of alien property protection. First, the massive destruction cau-

---

70 Ernest J Schuster, 'The Peace Treaty in Its Effects on Private Property' (1920) 1 British Year Book of International Law 168 and Andrew Martin, 'Private Property, Rights and Interests in the Paris Peace Treaties' (1947) 24 British Year Book of International Law 274.

71 The Office of the Historian of the USA Department of State <https://history.state.gov/milestones/1937-1945/mexican-oil> accessed on 15 May 2025.

72 Ibid.

73 Brownlie, *Principles of Public International Law* (6th edn, Oxford University Press 2003) 503–504, 509. I am relying on the 6th edition of treatise, because in my opinion it better represents the *status quo* of international law. The newer editions engage in progressive development of law, which is questionable: James Crawford and Ian Brownlie, *Brownlie's Principles of Public International Law* (8th edn, Oxford University Press 2012) 626. See also Doman 329; Dumberry also claims that the international minimum standard involved only the non-discriminatory aspect and the denial of justice: Dumberry 63–65.

74 Aspremont 10–11.

sed by the war, along with the ensuing state-led reconstruction effort, decolonisation and the rise of communism with nationalisations of entire economies, challenged the individualistic understanding of property and influenced the individual's relationship with the state.[75] The middle of the twentieth century yielded some nationalisations in France and the Netherlands,[76] but the scale of nationalisations was much wider in Eastern Europe. At the time, Eastern Europe was dominated by Soviet ideology, whose scholars emphasised Russia's distinctiveness from the Western world and denied the universality of international law,[77] especially rules regarding property. Tunkin argued that the doctrine of acquired rights and adequate compensation for nationalised property were common only to the Western tradition, but not to socialist, Asian and African states.[78] He further argued that Soviet states rejected the old principles and norms of international law because they were frequently used as means of enslavement and exploitation.[79] The Soviet Union supported the application of the national standard in the treatment of aliens and their property, as well as proclaimed principles of reciprocity and non-discrimination.[80] Thus, Soviet states recognised neither the universal nature of property nor the obligation to compensate for nationalised alien property.[81] Because the previous international practice had to deal with individual and sometimes arbitrary expropriations or failures to pay debts, the international law in the

75 Samuel Herman, 'War Damage and Nationalization in Eastern Europe' (1951) 16 Law and Contemporary Problems 498, 502–503.

76 Doman 1141–1142.

77 Mälksoo, 'The History of International Legal Theory in Russia: a Civilizational Dialogue with Europe' 226.

78 Grigorij I Tunkin, *Theory of International Law: Translation with an introduction* (William E Butler tr, Allen & Unwin 1974) 198.

79 Ibid 31.

80 Mark Abramovich Plotkin (tr R Biske), '*Legal status of foreigners in the USSR*' (1934) 51, 63; Edmund C Jann, 'Private International Law in the Soviet Union and Eastern Europe' (1965) 22 The Quarterly Journal of the Library of Congress 347, 349, 352, 360; Ferdinand Joseph Maria Feldbrugge, Gerard Pieter Van den Berg and William B. Simons, *Encyclopedia of Soviet law* (M. Nijhoff 1985) 40–41; V S Shevtsov, 'The legal status of foreigners in the USSR' (1975) 5 Denver journal of international law and policy 273–274; See also George Ginsburgs, *The Soviet Union and International Cooperation in Legal Matters* (Nijhoff 1992) 124.

81 Although the USA managed to conclude settlement agreements for lump sum compensations with Poland, Romania, Bulgaria, Hungary and Yugoslavia: Jann 372, 375. For the calculation of compensation for seizure of private property for public use see Peter B

mid-twentieth century was ill-equipped to deal with massive economy-wide general nationalisations.[82]

The challenge to the universal individualistic understanding of property was also exerted by former colonies and new states in Asia, the Middle East, Africa and Latin America, eager to assert their own sovereignty. The developing states wanted to have the freedom to carry out structural reforms, which affected property relations acquired during colonial times. The capital-exporting states, at the same time, preferred to preserve the *status quo* of wealth distribution, insisting on the universal idea of property. The assertiveness of the new and developing states was channelled into the New International Economic Order (NIEO). Whereas the 1803 Resolution on Permanent Sovereignty over Natural Resources of 14 December 1962 required 'appropriate compensation' for expropriated natural resources, the UN General Assembly Resolution 1301 of 1 May, 1974 on the Declaration on the Establishment of the New International Economic Order and the General Assembly Resolution 3281 of 12 December 1974 on the Charter of Economic Rights and Duties of States did not require compensation for the expropriation of alien property.[83] Aspremont argues that the opposition of developing, socialist and Latin American states prevented the emergence of a unified customary international regime of protection of property.[84] Furthermore, the property protection was never absolute 'even in states founded on private enterprise principles' and the vagueness of the principle posed certain problems for establishing the general practice of states.[85] Brownlie concludes that 'the general dogma as to the inviolability of private property can no more be erected into an international duty than other political and economic doctrines'.[86]

The second major factor defining twentieth-century legal development was various initiatives to consolidate the protection of alien property. The list of

Maggs, 'The Security of Individually-Owned Property under Soviet Law' (1961) Duke Law Journal 525, 533–534.

82 Doman 1125; Amerasinghe 127–128.

83 Sprankling argued that NIEO 'shattered the foundations of the pre-war idea of universal property right': Sprankling 12–14.

84 Aspremont 14. However, there are many governments and jurists mainly in Europe and North America, who argued that the protection of property was already established as a customary international law even before the NIEO: Mann, 'Outlines of a History of Expropriation', 203–208.

85 Brownlie, *Principles of Public International Law* (6th edn, Oxford University Press 2003) 509–512.

86 Ibid 512 (footnote omitted).

failed conventions and drafts is long.[87] It is generally agreed that efforts to codify the state responsibility for the damage to alien property in the mid-twentieth century were unsuccessful due to the opposition of Latin American and other developing countries.[88] From all the international initiatives to consolidate alien property protection, only the Convention on the Settlement of Investment Disputes between States and Nationals of Other States (ICSID Convention), which regulates the procedural aspect of disputes, and the Convention Establishing the Multilateral Investment Guarantee Agency of 11 October 1985, have been successful.[89] The success of multilateral procedural agreements is because they side-stepped the main problem; that is, the substantive aspect of property protection.[90]

Finally, the third important factor of the post-WWII developments was the emergence and rapid advancement of human rights law. However, infringements of human rights are still usually subject to the exhaustion of local remedies rule; the obligations under the human rights' instruments are seldom strict, and the enforcement mechanisms are much weaker in comparison with the investment arbitration awards. The parallels between the protection of human rights and property protection are analysed separately in Chapter 5.

The muddied waters of the customary status of property protection together with the frustrated multilateral codification efforts caused the capital-exporting states to turn their attention to consensual and bilateral instruments.[91]

3 Evolution into Investment under Treaty Law

Even in the nineteenth century, consensual protection of property was frequent in the treaties of friendship, commerce and navigation (FCN).[92] Ini-

87 United Nations documents concerning development and codification of international law, Supplement to American Journal of International Law, Volume 41, No 4, October 1947, 82–83; Harvard Law School, *Draft convention on 'Responsibility of States for Damage Done in Their Territory to the Person or Property of Foreigners'* 23 American Journal of International Law Special Supplement 133 (1929); Salacuse 95–96.

88 García-Amador, Sohn and Baxter viii; Nissel 320–344.

89 Aspremont 17.

90 Antonio R Parra, *The history of ICSID* (2017) 18–19.

91 Bernard Kishoiyian, 'The utility of bilateral investment treaties in the formulation of customary international law' (1994) 14 Northwestern Journal of International Law & Business 327, 372–373.

92 Salacuse 88–92. See other overviews of the historical evolution of investment treaties and ISDS: Van Harten 12; Escarcena 112; Slobodian 122.

tially, FCN named 'vessels, cargoes, merchandise and effects' for protection, which later transformed into 'property'[93] or 'property, rights and interests' (*biens, droits et intérêts* (fr)).[94]

The only instance where the ICJ addressed the question of the protection of property under the FCN was the *Elettronica Sicula SpA* (*ELSI*) case.[95] The dispute involved the ELSI's bankruptcy and possible influence on it by the mayor of the Italian town. The ICJ had to decide if the FCN between the United States and Italy applied to indirect ownership, i.e., to protect shareholders' interests in the company.[96] The majority of judges, being mindful that a phrase 'immovable property or interests therein' could include indirect ownership of property rights, in *obiter dictum* refused to extend the FCN protection to the shareholders and concluded that ELSI was insolvent even before the requisitioning order.[97]

The early FCNs were mainly aiming to protect property or goods. Even the first BIT, concluded in 1959 between Germany and Pakistan, and subsequent German investment treaties used the term 'capital' for the protection.[98] In the middle of the twentieth century, the linguistics of 'property' changed to 'investment' and, suddenly, all disagreements regarding the level of protection of private property were seemingly forgotten. This sudden change of opinion and course deserves an explanation, which could be twofold.

First, several private and governmental initiatives 'signal[ed] both a conceptual and semantic change from the traditional notions of protection of aliens and their property' to 'the protection of foreign investment',[99] which was mainly an economic and financial term that lacked a specific and local legal meaning. The Havana Charter for an International Trade Organization of 1948,[100] Draft Statutes of the Arbitral Tribunal for Foreign Investment and the

93 Kenneth J Vandevelde, 'The Bilateral Investment Treaty Program of the United States' (1988) 21 Cornell International Law Journal 205.

94 Redgwell 103.

95 *Elettronica Sicula SpA (ELSI) case (United States v Italy)* ICJ Rep (ICJ) [1989].

96 Ibid para 132.

97 Ibid para 135.

98 Treaty between the Federal Republic of Germany and Pakistan for the Promotion and Protection of Investments of 25 November 1959, International Investment Agreements Navigator, <https://treaties.un.org/doc/Publication/UNTS/Volume%20457/volume-457-I-6575-English.pdf> accessed on 15 May 2025.

99 Newcombe and Paradell 21.

100 Reprinted in UNCTAD, International Investment Instruments: A Compendium, vol 1 (New York, United Nations, 1996) 4.

Foreign Investment Court prepared by the ILA in 1948[101] and the International Code of Fair Treatment for Foreign Investment prepared by the (ICC) in 1949[102] did not use the language of protection of property and instead emphasised the protection of investment for the purpose of development and reconstruction. It seems that the new word 'investment' carried a promise that was disconnected from the past grudges of colonial property protection. Furthermore, the new term 'investment' could have been understood as promising a bargain – that there will be some developmental benefits for the host state arising from the new investment. Dolzer and Schreuer explain that the term 'investment' was used instead of 'property' because investment treaties were supposed only to protect things included in the definitions, not all property rights and interests.[103] For these and possibly other reasons, the term 'investment' seemed more acceptable for the developing countries, which started entering BITs frequently based on the template of the 1967 Draft OECD Convention on the Protection of Foreign Property.[104] However, because 'investment' was predominantly an economic and financial term, which lacked a precise legal meaning comparable to property, it later generated a fair amount of disputes and arbitrations.

Second, the change of opinion can at least partially be explained by a prisoner's dilemma. Developing states together objected to the international and allegedly higher levels of protection of private property. However, on an individual level, each separate developing state had much to gain from the deviation.[105] Thus, one by one, developing states started to abandon their previous positions on property.

Because the international customary law was uncertain and unable to identify the boundaries and priorities between private and communal interests, the treaties attempted to clarify what private interests were protected and how. However, the negotiators of BITs were eager to protect private investment and consciously or unconsciously failed to mention that the protection of private interests' is a result of a balance between private and public values.

---

101 Reprinted in UNCTAD, International Investment Instruments: A Compendium, vol 3 (New York, United Nations, 1996) 259.

102 International Chamber of Commerce, *Fair Treatment for Foreign Investment. International Code* (1949) Brochure No 129 reprinted in UNCTAD, International Investment Instruments: A Compendium, vol 3 (New York: United Nations, 1996) 273.

103 Dolzer and Schreuer 60.

104 Reprinted in UNCTAD, International Investment Instruments: A Compendium, vol 2 (New York United Nations, 1996) 113.

105 Andrew T Guzman, 'Why LDCs sign treaties that hurt them: explaining the popularity of bilateral investment treaties' (1998) 38(4) Virginia journal of International Law 643.

Most BITs concluded between 1960 and 2000 failed to mention that protection of investment is not absolute and has exceptions similar to those found in the national laws. Thus, in the majority of BITs, this lacuna appears ambiguous and allows for conflicting arguments. On the one hand, it could be argued that private interests were given priority over communal interests, leaving no regulatory space at all. On the other hand, it is plausible that the protection of private interests mentioned in the BITs did not limit or influence communal interests exercised via general legislation, even if the latter was not mentioned expressly. This controversy was resolved by adding the relevant 'right to regulate' language in the more recent BITs and investment agreements.[106]

The content of the early investment treaties usually covered at least three substantive issues: the range of economic interests that the treaty protects, the prohibition of expropriation and the standard and manner of compensation.[107] Below, each aspect is dealt with separately.

First, the continual transformation of property protection into the protection of investment is evident in the treaties and academic literature.[108] Early BITs often did not include the definition of investment at all, although they were using the term 'investment' or 'invest' throughout.[109] Germany, Switzerland, and the Netherlands were pioneers of concluding BITs, with Italy following in their footsteps. Capital-exporting states would usually draft the model treaty and use it as a basis for negotiations with other countries.[110] This explains many of the similarities between treaty texts as well as the tiny differences. Although German BITs in the German language used the term '*Kapitalanlagen*', all English translations used the term' investment'.[111]

---

106 For example, the Preamble of Malaysia – India FTA of 2011 <https://investmentpolicy.unctad.org/international-investment-agreements/treaty-files/2629/download> accessed on 15 May 2025; Preamble and Article 23(5) of Partnership and Cooperation Agreement between the European Union and its Member States, of the one part, and the Republic of Iraq, of the other part of 2012 <https://eur-lex.europa.eu/eli/agree_international/2012/418/oj/eng> accessed on 15 May 2025; Article 8.9(1–2) of CETA of 2016 <https://eur-lex.europa.eu/legal-content/EN/TXT/?uri=CELEX:22017A0114(01)#d1e2878-23-1> accessed on 15 May 2025.

107 Newcombe and Paradell 321. See also Dolzer, 'Indirect Expropriation of Alien Property' 41.

108 Article 9(b) of Abs-Showcross draft and Article 9 of 1967 OECD Draft Convention still speaks about 'all property, rights and interests, whether held directly or indirectly, including the interest which a member of a company is deemed to have in the property of the company'.

109 German – Cameroon BIT of 1962 <https://investmentpolicy.unctad.org/international-investment-agreements/treaty-files/588/download> accessed on 15 May 2025.

110 Salacuse 101.

111 Article 1 of German – Malaysian BIT of 1960 <https://investmentpolicy.unctad.org/international-investment-agreements/treaty-files/6606/download> accessed on 15 May 2025.

The 1965 Agreement between Malta and Switzerland on Trade, Protection of Investments and Technical Cooperation discussed protection without ever defining 'property, rights and interests'.[112] Similarly, the Treaty of Friendship and Commerce between Switzerland and Liberia of 1964 used the term '[*l*]*es investissements anciens ou nouveaux ainsi que les biens, droits et intérêts'* without providing a definition and used '*biens, droits et intérêts*' when speaking about expropriation.[113]

Early Dutch treaties containing investment protection did not define 'investment' either, even though this term was used throughout, for example, in the Agreement on Economic Cooperation between the Netherlands and Indonesia of 1968.[114] The Convention Concerning Encouragement of Capital Investment and the Protection of Property of 1963 between the Netherlands and Tunisia used the term 'investments, property, rights and interests',[115] and the Agreement on Economic Cooperation between the Netherlands and Kenya of 1970 used the term 'investments, goods, rights and interests' without defining what was protected.[116]

The United States followed the European lead and developed its model BIT text between 1977 and 1981,[117] which was a mixture of its previous FCNs and European BITs.[118] Following the OECD Draft Convention and European templates, the first USA model BIT from 1981–1983 'defines "investment" with a

112 The Agreement between Malta and Switzerland on Trade, Protection of Investments and Technical Cooperation of 1965 <https://investmentpolicy.unctad.org/international-investment-agreements/treaty-files/1978/download> accessed on 15 May 2025.

113 The Treaty of Friendship and Commerce between Switzerland and Liberia of 1964 <https://investmentpolicy.unctad.org/international-investment-agreements/treaty-files/4821/download> accessed on 15 May 2025.

114 The Agreement on Economic Cooperation between the Netherlands and Indonesia of 1968 <https://investmentpolicy.unctad.org/international-investment-agreements/treaty-files/3329/download> accessed on 15 May 2025.

115 The Convention Concerning Encouragement of Capital Investment and the Protection of Property of 1963 between the Netherlands and Tunisia <https://investmentpolicy.unctad.org/international-investment-agreements/treaty-files/5045/download> accessed on 15 May 2025.

116 The Agreement on Economic Cooperation between the Netherlands and Kenya of 1970 <https://investmentpolicy.unctad.org/international-investment-agreements/treaty-files/1793/download> accessed on 15 May 2025.

117 Vandevelde, 'The Bilateral Investment Treaty Program of the United States' 203–222, Kenneth J Vandevelde, 'U.S. Bilateral Investment Treaties: The Second Wave' (1993) 14 Michigan Journal of International Law 622.

118 Vandevelde, 'U.S. Bilateral Investment Treaties: The Second Wave' 626.

nonexclusive list of examples'.[119] The USA – Zaire BIT that was based on this model provided that:

> (c) 'Investment' means every kind of investment, owned or controlled directly or indirectly, including equity, debt, and service and investment contracts; and includes: (i) tangible and intangible property, including all property rights, such as liens, mortgages pledges, and real security; (ii) a company or shares of stock or other interests in a company or interests in the assets thereof; (iii) a claim to money or a claim to performance having economic value, and associated with an investment; (iv) intellectual and industrial property rights, including rights with respect to copyrights, patents, trademarks, trade names, industrial designs, trade secrets and know how, and goodwill; (v) licenses and permits issued pursuant to law, including those issued for manufacture and sale of products; (vi) any right conferred by law or contract, including rights to search for or utilize natural resources, and rights to manufacture, use and sell products; and (vii) returns which are reinvested.[120]

The typical letter of submittal of BIT to the Senate explained the USA notion of investment that greatly exceeded the constitutional notion of property:

> The BIT concept of 'investment' is broad and designed to be flexible; although numerous types of economic interests are enumerated, the intent is to include *all legitimate interests* in the territory of either Party, whether directly or indirectly controlled by nationals of the other, having economic value or 'associated' with an investment.[121]

Associated activities expanded the definition of investment even further, including:

119 Pamela B Gann, 'The US Bilateral Investment Treaty Program' (1985) 21 Stanford Journal of International Law 381.

120 Article 1 of the Treaty between the United States of America and the Democratic Republic of Congo (formerly Zaire) concerning the Reciprocal Encouragement and Protection of Investment, of 1984 <https://2001-2009.state.gov/documents/organization/43544.pdf> accessed on 15 May 2025.

121 The letter of submittal of the Treaty between the United States of America and the Republic of Turkey concerning the Reciprocal Encouragement and Protection of Investments, of 1985, <https://2001-2009.state.gov/documents/organization/43615.pdf> accessed on 15 May 2025 (emphasis added).

> the organization, control, operation, maintenance and disposition of companies, branches, agencies, offices, factories or other facilities for the conduct of business; the making, performance and enforcement of contracts; the acquisition, use, protection and disposition of property of all kinds including intellectual property rights; the borrowing of funds; the purchase, issuance, and sale of equity shares and other securities; and the purchase of foreign exchange for imports.[122]

Initially, the count of the concluded USA treaties was relatively low, likely due to inflexible negotiating practices;[123] only the second wave of BITs concluded after the collapse of the USSR was successful, which did not substantially alter the definition of investment.[124] Thus, towards the 1990s, the definitions of investment significantly exceeded the traditional concept of property.

Early BITs provided varying descriptions of what could be the subject of expropriation: 'property, rights or interests belonging [to somebody]',[125] 'investments or goods, rights and interests connected with such investments'[126] and 'investments'.[127] BITs concluded from the 1970s onwards began introducing definitions of 'investment' and 'property' that were protected from expropriation.[128] Many of the BITs defined the investments through assets in addition to a non-exhaustive and variable list of examples. Conflicting opinions exist regarding the relationship between investment, assets and specific examples. Cabrol argued that there is a distinction between 'investment' and 'assets' because if states wanted to protect any type of assets, they could have concluded 'an "asset protection treaty" instead of an "investment protection

122 Article 1(g) Treaty between the United States of America and the Republic of Turkey concerning the Reciprocal Encouragement and Protection of Investments of 1985, <https://2001-2009.state.gov/documents/organization/43615.pdf> accessed on 15 May 2025.

123 Vandevelde, 'U.S. Bilateral Investment Treaties: The Second Wave' 628.

124 Salacuse 104.

125 Article 3 of the Convention concerning the Encouragement of Capital Investment and the Protection of Property between the Netherlands and Tunisia of 1963.

126 Article 5 (1) of the Agreement on the encouragement and reciprocal protection of investments between Belgium and Indonesia of 1970 <https://investmentpolicy.unctad.org/international-investment-agreements/treaty-files/5309/download> accessed on 15 May 2025.

127 Article 3(1) of the Treaty between the United States of America and the Republic of Turkey concerning the Reciprocal Encouragement and Protection of Investments, of 1985.

128 Fortier and Drymer 296.

treaty"'.[129] Those who argue for the objective meaning of investment with objective characteristics – not only for the jurisdictional purposes of Article 25 of the ICSID but also for BITs – are opposed by those who insist that there is no need for an inherent meaning of investment, which could exclude some types of transactions from the protection of BITs.[130] The latter position seems counterintuitive to the aim of concluding BITs, which were intended to only protect investments, not any type of transaction or property. Otherwise, the change in terminology is unnecessary – the states could have continued to employ 'property' in their treaties, as was proposed in the countless draft treaties that did not come into effect.

In addition to bilateral initiatives, the only multilateral instrument that was successfully concluded was the Washington Convention that created the ICSID – a specialised machinery for the resolution of investment disputes. The failure of its drafters to agree on the definition of investment is notable, albeit well documented elsewhere.[131] Thus, the ICSID Convention became a 'procedural convention only, setting up machinery for the settlement of investment disputes through arbitration'.[132] World Bank officials contributed enormously to the successful creation of this institutional framework, which set the tone for the later neoliberal interpretations of investment protection.[133]

The second aspect of our inquiry looks at expropriation in the early BITs, where three conditions were usually attached to it as a reaction to the uncertainty of international customary law and the diversity of national property regimes. The lawful expropriation should be for a public purpose, non-discriminatory, and accompanied by compensation.[134] However, early German BITs attached only two conditions: '[i]nvestments of nationals or companies of

---

129 Emmanuelle Cabrol, 'Pren Nreka v. Czech Republic and The Notion of Investment Under Bilateral Investment Treaties. Does "Investment" Really Mean "Every Kind of Asset"?' in Karl Sauvant (ed), *Yearbook on International Investment Law & Policy* (Oxford University Press 2010) 224.

130 Peter Muchlinski, *Scope and Definition* (UNCTAD Series on Issues in International Investment Agreements II, 2011) 9.

131 Michael Hwang and Jennifer Fong Lee Cheng, 'Definition of "Investment": a Voice from the Eye of the Storm' (2011) 1 The Asian Journal of International Law 105; Emmanuel Gaillard, 'Identify or Define? Reflections on the Evolution of the Concept of Investment in ICSID Practice' in Christina Binder and Christoph Schreuer (eds), *International Investment Law for the 21st Century: Essays in Honour of Christoph Schreuer* (Oxford University Press 2009) 404–406; Christoph H Schreuer and others, *The ICSID Convention: A Commentary* (Cambridge University Press 2009) 125–134; Brigitte Stern, 'The Contours of the Notion of Protected Investment' (2009) 24 ICSID Review 534.

132 Sornarajah, *The International Law on Foreign Investment* 80.

133 St John 10, 13.

134 Amerasinghe 124, 127–133.

either contracting party in the territory of the other contracting party shall not be expropriated except for the public benefit and against just compensation'.[135] Dutch BITs implemented rather individualistic investment protection from the very beginning:

> Where one Party expropriates or nationalizes property ... or takes any measure which results directly or indirectly in the dispossession ..., it shall make provision for the payment of effective and adequate compensation, in accordance with international law. [...] Nevertheless, measures of expropriation, nationalization or dispossession shall be neither discriminatory nor inconsistent with a specific undertaking.[136]

Later, a 'due process' requisite became an official requirement for lawful expropriation. For example, early Belgian treaties were similar to Dutch treaties but with an additional 'due process' requirement:

> The nationals or legal persons of one Contracting Party may not be deprived, either directly or indirectly, of the property or enjoyment of their investments or goods, rights and interests connected with such investments, situated in the territory of the other Contracting Party, unless the following conditions are complied with: (a) the measures are taken in the public interest and under due process of law in accordance with international law; (b) the measures are neither discriminatory nor contrary to a specific engagement; (c) the measures are accompanied by provisions for the payment of just compensation.[137]

The USA model treaty of 1981 also included a 'due process' requirement:

> expropriation of covered investment unless the expropriation was nondiscriminatory, for a public purpose, in accordance with due process of law, accompa-

135 Article 3(2) of the Treaty between the Federal Republic of Germany and the Republic of Liberia for the promotion and reciprocal protection of investments of 1961, <https://investmentpolicy.unctad.org/international-investment-agreements/treaty-files/1360/download> accessed on 14 May 2025.

136 Article 3 of the Convention concerning the encouragement of capital investment and the protection of property between Netherlands and Tunisia, of 1963.

137 Article 5 (1) of the Agreement on the encouragement and reciprocal protection of investments between Belgium and Indonesia of 1970.

> nied by prompt, adequate, and effective compensation, and not inconsistent with any contractual obligation.[138]

The intent or purpose of a state's regulation never reached the level of the express provision of the BITs, and its application remained at the discretion of the tribunals with varying degrees of success.[139]

The main problem related to the expropriation is not even mentioned in the texts of the early BITs; that is, how to delimit expropriation, taking, and deprivation from a *bona fide* regulation, which is not compensable. As concluded by Brownlie, 'a lawful exercise of powers of government, may affect foreign interests considerably without amounting to expropriation' and 'in principle such measures are not unlawful and do not constitute expropriation'.[140] There was and still is 'little agreement about what the pre-existing customary international law had to say about the issue of regulatory takings'.[141] The problem was left to be resolved by the investment arbitration practice in the future.[142]

The third issue – the standard of compensation – was also problematic in the customary law because national laws and practices were very different. The contentious nature of the issue is mirrored in the variety of descriptions used by BITs for the standard of compensation. For example, German BITs provided for: 'a fair value of the investment affected; it shall be actually realisable, freely transferable and shall be made without undue delay'.[143] Dutch BITs required:

---

138 Vandevelde, 'U.S. Bilateral Investment Treaties: The Second Wave' 643–644 (emphasis added); Article 3(1) of the Treaty between the United States of America and the Republic of Turkey concerning the Reciprocal Encouragement and Protection of Investments, of 1985 provides: 'Investments shall not be expropriated or nationalized either directly or indirectly through measures tantamount to expropriation or nationalization ("expropriation") except for a public purpose; in a nondiscriminatory manner; upon payment of prompt, adequate and effective compensation; and in accordance with due process of law and the general principles of treatment provided for in Article II(2).'

139 Escarcena provides a review on all requirements for lawful expropriation: Escarcena 117.

140 Brownlie, *Principles of public international law* 509 (footnotes omitted).

141 Been and Beauvais 53.

142 N Jansen Calamita, 'The principle of proportionality and the problem of indeterminacy in international investment treaties' in N Jansen Calamita, David Earnest and Markus Burgstaller (eds), *The Future of ICSID and the Place of Investment Treaties in International Law* (2013).

143 Article 3(2) of the Treaty between the Federal Republic of Germany and the Republic of Liberia for the promotion and reciprocal protection of investments of 1961.

> *effective and adequate* compensation, in accordance with international law. The amount of such compensation, which shall be fixed at the time of expropriation, nationalization or dispossession, shall be paid to the due recipient without unjustified delay.[144]

Belgian BITs stated that:

> The amount of such compensation shall represent the *actual value* of the affected goods on the date on which the measure was taken. It shall be paid to the person entitled thereto and shall be freely transferable, without undue delay.[145]

The USA early-model BITs required the fair market value with additional conditions:

> Compensation shall be equivalent to the *fair market value* of the expropriated investment immediately before the expropriatory action was taken or became known.[146]

The language used to regulate the standard of compensation became stricter with each decade. Early BITs used the term 'fair value', which could consider the balance between private and public interests, whereas later BITs avoided balancing tasks by using the abstract term 'market value', which was common in accounting and financial contexts. Some authors opined that different variations used to describe the compensation due should be interpreted to mean the same thing: 'market value'[147] reflecting a broader commodification trend in modern property law.

In conclusion, the mounting number of similarly worded BITs inspired discussions that maybe BITs contribute to the formation of international custom-

144 Article 3 of the Convention concerning the encouragement of capital investment and the protection of property between the Netherlands and Tunisia, of 1963 (emphasis added).

145 Article 5 (2) of the Agreement on the encouragement and reciprocal protection of investments between Belgium and Indonesia of 1970 (emphasis added).

146 Article 3(2) of the Treaty between the United States of America and the Republic of Turkey concerning the Reciprocal Encouragement and Protection of Investments, of 1985 (emphasis added).

147 Burzū Sabahi, *Compensation and restitution in investor-state arbitration: principles and practice* (Oxford University Press 2011) 103. There is also a vivid discussion whether the standard of compensation should be different in cases of lawful and unlawful expropriation.

ary law[148] or at least to the consolidation and the crystallisation of customary rules.[149] The flaw of these claims is demonstrated by asking a question: why conclude new BITs if investment protection is already a mandatory international law custom? The answer is that no international tribunal will ever issue an award based on such a 'custom' alone as it stands today.

Even though on a general level, investment treaties could be seen as similar, the specific content of BITs differs.[150] As we could see in the previous subchapters, different BITs have slightly different definitions for investment and conditions for expropriation, as well as the standards of compensation. Thus, ascertaining which particular variation of the rule represents the custom is impossible. If the content of a specific rule is unclear, how could there be a uniform practice and *opinio juris* on it?

This variety of BIT provisions contrasts with other areas of international law, which were codified by treaties, such as the 1969 Vienna Convention on the Law of Treaties. It could be said that after a sufficient number of states have become bound by the same convention, uniform practice emerges due to the application of the identical instrument. However, this is not the case with numerous slightly different and individually negotiated BITs.[151]

---

148 For the general argument that treaties could be seen as an evidence of international customary law see Richard R Baxter, 'Multilateral Treaties as Evidence of Customary International Law' (1965) 44 British Yearbook of International Law 275 Stephen M Schwebel, 'The Influence of Bilateral Investment Treaties on Customary International Law' (2004) 98 American Society of International Law Proceedings27; Campbell McLachlan, 'Investment Treaties and General International Law' (2008) 57 International and Comparative Law Quarterly 365.

149 Patrick Dumberry, 'Are BITs Representing the 'New' Customary International Law in International Investment Law' (2010) 28 Penn State International Law Review 694; See also T Gazzini, 'The Role of Customary International Law in the Protection of Foreign Investment' (2007) 8 Journal of World Investment and Trade 710.

150 Sornarajah, *The International Law on Foreign Investment* 85.

151 Some authors claim not the existence of custom, but universal international law principles associated with regulatory takings: Ratner, 'Regulatory Takings in Institutional Context: Beyond the Fear of Fragmented International Law' 475. Such a claim has two problems. First, such a principle can be claimed only on such an abstract and general level that its application becomes impossible in a real dispute. The majority of the world's legal systems prohibit a theft but allows the regulation to interfere with the use and enjoyment of property. There is no universal agreement when regulation becomes a theft. Furthermore, there is no universal agreement on what compensation needs to be paid even for direct expropriation because national laws are very different on the issue. The second problem is that such a claim usually is based on the Western individualistic ideology and experience, ignoring other regions and traditions of the world.

If the strict traditional test for establishing customary law rules applies, it must be concluded that, besides some similarities on a very general and abstract level, BITs do not demonstrate or consolidate international customary law rules on either property or investment protection.

4 Impact of Investment Treaties and Arbitral Practice on the Development of Investment Law

The early texts of investment treaties were trying to imitate Western individualistic property regimes, but the wordings were still vague, and practice could have gone either way. However, the interpretation of investment treaties in investment arbitration acquired neoliberal content, and exceeded even the most individualistic national property regimes.

The Iran–US Claims Tribunal set the tone for the expansive investment protection.[152] Presided mainly by Western lawyers, the tribunal generated numerous arbitral awards, which influenced international jurisprudence on injuries to foreigners.[153] The Iran–US Claims Tribunal practice stretched alien property protection to new limits. This was possible due to the violent nature of the Iranian revolution and the broad jurisdictional clause of the Claims Settlement Declaration,[154] which allowed the tribunal to hear disputes on debts, contracts, transactions and other measures affecting property rights.[155] The tribunal also had wide discretion on applicable law.[156] Although the Iran–United States Claims Tribunal heard many contractual disputes, it employed the language

152 A policy-oriented approach of the New Haven School probably helped the interpretation: Myres Smith McDougal, Harold Dwight Lasswell and James C Miller, *The Interpretation of International Agreements and World Public Order: principles of content and Procedure*, vol 8 (M Nijhoff Publishers 1994) 3.

153 Rahmatullah Khan, *The Iran-United States Claims Tribunal: Controversies, Cases, and Contribution* (M Nijhoff 1990) 179; Allahyar Mouri, *The International Law of Expropriation as Reflected in the Work of the Iran-US Claims Tribunal*, vol 17 (M Nijhoff 1994) 37, 65; G H Aldrich, *The Jurisprudence of the Iran-United States Claims Tribunal: An Analysis of the Decisions of the Tribunal* (Clarendon Press 1996) 172–173.

154 Aniruddha Rajput, 'Problems with the Jurisprudence of the Iran–US Claims Tribunal on Indirect Expropriation' (2015) 30 ICSID Review 589, 600–601.

155 Article II of the Declaration of the Government of the Democratic and Popular Republic of Algeria Concerning the Settlement of Claims by the Government of the United States of America and the Government of the Islamic Republic of Iran (9 January 1981) (1981–1982) 1 Iran–USCTR 9, <https://iusct.com/foundingdocuments-2/#1691403316137-6fcd4efb-918f> accessed on 14 May 2025.

156 Article V of the Claims Settlement Declaration, <https://iusct.com/foundingdocuments-2/#1691403327893-9cca2d2b-cfac> accessed on 14 May 2025.

of expropriations,[157] relying only on soft law arguments supported by Whiteman,[158] an article of Christie,[159] the Harvard Draft Convention of 1962 and *Lena Goldfield*'s case,[160] none of which were robust evidences of international customary law because opinions on them differed, and no uniform or global state practice existed. The outcomes, such as *Starrett Housing*,[161] *Tippetts*,[162] *Phillips Petroleum*,[163] *Amoco*,[164] and *Mobil Oil*,[165] were possible only due to the wide jurisdictional and applicable law clauses in the Claims Settlement Declaration. The tribunal stretched the meaning of the term 'expropriations', and it would never be the same as before. Even though the early nineteenth and twentieth-century cases retained some, albeit weak, linkage between property rights and expropriation, after the Iran–US Claims Tribunal, not only could nearly anything fall under the protected property or investment, but it could also be considered for expropriation. Although generating controversies, the Iran–United States awards were frequently cited in later investment arbitration practice[166] and used to justify the expansive interpretations of investment protection, forgetting the revolutionary context and specific clauses of the Claims Settlement Declaration under which those awards were issued.

Another influence in the development of international investment law was the collapse of the USSR. Newly re-emerging states were eager to conclude BITs with Western countries to strengthen their status as independent and internationally recognised states.[167] This also prompted the second stage of a USA treaty programme that aimed to cement the regime changes in the former USSR countries as well as its satellites:

---

157 *Phillips Petroleum v Iran* 21 Iran-US CTR 81 [1989]; *Amoco v Iran Award* 27 International Legal Materials 301 (1988) [1987]; *Mobil Oil v Iran* 86 International Law Reports 231 (1988) [1988] 4.

158 Marjorie M Whiteman, Green Haywood Hackworth and others, *Digest of International Law*, vol 1–15 (US Department of State 1963).

159 Christie 338.

160 Aldrich 175.

161 *Starrett Housing Corp v Iran* (1983) 4 Iran-US CTR 122.

162 *Tippetts, Abbett, McCarthy, Stratton v TAMS-AFFA Consulting Engineers of Iran* 6 Iran-US CTR 219.

163 *Phillips Petroleum v Iran* 81.

164 *Amoco v Iran Award* 301.

165 *Mobil Oil v Iran* 4.

166 Tams 326.

167 For example Czech Republic in 1990 concluded nine BITs, Lithuania in 1992 concluded eight BITs, Poland – ten BITs; Romania in 1994 concluded fourteen BITs <http://investmentpolicyhub.unctad.org/IIA> accessed on 15 May 2025.

> U.S. BIT negotiators attached particular significance to the conclusion of BITs both with the former communist States and with Argentina. The Soviet bloc had been among the foremost opponents of international protection for property rights, while Argentina historically had been a firm adherent to the Calvo Doctrine.[168]

With socialist states embracing private property, 'the traditional opposition toward recognizing the right to property'[169] substantially weakened. Neo-liberal economic policies engrafted in BITs are usually explained by the need for legal stability – individual enterprises need stability to grow, expand, and earn a profit. So it is argued that, as a result, these enterprises will lift the economy of the whole society, and everyone will supposedly be better off. In a neo-liberal fashion, even communist China started implementing the BIT programme, which at least on the surface recognised a foreigner's right to property but still refused to arbitrate disputes on merit.[170] These geopolitical shifts encouraged the individualistic language in the BITs of the 1990s[171] and expansive interpretations of the investment protection standards that exceeded even the highest national property protection standards.[172] This trend was particularly reinforced by 'a consensus between the IMF, the World Bank and the USA Treasury on the policies for developing states', which included 'the promotion of [foreign direct investment] and the enforcement of property rights'.[173] In accordance with the ideology of the Washington Consensus, foreign direct investment was key to economic development and prosperity; thus, the numbers of concluded BITs skyrocketed at this time: between 1989 and 1995 nearly 900 BITs were concluded.[174] In the 1990s, 'developing States fundamentally

168 Vandevelde, 'U.S. Bilateral Investment Treaties: The Second Wave'631, 634–635 (footnotes omitted).

169 Sprankling 16.

170 Gallagher and Shan 143.

171 For example the Treaty between the United States of America and Ukraine Concerning the Encouragement and Reciprocal Protection of Investment of 1994 <https://investmentpolicy.unctad.org/international-investment-agreements/treaty-files/2366/download> accessed on 15 May 2025.

172 *Southern Pacific Properties (Middle East) Limited v Arab Republic of Egypt*; *Fedax NV v Venezuela*, Decision on Jurisdiction (ICSID) Case No ARB/96/3, (2002) 5 ICSID Rep 183; *Saar Papier Vertriebs GmbH v Republic of Poland* para 93; *Compañía del Desarrollo de Santa Elena v Republic of Costa Rica* 64.

173 Newcombe and Paradell 48.

174 Database of UNCTAD Investment Policy Hub <http://investmentpolicyhub.unctad.org/IIA> accessed on 15 May 2025.

changed their position [and] suddenly embraced treaties that provided the very basic legal protection that they had rejected for decades'.[175]

Even though more recent BITs and IIAs have retreated from the extremely wide language of the 1990s, it is still worth examining those treaties of the 1990s because they govern the majority of investment disputes arbitrated nowadays and frame the issues of the reform. Furthermore, BITs preceding 'balanced treaties' better illustrate the gap between investment protection and national property regimes. The following subchapters reflect what has been protected by the typical investment treaties, how expropriation has been understood, and what have been the methods and standards of compensation employed by the arbitral tribunals.

4.1 Scope of Protected Investments

The investment arbitration practice was still developing throughout the 1980s and 1990s. Even though the number of recorded investment disputes was relatively low, or maybe because the cases were rare, the definitions and coverage of investment instruments were interpreted expansively.[176] The expansive trend was supported by both arbitral practice and scholarly writings:

> [i]t is widely considered today that the definition of 'investment' has to be a broad one […]. The decision emphasizes that the definition chosen by the parties was a very broad one.[177]

The ICSID jurisprudence that flourished after the 1990s confirmed that 'investment' covered almost any economic activity:

> movable and immovable property, financial instruments, loans (except a bank guarantee and an option), participation in companies, including minority and indirect shareholdings, civil engineering, construction and infrastructure proj-

175 Dumberry, *The formation and identification of rules of customary international law in international investment law* 79.

176 Vaughan Lowe, 'Regulation or Expropriation?' (2002) 55 Current Legal Problems 447, 457; United Nations Conference on Trade and Development (UNCTAD), Bilateral Investment Treaties in the Mid-1990s, 8–10, UN Doc UNCTAD/ ITE/IIT/7, UN Sales No E98.II.D.8 (1998); Vandevelde, 'U.S. Bilateral Investment Treaties: The Second Wave' 621, 630–631.

177 Rudolf Dolzer, 'The notion of investment in recent practice' in Steve Charnovitz, Debra P Steger and Peter Van den Bossche (eds), *Law in the Service of Human Dignity: Essays in Honour of Florentino Feliciano* (Cambridge University Press 2005) 267.

> ects, provision of services in some cases, mining operations, construction and operation of hotels, banking and agriculture.[178]

The concern of the time was how to draft and interpret the definition of 'investment' to include all possible future forms of wealth.[179] Typical BITs of that era would explain 'investment' as 'every kind of asset' and would provide a 'laundry list' of non-exclusive forms or examples.

Scholars and tribunals focused on the question of whether 'investment' or 'assets' used in the *chapeau* of definitions had any qualifying meaning at all besides the 'laundry list'.[180] Even the tribunals that assumed the term 'investment' required substantial commitment, risk, duration, the regularity of profit, and the host state's development[181] frequently found that almost any economic activity could satisfy them because the criteria were not cumulative and could take a variety of forms.[182]

The scope of protected investments went far beyond traditional notions of property even in the Anglo-American legal systems. Investment treaties were protecting payments for import supervision services,[183] rights under the loan agreement,[184] claims to performance under the bareboat charter contract,[185]

178 Schreuer and others 125–128 (footnotes omitted).

179 Awards emphasizing that the definition of investment is broad: *Continental Casualty Company v Argentine Republic* (ICSID) para 84; *Millicom International Operations BV and Sentel GSM SA v Republic of Senegal* (ICSID) para 79; *Jan Oostergetel and Theodora Laurentius v Slovak Republic* (UNCITRAL) para 157–158; *Sanum Investments Limited v Lao People's Democratic Republic* (PCA) para 318–320.

180 Dolzer, 'The notion of investment in recent practice' 269; *Nordzucker AG v Republic of Poland* (UNCITRAL)para 166; *RosInvestCo UK Ltd v Russian Federation* para 383; *Anatolie Stati, Gabriel Stati, Ascom Group SA and Terra Raf Trans Traiding Ltd v Republic of Kazakhstan* (SCC) para 806.

181 *Salini Costruttori SPA and Italstrade SPA v Kingdom of Morocco* (ICSID) para 52. Other awards following *Salini* test: *Joy Mining Machinery Limited v Arab Republic of Egypt* (ICSID) para 53–57; *Patrick Mitchell v The Democratic Republic of Congo* (ICSID) para 27; *Jan de Nul NV and Dredging International NV v Arab Republic of Egypt* (ICSID) para 91–92; *Ioannis Kardassopoulos v Georgia* (ICSID) para 116.

182 *MCI Power Group, LC and New Turbine Inc v Republic of Ecuador* para 164–165; *Saipem SpA v People's Republic of Bangladesh* (ICSID) paras 99, 111; *Abaclat and Others (formerlyGiovanna a Beccara and Others) v Argentine Republic* (ICSID) para 364; *Philip Morris Brand Sàrl (Switzerland), Philip Morris Products SA (Switzerland) and Abal Hermanos SA (Uruguay) v Oriental Republic of Uruguay* (ICSID) para 204–206; *Hassan Awdi, Enterprise Business Consultants, Inc and Alfa El Corporation v Romania* (ICSID) paras 197–199.

183 *SGS Société Générale de Surveillance SA v Republic of the Philippines* (ICSID).

184 *OKO Pankki Oyj and others v Republic of Estonia* (ICSID).

185 *Inmaris Perestroika Sailing Maritime Services GmbH and others v Ukraine* (ICSID).

consulting services,[186] a shipwreck salvaging service,[187] and arbitral awards.[188] Each of those cases had its own motivation, and vaguely worded BITs, or investment contracts caused the outcomes of those cases to be as they are; however, those cases also illustrate the prevailing trend.[189] The refusals to uphold the jurisdiction due to the absence of investment were rare under the second-wave BITs.

While expanding the definition of investment and, together with it, the jurisdictional coverage of investment treaties, the drafters, tribunals, and counsels were actively promoting the neoliberal premise of investment.[190] If the understanding of investment covers almost all economic interests and many economic activities, that means that any state interference with individual priorities and the most profitable use of these investments needs to be compensated. Perrone calls it the wealth maximisation paradigm of international investment law.[191] The extensive application of investment protection to huge areas of economic activities in the host states leaves very little scope for permissible government regulation. The situation was dire because many of those economic activities had negative externalities, which imposed costs on the host society and needed to be regulated. The most often cited examples of such negative externalities are environmental pollution, health and safety degradation.

The international regime of investment protection effectively created extraterritorial regulatory pockets for protected interests in the sense that it required a state to abstain from regulating negative externalities arising from protected interests or prevented states from initiating legal reforms that affected the value of protected interests. The broader the protected interests are defined, the wider those regulatory pockets are and interfere with the 'usual' domestic property regime. Arato also concluded that international invest-

186 *Luigiterzo Bosca v Republic of Lithuania* (PCA) <https://www.italaw.com/cases/2076> accessed on 15 May 2025.

187 *Malaysian Historical Salvors Sdn Bhd v Government of Malaysia* (ICSID).

188 Loukas A Mistelis, 'Award as an Investment: The Value of an Arbitral Award or the Cost of Non-Enforcement' (2013) 28 ICSID Review – Foreign Investment Law Journal 64.

189 There were other and contradicting more recent examples: *Gustav FW Hamester GmbH & Co KG v Republic of Ghana* (ICSID); *Alps Finance & Trade AG v the Slovak Republic* (*UNCITRAL*); *Romak SA v the Republic of Uzbekistan* (UNCITRAL); *Energoalians SARL v Republic of Moldova* (UNCITRAL) para 288; *Poštová banka, as and Istrokapital SE v Hellenic Republic* (ICSID) paras 287–292.

190 Slobodian 145.

191 Nicolás M Perrone, 'The Emerging Global Right to Investment: Understanding the Reasoning behind Foreign Investor Rights' (2017) 8 Journal of International Dispute Settlement 673, 685.

ment law implicitly invades domestic systems of law, although he argued that this invasion does not 'distort the logic of property law' – the principle of standardisation and the fact that national law defines the contours of different types of property.[192] The proponents of the investment regime argue that an extremely wide definition of protected interests *per se* does not prohibit changing national legislation, if the compensation for the changes is paid.[193] However, the qualification of rights, interests, and other legal relations as proprietary for the purposes of investment arbitration and protecting them at a level higher than property protection distorts national legal systems, creating internal conflicts.[194]

Civil law countries have a narrower understanding of property,[195] but many investment tribunal reasonings go far beyond the traditional concepts of property. A relatively recent case based on the classic investment treaty between the UK and Hungary – *Magyar Farming and others v Hungary* – highlights the issue and demonstrates the general clash between local economic policy choices and neoliberal globalisation strategies.[196] At the centre of the dispute was the Hungarian agricultural land reform. While the ownership of agricultural land was reserved for Hungarian citizens, indicating certain protective and traditional attitudes to land, characteristic of many Central and Eastern European societies after the collapse of the communist order, some large enterprises managed to accumulate huge masses of land through leases.[197] In 2010–2011, the Fidesz party initiated regulatory changes prioritising small agricultural family farms and terminating statutory pre-lease rights. Claimants had a ten-year lease right to agricultural land, which was already extended by the time the dispute arose, and a pre-lease right, meaning a priority to extend the lease on the same terms as agreed with the third party.[198] The jurisdiction of the tribunal in that case was limited to legal disputes arising under the expropriation provision of the UK–Hungary BIT.[199] Hungary argued that pre-lease rights are not transferable, lack intrinsic value, and do not constitute

---

192 Julian Arato, 'The Private Law Critique of International Investment Law' (2019) 113 American Journal of International Law 1, 12, 14.

193 More detailed analysis of compensations mechanisms below in Subchapter 4.4.3.

194 For further analysis of assimilation of contractual rights and property in investment disputes, see: Martinkute, 'The delimitation of contractual rights and property in international investment law' 1.

195 AJ van der Walt, *Property and Constitution* (Pretoria University Law Press (PULP) 2012) 114.

196 *Magyar Farming and others v Hungary* (President Kaufmann-Kohler, Arbitrators: Alexandrov, Hanefeld).

197 Ibid para 111.

198 Ibid paras 117–118.

199 Ibid para 249.

'assets',[200] in other words, they do not qualify as property and do not bear separate hallmarks of investment, thus, cannot be expropriated. The tribunal paid lip service to Hungarian law on the qualification question[201] and concluded that the pre-lease right is a vested right,[202] thus capable of being expropriated separately from the main lease agreement, ignoring the whole civil law separation between contractual rights and proprietary rights. In doing so, the tribunal even ignored Article 1 of the applicable UK–Hungary BIT, which did not include statutory rights among protected interests, instead asserting that a pre-lease right amounts to some mythical international vested right.[203] Furthermore, the tribunal compared this pre-lease right to pension entitlements[204] – conflating business interest with a right to the main source of income closely related to human dignity under human rights instruments. The tribunal refused to exclude the pre-lease right from the protection of the BIT, questioning why *in rem* rights should be protected from expropriation, while a pre-lease right should not.[205]

Pre-contractual and statutory rights in domestic legal regimes usually have a specific protection, which does not amount to the protection of the property. Pre-contractual rights are usually non-transferable and cannot be separated from the main contract. Furthermore, specific remedies apply to the breaches of pre-contractual rights under national laws, usually, they do not entitle the relevant party to the conclusion of the contract and damages are limited to the costs, not future profits. The elevation of pre-contractual rights to the level of property protection disrupts the domestic legal system, making legal reforms more difficult and changes in economic policies more costly for host states.

Probably, it is not surprising that the UK–Hungary BIT was terminated after the award in *Magyar Farming and others v Hungary* was issued, which might imply that states are not satisfied with the way investment treaties are interpreted by investment tribunals.[206]

---

200 Ibid para 254.

201 Ibid para 341.

202 Ibid para 342.

203 The application of vested or acquired rights is also problematic in international law. Besides being very vague, historically, it was applied in situations involving territorial changes or as a procedural admission of parties, while a broad international consensus was lacking: Pierre A. Lalive, *The doctrine of acquired rights* (Matthew Bender 1965) 149.

204 *Magyar Farming and others v Hungary* para 344.

205 Ibid para 359.

206 Agreement between the Government of the United Kingdom of Great Britain and Northern Ireland and the Government of Hungary on Termination of the Agreement between the Government of the United Kingdom of Great Britain and Northern Ireland and the Government of the Hungarian People's Republic for the Promotion and Reciprocal Pro-

In *Emmis International Holding BV and others v Hungary* a similar question was addressed – whether contractual and statutory rights could be expropriated.[207] Like in the previous case, the tribunal's jurisdiction was limited to expropriation disputes.[208] According to Hungary, expropriation could only occur with regard to proprietary rights, which can be owned, acquired, transferred or sold.[209] Meanwhile, claimants argued that rights *in rem* are not a prerequisite to an expropriation claim and that statutory rights may be expropriated.[210] Applicable investment treaties, like in the previous case, protected any performance having an economic value and rights granted under public law.[211] The tribunal concluded that the term 'asset' presupposes property[212] and referred to Hungarian law to ascertain what rights claimants had after the expiry of the broadcasting licence.[213] The tribunal investigated whether claimants held 'contractual rights capable of constituting property or assets under Hungarian law'.[214] The tribunal, similarly to Douglas, identified that an underlying asset – not the contractual right itself – could be subject to expropriation.[215] But while reaching this conclusion, the tribunal intuitively relied on broad common law property features.[216] What the tribunal seems to have done is to check the national law answer (if there is property) against some mythical international concept of property, which only hides a neoliberal understanding of property geared towards the preservation of the current distribution of wealth.

Brownlie was a lone voice when he called for a restraint in international investment law:

---

tection of Investments and the Extending Exchange of Notes, 18 January and 6 July 2022, <https://investmentpolicy.unctad.org/international-investment-agreements/treaty-files/8578/download> accessed on 25 November 2025.

207 *Emmis International Holding, BV, Emmis Radio Operating, BV and MEM Magyar Electronic Media Kereskedelmi és Szolgáltató Kft v Hungary* Case No ARB/12/2, Award, 16 April 2014 (President: McLachlan, Arbitrators: Thomas, Lalonde) para 5.

208 Ibid para 110.

209 Ibid.

210 Ibid para 117.

211 Ibid paras 135 and 138.

212 Ibid para 159.

213 Ibid para 162 (footnote omitted).

214 Ibid paras 169–170.

215 Douglas, 'Property, Investment and the Scope of Investment Protection Obligations' 224–225.

216 *Emmis International Holding BV & Ors v Hungary* para 192.

> Investment does not include all kinds of property, and it is essential that arbitrators confer the benefits of investment protection treaties only on property rights that qualify as investment. To do otherwise would betray the intent – and consent – of the parties to arbitrate their disputes with aliens operating in their territory.[217]

NAFTA had started narrowing the definition of investment by excluding some economic interests: (i) claims to money from commercial contracts for the sale of goods or services, (ii) the extension of credit in connection with a commercial transaction, and (iii) certain other claims to money. The *Pope & Talbot v Canada* tribunal differentiated the NAFTA tribunal's jurisdiction from the jurisdiction of the Iran–US Claims Tribunal,[218] but it did not prevent the tribunal from maintaining that access to the market is a protected property right under Article 1110 of NAFTA.[219] If access to the market were protected as a property right under national law, it would paralyse any legal system. Thus, even though NAFTA had started narrowing down the definition of investment, its Chapter 11 still covered 'a great deal more than the property interests traditionally protected by the Fifth Amendment' of the US Constitution and 'establishes a very low threshold for obtaining Chapter 11 protections'.[220]

More recent BITs have also narrowed the scope of the term of investment[221] and introduced an *expresis verbis* requirement to give a meaning to the word 'investment' in the definitions.[222] Following this more restrictive approach in 2004, the term 'asset' was introduced into the definition of investment of the USA model BITs. The 2004 USA model BIT also added a note that 'other forms of debt, such as claims to payment that are immediately due and result from the sale of goods or services, are less likely to have [investment] characteristics'[223] and that licenses, authorisations, permits or concessions may qualify as investment depending on the nature and extent of rights under domestic law. The same wording has been maintained in the 2012 USA model BIT.[224]

---

217 *CME Czech Republic BV v Czech Republic* (UNCITRAL), Separate Opinion of Ian Brownlie 33.

218 The Iran-US Claims Tribunal's jurisdiction included 'other measures affecting property rights': *Pope & Talbot Inc v Government of Canada* para 104.

219 Confirmed in *Merrill & Ring Forestry LP v Government of Canada* para 143.

220 Been and Beauvais 42 (footnotes omitted).

221 Muchlinski 28.

222 Dolzer 'The notion of investment in recent practice' 264.

223 Article 1 of the 2004 USA model BIT <https://www.ustr.gov/sites/default/files/U.S.%20model%20BIT.pdf> accessed on 22 November 2025.

224 Article 1 of the 2012 US model BIT <https://www.ustr.gov/sites/default/files/U.S.%20model%20BIT.pdf> accessed on 15 May 2025.

Overall, changes in the scope of protected interests in investment treaties are rather cosmetic, and the prevailing wording and interpretation of investment are significantly broader than any understanding of protected property under national law.

4.2 Expropriation v Regulation

The investment treaties take the expropriation concept for granted, implying that substantive taking of a major part of an investment or reduction of its value would amount to expropriation. However, the Latin origin of the word '*ex-propriare*' itself signals that property, not other rights or interests, is taken from the rightful owner. Investment arbitration practice ignores the literal meaning of this word and is full of examples of expropriation of all types of interests and rights, which do not qualify as property.[225] This creates qualification problems, such as when a contract is lawfully terminated under governing law, but expropriation of contractual rights is alleged at the international level.[226] For the structural clarity of the system, those other non-proprietary interests should be protected by other treaty standards, leaving expropriation clauses only for property protection. Otherwise, if the injury to any interest having economic value can be couched in terms of expropriation or indirect expropriation, it is difficult to see why we need all other treaty standards.

This brings us to another crucial problem – state measures that leave the formal ownership intact but have effects equivalent or tantamount to expropriation. Indirect expropriation is understood as restrictions on the use of investment or a reduction in the value of the investment due to regulation.

The Iran–United States Claims Tribunal contributed a great deal to the expansion of the concept of indirect expropriation, which acquired many features characteristic of the US regulatory takings. For example, the *Starrett Housing*[227] *and Tippetts* cases[228] involved the imposition of temporary managers who interfered with the use of property or with the enjoyment of its benefits.[229] The tribunals viewed the problem in terms of 'indirect expropri-

---

225 *Magyar Farming and others v Hungary* para 359.

226 Douglas, *The international law of investment claims* 207.

227 *Starrett Housing Corp v Iran* 122.

228 *Tippetts, Abbett, McCarthy, Stratton v TAMS-AFFA Consulting Engineers of Iran* 219.

229 France had somehow similar constitutional case around the same time, where the power of the Minister of Commerce and Industry to appoint members of the board representing employees' in a company was proclaimed unconstitutional: French Constitutional Council decision No 93-162 DC, 19, 20 July 1983, *Democratization of the Public Sector.* Similar decision No 90-283 DC, 8 January 1991, *Tobacco and Alcohol Advertising.* However

ation', and the overall outcome of those cases may be understandable in the revolutionary context.[230] However, using those analogies in times of peace for 'ordinary' regulatory measures of the state is questionable. *Starrett Housing* is relied on by some investment arbitrations dealing with land planning, contractual disputes and regulation of utilities.[231] The latter measures may arguably represent a valid common interest and, without revolutionary and outrageous context, should not be treated as expropriation but rather as a permissible regulation.[232]

Land reforms, legal reforms seeking to improve the functioning of a market, or to reduce inequality, or address other socio-economic problems of the local society, represent one of those really difficult cases where regulation interferes with the rights of owners, but depending on the individualistic or communitarian understanding of property, the outcome could be very different.[233] These cases pose a philosophical question based on underlying values: to what extent an owner is obliged to contribute to the well-being of the society within which it operates? The traditional answer to that question provided by Western jurisprudence is that the owner alone should not bear the burden of improving the living conditions of the host society, also known as the principle of equality against public burdens.[234]

However, the traditional answer has weaknesses that are worth exploring more deeply. First, in the case of general reforms, it is not a single owner who bears the burden of benefiting society. Usually, during the economy-wide reforms, the circle of affected owners is wider. If a general law reform tries to solve a particular problem in society, it might be that proprietary interests of a small number of owners are part of the problem, and without affecting those interests, it is impossible to solve the problem. Monopolistic market reforms illustrate the point: if the problem is the concentration of the market, it is impossible to improve the functioning of the market without affecting the incumbent interests. If apartheid or inequality was the problem, it is impossible to address the problem without some redistribution of wealth or entitle-

---

it is unclear whether French practice was influenced by the Iran-Us Claims Tribunal or *vice versa*.

230 Been and Beauvais 58.

231 *AIG Capital Partners, Inc and CJSC Tema Real Estate Company v Republic of Kazakhstan* para 65; *Impregilo SpA v Argentine Republic* (ICSID) Case No ARB/07/17, concurring and dissenting opinion of Judge Charles N Brower, 21 June 2011 para 21.

232 Lowe 452.

233 The termination of pre-lease rights was qualified as expropriation in *Magyar Farming and others v Hungary* para 366. However, the forced sale of land in Hawaii was not considered expropriation in the USA: *Hawaii Housing Authority v Midkiff*.

234 *Magyar Farming and others v Hungary* para 367.

ments within the society.[235] Acemoglu and Robinson argue that inclusive institutions and economic structures tend to produce more prosperous societies.[236] However, a transition from extractive political institutions to inclusive economic structures will require general reforms negatively affecting the proprietary interests of incumbent owners. Some might argue that these conceptual reforms should be accomplished by paying the compensation from collected taxes, which brings us to the second argument. Often in developing states, general reforms are the only viable option for change because of the lack of strong state institutions, their inability to collect taxes for public projects and the general lack of administrative capacities. If these societies could change their situation, they would likely strengthen their administrative state apparatus, improve tax collection, and better satisfy the needs of society. However, there are reasons why developing states cannot change their ways. Sometimes, among those reasons are dire poverty, corruption, and path dependence.[237] As a consequence, it is more difficult to overhaul the whole state, than to undertake targeted reforms, such as land reform for which just enough votes can be mustered at the national parliaments. Thus, the targeted reform aimed at achieving some public good, involving changes in the proprietary interests, may be the only available pathway for progress in such circumstances. Almost all industrialised nations underwent such general land reforms, and very rarely were they compensated based on the market value.[238]

Christie, who was frequently relied on in the indirect expropriation awards of the Iran–US Claims Tribunal, did not provide answers on where the line between indirect expropriation and regulation should be drawn. Instead, he only argued that 'the question of what kind of interference short of outright expropriation constitutes a "taking" under international law' is best answered by 'the common law method of case by case'.[239] Investment treaties did not explicitly address this problem either, leaving it to the discretion of arbitral tribunals.[240] Due to the peculiar practices of arbitral tribunal formation and

235 Walt 125.

236 Acemoglu and Robinson 70.

237 Ibid 335.

238 Gediminas Vaskela, 'The Land Reform of 1919–1940: Lithuania and the Countries of Eastern and Central Europe' (1996) 1 Lithuanian Historical Studies 116; Joe Regan and Cathal Smith, *Agrarian Reform and Resistance in an Age of Globalisation: The Euro-American World and Beyond, 1780–1914* (Taylor & Francis Group 2020) 7; Rosemary L. Hopcroft, *Regions, Institutions, and Agrarian Change in European History* (University of Michigan Press 1999) 1.

239 Christie 338.

240 UNCTAD Series on issues in international investment agreements, Taking of Property (2000) 20; *Saluka Investments BV v Czech Republic* (UNCITRAL) para 263–264.

the dynamics of arbitration networks, Western arbitrators have started to dominate the field.[241] Together, they brought extremely individualistic views on property protection into the interpretations of investment treaties. Fragmented from other branches of international law and immune from other societal concerns and the need to balance competing interests in a democratic way, investment tribunals gave birth to the neoliberal world order, which is more individualistic than any other national property regime, including the USA.[242]

The wide coverage of protected interests coupled with the high level of investment protection allows investors to challenge not only new host state policies, measures or reform initiatives,[243] but also some state functions that are considered traditional even in the investor's home state.[244] Sometimes those challenges are successful just because the respondent states are not equipped or prepared to defend in those cases.[245] In such a legal framework, any reform becomes notably difficult because most reforms affect some proprietary interests.[246] Reforms tackling inequality become impossible because BITs have been specifically designed to prevent any redistribution of wealth.

The investment arbitration practice developed some factors helping to differentiate legitimate regulatory measures from indirect expropriation, which are similar to the USA regulatory takings criteria formulated in *Penn Central* case.[247] The severity of the impact of the indirect expropriatory measure has to be substantial for a measure to be recognised as indirect expropriation,[248] as well as the duration of the state interference on investment has to be per-

241 Sergio Puig, 'Social Capital in the Arbitration Market' (2014) 25 European Journal of International Law 387.

242 Been and Beauvais 63.

243 *Saar Papier Vertriebs GmbH v Republic of Poland* 78, 96–97, dissenting opinion of Dr habil Tadeusz Szurski, 17 August 1994 para 3.

244 *Tecnicas Medioambientales Tecmed SA v The United Mexican States* para 151; *CME (Netherlands) v Czech Republic (Partial Award)* (UNCITRAL) paras 599–602.

245 *SwemBalt AB v Republic of Latvia* para 38.

246 *Magyar Farming and others v Hungary* para 129.

247 *Penn Central Transportation Company v New York City* 438 US 104, 127 (1978).

248 *CME Czech Republic BV v Czech Republic* para 599–601; *Tecnicas Medioambientales Tecmed SA v The United Mexican States* para 115; *CMS Gas Transmission Co v Argentina* (ICSID) para 262–263; *Occidental Exploration and Production Company v Republic of Ecuador* (LCIA)para 89; *Eastern Sugar BV v Czech Republic* (SCC) Case No 088/2004, Partial Award 27 March 2007 para 210; *MCI Power Group, LC and New Turbine Inc v Republic of Ecuador* para 300; *AES Summit Generation Limited and AES-Tisza Erömü Kft v Republic of Hungary* (ICSID) Case No ARB/07/22, Award 23 September 2010 para 14.3.1; *Total SA v Argentine Republic* para 196; *RosInvestCo UK Ltd v Russian Federation* para 624.

manent or long-term.[249] The respect for legitimate expectations,[250] the proportionality of the measure,[251] and the character and intent of the governmental action[252] may play a role in differentiating legitimate regulation from indirect expropriation. The intent of a state measure was initially ignored by BITs drafters and the Iran–US Claims Tribunal. Most investment tribunals preferred to rely solely on the effects doctrine,[253] and German, British, Mexican and Swiss model BITs refused to address this trend of arbitral practice.[254]

These factors, designed to help the tribunals to differentiate between indirect expropriation and regulation, originate from Western constitutional jurisprudence, which protects an individualistic balance between individual and society. Furthermore, this balance is premised on a certain social contract in those Western societies. Paying taxes in Anglo-American societies externalises the needs of the society from private property, i.e., the needs of the community have to be satisfied from the state budget and taxes. Schools, roads, police, sanitary needs, ecology and even preservation of historical heritage are considered external to the fact of ownership.

The Western criteria for distinguishing the legitimate regulation from indirect compensation impose an individualistic understanding of property in investment disputes because the starting point of the analysis is a social contract of Western societies, where individual rights have a high value, and sep-

249 *Tecnicas Medioambientales Tecmed SA v The United Mexican States* para 116; *Azurix Corp v Argentine Republic* (ICSID) para 313; *Tza Yap Shum v Republic of Peru* para 163; *Ulysseas, Inc v Ecuador* (UNCITRAL) Final Award 12 June 2012 para 173; *Marion Unglaube v Republic of Costa Rica* para 226; *Reinhard Hans Unglaube v Republic of Costa Rica* para 226; *Bernhard von Pezold and others v Republic of Zimbabwe* para 516.

250 *Generation Ukraine v Ukraine* para 20.37; *Tecnicas Medioambientales Tecmed SA v The United Mexican States* paras 122, 150; *Azurix Corp v Argentine Republic* para 316–321.

251 *Tecnicas Medioambientales Tecmed SA v The United Mexican States* para 122 followed by *LG&E Energy Corp, LG&E Capital Corp and LG&E International Inc v Argentine Republic* (ICSID) para 195; *Azurix Corp v Argentine Republic* para 311–312; *Tza Yap Shum v Republic of Peru* para 174; *Deutsche Bank AG v Democratic Socialist Republic of Sri Lanka* (ICSID) para 522; Henckels argued that proportionality test may be the solution to many ISDS problems: Caroline Henckels, *Proportionality and deference in investor-state arbitration: balancing investment protection and regulatory autonomy* (Cambridge University Press 2015) 194. Henkels ignores that proportionality analysis is a value judgment itself.

252 *Telenor Mobile Communications AS v Republic of Hungary* para 70; *Spyridon Roussalis v Romania* (ICSID) Case No ARB/06/1, Award 1 December 2011 para 330.

253 *Tecnicas Medioambientales Tecmed SA v The United Mexican States* para 116; *Siemens AG v Argentine Republic* para 270; *National Grid PLC v Argentina Republic* (UNCITRAL) Award 3 November 2008 para 147; *SAUR International SA v Argentine Republic* paras 366, 441; *Burlington Resources Inc v Republic of Ecuador* (ICSID) Case No ARB/08/5, Decision on Liability 14 December 2012 paras 396–397.

254 Escarcena 120.

arate mechanisms address community interests. However, such basic premises do not always exist in other societies. Many developing states do not have an effective tax collection system for the satisfaction of community interests. Instead, the concept of property is adapted to satisfy the needs of the developing community. Thus the greatest tension the ISDS system experiences is when an individualistic concept of property protection is transplanted into the setting where a communitarian concept of property dominates.[255]

The perpetually expanding notion of state liability for any measures affecting economic interests caused a rethink among the most powerful states, primarily the USA and Canada.[256] The USA drafters attempted to narrow down the concept of indirect expropriation by providing criteria for the delimitation of indirect expropriation and permissible regulation. Naturally, their source of inspiration was the US constitutional jurisprudence. The 2004 US model BIT Annex B draws on the US regulatory takings doctrine, formulated in the *Penn Central* case and lists a number of issues that should be considered when distinguishing permissible regulation from indirect expropriation:

(i) the economic impact of the government action, although the fact that an action or series of actions by a Party has an adverse effect on the economic value of an investment, standing alone, does not establish that an indirect expropriation has occurred;
(ii) the extent to which the government action interferes with distinct, reasonable investment-backed expectations; and
(iii) the character of the government action.[257]

The USA drafters adopted the reasonableness factor that was prominent in the USA jurisprudence[258] and a 'police-powers exception for non-discriminatory regulatory measures aimed at public purposes' in its model BITs.[259] Furthermore, the idea to exclude orders or judgments from the definition of 'investment'[260] was borrowed from 'the US regulatory takings doctrine, where judi-

255 Arato presumed that IIAs and ISDS do not clash with 'the basic functions of domestic (Western-style) property law', just because he did not take into consideration other legal traditions and communitarian understanding of property: Arato 15.

256 Lowe, 456–457. Only one claim of expropriation under NAFTA was resolved in favour of a claimant: *Metalclad Corporation v United Mexican States* para 113. Seventeen other claims on expropriation were rejected under NAFTA.

257 Article 4 of Annexe B of the 2004 US model BIT.

258 Been and Beauvais 71, citing *SD Myers*.

259 Escarcena 120.

260 Fn 3 of the 2004 US model BIT.

cial decisions cannot constitute expropriation'.[261] The USA has been setting the trend and it has been followed by other states too.

After *Methanex*,[262] other states in their draft investment treaties began noting that regulation, except in rare circumstances, did not amount to expropriation.[263] However, all BITs from the 1990s – which are still applied primarily in disputes – do not even mention the state's right to regulate, making the protection of individual economic interests the priority of the BITs. Instead, investment treaties from the 1990s shun away from these complicated questions about the place and value of an investment in the host society and attempt to regulate derivative issues, that is, conditions for lawful expropriation: procedure provided by law, for a public purpose, with due process, non-discriminatory and accompanied by compensation.

The requirement for the expropriation procedure to be authorised by law is a mixed blessing. As discussed in Chapter 3, many national legal systems, especially those that lean towards a more traditional and narrower understanding of property, have such requirements in their respective constitutional jurisprudences. However, curiously, this requirement operates in a completely different way that actually limits the possibility of having a claim for indirect expropriation in the national legal system. General regulation, which limits the use or reduces the value of property, but does not expressly admit that it is a taking for a public purpose, usually will not be considered as indirect expropriation. Without an official statute expressly stating that a particular regulatory measure is an expropriation, starting a successful case for compensation is quite impossible. This leaves most indirect expropriation instances outside the remit of constitutional property protection in these countries. Consequently, only the takings of property that are expressly authorised by special statutes, the physical 'takings of something for pubic purposes', entitle the owners to compensation. The international treaty practice differs dramatically on this account.

Also, national laws and judicial practice are pretty flexible regarding the scope of public purpose and general interest. National courts usually are deferential to the legislative and executive powers on the question of whether a

261 Been and Beauvais 79.

262 *Methanex v US*, NAFTA award, 3 August 2005, part IV, chapter D, 4, para 7: 'as a matter of general international law, a non-discriminatory regulation for a public purpose, which is enacted in accordance with due process and, which affects, inter alia, a foreign investor or investment is not deemed expropriatory and compensable unless specific commitments had been given by the regulating government to the then putative foreign investor contemplating investment that the government would refrain from such regulation'.

263 Article 8.9 of the CETA.

particular measure serves a public purpose.[264] On the contrary, investment tribunals frequently tend to review *post facto* whether state measures were capable of furthering a public interest.[265] Although *Guaracachi America, Inc and Rurelec PLC v Plurinational State of Bolivia* award notes that 'the precise contours of public purpose and social benefit lie with the internal constitutional and legal order of the State',[266] investment tribunals frequently pay lip service to such a notion and conduct a substantial re-evaluation of state measures with the benefit of hindsight.[267]

The practice for other requirements for legal expropriation, like due process, is similarly unclear. The requirement is sometimes featured in national constitutional law, but is sometimes omitted from the language of BITs. The investment arbitration practice associated with this requirement is scattered and ranges from claims about a generic concept in international law,[268] demands on procedural and substantive due process[269] to the possibility of participating in weighing of interests and making decisions,[270] as well as concluding that the contracting parties did not agree on the due process requirement at all.[271]

The non-discrimination requirement is not typically included in constitutional property clauses but is frequently implied by other constitutional provisions and routinely mentioned in the expropriation clauses of BITs. Its application in investment arbitration does not appear problematic, except in cases of positive action when the very reason for a state action is to address historical injustices. The reasoning in the *Bernhard von Pezold and others v Republic of Zimbabwe* award suggests that any redistribution policy based on race would be contrary to the BITs.[272]

264 Johannes Hendrik Fahner, *Judicial Deference in International Adjudication: A Comparative Analysis* (1st edn, Hart Publishing 2020) 8.

265 *Waguih Elie George Siag & Clorinda Vecchi v Arab Republic of Egypt* (ICSID) para 429; *Bernhard von Pezold and others v Republic of Zimbabwe* para 502–503; *Vestey Group Ltd v Bolivarian Republic of Venezuela* (ICSID) para 294; *UP (formerly Le Chèque Déjeuner) and CD Holding Internationale v Hungary* (ICSID) para 414–419.

266 *Guaracachi America, Inc and Rurelec PLC v Plurinational State of Bolivia* (PCA) para 437. Also *Crystallex International Corporation v Bolivarian Republic of Venezuela* (ICSID) para 712; *Teinver SA, Transportes de Cercanías SA and Autobuses Urbanos del Sur SA v Argentine Republic* (ICSID) Case No ARB/09/01, Award 21 July 2017 para 984.

267 *SD Myers Inc v Canada* para 264; *Continental Casualty Company v Argentine Republic* para 181.

268 *Rusoro Mining Ltd v Bolivarian Republic of Venezuela* (ICSID) para 389.

269 *ADC Affiliate Limited and ADC & ADMC Management Limited v Republic of Hungary* para 435.

270 *Venezuela Holdings BV and others (formerly Mobil Corporation and others) v Bolivarian Republic of Venezuela* (ICSID) para 297.

271 *Saint-Gobain Performance Plastics Europe v Bolivarian Republic of Venezuela* para 400.

272 *Bernhard von Pezold and others v Republic of Zimbabwe* para 501.

Overall, if some generalisation is permitted, it must be concluded that national and international systems treat indirect expropriation very differently. Many national legal systems do not have and do not recognise the concept of regulatory taking. While international investment law drew some inspiration from the USA constitutional jurisprudence,[273] the investment arbitration practice in the hands of investment tribunals developed the neoliberal concept of indirect expropriation without national safeguards.

4.3 Compensation

The Iran–United States Claims Tribunal adopted a full compensation standard for expropriation cases,[274] which involved the notion of a market transaction between willing buyers and sellers. That standard, however, was not 'extended to other measures affecting property rights'.[275]

Almost all investment treaties require compensation for the expropriation of an investment. Several BITs expressly required full compensation, understood as market value, in case of expropriation, thus sparking suggestions that it may have become a customary rule.[276] This assumption of lawful expropriation requiring full market value compensation caused a controversy: what is the standard of compensation in the case of unlawful expropriation? A line of case law argues that compensation in cases of unlawful expropriation should be higher to discourage such behaviour.[277] However, according to a number of other cases, no such practical difference exists.[278] Another problem with the full market value standard is that, usually, no comparable transactions for the expropriated assets can be found. Thus, tribunals employ a variety of accoun-

273 Lucas Clover Alcolea, 'The importance of property in international investment law' (2025) 16 Journal of International Dispute Settlement 22.

274 C N Brower, 'Current Developments in the Law of Expropriation and Compensation: a Preliminary Survey of Awards of the Iran-United States Claims Tribunal' (1987) 21 The International Lawyer 662.

275 Escarcena 227.

276 *CME Czech Republic BV v Czech Republic* para 498; Sabahi 93.

277 *ADC Affiliate Limited and ADC & ADMC Management Limited v Republic of Hungary* para 481; *Siemens AG v Argentine Republic* para 352–353; *UP (formerly Le Chèque Déjeuner) and CD Holding Internationale v Hungary* paras 511–512, 560.

278 *Waguih Elie George Siag & Clorinda Vecchi v Arab Republic of Egypt* para 532–541; *Guaracachi America, Inc and Rurelec PLC v Plurinational State of Bolivia* para 613; *British Caribbean Bank Ltd v Government of Belize* (PCA) Case No 2010-2018/BCB-BZ, Award 19 December 2014 para 260–261.

tancy and financial techniques to calculate compensation.[279] Furthermore, Article 36 of the ILC Articles on State Responsibility has encouraged claims for the loss of future profits (*lucrum cessans*).[280] Even if profits of speculative nature were excluded, claimants encouraged the tribunals to be more creative than conservative when calculating damages.[281] For example, in *Magyar Farming and others v Hungary* the main object of the dispute was the statutory right to extend the lease term and its valuation.[282] Putting aside the question of whether such a right amounted to property and whether it was transferable at all, the tribunal evaluated it as 'the stream of profit that those rights could have been expected to produce'.[283] Usually, national laws provide different remedies for breaches of pre-contractual rights, while international investment practice tends to evaluate them as property.

Some investment treaties that resemble constitutional practices have employed the term 'just compensation' for expropriated assets, but even those BITs have been interpreted as meaning 'market value',[284] despite Sir Ian Brownlie's objection.[285] Other BITs employed the term 'appropriate compensation',[286] or 'adequate compensation',[287] that, under national constitutional jurisprudence, would mean that something less than full market value is due. However, investment tribunals routinely rejected that idea and interpreted them as requiring 'a full market value' compensation,[288] contradicting the literal meaning of the treaty text.

---

279 *Middle East Cement Shipping and Handling Co SA v Arab Republic of Egypt* (ICSID) para 127–128; *AIG Capital Partners, Inc and CJSC Tema Real Estate Company v Republic of Kazakhstan* para 12.1.1; *Suez, Sociedad General de Aguas de Barcelona SA and Vivendi Universal SA v Argentine Republic* (ICSID) Case No ARB/03/19, Award 9 April 2015 para 88; *AWG Group Ltd v The Argentine Republic* (UNCITRAL) Award 9 April 2015 para 88.

280 *Archer Daniels Midland Company and Tate & Lyle Ingredients Americas, Inc v United Mexican States* (ICSID) Case No ARB(AF)/04/5, Award 21 November 2007 para 281–282.

281 *Tecnicas Medioambientales Tecmed SA v The United Mexican States* paras 187–188, 191; *Crystallex International Corporation v Bolivarian Republic of Venezuela* para 875.

282 *Magyar Farming and others v Hungary* para 361.

283 Ibid para 374.

284 *CME Czech Republic BV v Czech Republic* para 501; *Venezuela Holdings BV and others (formerly Mobil Corporation and others) v Bolivarian Republic of Venezuela* para 307.

285 *CME Czech Republic BV v Czech Republic* separate opinion of Ian Brownlie para 31–32.

286 *AIG Capital Partners, Inc and CJSC Tema Real Estate Company v Republic of Kazakhstan* para 12.1.1.

287 *Total SA v Argentine Republic* (ICSID) Case No ARB/04/1, Award 27 November 2013 para 59.

288 *Compañía del Desarrollo de Santa Elena v Republic of Costa Rica* para 70; *Tecnicas Medioambientales Tecmed SA v The United Mexican States* paras 187–188, 191; *AIG Capital Partners, Inc and CJSC Tema Real Estate Company v Republic of Kazakhstan* para 12.1.1.

The link between arbitrators' nationality, educational and professional background and the outcomes of investment disputes on this question is hard to ignore. Arbitrators consciously and subconsciously interpret investment treaties' definitions and standards in a way that resembles their own national understanding of property and requirements for compensation. Consequently, arbitrators harbouring individualistic legal traditions tend to award 'a full market value' compensation.[289] By dismissing the practices and laws of a host state, arbitrators usually deny the existence of their own cultural bias and value judgments in the interpretation of investment treaties.[290]

In conclusion, the same neo-liberal trend that prioritises individualistic understanding of property has been dominating the interpretation of the standard of compensation. Such interpretation contrasts with the regulation of the issue at the national level, where full market value compensation for an expropriated property is not always required, and the judiciary has the discretion to award something less than the market value, taking into account the circumstances of the dispute between the individual and society.

5 Investment Protection Mimics Neoliberal Understanding of Property Protection

The journey through time, following the concept of property and its application in international settings, appears to confirm that, initially, both communitarian and individualistic understandings of property, which exist at the theoretical and national levels, could have been adopted by international practice.

However, with the Enlightenment and the emergence of classical international law, Western countries projected their individualistic understanding of property into international relations, which aligned with their economic interests.[291] International law's entanglement with capitalism and business enter-

289 Provided that party-appointed arbitrators balance each other, the president's views become prevalent: *Compañía del Desarrollo de Santa Elena v Republic of Costa Rica* para 70; *Crystallex International Corporation v Bolivarian Republic of Venezuela* para 882; *Rumeli Telekom AS and Telsim Mobil Telekomunikasyon Hizmetleri AS v Republic of Kazakhstan* (ICSID) Case No ARB/05/16, Award, 29 July 2008 para 786.

290 *Masdar Solar & Wind Cooperatief UA v Kingdom of Spain* (ICSID) Case No ARB/14/1, Award, 16 May 2018 para 580; Sornarajah, *The International Law on Foreign Investment* 465.

291 Gus Van Harten, 'Fortifying Inequality' in *The Trouble with Foreign Investor Protection* (Oxford University Press 2020) 11.

prises is well documented,[292] as well as the fact that 'the theories of sovereignty, rights, property and international law ... [are] inherently disposed towards Western interests and values'.[293] The understanding of property that prioritises the interest of the property owner over the interest of general society seemed to serve the Western interests: '[t]he adjective "civilised" came to serve as the justification for the imposition of a Western liberal vision of property rights'.[294] The combined role of business actors, neoliberal intellectuals, institutions, and arbitrators in the creation of the current investment protection regime is significant. However, it is important not to overstate the influence of any particular actor, as the international investment protection regime resulted from a combination of factors. Central among these was the prevailing neoliberal belief that safeguarding property rights and, by extension, investments – along with the prohibition of redistribution – represents the most effective policy for enhancing the wealth and prosperity of any society.

This chapter illustrates what Sundhya Pahuja called 'categorical cuts', but instead of an institutional prism, I am concerned with the concept of property and how international actors, such as negotiators, adjudicators, and counsels made the cut between individualistic and communitarian understandings of property.[295] This cut becomes obvious when international law on property is analysed alongside a variety of national property systems.

Even though 'Western international law has achieved a geographical spread, thematic expansion and claim to universality',[296] its claim about universal property protection remains in a constant flux of uncertainty. For example, Leiter–Bockley points out a number of decisions where the property protection rule was asserted as existing through the mental acrobatics of scholars and adjudicators trying to show that it existed in the past.[297] In that sense, the international property protection rule is nothing more than a belief system reinforced by circular references and the notion that property must be protected in an individualistic way.[298] The critical analysis of historic cases on

292 Ntina Tzouvala, *Capitalism As Civilisation: A History of International Law* (Cambridge University Press 2020) 34; Doreen Lustig, *Veiled Power: International Law and the Private Corporation 1886–1981* (Oxford University Press 2020) 14.

293 Fitzmaurice 11.

294 Leiter, *Making the World Safe for Investment: The Protection of Foreign Property 1922–1959* 17, 24.

295 Pahuja 26–27.

296 Tzouvala 18.

297 Leiter, *Making the World Safe for Investment: The Protection of Foreign Property 1922–1959* 3.

298 The parallel borrowed from Jean d'Aspremont, *International Law as a Belief System* (Cambridge University Press 2017).

the protection of property shows that the claim to universality, like many other international law concepts and rules, is circular and relies only on its own claim to be authoritative.[299]

The predominantly individualistic interpretation of investment protection was achieved through several legal innovations. First, investment treaties significantly expanded the scope of protected economic interests, well beyond national concepts of property. Second, investment arbitration provided a mandatory dispute resolution mechanism and tangible investment protection, grounded in the neoliberal understanding of property with accompanying prohibition of wealth redistribution. Third, investment treaties granted international procedural standing to individuals and corporations, who take the pursuit of individual economic rights very personally.

The substantive protection standards of investment treaties had the potential to be interpreted in both individualistic and communitarian ways. The procedural choices for the resolution of investment disputes determined the prevalence of neoliberal patterns. First, the widely adopted practice of appointing Western arbitrators in investment disputes, who consciously and subconsciously applied an extreme individualistic property protection without national safeguards,[300] entrenched and solidified the neoliberal interpretation in investment disputes.[301] Second, investment tribunals had a tendency to overlook domestic property regimes in favour of a poorly grounded notion of international property protection.[302]

Shirlow identified that only 42 per cent of international court and tribunal decisions relating to property engaged in some form of deliberation on whether the international or national regime should have priority.[303] Out of all investment arbitration decisions, Shirlow shows that 53 per cent refer to the possibility of deference, but ultimately refuse to defer to the domestic law or

299 Pahuja 26.

300 National property regimes do not prioritise individual interests, instead they try to balance owner's and social or public interests: Walt 129.

301 Slobodian 12–13; Perrone, *Investment Treaties and the Legal Imagination: How Foreign Investors Play By Their Own Rules* 2–3, 170; Batselé 415; Zarbiyev 525.

302 Schneiderman, *Investment Law's Alibis: Colonialism, Imperialism, Debt and Development* 172.

303 Shirlow argues that deference of international adjudicators to the domestic property regime varies in time and depending on context: Esmé Shirlow, *Judging at the Interface: Deference to State Decision-Making Authority in International Adjudication* (Cambridge University Press 2021) 198.

decisions.[304] The combination of these factors led to the marginalisation of national property laws, which protect public interests[305] and provide a systemic view of the property.[306]

304 Ibid 202.
305 Kulick 4.
306 Walt 130.

CHAPTER 5

Right to Property as a Human Right and Investment Protection

Human rights, their history, notion, status, and scope are passionately debated.[1] The right to property, although not at the core of human rights discussions, generates a fair share of its own controversy.[2] This chapter scratches the surface of the problems associated with the triangle of international investment protection, national property regimes, and human rights. Some of the problems stem from the disputed status of human rights: are they universal, regional, or local? Other problems originate from the contested nature of property rights: is it a natural phenomenon or a social consensus? Meanwhile, some people question whether the right to property is a human right at all and what it means for the substantial part of the population living in poverty.[3]

This chapter argues that property protection under different multilateral human rights instruments, in terms of the scope and level of protection, occupies an uneasy middle ground between national property regimes and international investment protection. Furthermore, the human rights agenda *per se* does not dictate a particular political economy. The problem arises only if human rights are infused with the extreme individualistic understanding of property, leaning towards neoliberal ideology. Such a version of the human right to property becomes a problem almost everywhere, even in the West, from which it originates. The claims that the individualistic understanding of property amounts to a human right, suffer from the fatal internal contradiction: if the content of the human right to property is Western, then it is necessarily limited to the Western scope of influence. If the human right to property

1 Samuel Moyn, *The Last Utopia: Human Rights in History* (Belknap Press of Harvard University Press 2010) 176; Samuel Moyn, *Not Enough: Human Rights in an Unequal World* (The Belknap Press of Harvard University Press 2018) 174.

2 Yannick Radi, 'Introduction: Taking stock of the societal and legal interplay between human rights and investment' in Yannick Radi (ed), *Research Handbook on Human Rights and Investment* (Edward Elgar Publishing Limited 2018) 5; Alvarez 580. See also Lorenzo Cotula, 'Property in a shrinking planet: fault lines in international human rights and investment law' (2015) 11 International Journal of Law in Context 113.

3 Anne Peters, *Beyond Human Rights: The Legal Status of the Individual in International Law* (Jonathan Huston tr, Cambridge University Press 2016) 318.

 | HTTPS://DOI.ORG/10.1163/9789004763517-006

has any pretence of universality, then it cannot have an exclusively Western and individualistic understanding of property.

The often-cited and influential jurisprudence of the European Convention on Human Rights (ECHR) merely reflects regional social consensus over property. This regional solution to the balance of individual and community interests, is not suitable for universal application because it promotes European values and the preservation of the *status quo* in wealth distribution. Any attempts to hijack human rights rhetoric in order to impose neoliberal policies on the rest of the world would be misplaced and harmful to the promotion of other fundamental human rights.

The antagonism between the right to property and other human rights is indirect, meaning that the right to property, if enforced in an extreme individualistic manner, might make legal reforms more challenging to implement. For example, a land reform aimed at improving the social and economic situation in the local society will inevitably interfere with the legal interests of the incumbent owners. Thus, an individualistic understanding of property affects many aspects of life in developing states.[4]

Even from a cursory overview, the teleological, substantive, and procedural differences between the protection of human rights, on the one hand, and the protection of property and investments, on the other, are apparent.[5] The differences between these two systems are numerous. For individuals, access to international human rights protection mechanisms is more complicated and less efficient than ISDS.[6] Many universal and some regional human rights instruments are not even strictly binding, while bilateral investment treaties are. The substantive state obligations under BITs are frequently interpreted as strict obligations, while human rights obligations are often treated as best efforts' obligations or aspirational.[7] Many human rights instruments do not have mandatory dispute resolution mechanisms, while BITs have mandatory

4 Further see Jesse Coleman, Kaitlin Y Cordes, and Lise Johnson, 'Human rights law and the investment treaty regime' in Deva Surya and Birchall David (eds), *Research Handbook on Human Rights and Business* (Edward Elgar Publishing 2020) 307; *Cf.* Alvarez adopts a neoliberal approach to societal problem solving, arguing that stronger, secure and even more individualistic understanding and protection of property rights may rectify inequalities within societies and globally: Alvarez 689.

5 Enrique B. Barrera, 'Property Rights as Human Rights in International Investment Arbitration: A Critical Approach' (2018) 59 Boston College Law Review 2638.

6 The victims of human right's abuses have to exhaust local remedies before applying to the regional human rights' courts, while the requirement of exhaustion of local remedies is abandoned in investment arbitration.

7 *Quasar de Valors SICAV SA and others (formerly Renta 4 SVSA and others) v Russian Federation* (SCC) para 22.

dispute resolution mechanisms. The compensations for breaches of human rights are also minimal, and enforcement relies a great deal on the goodwill of a respondent state.

These differences in interpretation, treatment and adjudication of human rights violations and protection of investments speak volumes about the current status of international law and the values that it actually and efficiently serves.[8] Cotula identifies that:

> international investment law and international human rights law protect different and possibly competing rights, reflect different balances of commercial and non-commercial considerations, and embody different standards of legal protection.[9]

The different dynamics of human rights and investment or property protection were conceptualised as fragmentation of international law.[10] Indeed, the interaction between investment arbitration and human rights practice was fairly limited for a long time.[11] Such historical compartmentalisation was quite convenient for the dominant powers after WWII when human rights courts and ISDS were intensely developing in the context of NIEO. It also served the emerging Washington Consensus about the separation between so-called economic issues (property and investment) and political questions (human rights). It was feared that the communitarian human rights' considerations might interfere with the neoliberal framework of investment protection.[12] This line of thinking is not entirely unreasonable:

> Taken in their most extreme form, these values are polar opposites. The values associated with the individual element of property posit that individual rights trump community rights to distribute property in accordance with a publicly conceived common good. … The values associated with the social element of

---

8 See also: Margot E Salomon, *Global responsibility for human rights: world poverty and the development of international law* (Oxford University Press 2007) 196.

9 Cotula 113.

10 Martti Koskenniemi and Päivi Leino, 'Fragmentation of International Law? Postmodern Anxieties' (2005) 15 Leiden Journal of International Law 553.

11 *Biloune and Marine Drive Complex Ltd v Ghana Investments Centre and the Government of Ghana* (UNCITRAL), Award on Jurisdiction and Liability, 27 October 1989, 95 ILR 184; *Patrick Mitchell v The Democratic Republic of Congo* para 62; *CMS Gas Transmission Co v Argentina* para 114; *Azurix Corp v Argentine Republic* para 254; *Siemens AG v Argentine Republic* para 75.

12 Bruno Simma, 'Foreign Investment Arbitration: a Place for Human Rights?' (2011) 60 The International and Comparative Law Quarterly 573, 567.

> property, on the other hand, posit unbounded community rights to distribute property entitlement in a manner that reflects community consensus of the proper or desirable economic order.[13]

Higgins was one of the early advocates of a comprehensive approach that includes the international protection of property and human rights, but her solutions were very Anglo-American.[14] Her understanding of the integration of property protection and human rights was that human rights law should help protect property from the state, insulating it from other competing interests and values of society. She noted the difficulties in finding a single European standard for property protection, but in all problematic questions, her interpretation favoured an individualistic understanding of property with an extensive scope of protection and minimal state interference.[15] Dupuy also acknowledged the procedural and substantive differences between human rights and international investment law, then argued against the fragmentation of these two branches of international law, but in favour of the individualistic understanding of property.[16] Simma summarised the traditional individualistic approach to the question – investment protection and human rights are not 'separate worlds', because 'the ultimate concern … is one and the same: the protection of the individual against the power of the State', ignoring the systemic view of the property.[17] Meanwhile, Alvarez argued that the fragmentation of different property protection systems is not a problem, but rather a strength of the global system, as it allows for the adaptation of property rights in different locations and forums.[18]

Overall, the human rights argument in investment disputes may play two contradictory roles: as a moral authority supporting an individualistic understanding of property behind investment claims or as a justification for state interference with private property.[19] Krommendijk and Morijn argued that

13 Michael R Antinori, 'Does Lochner Live in Luxembourg: An Analysis of the Property Rights Jurisprudence of the European Court of Justice Note' (1994) 18 Fordham International Law Journal 1778, 1848.

14 Higgins 370–373.

15 Ibid 357, 361.

16 Pierre-Marie Dupuy, Francesco Francioni, and Ernst-Ulrich Petersmann, *Human rights in international investment law and arbitration* (Oxford University Press 2009) 46–53.

17 Simma 576.

18 Alvarez 655.

19 James D Fry, 'International Human Rights Law in Investment Arbitration: Evidence of International Law's Unity' (2007) 18 Duke journal of comparative & international law 77, 106–107; Eric De Brabandere, Malgosia Fitzmaurice, and Panos Merkouris, 'The Interpretation and Application of the European Convention of Human Rights: Legal and Practi-

'the right to property within investment law should not be' isolated from the demands of other human rights, which inevitably involve a balancing of interests.[20] Arbitral tribunals have also realised the usefulness of balancing rhetoric.[21] However, investment arbitration allows wide discretion for arbitral tribunals to adopt solutions based on their own (usually Western and individualistic)[22] understanding of property and its place in the society, ignoring social consensus in the host state.[23] Thus, investment arbitration disputes increasingly feature different human rights arguments formulated both as claims and as defences.

Below, the regional differences in the protection of property under human rights mechanisms are analysed before turning to the problems arising out of the *mélange* of human rights, property, and investment. Although the fragmentation of human rights and investment arbitration is criticised, but mingling those concepts presents its own challenges. First problem is the alleged universality of the human right to property, which only masks the Western European content of the right; second issue is the prioritisation of the right to property over other recognised values, protected by human rights' conventions or constitutions.

1 Right to Property in Global Instruments and Regional Conventions

In 1948, the Universal Declaration of Human Rights (UDHR) proclaimed that '[e]veryone has the right to own property alone as well as in association with

cal Implications' in *Human Rights Considerations in International Investment Arbitration* (Brill | Nijhoff 2013) 184.

20 Jasper Krommendijk and John Morijn, '"Proportional" by What Measure(s)? Balancing Investor Interests and Human Rights by Way of Applying the Proportionality Principle in Investor-State Arbitration' in Pierre-Marie Dupuy, Francesco Francioni and Ernst-Ulrich Petersmann (eds), *Human Rights in International Investment Law and Arbitration* (Oxford University Press 2009) 429.

21 Yulia Levashova, 'The Right of Access to Water in the Context of Investment Disputes in Argentina: Urbaser and Beyond' 16 Utrecht Law Review 110; Ursula Kriebaum, 'The Right to Water Before Investment Tribunals' (2018) 1 Brill Open Law 16.

22 Pauwelyn Joost, 'The Rule of Law without the Rule of Lawyers? Why Investment Arbitrators are from Mars, Trade Adjudicators from Venus' (2015) 109 The American Journal of International Law 761, 773.

23 *Tecnicas Medioambientales Tecmed SA v The United Mexican States* para 116; *Saipem SpA v People's Republic of Bangladesh* paras 130 and 132; *Mondev International Ltd v USA* paras 138, 141–144.

others' and that 'no one shall be arbitrarily deprived of his property'.[24] However, rights are not absolute and may be limited 'solely for the purpose of securing due recognition and respect for the rights and freedoms of others and of meeting the just requirements of morality, public order and the general welfare in a democratic society'.[25] This text was the result of complex negotiations trying to combine socialist and capitalist ideologies regarding property.[26] Lacking the common denominator about the extent of property rights and what could be seen as an abuse by a state, the International Covenant on Civil and Political Rights (ICCPR) and the International Covenant on Economic, Social, and Cultural Rights (ICESCR) adopted in 1966 do not provide a separate right to property but instead only mention that property cannot be a basis for discrimination.[27] Some other international instruments aiming to protect the most vulnerable members of society also mention property in passing.[28]

Regional agreements on the right to property were slightly more successful than international instruments, maybe because consensus among states that shared a similar history and underlying values was easier to find.

While the European Convention on Human Rights (ECHR),[29] like the UDHR, remained silent on the right to property for the same reason – the impossibility of reconciling socialistic and capitalistic ideologies on property[30] – the solution was found in the adoption of a separate First Protocol

24 Article 17(1) and (2) of the Universal Declaration of Human Rights (1948) <http://www.un.org/en/universal-declaration-human-rights/> accessed on 19 May 2025.

25 Article 29(s) of the Universal Declaration of Human Rights.

26 See UN Docs E/CN.4/SR.230–232; E/CN.4/SR.302, 303; E/CN.4/SR.413–418.

27 Article 2(1) of the International Covenant on Civil and Political Rights (1966); Article 2(2) of the International Covenant on Economic, Social, and Cultural Rights (1966); See also Eibe H Riedel, *Theorie der Menschenrechtsstandards: Funktion, Wirkungsweise und Begründung wirtschaftlicher und sozialer Menschenrechte mit exemplarischer Darstellung der Rechte auf Eigentum und Arbeit in verschiedenen Rechtsordnungen* (Duncker & Humblot 1986) 39.

28 Convention relating to the Status of Refugees (1951); Convention relating to the Status of Stateless Persons (1954); the International Convention on the Elimination of All Forms of Racial Discrimination (1965); the International Convention on the Elimination of All Forms of Discrimination against Women (1979); International Labour Organization Convention No 169 concerning Indigenous and Tribal Peoples (1989); International Convention on the Protection of the Rights of All Migrant Workers and Members of Their Families (1990); Convention on the Rights of Persons with Disabilities (2006).

29 European Convention on Human Rights (1950) <https://www.echr.coe.int/european-convention-on-human-rights> accessed on 16 May 2025.

30 Wolfgang Peukert, 'Protection of Ownership under Article I of the First Protocol to the European Convention on Human Rights' (1981) 2 Human Rights Law Journal 37, 38.

that 'reflect[ed] the constitutional experiences in some European countries (like France and Germany)'[31] and allowed partitioning of the signatories along the ideological lines.[32]

The American Convention on Human Rights (ACHR) and the African Charter on Human and Peoples' Rights (AfCHPR), even though mentioning the right to property, do not have such strong enforcement mechanisms as in Europe, while Asian states failed to adopt a mandatory convention on any human rights, let alone right to property.[33]

The literature on regional human rights conventions and their property clauses is plentiful. Academics and practitioners, however, seem to pay the most attention to the ECHR jurisprudence. The ECHR jurisprudence is frequently cited and used for analogies in other legal systems, including in the ISDS. The Protocol 1 of the ECHR provides that:

> (1) Every natural or legal person is entitled to the peaceful enjoyment of his possessions. No one shall be deprived of his possessions except in the public interest and subject to the conditions provided for by law and by the general principles of international law.
>
> (2) The preceding provisions shall not, however, in any way impair the right of a State to enforce such laws as it deems necessary to control the use of property in accordance with the general interest or to secure the payment of taxes or other contributions or penalties.[34]

However, it is the case practice of the ECtHR that animates the prevailing understanding of property and its limits in Europe. Initially, only some proprietary interests were treated as protected property, and the use rights were not among them.[35] Only since *Sporrong and Lonnroth v Sweden,* property has been understood as including all economic interests.[36] The ECtHR interpreted the term 'possessions' in an autonomous way, which is allegedly independent of

31 Dupuy, Francioni and Petersmann 159.

32 Helen Mountfield, 'Regulatory Expropriations in Europe: the Approach of the European Court of Human Rights' (2002) 11 New York University Environmental Law Journal 136.

33 The ASEAN Intergovernmental Commission on Human Rights, inaugurated in 2009, is a consultative body, and the ASEAN Human Rights Declaration (2012) is a more aspirational document than binding: <https://asean.org/asean-human-rights-declaration/> accessed 20 May 2025.

34 Article 1 of Protocol 1 of the ECHR, <https://rm.coe.int/168006377c> accessed on 19 May 2025.

35 Peukert 42–45.

36 *Sporrong and Lonnroth v Sweden* (1982) 52 ECHR (Ser A) 26.

national understandings of property, but interpreted it very broadly, which coincides with the Western individualistic understanding of property that includes contractual rights with economic value, professional clientele, goodwill, entitlement to compensation, and future income.[37]

The practice of the ECtHR had a profound influence on the constitutional understanding of property in Eastern Europe, which initially under the Soviet law influence had a very traditional and narrow understanding of property. Since most Eastern European member states joined the ECHR already after *Sporrong and Lonnroth v Sweden* interpretation,[38] they had to accept as a *fait accompli* that, under the ECHR, property involves almost all pecuniary interests and even some claims, except the right to acquire property in the future.[39] The ECHR also extends protection to legal persons' property, while all other regional human rights conventions protect only natural persons and shun away from disputes involving business interests.[40]

Similarly, the ACHR also implies a very wide understanding of property[41] but is limited by the social function of property[42] where individuals are prioritised over commercial or economic interests or corporations.[43] In ACHR, property includes material things and intangible things, pensions, copyrights, or claims 'capable of having value', which may be part of a person's patrimony, as well as claims to land by indigenous people.[44] Perhaps to address the historical injustices, the claims to property by indigenous communities are pri-

---

37 Aida Grgic and others, 'The right to property under the European Convention on Human Rights: a guide to the implementation of the European Convention on Human Rights and its protocols' (2007) 6–9.

38 *Sporrong and Lonnroth v Sweden* para 61.

39 *Maltzan and others v Germany Applications Nos 71916/01, 71917/01 and 10260/02 (ECtHR)* para 74 (c); *Kopecký v Slovakia* Application No 44912/98 (ECtHR) para 35(c); *Slivenko and Others v Latvia* Application No 48321/99 (ECtHR) para 121; *Van der Mussele v Belgium* Application No 8919/80 (ECtHR) para 46.

40 Lorenzo Cotula, *Human rights, natural resource and investment law in a globalised world: shades of grey in the shadow of the law* (Routledge 2012) 47.

41 Articles 21(1) and (2) of the American Convention on Human Rights (1969).

42 Theo RG van Banning, *The human right to property* (Intersentia 2003) 62.

43 Dupuy, Francioni and Petersmann 20, 257.

44 *Yakye Axa Indigenous Community v Paraguay (ACtHR)* para 137; *Five Pensioners v Peru* Series C No 98 (ACtHR) para 103; *Ivcher-Bronstein v Peru Series C No 74 (ACtHR)* para 122; *Alejandra Marcela Matus Acun˜a and ors v Chile Report No 90/05 (ACtHR)* para 51; *Palamara-Iribarne v Chile Series C No 135* paras 102–106.

oritised over all other rights and interests, including foreign ones, in the Inter-American case practice.[45] The AfCHPR shares this view.[46]

The comprehensive understanding of property under the ECHR is balanced by a somewhat narrower understanding of the expropriation if compared to the investment arbitration practice. The ECtHR, in some cases, has refused to treat partial limitation of property rights as expropriation if the owners could still exercise at least some of their rights.[47] Furthermore, human rights courts and investment arbitration apply differently deference to national legal system and institutions, also known as the judicial self-restraint or 'a wide margin of appreciation' when balancing public and private interests.[48] The importance of the wide margin of appreciation is such that it was added to the preamble of the Convention by the Protocol No 15[49] explaining that:

> the Convention system is subsidiary to the safeguarding of human rights at national level and that national authorities are in principle better placed than an international court to evaluate local needs and conditions.[50]

In *James v. the UK,* the government was trying to reform the leasehold situation for social causes, allowing long-term tenants to purchase their homes. The ECtHR agreed that states have broad discretion over policies that serve public interest.[51] The European Court of Justice adopted a similar approach.[52]

45 Alvarez 606.

46 *Centre for Minority Rights Development (Kenya) and Minority Rights Group International on behalf of Endorois Welfare Council v Kenya* (African Commission on Human and Peoples' Rights) para 209.

47 Deborah Rook, *Property law and human rights* (Blackstone 2001) 74–75.

48 Shirlow 241.

49 Protocol No. 15 amending the ECHR Convention: <https://rm.coe.int/1680084831> accessed on 20 May 2025.

50 Explanatory Report to Protocol No 15 amending the Convention for the Protection of Human Rights and Fundamental Freedoms <https://rm.coe.int/1680a5278a> accessed on 20 May 2025. The principle of margin of appreciation was developed by the ECtHR jurisprudence: *Sporrong and Lonnroth v Sweden* para 61; *Viaşu v Roumanie Requête No 75951/01 (ECtHR)* para 72, 83; *Former King of Greece and others v Greece* (ECtHR); Michael R. Hutchinson, 'The margin of appreciation doctrine in the European Court of Human Rights' (1999) 48 International and Comparative Law Quarterly 638, 640.

51 *James and others v The United Kingdom* para 67. The USA Supreme Court has a similar case regarding land ownership in Hawaii: *Hawaii Housing Authority v Midkiff* 467 US (1984).

52 *Liselotte Hauer v Land Rheinland-Pfalz* Case 44/79 (ECJ); *Hubert Wachauf* Case 5/88 [1989] (ECJ); the EU case law can be accessed here <https://eur-lex.europa.eu/collection/eu-law/eu-case-law.html> accessed on 20 May 2025.

The recent investment arbitration case *Philip Morris et al v. Uruguay* also employed this doctrine when deciding on the government's measures in matters of public health.[53]

The wide margin of appreciation in the ECtHR jurisprudence is counterbalanced by the principle of proportionality.[54] The proportionality test between a state measure affecting property and the desired aim in practice is quite flexible. It varies depending on the nature of a state measure: if a state takes the title of property, the test is stricter. If a regulation interferes only with the use and control of the property, the test is looser. The proportionality test with the underlying distributional effects is embedded in European administrative practices and European values. Investment arbitration practice selectively borrowed the proportionality tests but ignored the wide margin of appreciation.[55] In an investment dispute with a factual pattern similar to *James v UK,* the claimant would have, most likely, prevailed.[56]

The ACHR also represents a flexible understanding of interference with property,[57] but such flexibility has always been a derivative question of some other fundamental human rights such as personal freedom, due process, etc.[58] The courts have never addressed the genuine conflict between communitarian and individual interests directly. Under the Inter-American human rights jurisprudence, 'arbitrariness against private economic activity' is not treated as a breach of human rights,' and, generally, economic interests yield to fundamental human rights.[59]

The African Commission on Human and Peoples' Rights adopted a similar position: in the *Endorois* case, the interests of indigenous communities were given priority over commercial and economic interests as in the ACHR practice.[60] The AfCHPR does have a property clause but acknowledges that the public need and the general interest of the community may legitimately

---

53 *Philip Morris Brand Sàrl, Philip Morris Products SA and Abal Hermanos SA v Oriental Republic of Uruguay* (ICSID) para 399, 418.

54 *Tre Traktörer Aktiebolag v Sweden* para 46; Yutaka Arai-Takahashi, *The margin of appreciation doctrine and the principle of proportionality in the jurisprudence of the ECHR* (Intersentia 2002) 148.

55 *Tecnicas Medioambientales Tecmed SA v The United Mexican States* para 122.

56 *El Paso Energy International Company v Argentine Republic* (ICSID) para 488, 519.

57 Dupuy, Francioni and Petersmann 250.

58 Ibid 254.

59 Ibid 259, 270.

60 *Centre for Minority Rights Development (Kenya) and Minority Rights Group International on behalf of Endorois Welfare Council v Kenya* para 211–219.

limit it.[61] Besides the requirement for the limitation of rights to be provided by the law, the African Commission on Human and Peoples' Rights, similarly to the ECHR practice, applies the principle of proportionality. Overall, the property protection clause in AfCHPR is viewed as considerably weaker than the European counterpart.[62]

The First Protocol of the European Convention fails to specify the standard of compensation *expressis verbis* because of the disagreements and because, initially, compensation requirement was thought to apply only to foreigners.[63] Interestingly, in order to interpret the First Protocol of ECHR, the argument of national law was advanced, that is, that national laws of the UK, Germany, and France normally require compensation.[64] Subsequently, the ECtHR developed a practice where a total deprivation of property requires compensation at the amount reasonably related to the market value, but general regulation, even though interfering with property rights, does not require compensation.[65] According to the ECtHR, legal reforms for 'public interest' may warrant compensation at less than the full market value.[66] Compensation is viewed as part of the balance between communitarian and individual interest.[67] The standard of fair compensation paid in good time is required by the Charter of Fundamental Rights of the European Union,[68] while in all other material aspects, the European Court of Justice follows the interpretations of the ECtHR.[69] Article 26(1) of the 1995 Commonwealth of Independent States Con-

61 Article 14 of the African Charter on Human and Peoples' Rights (1981); Gino J Naldi, 'Limitation of rights under the African Charter on Human and Peoples' Rights: the contribution of the African Commission on Human and Peoples' Rights' (2001) 17 South African Journal on Human Rights 109, 118.

62 Cotula, *Human rights, natural resource and investment law in a globalised world: shades of grey in the shadow of the law* 45–46.

63 Higgins 361; R. Anthony Salgado, 'Protection of nationals' rights to property under the European Convention on Human Rights: Lithgow v. United Kingdom' (1987) 27 Virginia Journal of International Law 865, 883; Peter Van Den Broek, 'The protection of property rights under the European Convention on Human Rights' (1986) Legal Issues of European Integration 52, 54.

64 Higgins 361.

65 Banning, 102; *James and others v The United Kingdom* para 54; *Former King of Greece and others v Greece* para 75–79; *Scordino v Italy (No 1)* (ECtHR) para 250–253.

66 *Lithgow and Others v the United Kingdom* (ECtHR) para 121.

67 Ursula Kriebaum, 'Regulatory Takings: Balancing the Interests of the Investor and the State' (2007) 8 The Journal of World Investment & Trade 717, 719, 720.

68 Article 17 of the Charter of Fundamental Rights of the European Union (2009).

69 Dupuy, Francioni and Petersmann 201; *European Commission v Hungary Case C 235/17* (ECJ (Grand Chamber)) [2019] para 128.

vention on Human Rights and Fundamental Freedoms does not mention compensation at all.[70]

The Arab Charter on Human Rights of 2004 also provides for the protection of property, but the inter-state court has yet to be established.[71] Although there is no jurisprudence on the Arab Charter on Human Rights to illuminate its provisions, it would be rather shocking, given the legal traditions in the region, if the court ascribed a very individualistic meaning and a high level of property protection to it.[72]

The overall European practice of property protection is a regional phenomenon guarded by the ECtHR, far from uniform and not uncontested:

> There are inevitable constitutional differences among the Member States even in interpreting norms which look alike. The adoption of an outcome corresponding to a balancing choice in one Member State will be in contrast to a balancing choice adopted elsewhere. The Court should reject, and in fact has rejected, the notion and the language of trying to adopt the maximal standard prevailing among the Member States, not simply because it will in effect subject the Community to the constitutional dictates of the different Member States, but because it is an impossible exercise.[73]

The relatively broad interpretation of property and its equation to possessions together with the high level of protection under the ECHR was successfully exported to the outskirts of Europe. Two factors have contributed to the successful imposition of the more or less uniform European understandings of property. First, after the collapse of the Soviet Union, Eastern Europe eagerly followed the vision of private property, promoted by the ideologically close Western European countries.[74] Second, unlike investment tribunals, ECtHR allowed for flexibility by repeatedly deferring to national courts and acknowledging the importance of national priorities and peculiarities.[75] However, the

70 The convention remains controversial, see ECtHR Decision on the Competence of the Court to Give an Advisory Opinion, 2 June 2004.

71 Ahmed Almutawa, 'The Arab Court of Human Rights and the Enforcement of the Arab Charter on Human Rights' (2021) 21 Human Rights Law Review 506.

72 Article 31 of the Arab Charter on Human Rights (2004) <https://digitallibrary.un.org/record/551368?v=pdf> accessed on 20 May 2025. Although the Agreement on Promotion, Protection and Guarantee of Investments amongst the Member States of the Organisation of the Islamic Conference (1981) follows an individualistic template of investment treaties.

73 Weiler, 1128.

74 Dupuy, Francioni and Petersmann 159.

75 Shirlow 201; Peat 144–145.

process of internalising the individualistic understanding of property in the national laws and practices may never be completely finished, and conflicts about the balance between individual and community interests still abound.[76]

While this expanded European understanding of property is deeply embedded within the historical and economic structures of Europe, it is not the only one globally. Despite similar treaty language and occasional reliance on the ECtHR practice by other regional human rights conventions or institutions, both Latin American and African understandings of property and its place in society are more communitarian, let alone Asian views on property, where a binding treaty on human rights does not exist.

Alvarez brushes aside the discussed regional and national differences, the divide between socialist and market economies, as well as the long list of historical, philosophical and religious problems of property and, similarly to Sprankling, argues that the list of 21 international instruments mentioning the word 'property' have begun to delineate what constitutes property internationally.[77] This argumentation holds an irreconcilable contradiction. While Alvarez calls the human right to property a universal value, he admits that there has been no global consensus over the regime for property protection, despite the fact that property is mentioned in almost every single national constitution.[78] His argument for the human right to property is based on a very superficial assessment by Hegel and the moral principles of the European Enlightenment, primarily – human dignity.[79] The following subchapter analyses whether the alleged universal human right to property can overcome regional limitations to become a backbone for international property law.

2 European Version of Human Right to Property and the Claim to Universality

The similarities or overlaps between national property regimes, the international system of investment protection, and human rights protection are few and superficial.[80] The most obvious problem is that, besides much-idealised *lege ferenda* idea about the human right to property, a single universal, globally accepted standard is a myth. The existing conventions and consents are

76 *Magyar Farming and others v Hungary* para 129.
77 Alvarez 654.
78 Ibid 650.
79 Ibid 681.
80 Barrera 2644.

only regional at best,[81] even when all national law regimes have an idea of property and some system of property.

The European human rights practice – the pioneer in the field with the most developed jurisprudence – is often looked up to in investment arbitration because it helps to cement the Western and individualistic understanding of property. In very general terms, the ECtHR jurisprudence on property protection could be situated somewhere in the middle between international investment protection and the average European national property regime. The ECtHR practice provides for a broad definition of property, but it refuses to treat limitations on the use of property as indirect expropriation if an owner can still exercise at least some ownership rights. Investment arbitration practice is neoliberal and individualistic in that regard, and indirect expropriations are pronounced more frequently than under ECHR practice.[82] Also, the ECtHR widely acknowledges and applies the margin of appreciation, while investment tribunals paying lip service to the concept, very often decide on their own and *post factum* what the best solution to a governance crisis was.[83] Finally, the quantum of compensation is much lower in the practice of human rights courts than in investment arbitration.[84]

The ECtHR practice on property protection may be on par with the constitutional jurisprudence of Western European states, but it still is more individualistic than the property protection in most of Eastern Europe, even though the latter states are coming to accept and internalise the ECtHR practice on property. A glimpse at the overlap of isolated instances in European human

---

81 Alvarez 650.

82 *Metalclad Corporation v United Mexican States* para 107; *Antoine Goetz and others v Republic of Burundi* [II] (ICSID) Case No ARB/01/2, Award 21 June 2012 [French] para 244; *Abengoa, SA y COFIDES, SA v United Mexican States* para 610; *Gavrilovic and Gavrilovic doo v Republic of Croatia* (ICSID) para 922–923; *Occidental Petroleum Corporation and Occidental Exploration and Production Company v Republic of Ecuador* (ICSID) Case No ARB/06/11, Award 5 October 2012 para 455. Metalclad approach was criticised in other awards as too wide: *Fireman's Fund Insurance Company v 111 United Mexican States* (ICSID) para 177; *ECE Projektmanagement International GmbH and Kommanditgesellschaft PANTA Achtundsechzigste Grundstücksgesellschaft mbH & Co v Czech Republic* (PCA) Case No 2010-2015, Award 19 September 2013 para 4.812.

83 *Siemens AG v Argentine Republic* para 271; *Tecnicas Medioambientales Tecmed SA v The United Mexican States* para 151.

84 Yukos cases: *Veteran Petroleum Limited (Cyprus) v Russian Federation* (PCA) Case No AA 228, Final Award 18 July 2014 para 1787; *Yukos Universal Limited v Russian Federation* (PCA) Final Award para 1787; *Hulley Enterprises Limited (Cyprus) v Russian Federation* (PCA) Case No AA 226, Final Award 18 July 2014 para 1787.

rights practice (which, arguably, is the most similar to investment protection) and investment arbitration reveals a number of issues.

First, like BITs, human rights' conventions were drafted in a very broad manner, using vague language. Unfortunately, that vagueness did not translate into effective protection of human rights, while the broad language efficiently protected investments.[85]

Second, both investment arbitration and human rights' jurisprudence define property in an extensive manner, stretching the domestic understandings of property. This liberal interpretation of 'possessions' in human rights courts could be justified by the claimants' need to overcome substantial procedural obstacles before they can submit a claim (such as exhaustion of local remedies or the fact that not all human rights courts have mandatory jurisdiction). Meanwhile, in investment disputes, such obstacles do not exist. Consequently, broad interpretation of investment just makes sure that arbitral tribunals have jurisdiction over the majority of a claim that has been brought before them.

The third issue is the occasional application of deference and proportionality test by both human rights courts and investment tribunals.[86] In its reasoning, the ECtHR reach the proportionality test after applying the margin of appreciation that recognises that local governments are inherently better informed and equipped to deal with local problems or difficult choices between individual and communitarian interests.[87] Investment arbitration practice on the issue is not uniform: cases range from 'the high measure of deference',[88] just 'deference',[89] modest 'margin of appreciation'[90] to doubts about the possibility of applying 'deference' to regulatory policies.[91] Differences in

85 Dupuy, Francioni and Petersmann 143.

86 Shirlow 200.

87 Sornarajah, *Resistance and change in the international law on foreign investment* 375.

88 *SD Myers Inc v Canada* para 263; See also *Philip Morris Brand Sàrl, Philip Morris Products SA and Abal Hermanos SA v Oriental Republic of Uruguay* para 399, 418; *Marion Unglaube v Republic of Costa Rica* para 258; *Reinhard Hans Unglaube v Republic of Costa Rica* para 258; *Crystallex International Corporation v Bolivarian Republic of Venezuela* paras 583, 585.

89 *Mercer International Inc v Government of Canada* (ICSID) Case No ARB(AF)/12/3, Award 6 March 2018 para 7.42; *Les Laboratoires Servier, SAS, Biofarma, SAS and Arts et Techniques du Progres SAS v Republic of Poland* para 568; *Invesmart, BV v Czech Republic* (UNCITRAL) Award (Redacted) 26 June 2009 paras 484–488.

90 *Electrabel SA v Republic of Hungary* (ICSID) Case No ARB/07/19, Decision on Jurisdiction, Applicable Law and Liability 30 November 2012 para 6.92.

91 *Glamis Gold Ltd v The United States of America* para 617; *Quasar de Valors SICAV SA and others (formerly Renta 4 SVSA and others) v Russian Federation* para 22; *Bernhard von Pezold and others v Republic of Zimbabwe* para 465–466.

interpretation and application of the concepts lead to the fact that many tribunals after consulting the deference and proportionality principles decide that the government's actions were in breach of the BIT.[92] One of the possible reasons is that the investment tribunals subconsciously interpret and apply those concepts in a manner that mirrors Western European governance standards.

The concept of margin of appreciation or the doctrine of deference sometimes appears in the reasoning of investment tribunals on indirect expropriation,[93] where tribunals often jump directly to the test of proportionality that is frequently used to circumscribe the margin of appreciation.[94] In *Blusun SA, Jean-Pierre Lecorcier and Michael Stein v Italian Republic*, the tribunal suggested that concepts of public interest, reasonableness and the deference to the local government are intrinsically indeterminate and subjective, therefore, should be abandoned in favour of proportionality.[95] Such reasoning overlooks the fact that the latter concepts also involve an element of subjective judgment – what weight is attributed to individual interests and preferences, and what weight is attributed to the public interests, both of which are informed by the prevailing values about the basic organisation of social and economic life in a particular state.

This prevailing human rights discourse originates from the Western historical experience and is deeply embedded in the philosophy of Enlightenment and natural law. The majority of the remaining world still faces rather prosaic problems: how to feed the population, where to get fresh water, how to ensure sanitation and education and how to deal with natural and human-made disasters. Distanced from the basic problems of the Global South, the Western tradition of human rights focused on the protection of an individual from her own state. The aim of the reduction of human suffering through the limitation

92 *Les Laboratoires Servier, SAS, Biofarma, SAS and Arts et Techniques du Progres SAS v Republic of Poland* para 568, 676; *Saluka Investments BV v Czech Republic* para 281; Ortino, 75.

93 Shirlow 15.

94 *Tecnicas Medioambientales Tecmed SA v The United Mexican States* para 122; *LG&E Energy Corp, LG&E Capital Corp and LG&E International Inc v Argentine Republic* para 195; *Deutsche Bank AG v Democratic Socialist Republic of Sri Lanka* para 522, *PL Holdings SARL v Republic of Poland* (SCC) para 410; See also Valentina Vadi, *Proportionality, Reasonableness and Standards of Review in International Investment Law and Arbitration* (Edward Elgar Publishing 2018).

95 *Blusun SA, Jean-Pierre Lecorcier and Michael Stein v Italian Republic* (ICSID) Case No ARB/14/3, Award 27 December 2016 para 318. See also *Fireman's Fund Insurance Company v 111 United Mexican States* para 176; *Occidental Petroleum Corp v Ecuador* (ICSID) Case No ARB/06/11 Award 5 October 2012 para 419.

of state abuse and authority has very little to say about the required economic structure of the society and has no recipe for how to deal with the problems of the Global South in the fastest way.[96] Barerra argues that cases about extreme violence and arbitrariness are not the same as disputes about the technical boundaries of the right to use of property and should not be equated.[97] Arguably, both capitalist and social economic systems should be capable of existing without breaching the fundamental human rights relating to physical and mental security and dignity if those notions of human rights do not go as far as ensuring certain profitability from property. If liberal economic structures become engrafted to the protection of human rights, the spectre of economic policies for development available to a state (without breaching those human rights) becomes limited:

> [t]he influence of international economic organizations, the impact of external actors advancing the requirements of a global free-market, and the corresponding diminution in domestic autonomy ... limits the ability of states independently to decide their own economic and social policies.[98]

Humans are not entitled to the neo-liberal economic order just by the mere existence, and any attempt to induce the neoliberal scope and standard to the property (or investment) is an overreach. Despite the fall of communism that opposed the consolidation of the individualistic understanding of property in international covenants, the majority of the world population still harbours solid communitarian notions of property, and human rights' instruments should recognise that.[99]

Outside of Europe, the gap between the prevailing standards on investment protection, human rights conventions and national property regimes is even greater. With the exceptions of a few highly industrialised, developed and stable states, most other regional human rights instruments and domestic regimes for property protection would fall below the ECtHR practice for property protection. Thus, even if we assume that the international investment protection standard should aim at the European human rights' practice and constitutional consensus about the proper balance between individual and

96 David Kennedy and Joseph E Stiglitz, *Law and Economics with Chinese Characteristics: Institutions for Promoting Development in the Twenty-First Century* (Oxford University Press 2013) 187.

97 Barrera 2661.

98 Salomon 196.

99 Antinori, 1787; Mary Ann Glendon, *Rights talk: the impoverishment of political discourse* (The Free Press 1991) 32–40.

communal interests with regard to property, we should not forget that this solution might not be optimal for other parts of the world where local problems might require a different approach.[100] On the contrary, addressing global injustices, inequality, and climate change will likely require collective actions through state organs that will tackle the *status quo* and affect the distribution of wealth in a neoliberal sense. The individualistic structures and practices of even recent IIAs are too rigid for such a task and will have to adapt, giving way to a more flexible and communitarian understanding of property, investment, and permissible regulation.

3 The Right to Property in the Context of Other Human Rights

Even if, for the sake of argument, we accept that the global human right to property has European content, investment arbitration is prone to another problem – investment protection exceeds the European balance between individual and community interests. In investment arbitration practice, the scope of protected interests, the prohibition to interfere with separate consisting rights and the prohibition to reduce their value, the methods of damage calculation lean towards a neoliberal balance between individual and community. The reframing of investment protection as a human right enables the selective adoption of the strongest elements from national legal systems, with the aim of securing the most profitable use of investment, while overlooking the adverse effects on the host society.

The cross-fertilisation of various legal systems is not an unheard-of phenomenon,[101] especially in the area of property law, where the general process of commodification of property could be observed first in some Anglo-American legal systems and then in the ECtHR practice. Also, international investment practice was partially the result of neoliberal ideology and globalisation trends. As such, international investment law is facilitated by the use of the same legal terminology that acquires different meanings and causes different consequences in different contexts. For example, English, American, French, and Dutch laws developed a very wide definition of property, and the ECtHR practice followed it. However, all those national laws have a distinction between property used in horizontal legal relations with other private persons and vertical legal relations with a state, i.e., not all property in a commercial

100 Antinori 1797.

101 Tushnet calls it '*bricolage*': Mark Tushnet, 'The Possibilities of Comparative Constitutional Law' (1999) 108 The Yale Law Journal 1225, 1229.

sense will be protected against the interference (or regulation) of the state. Similarly, in human rights jurisprudence, property is interpreted broadly because there are other safeguards for the state's regulatory power. Investors and, subsequently, tribunals picked only the broad understanding of property from national legal systems and the ECtHR practice, ignoring limitations on the concept imposed by national law or human rights conventions.[102]

It is interesting to note that the trend works only one way – due to the obscure relationship between the legal systems, investors can invoke wider understandings of property, higher levels of property protection or additional procedural guarantees.[103] Human rights' claimants cannot use any of the procedural advantages of BITs, because their access to legal recourse is strictly limited. Meanwhile due to the fragmentation of system, investors' rights under the investment treaties are seemingly made immune from the considerations of human rights.[104]

Furthermore, human rights instruments, as well as national legal systems, contain a constellation of values and virtues that deserve protection in human society, such as, protection of life, liberty, and human dignity, while investment treaties do not. BITs do not expressly acknowledge other protected interests and values besides investment protection – the right to development is not even a part of the bargain and is not enforceable.[105] Too often, investment tribunals have pronounced that states are bound by both human rights and investment treaty obligations, absolving the investor of the shared burden over the wellbeing of a society at the time of crisis.[106] This approach, besides being highly investor-friendly, is characteristic of neoliberal world order and is at odds with other legal systems, which harbour a more communitarian understanding of property.

The conflation of human rights with investment protection in order to strengthen the absolute notion of property protection in most investment

---

102 *El Paso Energy International Company v Argentine Republic* para 311–312; *The Rompetrol Group NV v Romania* (ICSID) Case No ARB/06/3, Award 6 May 2013 para 172.

103 *Tulip Real Estate and Development Netherlands BV v Republic of Turkey* (ICSID) Case No ARB/11/28, Decision on Annulment 30 December 2015 para 92.

104 *SAUR International SA v Argentine Republic* para 330–331.

105 John Linarelli, Margot E Salomon and M Sornarajah, *The misery of international law: confrontations with injustice in the global economy* (Oxford University Press 2018) 145; Barrera 2635.

106 *Urbaser SA and Consorcio de Aguas Bilbao Biskaia, Bilbao Biskaia Ur Partzuergoa v Argentine Republic* (ICSID) para 1200; *Suez, Sociedad General de Aguas de Barcelona SA and Vivendi Universal SA v Argentine Republic* (ICSID) Case No ARB/03/19, Decision on Liability 30 July 2010 para 262.

cases is misguided. Such a conflation is flawed not only because the absolutist notion of property protection cannot exist isolated from other values in any society,[107] but also because it ignores the context of the protection of human rights – those are not forums for commercial disputes. Reliance on exclusively one element – prohibition of interference with property – is inappropriate and ignores the whole spectrum of other protected values and interests. In other words, giving full effect to the protection of property while ignoring hunger, extreme poverty, inequality, lack of sanitation, and access to education on a massive scale is a huge hypocrisy and contravenes the basic premises of the property system even in Western European terms.

Thus, a superficial comparison of human rights mechanisms and investment protection only obscures the fact that those systems were created for different purposes.[108] Their partial integration, while providing moral justification for investment protection, is most likely harmful to the protection of human rights. If states are allowed to rely on human rights for their defence in investment disputes, they will have an incentive to observe human rights themselves and be more willing to protect human rights in a broader context, if they want to appear consistent. However, investment claims are very often business disputes over profits. Though the amounts at stake are sometimes huge, they rarely involve a threat to the life and liberty of an investor. Given the history of human rights, fundamental rights, such as the right to life, liberty, security, and dignity, should take precedence over economic rights. Human rights' forums are not suited for commercial disputes. Thus, if commercial disputes are routinely framed as human rights issues,[109] it will undermine the moral authority of the human rights' rhetoric and will weaken the human rights' mechanisms, which are not very strong, to begin with.

Overall, the existing dominant interpretation of human rights law protects human dignity and immediate personal surroundings from arbitrary interference and abuse by the state. It has nothing to say about how much profit an individual should earn or how cheap or expensive she can sell.[110] Those economic matters are and should be influenced by the democratic consensus within a local society, with specific needs in mind. Human rights conventions seem to be flexible enough to support the idea that the government should be

107 James L Kainen, 'The Historical Framework for Reviving Constitutional Protection for Property and Contract Rights' (1993) 79 Cornell Law Review 87, 88.

108 Barrera 2644.

109 For example *Anglia Auto Accessories Ltd v Czech Republic* (SCC) para 135.

110 There are convincing arguments for the shared international responsibility for elimination of the global injustices, primarily by providing at least decent living conditions for humans: Salomon 198.

entitled to undertake genuine economic reforms that substantially affect property rights without buying its way through.

This chapter cautions against the partial integration of international investment law and human rights rhetoric for property protection. The use of human rights for neoliberal aims is misguided and inappropriate, not only because the absolutist version of property protection does not exist anywhere in the world but also, because international investment law, as it is practised now, lacks the complexity and appreciation for other values and interests, protected by the human rights conventions and national legal systems.

CHAPTER 6

The Divergence between Property and Investment Protection

The previous chapters have identified some ideological and terminological similarities between property protection in Western legal systems and international investment. These similarities and overlaps are not surprising since investment protection was inspired by the Western system of property protection.

What is surprising is that investment protection exceeded even Western property protection standards.[1] The investment protection appears to be a Western property regime without the safety checks and balances that exist in national property regimes. The main reason for this conclusion is that, within many national property regimes, general public interests are recognised at a statutory or even constitutional level and used as a counterweight to balance property protection. This balancing feature was absent in international investment law and investment arbitration. As a result, investment protection as interpreted and applied by the investment tribunals was neoliberal – geared towards the maximisation of the owners' benefit.

The similarities between international investment law and the way the protection of property is understood and applied outside the Western sphere of influence are minimal, despite similarities in terminology. Developing states and states in transition usually harbour a more communitarian understanding of property[2] and tolerate greater levels of state activism regarding private property rights.[3]

This chapter further discusses the mismatch between international investment protection and national property laws and its implications. The ideology of globalisation, neoliberalism, multilateralisation, and commodification of property dominated the legal discourse at the end of the twentieth century. International investment law and investment arbitration were children of

1 Many practitioners and scholars claim the opposite, for example: Parvanov and Kantor 836. However, such a conclusion is usually reached by ignoring those aspects of the domestic property regime which serve communitarian purposes.

2 Some developing states, like India and the Philippines, have conflicting ideas about property protection: constitutions provide for a communitarian understanding of property, but the judiciary interprets it in an individualistic manner.

3 Many Asian, African, Latin American, and Eastern European states.

 | HTTPS://DOI.ORG/10.1163/9789004763517-007

globalisation and neoliberalism. The legal profession also actively supported the extreme individualistic approach to investment protection and claimed its alleged global reach. It was a common and convenient practice to ignore the variety of national legal systems and communitarian approaches to property, which have been present even in the Western legal tradition. Even the new generation of investment treaties is drafted based on old templates and frameworks. Disputes arising from the new so-called 'balanced' treaties tend to replicate old interpretations and deliver results similar to the old case law.[4] ISDS, as a system and practice, fails to address the most contested issues and fails to convince the global audience that neoliberal investment protection significantly contributes to the development and increases prosperity and wealth for those states that are usually required to pay under investment awards.

1 Investment Protection Is an Extreme Version of Property Protection

This sub-chapter summarises how investment protection provided by investment treaties compares to domestic property regimes and how international investment protection exceeds national laws and human rights instruments in four parameters of comparison: (i) the scope of protected interests, (ii) permissible interferences with protected interests that do not require compensation, (iii) the conditions for lawful expropriation, and (iv) the standard of compensation.

1.1 Scope of Protected Property and Investment

The definition of investment in the practice of investment arbitration is extensive and much broader than most national understandings of property.[5] For example, NAFTA jurisprudence protected interests with economic value or claims as investment,[6] but such interests or claims are rarely recognised as property; seldom are they protected *vis-à-vis* a state interference under nat-

4 Wolfgang Alschner, *Investment Arbitration and State-Driven Reform: New Treaties, Old Outcomes* (Oxford University Press 2022) 14–15.

5 In *Casinos Austria International GmbH and Casinos Austria Aktiengesellschaft v. Argentine Republic* para 229 it was held that revocation of a licence *prima facie* may amount to expropriation.

6 *Pope & Talbot Inc v Government of Canada*; *Merrill & Ring Forestry LP v Government of Canada* (UNCITRAL, ICSID Administrated) [2010] para 143.

ional law.[7] Furthermore, some BITs extend the definition of investment to any business activities,[8] short of the right to formal negotiations.[9] Goodwill and know-how are also routinely included in the definitions of investment but rarely enjoy the level of protection afforded to property under national laws.[10]

Common law definitions of property come closest to the wide scope of interests defined as investment in investment treaties. In particular, American and English legal systems embrace a vast understanding of property that encompasses any assets, including contractual rights and other interests, with quite narrow exceptions.[11] What is wrong with giving other interests the level of property protection? There is a reason why national law makes a distinction between property rights and other rights – property rights have a priority over other rights and serve a unique function in the legal order. They apply *erga omnes*, allow vindication, and enable exclusion. Thus, national laws do not protect contracts and other rights in the same way as property. The ownership of property presumes validity, especially in civil law countries, where the most valuable and important property objects have to be registered. Meanwhile, contractual rights are *inter partes*, inherently more confidential, fluid, contested, and subject to disputes.[12] Many investment disputes over contractual rights involve counterclaims. Contractual rights can be difficult to trace and easy to manipulate. National legal systems have developed other principles and mechanisms for the protection of valuable interests and rights, such as the protection of legitimate expectations, protection of reliance, principles of proportionality, good administrative practice, equality before public burdens, etc. However, these interests are not protected under national constitutional property protection clauses, which are reserved for property.

---

7 *British Medical Association v The Commonwealth (1949) 79 CLR 201, 270–271*; *Saghir Saghir Ahmad v The State of Uttar Pradesh* [1955] SCR 707 707; *Authorson v Canada (Attorney General)* [2003] 2 SCR 40.

8 Article 1(g) of the Treaty between the United States of America and the Republic of Turkey concerning the Reciprocal Encouragement and Protection of Investments (1985) provides the protection to associated activities, such as the organisation, control, operation, maintenance and disposition of companies, branches, agencies, offices, factories or other facilities for the conduct of business; the making, performance and enforcement of contracts; the acquisition, use, protection and disposition of property of all kinds.

9 *Oxus Gold plc v Republic of Uzbekistan* (UNCITRAL) [2015] para 301.

10 *Tidewater Investment SRL and Tidewater Caribe, CA v Bolivarian Republic of Venezuela* (ICSID) [2015] para118.

11 Allen, *The Right to Property in Commonwealth Constitutions* 122–123; Gray 281; Palmer and McKendrick 187–206.

12 Martinkute, 'The delimitation of contractual rights and property in international investment law' 3.

Another problematic area, where investment exceeds even common-law understanding of property, is the use of economic value as one of the primary indicia of assets. The extensive debate over the US cases *Pennsylvania Coal Company v Mahon*[13] and *Keystone Bituminous Coal Ass'n v DeBenedictis* illustrates the controversy,[14] but the economic value of interest not amounting to property is still widely used in investment disputes.[15]

The Anglo-American concept of property and the scope of its protection undeniably have global reach due to the power of their respective economies.[16] There is a great deal of overlap between the definitions of investment in investment treaties and the common law approach to property. International investment law would recognise almost any economic activity or interest with economic value as a protected investment.[17]

The difference in scope between investment protection and property protection lies in the safeguards provided by national laws. In order to balance the exorbitant scope of property, the USA, the UK, and even the ECtHR practice separate between 'constitutional property', which is protected from state interference, and property used for the private and commercial turnover. It means that in private horizontal relations among citizens and companies, a wide scope of property is recognised, but only a narrower scope of those interests is protected from state interference. This separation allows the state to

13 260 US 393 (1922). For a detailed analysis of *Pennsylvania Coal Co v Mahon*, see William A Fischel, Regulatory Takings: Law, Economics, and Politics (Cambridge, Mass. and London: Harvard University Press, 1995); Lawrence M. Friedman, 'A Search for Seizure: Pennsylvania Coal Co v Mahon in Context', (1986) 4 Law and History Review 1; Carol Rose, 'Mahon Reconstructed: Why the Takings Issue is still a Muddle', (1984) 57 Southern California Law Review 561.

14 480 US 470 (1987).

15 *DR Energy Holdings Limited and Empresa Distribuidora de Electricidad del Este SA v Dominican Republic* (UNCITRAL) para 48; *Alpha Projektholding GmbH v Ukraine* (ICSID) para 303; *Quiborax SA and Non Metallic Minerals SA v Plurinational State of Bolivia* (ICSID) para 238–239; *UP (formerly Le Chèque Déjeuner) and CD Holding Internationale v Hungary* para 304–305.

16 Koskenniemi, 'Sovereignty, Property and Empire: Early Modern English Contexts' 388.

17 Schreuer and others 125–128; *Continental Casualty Company v Argentine Republic* para 84; *Millicom International Operations BV and Sentel GSM SA v Republic of Senegal* para 79; *Jan Oostergetel and Theodora Laurentius v Slovak Republic* para 157–158; *Sanum Investments Limited v Lao People's Democratic Republic* para 318–320. Whether arbitral awards constitute protected investment is still debated, see *Saipem SpA v People's Republic of Bangladesh* para 128; *White Industries Australia Limited v Republic of India*, (UNCITRAL) Final Award, 30 November 2011 paras 7.6.1–7.6.10; *GEA Group Aktiengesellschaft v Ukraine* (ICSID) Case No ARB/08/16, Award, 31 March 2011 paras 161–163.

operate, albeit on rather minimalistic terms.[18] However, the distinction becomes blurred in the practice of investment tribunals and scholarly works by arguing that a wider scope of interests, i.e. everything that is recognised as property in a private and commercial sense, should be protected from the interference of foreign states. The investment arbitration does not envisage the possibility of such separation between protected investments and other economic interests that might be the objects of civil turnover, accounting, and evaluation, but should not be protected from the interference of general regulations.

Western European legal systems are approaching the scope of the Anglo-American understanding of property.[19] Developed economies of civil law tradition, such as the Netherlands and France, embraced the expanding scope of property at an early stage, but they balance it with robust protection of public interests in their national legal systems.[20] Within this expansive trend, there is a peculiar approach towards pensions and other primary sources of personal income necessary for a decent living. Such pensions or government payments, although lacking the apparent attributes of property, are recognised by the German and Indian judiciary as property and protected as such, probably recognising the social importance of preserving the means for basic living.[21]

Furthermore, many legal systems around the world have property rights limitations conceived as part of the content of property, not as state interferences. For example, in Germany, the principles of self-determination and social obligation substantially qualify the expansive scope of protected property.[22] In practice, it means that the German Constitutional Court refused to recognise and protect the right to use and dispose of a property (*Anspruch*) that is expressly mentioned by the German Civil Code.[23] In France, there is a separate public domain regime for things that cannot be privately owned

18 Allen, *The Right to Property in Commonwealth Constitutions* 127–128; Underkuffler 46, 70; Douglas, *The international law of investment claims* 206.

19 Jansen and Van Erp, 'Comparative Property Law', 1054.

20 Milo 732; Praduroux 63.

21 *Madhav Rao Scindia v Union of India* AIR 1971 SC 530; *Egualisation of Pensions upon Dissolution of Marriage Decision* BVerfGE 53, 257 (1980). Such practice was followed in the ECHR practice and Lithuania: *Decision on the state pensions of officials and servicemen in a cases No 46/2001-48/2001-50/2001-2/2002-6/2002-18/2002.*

22 *Co-fetermination Decision* 50 BVerfGE 339 (1979); Alexander, *The global debate over constitutional property: lessons for American takings jurisprudence* 97.

23 *Groundwater cases* 58 BVerfGE 300 (1981) 341, citing 10 BVerfGE 113; See also the *Right of Pre-emption* case BVerfGE 83, 201 (1991); Alexander, 'Property as a fundamental constitutional right?: the German example' 733.

because of the public interest in them.[24] Furthermore, in France, even private property is heavily socialised, confirming the community's interest in it.[25] Thus, the expectation of the renewal of a concession or the authorisation to operate public transport or energy infrastructure have not been recognised as property rights,[26] in contrast to international investment law, which includes concessions under the definition of investment and, in its heyday, protected the right to the renewal of administrative permits.[27]

Eastern Europe and most other legal systems outside Europe have an even narrower understanding of property than Western European states. For example, in Poland, contractual rights, pre-emption rights, permits, licences, awards, or judgments are not considered as property and are not protected as such. Therefore, their termination is not treated as expropriation. Moreover, extensive regulations are not seen as a limitation but as an integral part of property, beyond which the right to ownership does not exist.[28] The property understanding in the Baltic states resembles the German understanding but has even stronger communitarian connotations and favours state activism to the extent that the ECHR allows it.[29] Russia uses the German system as the backbone for its Civil Code and sticks to the rather conservative and traditional interpretation that 'a commodity in the economic sense does not always constitute an object of the right of ownership in the law'.[30] The clash between different understandings of property and investment is illustrated by the recent case *Gavrilovic v Croatia*, where, quintessentially, the continental law tradition of property registration was deemed expropriatory by an investment tribunal.[31]

Recognising this Eastern European traditional and narrower scope of property and its protection, Eastern European BITs frequently include clauses limiting the jurisdictional authority of the arbitral tribunal to expropriation dis-

24 Bell, Boyron and Whittaker 274.

25 Bermann and Picard 148.

26 *Transport Law case (French Constitutional Council)* [*1982*]; Praduroux 64. In a similar case in Australia *Commonwealth v WMC Resources* the High Court refused to recognise mandatory acquisition.

27 *Metalclad Corporation v United Mexican States* (ICSID) [2000] para 107, 111; *Tecnicas Medioambientales Tecmed SA v The United Mexican States* (ICSID) [2003] para 113–114; *Copper Mesa Mining Corporation v Republic of Ecuador*, PCA Case No 2012-2, Award (Redacted), 15 March 2016 6.677, 6.123; *Abengoa, SA y COFIDES, SA v United Mexican States* (ICSID) [2013] para 610.

28 Habdas, *Property and trust law in Poland* 205.

29 Varul, 107–108.

30 Sukhanov, 'The Concept of Ownership in Current Russian Law' 103.

31 *Gavrilovic and Gavrilovic doo v Republic of Croatia* paras 922–923, 949.

putes with a limited number of other complaints.[32] The existence of such jurisdictional clauses underscores the importance of the concept of what can be expropriated and the relevance of domestic law that establishes which rights can benefit from international protection.

In Asia, the 'institution of private property' did not develop in a Western sense as a tool for limiting the absolute power of monarchs.[33] Even if the constitutional language, at first sight, might seem similar to Western notions, its application is quite different from the liberal and individualistic understanding of property.[34] In most developing Asian states, the administrative tradition of state planning is quite strong, and even developed states feature aspects of the communitarian understanding of property because historically Asian societies relied heavily on social hierarchy and communal property.[35]

Although Latin American countries initially adopted the liberal concept of property, later most of them introduced communitarian ideals,[36] and almost all Latin American constitutions refer to the social function of property. Many independent Latin American civil codes define ownership through power over tangible things, which means that intangible things and contractual rights are not perceived as property and thus are not protected as such.[37]

In Africa, people also lean towards the communitarian understanding of property[38] and have a much higher proportion of communal land.[39] The current constitutional regimes in Africa are aimed at eliminating the social and economic consequences of colonial and apartheid policies,[40] but support a rather broad civil law definition of property, which inevitably leads to clashes between individual and communal interests.[41]

---

32 *Emmis International Holding, BV, Emmis Radio Operating, BV and MEM Magyar Electronic Media Kereskedelmi és Szolgáltató Kft v Hungary* (ICSID) [2014] para 64; *Telenor Mobile Communications AS v Republic of Hungary* para 80; *Anglia Auto Accessories Ltd v Czech Republic* para 189.

33 Zhang 324.

34 Wang 81.

35 Walt 258; Shin 396.

36 Dixon and Ginsburg 7, 15.

37 Amunategui Perello 108.

38 Bentsi-Enchill 74–77.

39 Home 404.

40 Merwe, Waal and Miller 164; Atuahene 771.

41 Article 16 of the Constitution of the Republic of Namibia; *Cultura 2000 and Another v Government of the Republic of Namibia and others*; Section 71 of the Constitution of Zimbabwe Amendment (No 20) Act (2013); *Re Certification of the Constitution of the Republic of South Africa* 27; Schneiderman, *Constitutionalizing Economic Globalization: Investment Rules and Democracy's Promise* 144–145.

Due to socio-legal ethos, and probably also for historical reasons, the majority of developing states favour state activism, where individual interests yield to community interest. These insights suggest that the individualistic premise of international investment law diverges significantly from the understanding of property in many parts of the world.

The divergence between the understanding of the scope of property and the scope of investment works to the detriment of host (more often developing) states. Two major problems result. First, the legal concepts of the international economic order are interpreted in the broad 'common law way', even though this basis of interpretation is not openly acknowledged either during the signing stage of BITs or during adjudication. Second, the investment protection regime, although formally recognising the states' right to regulate, approaches this power from a very individualistic and neoliberal perspective. This is an issue because, at the national level, a broad interpretation of property is qualified by the understanding that not all of that property will be protected from state regulation or interference. In contrast, on the international level, an even wider definition of investment is protected from the regulation and interference of host states, and only recent examples of international investment agreements expressly recognise states' right to regulate.[42]

The remedy to both problems could be a neutral interpretation of the basic legal concepts used in investment arbitration, such as investment and expropriation. However, as we observe in practice, these tend to be interpreted in light of the individualistic understanding of property, given the educational backgrounds of arbitrators and representing counsels.[43] Alternatively, the adequate recognition of the domestic legal regime of the host state and local understandings of property and its contours *vis-à-vis* a state could remedy the disadvantage that the developing states experience in investment arbitration. At the bare minimum, the property regime of a host state should not be ignored and overridden by some mythical investment standard under IIAs. If applicable investment treaties refer to a host state law or qualification require to apply host state law, arbitral tribunals should exercise a greater degree of deference to local needs and priorities expressed through the democratic process.[44]

---

42 Some authors argued that the state's right to regulate is customary international law, therefore there is no need to include it in treaties: Aniruddha Rajput, *Regulatory Freedom and Indirect Expropriation in Investment Arbitration* (Kluwer Law International 2018) 103.

43 Puig 387; Michael Waibel, 'ICSID Arbitrators: The Ultimate Social Network?' EJIL: Talk! <https://www.ejiltalk.org/icsid-arbitrators-the-ultimate-social-network/> accessed 28 November 2025.

44 Shirlow 5.

A contrasting and widely disseminated perspective on the divergence is that the wider definition of investment would be beneficial for commerce and ultimately for the developing states because commodification is supposed to create more efficient distribution mechanisms for resources and, ultimately, a wealthier society. There are two problems with this view. First, the wide definition of investment found in the investment treaties and supported by investment arbitration practice does not translate into internal state practices.[45] The wider protection of investments remains a privilege of foreigners with very limited spillover effects. Second, if the law allows indefinite expansion of the concept of property and still insists on a high level of its protection, it will eventually make a common regulation in the interests of society very hard and reforms difficult. With the pressing global and national issues, where societies require joint action, this option is untenable. The alternative, which seems to have been happening for quite some time, is to lower the level of protection to allow for laws that regulate the various spheres of human life, such as the environment, healthcare, historical heritage, security, etc.

Another aspect of the equation is that the process of commodification is at different stages in different parts of the world. In developed states, it is at an advanced stage; in developing states, it is just beginning, with some inevitable variations. A conflict often emerges when an investor with a very wide understanding of property stumbles into a developing state that has a narrow and conservative understanding of property. Those understandings are very deeply embedded in the social fabric of society. Even the signing of dozens of investment treaties and many lost investment disputes are not going to change the foundational values of a host state community. That is because property regimes and the acceptable balance between individual and community are among the most difficult to change in society.[46]

Despite this significant overlap between investment and property understanding in developed states, the far bigger part of the world, in terms of geography and population, does not consider that certain interests, such as market share, permits, licences, confidential information or contractual rights, should be elevated to the status of property with an accompanying level of protection. That conclusion is probably reasonable when considering the developmental

45 N Jansen Calamita and Ayelet Berman, *Investment Treaties and the Rule of Law Promise: An Examination of the Internalisation of International Commitments in Asia* (Cambridge University Press 2022) 6.

46 Russell Brown, 'Possibilities and pitfalls of comparative analysis of property rights protections and the Canadian regime of legal protection against takings' in Susy Frankel (ed), *Learning from the Past, Adapting for the Future: Regulatory Reform in New Zealand* (LexisNexis NZ 2011) 161.

needs of the majority of the world and the fact that developing states could not sustain a very broad scope of protected interest at the relatively high level of protection that is afforded to property.

1.2 Where Does Private Property End and Regulation Begin?

This subchapter compares the level of protection afforded to property and investment under national and international legal orders.[47] More specifically, it examines what restrictions on private property are tolerated as permissible without compensation under national laws and how those measures are viewed in the light of IIAs.

The general common law approach is that regulation does not warrant compensation, even if it affects the value of a property.[48] This is also a general approach in India.[49] In Canada, a general regulation that affects the economic value of a property is not compensable either, unless such compensation is required by a statute.[50] Australia and New Zealand recognise that certain limitations on property rights derive from the concept of property itself,[51] and general regulations in the interests of the common good are not compensable.[52] In several the USA cases, when legislation affected property in the interest of public health, safety, morals, urban planning, environment, historic preservation and monopoly regulations, etc., no compensation was awarded.[53]

47 The phrase 'Where does private property end and regulation begin?', first used in *Goldblatt v Hempstead,* shows that even the language used for international investment law is largely framed by the USA constitutional takings jurisprudence.

48 Restrictions on land use were not compensable when the purpose of the restriction is public amenity and health: *Belfast Corporation v OD Cars* 490.

49 Article 300A of the Constitution of India provides that 'No person shall be deprived of his property save by authority of law.'

50 Levesque and Newcombe 56; *Cream Silver Mines Ltd v British Columbia* 208; *Canadian Pacific Railway Co v Vancouver (City)* 227.

51 *British Medical Association v The Commonwealth* 201 and *Commonwealth v Tasmania*; Boast and Quigley 130.

52 *Commonwealth v WMC Resources* (1998) 194 CLR 1; *Murphyores Inc Pty Ltd v Commonwealth* [1976] HCA 20, (1976) 136 CLR 1 (14 April 1976), High Court. In similar investment arbitration cases, investors have been prevailing: *Copper Mesa Mining Corporation v Republic of Ecuador,* PCA Case No 2012-2, Award (Redacted), 15 March 2016 6.677, 6.123; *Abengoa, SA y COFIDES, SA v United Mexican States* para 610; *Metalclad Corporation v United Mexican States* para 107, 111.

53 Underkuffler 45–46 citing *Hadacheck v Sebastian* 239 US 394 (1915); *Reinman v Little Rock,* 237 US 171 (1915); (33) *Mugler v Kansas,* 123 US 623 (1887); (34) *Bowditch v Boston,* 101 US 16, 18–19 (1879); (35) *Goldblatt v Hempstead* 369 US 590 (1962); *Calhoun* v *Massie,* 253 US 170, 175 (1920); *Corn Products Refining Company* v *Eddy,* 249 US 427 431–432 (1919); *Walls v Midland Carbon Company,* 254 US 300 (1920); *Miller v Schoene,* 276 US 272 (1928).

However, the solution is not clear-cut everywhere all the time because in some cases, when a regulation gives a state the power of an owner, equivalent to the acquisition of property, the UK courts would order compensation.[54] In some earlier cases, Canadian courts also interpreted statutory ambiguities in favour of the owners.[55] In the USA, the separation between permissible regulations and regulatory takings has also fluctuated over time: in *Mugler v Kansas*, the ban on the manufacturing of liquor that affected the value of the property was deemed permissible regulation.[56] In *Pennsylvania Coal v Mahon*, the prohibition to mine coal under residential homes was deemed a taking,[57] but later in *Keystone Bituminous Coal Ass'n v DeBenedictis* it was treated as a permissible regulation.[58] In *Penn Central Transportation Co v New York City*, it was held that a regulation protecting historical heritage and freezing then current use of New York's Grand Central Terminal is not a taking, despite prohibiting owners from building on top of the historic train station.[59] In *Lucas v South Carolina Coastal Council*, the situation was similar, except that the regulation for environmental purposes aimed to regulate commercial development on beaches.[60] The owner of two land plots on the beach was prevented from constructing new houses on it but could continue using it in a way that they were used historically. The USA Supreme Court decision, in this case, was quite controversial because, on the one hand, it established that the threshold for a regulatory taking is when the owner is deprived of all benefit of the property (relatively high threshold). On the other hand, the USA Supreme Court held that prohibition of construction meant that the owner was deprived of all beneficial use of the property, although as noted by Justice Blackmun the owner could still sell it, exclude others, 'picnic, swim, camp in a tent or live

54 Allen, *The Right to Property in Commonwealth Constitutions* 125; *Government of Mauritius v Union Flacq Sugar Estates Co Ltd* [1992] 1 WLR 903, 911, but see *Attorney-General v Lawrence the Court of Appeal of St Christopher and Nevis* [1985] LRC (Const) 921, 930.

55 *Manitoba Fisheries v The Queen* (1978) 88 DLR (3d) 462; *the Queen in right of British Columbia v Tener et al* (1985), 17 DLR (4th) 1 (SCC); *Casamiro Resource Corp v British Columbia (Attorney-General)* (1991), 80 DLR (4th) 1 (BCCA).

56 123 US 623, 668–669 (1887). Tobacco marketing restrictions were deemed as permissible regulation in *Philip Morris Brand Sàrl, Philip Morris Products SA and Abal Hermanos SA v Oriental Republic of Uruguay (ICSID)* [*2016*].

57 260 US 393 (1922).

58 480 US 470 (1987).

59 It was an important argument that owners could continue using the property in accordance with the historical use of that property: 438 US 104, 127 (1978). A similar conclusion was reached in Canada: *Canadian Pacific Railway Co v Vancouver (City)* SCC 5, (2006) 1 SCR 227.

60 *Lucas v South Carolina Coastal Council* para 1003.

on the property in a movable trailer', i.e. usages that a not necessarily the most profitable.[61] In other USA cases, environmental regulations and market regulations were treated as permissible.[62] In contrast to *Lucas* case, the ban on commercial development in the vicinity of the Egyptian pyramids was deemed expropriatory by an investment tribunal,[63] and environmental prohibitions were deemed expropriatory in the investment dispute against Poland.[64]

The intent of state measures is not the sole decisive factor in deciding whether a permissible regulation or regulatory taking occurred. The USA Supreme Court emphasised that the question needs to be evaluated in the context of the totality of possible use of the property and the extent of interference with those usages by the regulation.[65] The outcomes in these USA cases led some scholars to believe that the US law on property protection does not surpass Western European legal systems.[66] Such an impression could be formed when looking at the zoning and planning cases only, where indeed the USA practice is much more tolerant of various restrictions on land use, but not so in cases of active permanent physical occupation of a property, even if minimally intrusive, such as the installation of telecommunication cables on the exterior of a building.[67]

Continental legal systems are more likely to compensate for restrictions on land use due to planning and zoning, especially after the ECtHR decision in *Sporrong*.[68] In most other areas, continental legal systems seem to give priority to communitarian interests, particularly concerning environmental matters (access to seas, rivers, free-roaming, and rights of access for public services).

French courts, more often than Anglo-American courts, endorse the communitarian understanding of property with limitations in the name of public interest.[69] Contrary to USA courts, which in *Loretto* ruled that permanent although minimal presence of TV cables on a building constituted a regulatory

---

61 Ibid 1044.

62 *Tahoe-Sierra Preservation Council Inc v Tahoe Regional Planning Agency* 535 US 302 (2002); *Lingle v Chevron USA Inc* 544 US 528 (2005).

63 *Wena Hotels LTD v Arab Republic of Egypt* (ICSID) para 99.

64 *Saar Papier Vertriebs GmbH v Republic of Poland*, UNCITRAL, Interim Award, 17 August 1994, 17.

65 *Penn Central Transportation Co v New York City* 438 US 104, 127 (1978).

66 Brown 152.

67 *Loretto v Teleprompter Manhattan CATV Corp* 458 US 419 (1982).

68 *Sporrong and Lonnroth v Sweden*; FAM Hobma and P Jong, *Planning and Development Law in the Netherlands: An Introduction* ('s-Gravenhage: Instituut voor Bouwrecht 2016) 18–20; Alterman and Balla 64.

69 *TGV Nord* decision No 89-256 DC, 25 July 1989; Bell 176.

taking,[70] French courts ruled in *the Eiffel tower* case that the regulation requiring owners to accept telecommunication equipment on their buildings without compensation was not a deprival of property rights,[71] since it did not prevent the use of the property, and left the principal use intact.[72] Similarly, in Germany, regulation is not perceived as external to property but rather internal, as long as the regulation complies with the principles of proportionality and non-discrimination,[73] widely accepted in the ECtHR practice. In the *Groundwater* case, the new regulation prohibited the owner from excavating gravel.[74] The German courts refused compensation because the legislation did not deprive the owner of his property completely; that is, it left the principal use of the land plot intact and only limited its use.[75] Even rent regulations preventing the termination of tenancies in Germany that lowered the value of the property were considered legitimate and proportionate without compensation.[76] Likewise, the Dutch courts stated that the requirement for the ownership unbundling of certain businesses is not a regulatory taking, because the effect on the ownership rights is proportional to the general public interest.[77]

Thus, it appears that under Western civil law systems, compensation will not be granted if a regulation only affects some rights of a property owner but does not affect the main purpose of the property's use, especially if the owner uses the property for commercial purposes. The situation is somewhat different if the owner is a natural person. The European solution to the balance of individual and communitarian interest seems to be more sensitive to the interests of natural persons and protective of their immediate material vicinity.[78] However, the European continental courts, as well as ECtHR, are unlikely to protect the most profitable use of property if the property, after a new regulation can still be used for other purposes. The main difference in USA practice seems to lie in the popular belief that ownership is a bundle comprising various property rights, also known as the doctrine of 'conceptual

---

70 *Loretto v Teleprompter Manhattan CATV Corp.*

71 Decision No 85-198 DC (French Constitutional Council) 13 December 1985, Rec 78.

72 Bell 183. See also *Adapting Agriculture to the Environment*; *Town Planning*; *Application of Privatization*; *Structure of Agricultural Law*; Alterman and Balla 30.

73 Michalowski and Woods 322.

74 58 BVerfGE 300 (1981) 345.

75 58 BVerfGE, 345. It was later confirmed in *Right of Pre-emption* case BVerfGE 83, 201 (1991).

76 *First Termination for Personal Use Decision* BVerfGE 68, 361 (1985).

77 Case Nos 293142/HA ZA 07-2538, 296094/HA ZA 07-3089 and 306147/HA ZA 08-756.

78 *Sporrong and Lonnroth v Sweden.*

severance'.[79] The latter, at least in the USA, allows arguing that taking one of the property rights by regulation constitutes a taking *per se*, while the civil law countries are unlikely to separate rights but will evaluate if the totality of property was affected by the regulation.[80] International investment arbitration leans closer to American practice than continental law systems on that question.[81]

Despite the very liberal constitutional language in Central and Eastern Europe, in practice, very often, communitarian interests and values are prioritised over individual interests.[82] The limitations of property rights imposed by local laws are not compensated, and most are not even challenged as takings because a greater community interest is taken for granted. For example, in Lithuania, the prosecutor general is entitled to challenge construction or development permits in the name of public interest, and many of them are invalidated as posing a threat to cultural heritage.[83] In comparison, in investment arbitration, the annulment of administrative permits is very often treated as a taking of rights.[84] In Latvia, tax changes were unsuccessfully challenged as a breach of property rights,[85] while the practice of investment arbitration is that substantial fiscal measures may constitute an expropriation.[86] In *Revere Cop-*

---

79 Margaret Jane Radin, 'The Liberal Conception of Property: Cross Currents in the Jurisprudence of Takings' (1988) 88 Columbia Law Review 1667, 1674.

80 Alexander, *The global debate over constitutional property: lessons for American takings jurisprudence* 144.

81 *Tecnicas Medioambientales Tecmed SA v The United Mexican States*; *CME (Netherlands) v Czech Republic (Partial Award)* (UNCITRAL) [2001] para 166; *Saar Papier Vertriebs GmbH v Republic of Poland* (UNCITRAL) [1995] para 87; *Pope & Talbot Inc v Government of Canada*, UNCITRAL, Interim Award, 26 June 2000, para 96; *Merrill & Ring Forestry LP v Government of Canada* para 143; *Les Laboratoires Servier, SAS, Biofarma, SAS and Arts et Techniques du Progres SAS v Republic of Poland* (UNCITRAL) [2012] para 674. *Contra* see *Cargill, Incorporated v Republic of Poland* (ICSID) Case No ARB(AF)/04/2, Award 5 March 2008, para 583–585.

82 Alterman and Balla 46; Svilpaite 68.

83 Decision in case No AS-143-92-09 (Lithuanian Supreme Administrative Court) [2009] <https://eteismai.lt/byla/36007983132911/AS-143-92-09> accessed on 1 June 2025; Decision in case No 3K-3-143/2010 (Lithuanian Supreme Court) [2010] <http://liteko.teismai.lt/viesasprendimupaieska/tekstas.aspx?id=818d0e60-1de1-4927-b2ae-9b2d7c448ba6> accessed on 1 June 2025.

84 *Metalclad Corporation v United Mexican States* para 107, 111; *Abengoa, SA y COFIDES, SA v United Mexican States* para 610.

85 Decisions of the Latvian Constitutional Court of 3 July 2015 in case No 2014-12-01; of 25 March 2015 in case No 2014-11-0103; of 10 October 2014 in case No 2014-04-03; of 8 June 2007 in case No 2007-01-01; of 26 April 2007 in case No 2006-38-03.

86 *Yukos Universal Limited v Russian Federation* para 1434; *Ampal-American Israel Corporation and others v Arab Republic of Egypt* (ICSID) Case No ARB/12/11, Decision on Liability

per case, the radical increase of taxes and the breach of the stabilisation clause were equated to the total loss of effective use and control of the properties, thus, warranted compensation.[87]

The standard of review in national and ECHR cases is usually deferential to the legislative powers, checking only if there are rational considerations for the regulation.[88] For example, in Russia, rights are viewed primarily as arising from a statute; thus, regulations affecting property rights in Russia are unlikely to be challenged or compensated.[89] In China and the majority of Asia, the administrative tradition is still very strong, and the concept of regulatory taking or indirect expropriation is non-existent.[90] Although coming from a very different perspective, developed Asian states share communitarian attitudes towards property, which sets them apart from Western individualistic societies.[91] Similarly, in Latin America, regulatory measures are extensive, and property is considered to serve a social function.[92] Consequently, as in Brazil, partial loss of some property rights due to regulation does not amount to expropriation.[93]

On the African continent, regulation is usually not considered a deprivation of property rights as long as it is authorised by law, general, non-arbitrary, and follows clear and fair procedures.[94] Legislative reforms are primarily viewed as allowing 'the concept of ownership to fulfil its social function', including eliminating inequalities.[95] Recent constitutional jurisprudence also tends to exclude the possibility of indirect expropriation.[96]

---

and Heads of Loss, 21 February 2017 para 186; *NextEra Energy Global Holdings BV and NextEra Energy Spain Holdings BV v Kingdom of Spain* (ICSID) Case No ARB/14/11 Award, 12 March 2019.

87 *Revere Copper & Brass Inc v Overseas Private Investment Corporation*, 56 International Legal Materials 258.

88 Decisions of the Latvian Constitutional Court of 3 July 2015 in case No 2014-12-01; of 25 March 2015 in case No 2014-11-0103; decisions of the Estonian Supreme Court of 8 November 1996 in case No 3-4-1-2-96; of 28 October 2002 in case No 3-4-1-5-02; of 12 April 2006 in case No 3-3-1-63-05.

89 Raff and Taitslin 157.

90 Valerie J Washburn, 'Regular takings or regulatory takings? Land expropriation in rural China' (2011) Pacific Rim Law & Policy Journal 124 124.

91 Shin 396; Suh 170; Hamamoto and Nottage 349.

92 Léon Duguit, Frida Laski and Harold J Laski, *Law in the Modern State* (BW Huebsch 1919) 50.

93 Munhoz 93; *Serra do Mar State Park* case 147.

94 Merwe, Waal and Miller 167–168.

95 Ibid 162; Andre van der Walt, ' Towards the Development of Post-apartheid Land Law: An Exploratory Survey' (1990) 23 De Jure 1.

96 Walt and Walsh 212.

A number of scholars conclude that the level of investment protection is higher than the protection of property under the national laws of even the most developed and individualistic countries.[97] Indeed, as a way of exception, in some civil law countries, the regulation of historical heritage and nature reserves that freezes the current use of property and prohibits its commercial development warrants compensation,[98] but it has to be borne in mind that those civil law countries are also very protective of communitarian interests through other means.[99] There is an infinite variety of legitimate public interests that are protected by national legislations: from health, safety, security, nature, and heritage, to economic development and competition. National systems will not usually regard such regulatory measures as breaches of property rights if the legislation has rational considerations, lacks arbitrariness or discrimination, and leaves the main historical use of a property intact. National laws, except in the USA, rarely mention the diminution of value as the defining characteristic of compensable regulatory takings and interference with reasonable and property-backed expectations. Moreover, at the national level, there is an understanding that 'there is no scientific or politically neutral basis upon which to decide how far regulation may legally interfere with property'.[100]

On the contrary, international investment law is focused on the question '[t]o what extent may a government affect the value of a property by regulation?'[101] and frequently disregards the intent as a relevant factor for the question of indirect expropriation.[102] Moreover, the discourse in investment arbitration leans towards the conceptual severance doctrine and is more willing to

97 Been and Beauvais 30; Russell Brown 'The Constructive Taking at the Supreme Court of Canada: Once More, Without Feeling' (2007) 40 UBC Law Review 315, 316.

98 Japanese Supreme Court Decisions of 6 June 1963, 17 Keisyu 521 [1963]; of 27 November 1968, 22 Keishu 12, 1402 [1968]; *Sporrong and Lonnroth v Sweden*; Alterman and Balla 46, 64; Hobma and Jong 18–20.

99 Bell 182; Colly135, 174, 180; *Allotment decision* BVerfGE 52, 1 (1979).

100 Alexander, *Commodity and Propriety: Competing Visions of Property in American Legal Thought, 1776–1970* 331.

101 Catherine Yannaca-Small and Organisation for Economic Co-operation and Development, *'Indirect Expropriation' and the 'Right to Regulate' in International Investment Law* (2004) 2; *Isolux Infrastructure Netherlands, BV v Kingdom of Spain* (SCC) para 839; *UP (formerly Le Chèque Déjeuner) and CD Holding Internationale v Hungary* para 304–305.

102 *Tippetts, Abbett, McCarthy, Stratton v TAMS-AFFA Consulting Engineers of Iran* 219; *Phelps Dodge* case 10 Iran-US CTR para 130; *Metalclad Corporation v United Mexican States* para 111.

recognise indirect expropriation than national laws.[103] National constitutions rarely mention indirect expropriation, and national state practice on the issue is controversial, while most investment treaties expressly allow claims based on indirect expropriation, increasing the level of investment protection to such heights, which lock the current wealth distribution and make the implementation of substantive reforms more difficult.

It is argued that a higher level of property protection is conducive to wealth creation and development. It is said that a single person should not be made to bear the burden of benefiting society. Therefore, she has to be compensated from the state coffers.[104] However, the individualistic interpretation and application of IIAs also entrench the current wealth distribution within society, which is characterised by increasing inequality with associated security risks and makes changes more difficult to implement for developing countries. If the German administrative standard is taken as a benchmark for the international level, what transpires from the recent *Philip Morris* and *Vattenfall* cases is that BITs are susceptible to an interpretation that goes beyond the German level of property protection.[105] Such a high level of investment protection is problematic, as even stable and wealthy states cannot live up to that standard, not to mention developing states.

Furthermore, the relationship between the higher level of property protection and development is questionable. It is evident that stable, prosperous, and developed states provide for higher property protection, but there are some striking examples when developing countries introduced a high level of property protection and did not achieve the desired prosperity.[106] On the contrary, it seems that countries that engaged in the creative destruction of property rights and introduced legal reforms involving partial redistribution fare better in the long term.[107] Evidence from Allen's study suggests that a high level of property protection at the early developmental stage becomes a burden for reforms in developing countries.[108] The tendency is partially con-

103 *Compañía del Desarrollo de Santa Elena v Republic of Costa Rica*; *PL Holdings SARL v Republic of Poland* para 320–323; *Bear Creek Mining Corporation v Republic of Peru* (ICSID) [2017] para 416.

104 The argument first used in *Armstrong v United States*, 364 US 40 (1960).

105 *Philip Morris Brand Sàrl, Philip Morris Products SA and Abal Hermanos SA v Oriental Republic of Uruguay* para 192; *Philip Morris Asia Limited v Commonwealth of Australia* para 539–554; *Vattenfall AB, Vattenfall Europe AG, Vattenfall Europe Generation AG & Co KG v The Federal Republic of Germany*.

106 India, Malaysia, Philippines: Allen 266.

107 Upham 2.

108 Allen 266.

firmed by Singapore's and China's example, which, after reaching a certain level of development and accumulating wealth, started to increase property protection at the national level, not *vice versa*.[109]

The separation of bona fide regulation from malicious indirect expropriation is not an easy task. Failures to articulate the golden rule for separation lead to the suggestion by Christie that indirect expropriation in international law must be established on a case-by-case basis,[110] giving broad discretion to the arbitral tribunals. However, those tribunals come with their own structural and substantive bias.[111] Western arbitrators or arbitrators educated within the Western legal systems will be imposing a more individualistic understanding of investment protection than arbitrators from jurisdictions that have a prevailing communitarian property regime.

An interim conclusion follows that an overlap exists between the Western legal systems, and, in particular, the USA constitutional jurisprudence on takings and the international law that prioritises the right to exploit investment for its highest economic value. The investment protection under BITs and the ISDS as a system overlooks communitarian interests. On the other hand, national legal systems balance competing interests, including communitarian. In most developed economies, property protection is limited by a wide range of regulatory mechanisms that are created in the interest of the general society and that are considered to be an integral part of the concept of property and the ecosystem that supports it. Developing states and states in transition have an even more communitarian understanding of property that allows for much more public control over properties and how they are used. Eastern European, Asian, Latin American, and African states usually adapt and change the content of property rights. Such adaptations are not considered to be indirect expropriations and, consequently, do not require compensation. Therefore, property protection and investment protection diverge quite significantly in those regions.

109 Also the fact that those countries became exporters of capital probably played an important part: Sornarajah, 'The past, present and future of the international law on foreign investment' 41.

110 Christie 338.

111 C Chatterjee, 'Bias in Arbitrators and Bias against Arbitrators?' (2002) 3 The Journal of World Investment & Trade 369; Joost 364; Julian Donaubauer, Eric Neumayer and Peter Nunnenkamp, 'Winning or losing in investor-to-state dispute resolution: The role of arbitrator bias and experience' (2018) 26 Review of International Economics 892.

1.3 Expropriation Clauses in National and International Settings

The principle of territorial sovereignty manifests through a state's power to define property and sometimes to take property altogether from private citizens and companies. Most jurisdictions either include the concept of expropriation in their constitutions or some equivalent of it in their legal systems. Often, the wording of Western constitutions is formulated in the liberal spirit of Enlightenment: 'nor shall private property be taken for public use, without just compensation'[112] or 'no one shall be deprived [of property] except where public necessity, legally determined, shall clearly demand it, and then only on condition that the owner shall have been previously and equitably indemnified'.[113] This attitude defines the essence of the Western relationship between individual and society at large.

However, even within the Western legal tradition, constitutional property clauses differ regarding the level of specific conditions required to deem expropriation legal. Constitutions of countries with different legal traditions and development stages are more diverse. Venturing further from the Western centre of gravity, the influence of individualistic ideology decreases and with it the expectation that interference with private property has to be compensated, because communitarian interests are given priority over individual preferences. Thus, the judicial interpretation and practical application of expropriation clauses in various states and international law vary to such an extent that similarities remain only at a very general and superficial level.

Attitudes towards individualism or communitarianism can better explain what is happening on the ground than the plain text of constitutional clauses. For example, in the USA, where individualism is a prominent ideology, partial and indirect interference with property rights might be recognised as a taking.[114] Even Australian courts, in line with common law tradition, broadly interpret acquisition to include any form that in substance constitutes a transfer of property.[115] On the other hand, in, for example, Brazil, the qualification of expropriation requires the total loss of ownership rights or the impossibility of using the property.[116] In fact, the majority of national legal systems utilise

112 The Fifth Amendment of the USA Constitution <https://constitution.congress.gov/constitution/amendment-5/> accessed on 1 June 2025.

113 Article 17 of the Declaration of the Rights of Man and of the Citizen.

114 *Loretto v Teleprompter Manhattan CATV Corp.*

115 *Georgiadis v Australian and Overseas Telecommunications Corporation*, (1994) 179 CLR 297.

116 Munhoz 93.

mechanisms that preserve and advance communitarian interests, even when affording a high level of private property protection.

These communitarian interests manifest through the universal exception to the property protection clause – property may be expropriated for a public purpose. On a very general level, almost all national systems allow expropriation for a public purpose or general interest, but the content and extent of public interest differ depending on the local situation and needs. For example, in the Netherlands, the public interest is not expressly mentioned in the Constitution[117] but is presumed in 'dams and military works, infrastructure, water supply, and removal of waste, fire and flooding, spatial planning and public housing, and land use and nature protection'.[118] In the USA, Germany and South Korea, economic development is considered a sufficient and legitimate reason for expropriation.[119] Similarly, Japanese and South Korean laws interpret public interest widely, even including the redistribution of land to private users.[120] In the USA, regulations addressing market failures are deemed for the common good of society.[121] In the Baltic states, expropriation laws identify long lists of public interests[122] (in some cases arising out of the 2008 financial crisis, it was ruled that state measures designed to save money failed to establish public interest).[123] In Russia, state and municipality needs are understood very broadly, although at least in one case, the taking of a land plot was deemed illegal because the municipality failed to prove public interest.[124] In China, public interest is also defined very broadly, but, at least in the formal law, the expropriation of urban houses for non-public purposes is prohib-

117 The Constitution of the Kingdom of the Netherlands; Expropriation Act (Netherlands).

118 Schrijver and Prislan 537 fn 7.

119 *Kelo v City of New London* 545 US 469 (2005); *Boxberg Decision* BVerfGE 74, 264 (1987); The decisions of the Korean Constitutional Court in Private Taking Case of 24 September 2009, No 2007 Hun-Ba 114 and in Granting a Private Developer to Claim Transfer of Land from Private Owner Case of 26 November 2009, No 2008 Hun-Ba 133.

120 The Korean Act on Expropriation (2002); the Japanese Land Expropriation Law No 219; the Japanese Law of Special Measure for Land Acquisition No 150; Walt, *Constitutional property clauses: a comparative analysis* 261.

121 *Hawaii Housing Authority v Midkiff*; See also *People v Pullman's Palace-Car Co* 51 NE 664,674 (Ill 1898).

122 Article 45 of Lithuanian Land law No I-446 (1994); Article 3 of Estonian Immovables Expropriation Act No 274; Article 2 of the Latvian Law on Expropriation of Real Estate Necessary for Public Purposes (2010).

123 Decisions of the Latvian Constitutional Court of 19 March 2014 in case No 2013-13-01; of 19 October 2011 in case No 2010-71-01.

124 Judgment of the Russian Supreme Court of 14 August 2015 No 303-es15–5520.

ited.[125] The Brazilian laws interpret public purposes and social interest very broadly as well.[126]

Another aspect through which communitarian interests find their expression in national legal systems is through the review and control, who decide whether the general interest in a particular situation takes priority over private interest and property. Many jurisdictions accept legislative or executive powers' decisions on what a public purpose is, but the degree of deference to that decision varies depending on the local tradition. For example, the USA Supreme Court repeatedly accepted the government's judgment that the disputed action was for 'public use', except in the most outrageous cases.[127] The French Constitutional Council declared that the question of public necessity is for the legislature to decide and that the Council will only intervene in cases of a manifest error in evaluation.[128] The Canadian Supreme Court applied deference as well, requiring a rational balance between public needs and state measures that affect private property.[129] In more communitarian states, the judicial deference is unconditional, and independent judicial re-evaluation of what constitutes a public purpose is almost non-existent.[130]

Many jurisdictions in Central and Eastern Europe insist on very formal expropriation procedures. For example, Baltic states require expropriation acts to be embodied in the laws.[131] On the one hand, such a requirement purports to provide stronger protection for property rights. On the other hand, it inhibits the recognition of indirect expropriation, meaning that if the statute does not expressly acknowledge expropriation, the judiciary will refuse to treat any other interferences with property rights as expropriations. This ten-

125 'China issues new regulations on house expropriation' China Daily, 22 January 2011 <http://www.chinadaily.com.cn/china/2011-01/22/content_11900647.htm> accessed on 1 June 2025; Wang 127, 129.

126 Brazilian Federal Decree-Law on Expropriation for Public Purposes No 3365 (1941); Brazilian Federal Law on Expropriation for Social Interest No 4,132 (1962).

127 *Hawaii Housing Authority v Midkiff* 240; *Old Dominion Company v United States*, 269 US 55, 66 (1925); *United States v Gettysburg Electric Railway Company*, 160 US 668, 680 (1896); *Nollan v California Coastal Commission* 483 US 825 (1987) 837; *Dolan v City of Tigard*, 512 US 374 (1994) 391; *City of Monterey v Del Monte Dunes*, 526 US 687 (1999), 702–703.

128 Bell 178.

129 *R v Oakes* (1986) 26 DLR (4th) 200, 227.

130 Ho, 'Singapore' 626 citing *Eng Foong Ho & Ors v Attorney-General* [2009] 2 SLR 542; [2009] SGCA 1; L Garlicki, 'Artykuł 21' in *Konstytucja Rzeczypospolitej Polskiej. Komentarz*, vol 3 (Warsaw 2003) 18; Tavela and Andrade 120.

131 Rulings of the Lithuanian Constitutional Court of 26 October 1995 in case No 2/95; of 16 December 2005 in case No 2005-12-0103; of 21 October 2009 in case No 2009-01-01; of 12 February 2016 in case No 2015-13-03.

dency is also reflected in the jurisprudence of the Russian Constitutional Court which emphasises the procedural legality of expropriation.[132]

The attitudes and practices of national laws and international investment law on due process in the context of expropriation also differ significantly. Only a few jurisdictions, primarily influenced by USA law, require a procedural or substantive due process,[133] let alone in expropriations, while the majority of investment arbitration practices require such a process with confidence that is lacking in national settings.[134] Some investment tribunals apply the due process requirement for expropriation even in cases when the applicable BITs do not mention it.[135] These instances only illustrate that the arbitrators apply Western notions and interpretations which comply with their own stereotypes about property.

Moreover, international law and national laws have different attitudes towards the non-discrimination requirement in the context of property protection. While most European constitutions and human rights instruments contain a general non-discrimination clause prohibiting discrimination with regard to the ability to own property,[136] not all national constitutions specifically mention a non-discrimination requirement in the context of expropriation. Many national constitutions accommodate positive action (and positive discrimination with some public good in mind),[137] even though investment arbitration practice does not have sufficient tolerance for it.[138]

Overall, the standard texts of BITs and IIAs have more stringent requirements for expropriations than national laws:

---

132 Rulings of the Russian Constitutional Court of 16 July 2008 No 9-P; of 24 February 2004 No 3-P; of 11 May 2012 No 758-O; of 3 July 2007 No 714-O-P.

133 Richard Vogler, 'Due Process' in Michel Rosenfeld and András Sajó (eds), *The Oxford handbook of comparative constitutional law* (Oxford University Press 2012) 930; Fiona Wheeler, 'Due Process' in Cheryl Saunders and Adrienne Stone (eds), *The Oxford Handbook of the Australian Constitution* (Oxford University Press 2018) 928.

134 *ADC Affiliate Limited and ADC & ADMC Management Limited v Republic of Hungary* para 435; *Rusoro Mining Ltd v Bolivarian Republic of Venezuela* para 389. Contra see: *Saint-Gobain Performance Plastics Europe v Bolivarian Republic of Venezuela* para 400.

135 *AIG Capital Partners, Inc and CJSC Tema Real Estate Company v Republic of Kazakhstan* para 10.5.1; *Ioannis Kardassopoulos v Georgia* para 395–408; However the tribunal in *Guaracachi America, Inc and Rurelec PLC v Plurinational State of Bolivia*, refused to infer due process requirement to the BIT clause or customary international law: para 439.

136 Tarunabh Khaitan, *Discrimination* (2017).

137 T Loenen and P R Rodrigues, *Non-discrimination law: comparative perspectives* (Kluwer Law International 1999) 428.

138 *ADC Affiliate Limited and ADC & ADMC Management Limited v Republic of Hungary* para 442; *Waguih Elie George Siag & Clorinda Vecchi v Arab Republic of Egypt* para 438–439; *Tidewater Investment SRL and Tidewater Caribe, CA v Bolivarian Republic of Venezuela*

> [i]nvestments shall not be expropriated or nationalized either directly or indirectly through measures tantamount to expropriation or nationalization ('expropriation') except for a public purpose, in a nondiscriminatory manner, upon payment of prompt, adequate and effective compensation, and in accordance with due process of law and the general principles of treatment provided for in Article II (6).[139]

The individualistic content of BITs masked under the abstract language might come as a surprise for some communitarian-minded states having to deal with investment disputes.

Some investment awards make a connection between the expropriation clauses in investment treaties and customary international law.[140] However, such a claim is questionable when considering such a variety of constitutional practices. The scope of protected property, as well as the contrasting interpretation of expropriation clauses, leads to significant differences in its practical application, even if constitutional clauses look similar. The case of the USA constitutional jurisprudence on takings being dressed as an international standard and passed as the correct interpretation of BIT, without the slightest acknowledgement of the host state's law on the issue, is particularly startling.[141]

The differences between individualistic and communitarian approaches to investment and property protection become even more evident when considering the compensation standard, addressed below.

1.4 Standard of Compensation in Expropriation Cases

The differences between international law and national laws regarding the standard and calculation of compensation are substantial, and this gap has been a primary driver for the creation of the investment treaty network and the ISDS system.

---

para 127; *Bernhard von Pezold and others v Republic of Zimbabwe* para 501; Nicolas F Diebold, 'Standards of Non-discrimination in International Economic Law' (2011) 60 International and Comparative Law Quarterly 831.

139 Article 7(1) of the Treaty Between the United States of America and the Republic of Poland Concerning Business and Economic Relations (1990).

140 *Waguih Elie George Siag & Clorinda Vecchi v Arab Republic of Egypt* para 427–428; *Generation Ukraine v Ukraine* para 11.3; *Glamis Gold Ltd v The United States of America* para 354; *M Meerapfel Sohne AG v Central African Republic* para 300; Dolzer and Schreuer 99–100.

141 *AIG Capital Partners, Inc and CJSC Tema Real Estate Company v Republic of Kazakhstan* para 10.3.1.

International arbitration practice leans towards a full compensation standard calculated on the basis of the most profitable use of property.[142] For example, the Iran–US Claims Tribunal adopted full compensation standards for the expropriation cases,[143] and several investment treaties expressly provided for full compensation.[144] Even though some BITs employ such terms as 'just compensation', 'appropriate compensation',[145] or 'adequate compensation',[146] those terms in investment arbitration practice have often been equated to the full market value,[147] ignoring the different choices of terms for compensation standards and ignoring different national practices on the issue.[148]

The national property regimes intrinsically link the standard of compensation with the general balance between individual and general interests of the society. The more individualistic the society is, the more likely it is to compensate for the loss of individual preferences of the owner and *vice versa*. In that sense, the rules of compensation in the context of expropriation reflect the general societal attitudes towards the value of private property in that particular society.

Many national law systems link the compensation to the purpose of state interference with property and the historical use of the property. That is, future-oriented regulations that allow the historic use of the property but limit some more profitable use are unlikely to trigger the compensation requirement under national laws. Obviously, variations among national property regimes exist, and those variations can be better explained with the individualistic and communitarian leanings of societies in mind. Individualistic societies tend to offer higher compensations, and communitarian societies tend to offer lower standards of compensations, if any.

For example, although UK laws do not define a general compensation standard, the market value is usually paid in cases when the state acquires the

142 Borzu Sabahi, *Compensation and Restitution in Investor-State Arbitration: Principles and Practice* (OUP 2011) 92, 108.

143 Escarcena 227.

144 *CME Czech Republic BV v Czech Republic* para 498.

145 *AIG Capital Partners, Inc and CJSC Tema Real Estate Company v Republic of Kazakhstan* para 12.1.1.

146 *Total SA v Argentine Republic* (ICSID) Case No ARB/04/1, Award 27 November 2013 para 59.

147 *CME Czech Republic BV v Czech Republic* separate opinion of Ian Brownlie para 31–32.

148 Matthew Porterfield, 'State Practice and the (Purported) Obligation under Customary International Law to Provide Compensation for Regulatory Expropriations' (2011) 37 North Carolina Journal of International Law and Commercial Regulation 159, 162–163.

powers of an owner.[149] The Land Compensation Act 1973 c 26 p I s 4–7 specifies that compensation for the land shall be assessed on the first claim day, excluding any benefits associated with public works, any possible change of use of a land plot, and a certain minimal amount.[150] The Netherlands, like Israel, offer generous compensation levels for any state interference with private property rights.[151] The French Constitutional Council also insists on the market value[152] as 'cover[ing] the totality of the direct, material, and certain harm caused by the expropriation'.[153] However, in reality, interferences with property rights over land offer only modest compensation in France, as well as in Greece.[154] In Germany, compensation is usually offered at the market value, but it also plays an important role in balancing individual and community interests,[155] meaning that certain interferences with private property that have a great public interest may be compensated at a lower value. The German approach is followed in Austria,[156] Finland, and Sweden.[157]

Another interesting observation from national practices is that when societies undergo such major transformations as land reforms, the full compensation for expropriation or nationalisation is rare. For example, in Japan, the post-WWII land reform was only symbolically compensated.[158] At least in one case, compensation amounting to less than the full market value for legal reforms or restrictions aimed at public welfare was deemed sufficient.159 Now that major land reforms have been completed, the current Japanese law requires that expropriation be fully compensated at fair market value, excluding the loss of profit.[160]

A further overview of the various national legal systems reveals different compensation standards for expropriation, none of which match the international investment protection practices. For instance, in South Korea, 'just

149 Allen, *The Right to Property in Commonwealth Constitutions* 195.
150 Land Compensation Act (UK).
151 Alterman and Balla 36.
152 Bell 180.
153 Ibid 186.
154 Alterman and Balla 26, 31, 41.
155 *Hamburg Dyke Order Act* Case BVerfGE 24, 421 (1968).
156 Reinisch 16.
157 Alterman and Balla 32, 35.
158 Upham 77.
159 Walt, *Constitutional Property Clauses: A Comparative Analysis* 263; Judgment of the Japanese Supreme Court of 18 October 1973, 27 Minshu 9, 1210 [1973].
160 Japanese Cabinet decisions on the Guideline of Standard for Compensation for Loss Caused by Acquisition of Land for Public Use (1962) and the Guideline of Standard for Compensation for Public Loss Caused by Execution of Public Project (1967).

compensation' refers to the full market price, or in other words, a reasonable sale price,[161] but in some instances, it is possible to compensate with the project operator's bonds.[162] The Polish Constitution only provides for just compensation, implying that there is no requirement to compensate at full market value.[163] In the Baltic states, the general standard of compensation guaranteed by the constitutions is not 'full market' value,[164] but special laws may provide for a 'full' market compensation standard.[165] In Russia, expropriation is subject to prior and fair compensation,[166] meaning reasonable and proportionate with the public interest.[167] In China, local governments and agencies are to decide on compensation standards, taking local needs into account.[168] For example, compensation for agrarian land could amount to the production value for six to ten years[169] in addition to certain social security measures.[170] Compensation standards in Latin American states also tend to favour fair compensation[171] and consider various aspects, including the purpose of the state measure, and previous use and income from the property, but rarely full market value, including lost profit. Similarly, African constitutional jurisprudence does not recognise the full compensation standard. For example, Article 25 (3) of the South African Constitution provides that compensation must be 'just and equitable, reflecting an equitable balance between the public interest and the interests of those affected, having regard to all relevant circumstances'. Other African constitutions include similar limitations on compensation guarantees and rarely provide for a full market value compensation standard.[172]

Again, like with other points of comparison, the current status of law and practice on compensation standards could be better understood by looking

---

161 Shin 396; Article 63(1)(2) of the Korean Act on Expropriation.

162 Art 63(7–8) of the Korean Act on Expropriation.

163 Decision of the Polish Constitution Tribunal No K20/02.

164 Decision of the Latvian Constitutional Court of 16 December 2005 in case No 2005-12-0103; Judgment of the Estonian Supreme Court of 18 March 2005 in case No 3-2-1-59-04.

165 The Article 4:100(2) of the Lithuanian civil code (2000); Section 22 of the Latvian Law on the Expropriation of Real Estate Necessary for Public Purposes.

166 Article 35 of the 1993 Constitution of the Russian Federation.

167 Trochev 58.

168 Yao Hong, Detailed Explanations to the Property Law of the People's Republic of China 8 (People's Press 2007) 71; Hu Kangsheng, Explanations to the Property Law of the People's Republic of China 7–9, 102–103.

169 Article 47 of the Chinese Law on the Administration of Land.

170 Rehm and Julius 221.

171 Article 32 and Article 184 of the Constitution of the Federal Republic of Brazil.

172 Walt, *Constitutional Property Clauses: A Comparative Analysis* 489.

through the prism of two opposites: individualistic and communitarian understanding of property. States and societies leaning towards the individualistic end of the spectrum tend to grant higher compensation for frustrated individual preferences of the owner, while states and societies leaning towards the communitarian understanding of property tend to offer lower compensation for interference with private property. These legal solutions reflect the legislative and judicial choices about the value of property in society and the balance between individual and broader community.

This overview underscores the lack of a universal compensation standard for expropriation. Scholars may speculate about the reasons, cause and effect, but most will probably agree that different national consensuses about compensation standards also reflect much deeper societal beliefs about the value of property and the place of the individual within a society. A similar consensus is lacking on the international level among the members of the international community; therefore, compensation standards and calculation methodologies are repeatedly contested.

2 Implications of the Divergence between Property and Investment

The definition of investment in arbitration practice is expansive, and investment protection, accompanied by compensation mechanisms, is geared toward protecting individual interests for the use and disposal of investment in the most profitable manner. Since the main goal of BITs and IIAs has been to protect investments from the interference of states, the main paradigm of ISDS is that the common interests of society are external to investment and are secondary to the interests of an owner. This attitude exemplifies a significant departure from the multitude of local property regimes where property is routinely subordinated without compensation in the name of public interest.

The discrepancies between property protection and investment protection reflect fundamental values promoted by national and international legal orders. This book does not argue whether individual or community interest should prevail on the international level or which system is better from an economic point of view. Instead, this book tries to expose how different property and investment protection regimes serve individual or community interests and what implications that entails. On a more practical level, the analysed differences between investment and property protection explain the underlying cause of tensions in investment arbitration. These differences also explain the growing resistance to and instability of the system, questioning its future.

A look through the property lens allows broadening of the analysis beyond the immediate field of international investment law and to theorise about the shortcomings of the conceptual foundations of investment protection.

The broad geographical comparison has identified two particular points of pressure between national and international legal systems, as explained below.

2.1 Investment Protection Exceeds Western Property Protection Standards

The first and obvious problem is that international investment protection, on some accounts, exceeds even the most individualistic property regimes, such as the USA or UK, because ISDS is neither structurally nor institutionally equipped to balance investment protection with other interests and values of the international community that are expressed in other binding international conventions and soft international law instruments.[173] If some of the most famous USA constitutional takings disputes were reheard by investment tribunals applying BITs, the outcomes would be overwhelmingly in favour of property owners because the individualistic understanding of property protection is not absolute in national law, even in the USA. Under national property regimes, the interests of owners stand *on par* with environmental, public health and safety, conservation and protection of heritage, financial stability, social security, and other concerns. Many of those interests are the concerns of communities, which, like ecosystems, support their own property regimes. This balance at the national level is fragile and frequently contested through the democratic process.

International investment protection prohibits the redistribution of wealth and prioritises legal stability over change. In this regard, investment arbitration differs from national legal systems because, as a system, formally, it is geared to protect only investments and does not have to bother about other interests that are protected by national laws. From this perspective, investment protection is one-sided and lacks the plurality of philosophical, ethical, moral, and economic considerations present at the national level.

International law, as a whole, offers super-effective tools for investment protection, but lacks mandatory safeguards of other global community interests or efficient dispute resolution mechanisms. This prioritisation of investment protection over other general interests exacerbates tensions in the ISDS.

173 See Chapter 4.

Even those states that prefer the individualistic property regime may need more regulatory flexibility in order to address the modern challenges of a globalised world. A good example of such a challenge is climate change. Even though renewable energy is a priority solution, the transformation from fossil fuels to renewable energy without state facilitation may take too long. Many states have introduced subsidies or other administrative support mechanisms in order to encourage the development of renewable energy and to minimise climate change. Initial support mechanisms were premised on certain assumptions about the price of equipment. However, when the prices decreased substantially, the support mechanisms became much more profitable than the usual business. The prioritisation of renewable energy over other needs and interests of Western societies became intolerable, and many states have changed the support mechanism, reducing the profitability of renewable energy projects. Some states successfully defended investment claims arising from the renewable energy sector, but some states were penalised for regulatory changes. The lost investment arbitration cases will probably make states reluctant to provide any support for the renewable energy sector in the future, or will make states more cautious before offering such support mechanisms. As a result, the renewable energy sector will develop more slowly than it would be possible if states were not penalised for regulatory experimentation.

Similar examples where even developed and stable legal systems are challenged by investment protection would be tobacco control and nuclear phase-out cases. In both cases, the basis for investment disputes was state interference with certain business models of investors. The dismissal of the tobacco control cases and the settlement of the nuclear phase-out case did not mean the absence of tension between property and investment protection. The outcomes of both tobacco control and nuclear phase-out cases have prompted some authors to argue that no significant discrepancies between national laws and investment law exist.[174] However, such arguments are hasty, as elucidated below.

Philip Morris v Australia case regarding Australia's tobacco control measures was dismissed on jurisdictional grounds and did not have a chance to rule on the substance. *Philip Morris v Uruguay* received a lot of attention, and

174 Nikos Lavranos, *The German Constitutional Court Judgment in the Vattenfall case: Lessons for the ECT Vattenfall Arbitral Tribunal* (2016) <http://arbitrationblog.kluwerarbitration.com/2016/12/29/german-constitutional-court-judgment-vattenfall-case-lessons-ect-vattenfall-arbitral-tribunal/#comments> accessed on 1 June 2025.

Uruguay received significant support in this case. Another less prepared and equipped respondent state could easily lose a similar claim on the interference with foreign-owned intellectual property.

Investment case *Vattenfal v Germany* regarding a nuclear phase-out has a national analogue – a German constitutional case initiated by EON Kernkraft GmbH, RWE Power AG, Kernkraftwerk Krümmel GmbH & Co oHG, and Vattenfall Europe Nuclear Energy GmbH.[175] In the national case, the German Constitutional Court emphasised that a licence did not constitute property and found no expropriation,[176] but found a breach of the German Constitution because the revocation of allowances based on a specific compensatory mechanism was found to be unequal, disproportionate and in breach of legitimate expectation.[177]

In the European constitutional jurisprudence, the careful balance of competing interests plays a massive role, and public interest often takes priority over commercial interests. Even if a state liability is found, national cases almost always provide smaller compensations than investment awards, or require an amendment in the regulation without any monetary compensation at all. On those fundamental facets, international investment protection exceeds national property protection.

Even if some cases conducted on national and international levels reach similar outcomes, they do not eliminate conceptual differences between how property and investment are protected. The differences in systems and how they operate create tensions sufficient to challenge the authority and broad acceptance of ISDS as legitimate. However, there is also another point of tension to which we turn next.

2.2 Neoliberal Investment Protection Freezes the Current Distribution of Entitlements

The difference between investment and property protection mechanisms in Western societies is noticeable, but the disparity is startling in other regions of the world that have a more communitarian orientation. Social tensions created by the mismatch between property and investment are more prominent in developing states than in Western states. Thus, international investment protection lacks social acceptance in states favouring the communitarian app-

175 BVerfG, Judgment of the First Senate of 6 December 2016–1 BvR 2821/11.
176 Ibid paras 231, 242 and 252.
177 Ibid para 262, 312 and 344.

roach to property, and the internalisation of investment treaties in the local legal systems is very low.[178]

This variety of national property regimes represents different choices for economic policy, different expectations about the state's role in the economy and relations between individuals and the community. It is not that individualistic legal systems, aiming to preserve individual wealth and to ward against change and redistribution, do not recognise or protect community interests. They do, but not through property regimes. Instead, public interests are safeguarded by other statutory laws and institutions. For instance, Western courts are obligated to weigh individual interests against those of a community. The national administrative apparatus ensures adequate healthcare, education, social security, environmental and heritage protection, and other general societal interests. Developing countries do not have an equivalent of such parallel public interest protection mechanisms. Consequently, when Western property protection standards, which prioritise investment protection over all other community concerns, are imposed in developing states, it causes tensions.

Existing literature emphasises that investment protection, akin to property protection, should encourage productive economic exchange and the creation of wealth in a society.[179] However, the data on the causal relationship between property protection and economic growth is controversial. For example, Leblang claimed that 'economies of nations that protect property rights grow more rapidly than those of nations that do not protect property'.[180] However, his study relies on a very imperfect substitution of property with some business indicators. He arrives at the conclusion having analysed not property, but exchange controls and credit available to private enterprises, which better illustrate a favourable business environment. Obviously, limited exchange controls and available credit are beneficial for transactions and potentially for the growth of the economy. Unfortunately, these and similar conclusions colour many discussions in the field of international investment law.

178 Calamita and Berman 7.

179 North 139; Demsetz 347; Arthur A. Goldsmith, 'Democracy, property rights and economic growth' (1995) 32 The Journal of Development Studies 157; Stephen Knack and Philip Keefer, 'Institutions and economic performance: Cross-country tests using alternative institutional measures' (1995) 7 Economics & Politics 207; Silvio Borner, Aymo Brunetti and Beatrice Weder, *Political credibility and economic development* (St Martin's Press 1995) 14.

180 David A Leblang, 'Property Rights, Democracy and Economic Growth' (1996) 49 Political Research Quarterly 5, 11–12.

International investment agreements are concluded and interpreted on the basis of the economic presumption that investment protection will increase the level of investments, which in turn will generate additional economic benefits to a host society.[181] This view is based on the Western experience of industrialisation, which is impossible to replicate in the twenty-first century. It ignores recent examples of accelerated development, which were mainly state-led and involved legal reforms affecting proprietary rights. A closer look at the variety of national property regimes and their development leads to the conclusion that clear and secure property rights do not necessarily lead to higher social and economic prosperity.[182] Instead, economic development requires a basic property system that is flexible enough to keep pace with the changing needs of society. Recognising the importance of this flexibility, some countries have strengthened property rights only after reaching a certain level of development and industrialisation in order to preserve the accumulated wealth.[183] As a result, due to serious doubts that imposing an individualistic investment protection standard for a limited number of investors could lead to the desired economic results across the national economy, policy makers, scholars, and economists should continue searching for other recipes for successful economic development.

The need for adaptive and flexible property rights is dire in the Global South which requires urgent reforms to resolve numerous problems affecting billions of people. The region needs active states and strong state institutions to facilitate speedy reform implementation. Adaptive and flexible property rights would allow faster industrialisation and economic development. The stagnation of a legal regime afraid to interfere with expansively defined private property rights is not an option for developing states because such a regime is geared towards the preservation of the *status quo*, which is quite miserable in many parts of the world. International investment protection should not come as a barrier to legal reforms and change. Imposing a Western equilibrium between individual and community interests may impede the change in the Global South and slow reforms down.

---

181 This presumption lacks empirical evidence: Emma Aisbett, 'Bilateral Investment Treaties and Foreign Direct Investment: Correlation Versus Causation' in Karl P. Sachs Lisa E. Sauvant (ed), *The effect of treaties on foreign direct investment: bilateral investment treaties, double taxation treaties, and investment flows* (Oxford University Press 2009) 396.

182 States that implemented land reforms, redistributing land, tend to perform better economically: Allen, 'Constitutional Law, Social Justice and the Redistribution of Land' 65. See also Jonathan Bonnitcha, *Substantive protection under investment treaties: a legal and economic analysis* (Cambridge University Press 2014) 331.

183 See Chapter 3 of the book.

The international level of investment protection should not be modelled after the level of property protection practised in industrialised and developed states because individualistic property regimes serve different functions and needs. Instead, in developing states, investment protection should allow for experimental policies and redistributional reforms. Furthermore, there is no single optimal level of investment protection that would work around the globe, despite the convenience of a single standard. The least developed and developing states will have different priorities and needs. What is a stretch for one may be impossible to achieve for another. Thus, international tribunals should differentiate investment protection standards depending on the local situation, values, and needs.

2.3 ISDS in the Age of Neonationalism and Protectionism

Despite the collapse of the capitalism – socialism binary, the majority of states function as mixed economies, favouring community interests and an activist state. Failing to appreciate the complexities of such mixed economies, the current international investment law is the combination of drafting techniques, interpretations and biases favouring the neoliberal understanding of property, oriented towards the preservation of current wealth distribution and stability.

This tendency is not openly acknowledged, and the decentralised ISDS system allows obscuring it.[184] However, the myth of an abstract and universal investment protection standard has been cultivated by scholars and arbitral tribunals, even though diverse national property regimes and the investment protection regime exist in parallel, creating multiple opportunities for confusion and misunderstandings.

The initial definitions and standards of investment treaties' are vague and allow for competing and equally legitimate interpretations. Since the majority of arbitral tribunals are staffed by Western lawyers, the Western and rather specific balance between individual and community prevails in investment arbitration practice. The interpretation of investment treaties and investment arbitration practice has been leaning toward an extreme individualistic understanding of property without the 'normal' democratic safeguards existing in the national legal systems.

184 The possible reasons may be several. First, the relative differences of regimes are difficult to grasp without global comparative studies, which are very limited. Second, the neoliberal narrative for property was compelling and occupied popular imagination. Third, countries which benefited from higher investment protection regime did not care about the gap, as long as other countries obeyed the system.

The conflicts between communitarian property regimes and neoliberal investment protection erupted as a backlash against the ISDS and globalisation agenda. The main tension in investment protection is that it promotes a 'one size fits all' approach to political economy. Such a neoliberal approach ignores local communitarian attitudes to property and fuels anti-globalist and populist rhetoric.

Besides penalising the discriminatory and unjustified takings of property, the interpretation and application of investment treaties that are still in force and that generate the majority of investment disputes are unfavourable to development and change-oriented legal systems.

Thus, an effective ISDS reform should address two critical questions: first, do we need a single investment protection standard, and, second, if we do, what is the optimal level of investment protection for sustainable economic development? Is it the American individualistic understanding of property based on the most profitable use of property? Or is it the European model of property protection with embedded social function and a well-functioning state administrative apparatus?[185] The comparison of the national property regimes in the context of investment protection provides a crucial perspective on the problem.

The idea of one universal investment protection standard embedded in the network of investment treaties looks rather attractive and has many advantages. It makes the movement of capital easier and simplifies the comparison of different business opportunities for decision-making purposes. The convergence also makes investment arbitration practice predictable and consistent – qualities frequently praised by practising lawyers and businesses.

The disadvantage of this approach is that 'one size does not fit all' economies and situations. The Western standard is the best fit for stable and wealthy Western economies. It is too stringent for reform-oriented developing states. The European model may be too rigorous for economies in transition. Despite all the advantages of the European model, it might not be sufficiently flexible for states that need fast industrialisation because developing states need adaptive and flexible property rights in order to help their economies transform.[186] It seems that investment protection set at the level of European property protection can do more damage in the Global South than good.

185 Bearing in mind that both American and European models for property protection fall below investment protection.

186 English enclosure movement and American coal mining industries were aided by judiciary in destroying old property rights and creating new: Upham 34.

This leads to the conclusion that investment protection should be graduated depending on the stage of the development of the host state. The level of protection could be ambitious, but the field should abandon the illusion of one universal investment protection standard and recognise the variety of national boundaries of private property rights against state interference. This targeted approach could be better suited for finding the right balance between individual and communitarian interests at the international level.[187] The redistributive aspects of property regimes, addressing inequality or historical injustices, which are present in most developing states, should be recognised as valid considerations in investment arbitration, thus lowering the tensions in the system and enhancing the reasoning and perceived legitimacy of investment awards.

In particular, more regulatory flexibility could be achieved if the scope of protected interests could be narrowed down. For example, the definition of investment should have an exhaustive list of protected assets. If an asset cannot be named, maybe it is not worth the protection of property? This should eliminate various interests and rights that are on the outer limits of property and are not recognised as property in either one of the contracting parties to the BIT. A tighter investment definition could eliminate a great deal of uncertainty in investment arbitration and would limit the interpretative powers of arbitral tribunals. Unfortunately, changing or terminating the thousands of investment treaties, given the inert nature of states and their officials, would be difficult to accomplish. A partial success could be achieved through the interpretation of investment treaties.

Furthermore, when seeking to calibrate investment protection with national property regimes, the concept of indirect expropriation should be severely curtailed or even eliminated. The indirect expropriation is rarely recognised at all in communitarian legal systems. It poses a myriad of problems associated with the margin of appreciation, proportionality and arbitrators' unconscious bias in favour of neoliberal balance between individual and society.[188] It is not enough to limit indirect expropriation to 'rare cases' seeking to allow regulatory experimentation. The reform should go further and rule that in case of regulatory change, investors cannot expect the most profitable use of investment, but only a reasonable rate of return. This should only allow com-

187 The targeted approach to investment protection can be criticised for the lack of consistency and predictability in investment awards, creating a myriad of different regimes around the world with little difference from national property regimes. The targeted approach is still preferred to the current system, which is not transparent about its bias towards the extreme individualistic understanding of property.

188 Bonnitcha 333; Henckels 195.

pensation for the current or historical use of the investment. The regulation could prohibit future development of property, but would compensate if the current use of the property becomes impossible due to the regulation. Such an approach could eliminate most of the speculative claims, and it corresponds with the psychological findings that people hate to lose what they already have and are less resentful if they lose something that they may gain in the future.[189]

However, in some specific areas of public concern that are subject to changes, such as the environment or urban planning, even the freezing of current use of property might not be enough, and regulations might need to go further in limiting its use or management. In such circumstances, gradual, general, non-discriminatory regulation for public interest based on scientific methods should not amount to expropriation. This should reverse the current investment arbitration practice that puts the burden of proof on states to justify a legislative change.

Overall, compensation standards should be more flexible, allowing for more diverse approaches than full market value in recognition of intertwined relations between individuals and society.

Thus far, the main argument of the book has been that investment protection has become neoliberal and needs to adopt more communitarian attitudes present in national legal systems. However, the alternative should also be considered: what is wrong when national laws provide for lower protection of property and international – for higher protection of investment? In principle, nothing is wrong with having two systems set at different levels. As a matter of fact, it has existed for decades already. Furthermore, it has been argued that higher investment protection standards may improve the governance standards of host states.

The problem is the lack of transparency of what goals international investment law is promoting and what are negative externalities for different societies. The lack of attention to the interplay and discussion about the diversity of property regimes and their implications creates an illusion of consent about a universal property protection standard when, in fact, there is none. The book theorises that the push for neoliberal content of investment protection is the real reason behind the backlash against the ISDS and, more generally, against neoliberal globalisation. It is only ironic that the main driving force behind the Washington Consensus – the USA – turned against it. Protectionism and eco-

189 Stephanie M Stern, Daphna Lewinsohn-Zamir and Linda J Demaine, *The Psychology of Property Law* (NYU Press 2020) 28, 104.

nomic nationalism are on the rise not only in the USA but in other major economies, fuelled by national security concerns and geopolitical rivalry.[190]

In order to survive these changing trends, the ISDS, as a system, must adapt and respond adequately. The investment arbitration practice should be conscious that investment protection, like property regimes, is not technical and neutral but has direct economic and social implications for local societies. The balance between the stability of possessions allowing longer-term planning with associated economic gains and the need for legal, social, and economic changes is not straightforward. Thus, solutions should attribute more weight to the communitarian notions of property present in host societies. Property is not an absolute right in national laws.[191] Active state participation in economic life, including creative destruction and interference with private entitlements, which is actively exercised by the Western states themselves, might be necessary and unavoidable to address the future global and security challenges, such as pandemics, climate change, populism, radicalism, migration, and even terrorism. Investment should not get absolute protection, especially from other competing interests and values of society as defined and protected by national laws. That means that in order to reduce the tensions that investment arbitration now causes, it is imperative to attribute more value to the communitarian understandings of property present in national laws.

3 Trends in New Investment Treaties and Model BITs

Old generation investment treaties still cover around half of foreign direct investment and are the basis for 97% of new investment arbitrations,[192] but efforts to reform international investment law and practice are underway. The draft Trans-Pacific Partnership Agreement was negotiated but later abandoned by the USA.[193] The remaining countries of the Trans-Pacific Partnership

190 Johannes Späth, 'The End of an Era: The Decline of Neoliberalism and the Emerging Interregnum' Trend Report <https://www.oiip.ac.at/en/publications/the-end-of-an-era-the-decline-of-neoliberalism-and-the-emerging-interregnum/> accessed on 28 November 2025.

191 Andries van der Walt, *Property in the Margins* (Bloomsbury Publishing (UK) 2009) 13.

192 UNCTAD, 'International investment agreements trends: The increasing dichotomy between new and old treaties' IIA Issues Note No 2 <https://unctad.org/publication/international-investment-agreements-trends-increasing-dichotomy-between-new-and-old> accessed on 28 November 2025.

193 Summary of the Trans-Pacific Partnership Agreement, 4 October 2015 <https://ustr.gov/about-us/policy-offices/press-office/press-releases/2015/october/summary-trans-pacific-partnership> accessed on 1 June 2025; Withdrawal of the United States From the Trans-

continued with the adoption of the amended Comprehensive and Progressive Agreement for Trans-Pacific Partnership.[194] Similarly, the draft Transatlantic Trade and Investment Partnership between the USA and the EU was abandoned too.[195] Meanwhile, NAFTA was transformed into the United States–Mexico–Canada Agreement[196] and the Regional Comprehensive Economic Partnership initiated by ASEAN was concluded and entered into force among Asia-Pacific countries.[197] Since 2012, when the new USA model BIT was adopted, more than a dozen other countries updated their model BITs in response to the critique of ISDS.[198]

The negotiation of new regional free trade agreements with investment chapters revealed the controversial nature of these arrangements and was not always widely supported.[199] Some initiatives and drafts fell victim to the isolationist and populist forces, partially because they failed to resolve earlier tensions between neoliberal globalisation strategies and national priorities. The new investment protection clauses in multilateral agreements are largely carried by inertia and old templates. They fail to consider the differences in national property regimes and to bridge the gap between diverse local understandings and expectations.

Pacific Partnership Negotiations and Agreement, 23 January 2017 <https://www.federalregister.gov/documents/2017/01/25/2017-01845/withdrawal-of-the-united-states-from-the-trans–pacific-partnership-negotiations-and-agreement> accessed on 1 June 2025.

194 Charlotte Greenfield, Reuters, Countering global protectionism, Pacific trade pact nears takeoff, 30 October 2018 <https://www.reuters.com/article/us-trade-tpp/trans-pacific-trade-deal-to-come-into-force-on-dec-30-nz-minister-idUSKCN1N42QV> accessed on 1 June 2025.

195 The EU Council Decision No 6052/19 authorising the opening of negotiations with the United States of America for an agreement on the elimination of tariffs for industrial goods, 9 April 2019 <https://www.consilium.europa.eu/media/39180/st06052-en19.pdf> accessed on 1 June 2025.

196 Agreement between the United States of America, the United Mexican States, and Canada, 1 July 2020, Office of the United States Trade Representative <https://ustr.gov/trade-agreements/free-trade-agreements/united-states-mexico-canada-agreement/agreement-between> accessed on 1 June 2025.

197 The Ministry of Foreign Affairs of Japan, Press release, The date of the entry into force of the Regional Comprehensive Economic Partnership Agreement, 3 November 2021 <https://www.mofa.go.jp/press/release/press4e_003051.html> accessed on 1 June 2025.

198 UNCTAD, Investment Policy Hub, Model Agreements <https://investmentpolicy.unctad.org/international-investment-agreements/model-agreements> accessed on 1 June 2025.

199 BBC, Protests in Germany against transatlantic TTIP and CETA trade deals, 17 September 2016 <https://www.bbc.com/news/world-europe-37396796> accessed on 1 June 2025.

One example is Chapter 8 of the EU–Canada Comprehensive Economic and Trade Agreement (CETA) between the EU and Canada.[200] It imposes *Salini* criteria for investment definition and excludes claims to money but still retains a rather long laundry list of assets.[201] CETA expropriation clause is typical of investment treaties, with the explanations in Annexe 8-A similar to the USA constitutional jurisprudence, although it expressly mentions the state's right to regulate.[202] These changes arguably balance investment protection with the state's right to regulate (police power) and make it possible to protect community values and interests locally through general non-discriminatory legislation.[203] However, those changes mimic the USA constitutional jurisprudence, and the USA practice is already on the individualistic side, with a very wide scope of protected interests and a high level of protection aimed at the preservation of current wealth distribution.

The 2015 Indian model BIT tries to break with tradition, suggesting a more ambitious reform and narrowing down the definition of investment by imposing additional *Salini*-type requirements. However, even the Indian model BIT leaves loans, licences, permits, authorisations, contractual rights, know-how, and other interests within the scope of protection, excluding portfolio investments, some claims to money, goodwill, brand value, market share, arbitral awards, judgments, and other intangible rights.[204] It also defines indirect expropriation in the *Penn Central* style.[205]

The Dutch model BIT of 2019 also introduced a state's right to regulate, and explains indirect expropriation in the *Penn Central* style, copying the USA model.[206] It limited the scope of the treaty application and the definition of investment, introducing *Salini* criteria, excluding claims to money, but left all

---

200 The EU–Canada Comprehensive Economic and Trade Agreement (2016) entered into force provisionally on 21 September 2017, except the investment chapter: <http://data.consilium.europa.eu/doc/document/ST-10973-2016-INIT/en/pdf> accessed on 2 March 2019.

201 Article 8.1 of CETA <https://eur-lex.europa.eu/legal-content/EN/TXT/?uri=CELEX:22017A0114(01)#d1e2899-23-1> accessed on June 2025.

202 Annexe 8-A to the CETA <http://data.consilium.europa.eu/doc/document/ST-10973-2016-ADD-3/en/pdf#page=64> accessed 1 June 2025.

203 Titi 303.

204 Article 1.4 of the 2015 Indian model BIT < https://investmentpolicy.unctad.org/international-investment-agreements/treaty-files/3560/download> accessed 29 November 2025.

205 Ibid Article 5.3.

206 Netherlands model Investment Agreement, 22 March 2019 < https://investmentpolicy.unctad.org/international-investment-agreements/treaty-files/5832/download> accessed 29 November 2025.

statutory rights under public law within the scope of protected interests.[207] The model outlines the investor's responsibilities and the potential establishment of a multilateral investment court.[208]

Free trade agreements with investment chapters that have recently been concluded approach the issues similarly by narrowing down the scope of protected interest and lowering the level of protection incrementally. For example, due to the controversy surrounding the ISDS during the negotiations between the EU and Singapore regarding the free trade agreement the investment protection agreement was separated from the main text and its entry into force is postponed until the ratification by all national parliaments.[209] In this agreement, the investment definition is still very broad,[210] but it expressly recognises that regulation for legitimate public policy objectives that negatively affect investments will not be treated as a breach of the agreement, also, some other administrative measures are excluded.[211] The treatment standards are formulated narrower as well. The expropriation has interpretation Annexes 1–3 very similar to the 2012 USA model treaty, explaining the desired application of indirect expropriation in accordance with *Penn Central* criteria and emphasising the exceptional nature of indirect expropriation.[212]

Likewise, the objective of the EU–Vietnam investment agreement is to enhance investment relations, not sustainable development.[213] The definition of the investment is extremely wide,[214] but reaffirms the state's right to regulate: 'to achieve legitimate policy objectives, such as the protection of public health, safety, environment or public morals, social or consumer protection,

207 Agreement on reciprocal promotion and protection of investments (Netherlands) <https://investmentpolicy.unctad.org/international-investment-agreements/treaty-files/5832/download> accessed on 1 June 2025.

208 Eric De Brabandere, 'The 2019 Dutch Model Bilateral Investment Treaty: Navigating the Turbulent Ocean of Investment Treaty Reform' (2021) 36 ICSID Review – Foreign Investment Law Journal 319, 331.

209 The Ministry of Trade and Industry of Singapore, press release, 13 February 2019 <https://www.mti.gov.sg/-/media/MTI/Microsites/EUSFTA/Press-Release-on-Approval-by-European-Parliament-of-EUSFTA-and-EUSIPA-final.pdf > accessed 1 June 2025.

210 Article 1.2 of the EU – Singapore Investment Protection Agreement (2018) <https://eur-lex.europa.eu/resource.html?uri=cellar:55d54e18-42e0-11e8-b5fe-01aa75ed71a1.0002.02/DOC_2&format=PDF#page=7> accessed 1 June 2025.

211 Article of 2.2 the EU – Singapore Investment Protection Agreement.

212 Article 2.6 and Annexe 1 of the EU – Singapore Investment Protection Agreement.

213 The EU–Vietnam Investment Protection Agreement (2019) <https://policy.trade.ec.europa.eu/eu-trade-relationships-country-and-region/countries-and-regions/viet-nam/eu-viet-nam-agreement/texts-agreements_en> accessed on 1 June 2025.

214 Ibid Article 1.2.

or promotion and protection of cultural diversity'.[215] The expropriation formula of the EU–Vietnam investment agreement is standard,[216] and it should be interpreted in accordance with the Annexe 4, which is similar to the respective CETA Annexe and the USA constitutional jurisprudence.[217]

The EU model agreement of 2023 aims to enhance the investment climate, while reaffirming the state's right to regulate, particularly in relation to subsidies.[218] The model provides numerous carve-outs and exceptions for financial systems, national security interests, environmental protection, labour standards, denial of benefits, etc. It provides the traditional list of assets qualified by the *Salini* criteria, but excludes sales, services, judgments, and awards from the definition of investment. Notably, the model includes contractual rights, but does not include general statutory rights. The model agreement includes a traditional direct and indirect expropriation clause, accompanied by Annexe 1 for interpretation in the *Penn Central* style. For the compensation, the model agreement uses the term 'adequate', but then explains it as 'fair market value'. The most important EU innovation is the push for a permanent multilateral investment court that should address many shortcomings of the ISDS.[219] However, the success of the institutional reform will depend a lot on the selection and appointment procedure of the judges. If the profile of the judges is similar to that of investment arbitrators, the old interpretations will be back with no significant changes, as happened with the awards under new balanced treaties.[220]

Mostly, the new investment agreements and model BITs only tinker around the main problem – what kind of economic policy and what kind of balance between individual and community those investment treaties are trying to promote: American, European, or the optimal for the developing world? Besides the value dilemma, the incremental approach to the reform has several additional problems.

---

215 Ibid Article 2.2.

216 Ibid Article 2.7.

217 Annexe 4 to the EU–Vietnam Investment Protection Agreement.

218 Annotations to the Model Clauses for negotiation or re-negotiation of Member States' Bilateral Investment Agreements with third countries, 21 September 2023 <https://investmentpolicy.unctad.org/international-investment-agreements/treaty-files/8390/download> accessed 29 November 2025.

219 The European Commission, Multilateral Investment Court project <https://policy.trade.ec.europa.eu/enforcement-and-protection/multilateral-investment-court-project_en> accessed 29 November 2025.

220 Alschner 14–15.

First, those recent drafting innovations are still framed as defences to state liability.[221] In case of an investment dispute, states will have to prove that a disputed measure is non-discriminatory, designed and applied to protect legitimate public objectives. Thus, the burden of proof is on a state, not on an owner, which carries the flavour of American regulatory takings practice where a state has to prove the need and the means of regulation of property rights.

Second, the recent drafting innovations still operate within the Western individualistic value framework,[222] which prioritises the most profitable use of the property as decided by the owner,[223] not the historical use of the property or the use that is most beneficial for the community. If the decision makers in the reformed institutions will remain the same, we can expect the same results.

Third, the changes in IIAs do not address the fact that indirect expropriation (regulatory taking) as a possible cause of action exists mostly in developed economies and is rare anywhere else. The requirement of full market value compensation is also rare in developing states. This standard of compensation makes it impossible to address historical injustices (such as apartheid) or economic policies that cause inequality. If any change in the status or rights of the property owner needs to be compensated at full market value from the state budget, it means that no real change is possible – the owner will own a different class of assets, but no structural change in society will be achieved. Furthermore, if investment is still perceived as economic value, any regulation can be potentially challenged, diverting administrative and human resources of developing states to the defence in investment disputes instead of reforms.

Finally, the recent changes in IIAs raise the question of how to interpret older, still valid investment treaties. Should they be interpreted in line with this (re)discovered state's right to regulate or prioritise absolute investment protection, which was implied in the structure of investment treaties and ISDS? Some authors have argued that the residual power of a state to legislate for the public interest remains sufficient despite the silence of the early BITs on how to resolve a conflict between investment protections and a state's regulatory power.[224] However, some arbitral tribunals reach the opposite conclusion, that the list of legitimate public welfare objectives in the new interna-

---

221 This creates other problems, as discussed in Sornarajah, *Resistance and Change in the International Law on Foreign Investment* 302.

222 Ibid 347, 373.

223 *Lucas v South Carolina Coastal Council* 505 US 1003 (1992).

224 OECD, 'Indirect Expropriation' and the 'Right to Regulate' in International Investment Law, OECD Working Papers on International Investment 2004/04, 8.

tional investment agreement should be interpreted exhaustively, thus requiring compensation for any regulatory changes outside of this list.[225] Alschner also observes that new generation investment treaties produce old results.[226]

Overall, the new drafts and recent investment treaties fail to pay sufficient attention to national property regimes and the socio-economic implications that they represent. As a consequence, they largely fail to recalibrate national property laws with international investment law. Thus, the unresolved tensions within ISDS are more likely to persist with uncertain outcomes for international investment law.

225 *Bear Creek Mining Corporation v. Republic of Peru*, ICSID Case No. ARB/14/21, Award, 30 November 2017, para. 473.

226 Alschner 14–15.

CHAPTER 7

Conclusions

The focus of the book is the relationship and interaction between national property regimes and international investment protection. The parallel is important for several reasons. First, investment protection historically originates from property protection. Second, investment protection is justified by neoliberal ideology, which does not provide a comprehensive view of property theory. Third, international law does not create property rights; only national law does. Thus, national concepts are reintroduced through definitions, and the interpretation of investment treaties is heavily influenced by the mixture of national ideas about property. Finally, the legality of investment is, and should be, determined by national laws, but investment arbitrators have wide powers to rule that national laws violate international law, thus effectively ignoring national laws.

The interplay of substantive norms on property and investment protection has intrigued scholars; however, previous global studies have been very limited.[1] The previous comparisons focused on Western property regimes, which led to the impression that a universal property protection standard exists.[2] This book attempts to dispel that myth by reminding readers that the status of property in international law has always been disputed and challenged. Besides a very general recognition of private property and condemnation of theft, there is very little in terms of details and practicalities that could form the basis for a common denominator.

The comparison allows us to conclude that the interplay between national property regimes and international investment law consists mainly of substantial and selective borrowing from Western individualistic views on property, without due regard for the communitarian ideas and practices, which form the basis of the societal fabric. The communitarian understandings of property are lacking in international investment law and practice.

The comparison is structured around four elements: (i) how broadly or narrowly property and investment are understood and interpreted in practice;

---

1 Dolzer, 'Indirect Expropriation of Alien Property' 61, 65; Conclusions 297; Eftekhar 39; Martina Conticelli, 'Property Rights, Administrative Limits and Procedural Requirements in the EU, the ECHR, and the IIL' in Martina Conticelli and Thomas Perroud (eds.), *Procedural Requirements for Administrative Limits to Property Rights* (Oxford Academic, Oxford University Press 2022) 305; Perrone, 'Expropriation' 64.

2 Sprankling 23, 219.

 | HTTPS://DOI.ORG/10.1163/9789004763517-008

(ii) when and how regulation will be treated as interference with property rights or investment; (iii) what are the conditions and procedures for compensable expropriation; and (iv) what is the standard of compensation. The findings and insights from the comparison are summarised below.

First, the scope of interests that is defined and protected as property at the national level is influenced by two factors: legal tradition and the stage of development. The common law tradition embraces a very wide understanding of property that encompasses almost anything of value, including contractual rights, with quite narrow exceptions. Some industrialised states follow that trend, expanding the concept of traditional property. The scope of investment definitions used in the investment treaties reflects this common law wide approach to property. However, at the national level, the US and UK laws separate 'constitutional property', protected from interference by the state from property in the private and commercial sense. This conceptual separation is absent in international investment law.

The civil law tradition has a narrower understanding of property historically associated with tangible property. However, some civil law systems of developed economies, such as the Netherlands and France, have embraced the expanding scope of property while still reserving substantial areas for state activism and the public domain at the national level. Industrialised states tend to have a broader understanding of property; however, it is unclear whether this broader understanding of property is the cause of prosperity and higher standards of living, or *vice versa*. It is possible to conclude that the stage of economic development has a greater influence on the understanding of property than the legal tradition. Therefore, the gap between the understanding of property and investment is not so startling in the developed Western countries. Eastern Europe and most other legal systems outside Europe, especially developing countries, have a narrower understanding of the scope of interests that are protected as property.[3] In communitarian-leaning societies, there is a strong belief that only traditional property can be expropriated. This difference in the scope of protected interests (under national law and internationally) in the mindsets of public officials dealing with investments could be one of the reasons behind many investment disputes.

Second, the regulatory taking and indirect expropriation, consisting of the limitation of or interference with property rights, is a relatively recent invention inspired by individualistic ideology and neoliberal economic policies.

3 There are interesting exceptions, for example, many ex-colonies inherited a common law broad understanding of property, but did not attain the levels of prosperity equal to industrialised states.

Traditionally, states had and exercised broad police powers to regulate the allocation of entitlements and the use of property. The general common law approach is that regulation does not warrant compensation, even if property values are affected. Under Western civil law systems, compensation is not usually granted if a regulation substantially affects some rights of a property owner but does not affect the main historical use of the property, especially if the owner uses the property for commercial purposes. Western European countries are also very protective of general interests, with a wide range of regulatory mechanisms that are created in the interest of society and are considered to be an integral part of the concept of property and the ecosystem that supports it. However, because the range of protected rights and interests is so wide, involving very different life spheres and situations, the balance between individual and community interests is often contested. From time to time, there will be cases like *Lucas v South Carolina Coastal Council* in America, which prioritise the most profitable use of the property for the owner;[4] or like *Sporrong* in Europe, which held that exceedingly long expropriation procedures and the prohibition of construction violated property rights.[5]

Outside Europe and developed states, regulatory takings or indirect expropriation are rarely recognised at all, because property tends to be viewed as unitary, not as a bundle of separate rights. Thus, interference with a separate right usually does not amount to the conclusion that expropriation occurred. This approach to property leaves more policy options for states to implement legal reforms affecting private entitlements. The standard of review in national cases is usually deferential to legislative or executive powers, only checking if rational considerations support the regulation or state measure. Developing states and states in transition have a more communitarian understanding of property, which allows for greater public control over properties and their use. Overall, investment arbitration practice regarding questions of indirect expropriation to some degree overlaps with Western property regimes found in developed states, while national practices in developing states diverge substantially.

Third, constitutional property clauses are very often formulated in the spirit of the Enlightenment and post-Revolutionary absolutism: property is lauded as an inviolable and sacred right. In this regard, it resembles the absolutist nature of investment protection in investment treaties, which prohibits any interference with investments without compensation, that is, any wealth red-

4 *Lucas v South Carolina Coastal Council* para 1003.

5 *Sporrong and Lonnroth v Sweden* para 61.

istribution. However, the judicial interpretation and practical application of property clauses at the national level and expropriation clauses in investment treaties differ so much that similarities appear only at a very general and superficial level. Within national legal systems, property protection is not absolute because other interests and values balance it. The ISDS is centred on investment protection and has difficulties fully integrating other community interests, such as human rights, the environment, heritage, and other public welfare objectives. All national systems, in addition to extensive regulation of property, allow expropriation for a public purpose or general interest. The nature of public interest will vary depending on the local situation and needs. Many jurisdictions accept legislative or executive powers' decisions on what constitutes a public purpose; however, the degree of deference will differ depending on the local tradition. Only a few jurisdictions, primarily influenced by the USA law, require procedural or substantive due process. Not all national constitutions specifically mention a non-discrimination requirement in the context of expropriation.

The fourth element of the analysis is the standard of compensation in expropriation cases. Recent international arbitration practice leans towards a full market value standard. However, some investment treaties still employ terms such as 'just compensation', 'appropriate compensation', or 'adequate compensation'. National jurisprudence is also poles apart. Although UK laws do not postulate a general compensation standard, the market value is usually paid. The Netherlands, like Israel, offers generous compensation levels for any state interference with private property rights. In Germany, compensation is typically offered at market value, but the specific level of compensation plays a crucial role in striking a balance between individual and community interests. Interferences with property rights over land offer a low level of compensation in France, as well as in Greece. The Eastern European constitutions provide for just compensation, implying that there is no requirement to compensate for full market value. Asia, Latin America, and Africa favour a fair compensation standard instead of full market value, as well as prioritising reforms that could benefit many people instead of one owner.

Based on the abovementioned four accounts, the international investment protection exceeds the property protection levels of even the most individualistic states because developed states have other mechanisms for expressing and protecting communitarian interests at the national level. The developing states and states in transition might lack strong legal systems and state administrations protective of communitarian interests, but they have come to rely on the concept of property that integrates communitarian interests. This communitarian understanding of property tends to accept limitations on the use and enjoyment of property, necessary or beneficial for the greater society, as an integral part of the property, not as a limitation on the right that needs to be compensated.

The mismatch between the dominant interpretation of investment protection and the principles of property protection under national laws creates tensions all over the world because national consensuses about the place and value of property in society are different from the neoliberal investment protection standards. Investment arbitration practice was, and still is, predominantly oriented towards wealth preservation and against wealth redistribution. Investment protection, with its broad scope of protected interests and high level of protection, as well as immunity from local concerns, entrenches the *status quo*.

Recent studies and drafting initiatives emphasise the need for balance between individual and communitarian interests. However, the balance itself depends on the initial values that are attributed to the individual and community. That balance is the outcome of local, historical, and social consensus that was born out of particular circumstances, needs, and different interests.

While the early investment treaties were inspired by the Western balance between individual and community interests, albeit a truncated one, theoretically, those BITs were vague and abstract enough to accommodate different versions of social consensus. Subsequently, investment tribunals interpreted investment treaties in such a neoliberal manner that cannot be found anywhere in the national property regimes. The background education, prevailing ideology, and ideas of decision-makers about the optimal state-individual balance had significant influences on the outcomes of investment disputes. Eventually, ISDS became a victim of its own success: the protection of investment was so efficient and individualistic that it raised a backlash. The tensions created by the mismatch between investment protection and property protection are emblematic of the recurring tensions between cosmopolitan globalists and national politicians favouring protectionist policies. It is not only investment treaties that are terminated in large numbers, but also international trade and even security agreements are under threat or paralysed, questioning all post-Cold War progress of international law.

The main implication of the divergence between national property regimes and investment protection, besides an increasing number of investment disputes, is that the future of the ISDS system is compromised. Without significant accommodations to local needs, practices, and values, the whole ISDS system might be abandoned as an untenable neoliberal globalisation project.

Examining the potential avenues for ISDS reform, it must be concluded that incremental and evolutionary changes to the system risk remaining within the dominant individualistic paradigm, which will be unsatisfactory for the developing world and sometimes inconvenient even for the Western world. Instead, inspiration for solutions must be sought externally, including national legal systems with a communitarian understanding of property. The comparison of national constitutional jurisprudence suggests that a substantial limitation of the scope of protected interests could ease the tensions in the system. Furthermore, the expropriation should be limited to property, not other rights and interests. For the protection of other rights, other investment treaty standards should be used. The indirect expropriation should be severely curtailed, and the general interest of the regulation should play a more significant role in the reasoning of the tribunals. Finally, the variety of compensation standards should be recognised by investment arbitration practice, reflecting a variety of situations where the interests of the community and the individual have to be balanced.

The existing schism between investment protection and property protection is not sustainable and should be reversed by bridging the gap between them. The recalibration of property and investment protection could help reduce tensions, improve the reasoning of awards and perceived legitimacy, and promote acceptance as well as the internalisation of international investment law. The communitarian approach to property has yet to gain more understanding and appreciation in investment arbitration practice. In a way, this book is an attempt to articulate alternative visions for international investment law. If economic development is the true object and purpose of investment treaties, ISDS should embrace more change-oriented and redistributive aspects of investment protection.

However, the new investment protection clauses in international investment agreements, despite mentioning the state's right to regulate and limiting regulatory takings to rare exceptions, are to a large extent carried by inertia and old templates. They presume stability in the legal and economic relations that verge on stagnation. This is a high standard even for developed Western states and impossible to achieve for developing states. Instead, investment treaties should presume a constant change in the legal systems of developing states and should take into account the existing variety of national property protection practices. Currently, the newly negotiated investment treaties fail to consider and appreciate the differences in national property regimes, instead tinkering around the main problem rather than addressing it directly.

The book opens up several other topics for further research. It is only the start of comparative work that could serve as a stepping stone for further in-depth comparisons among national property regimes and investment protection. Due to the broad geographical coverage of this study, entire continents had to be reduced to several pages, but they deserve much deeper analysis and possibly separate books. Plenty of unverified historical assumptions in the field need to be tested, such as the customary nature of property protection under international law and its relation to the protection of vested (acquired) rights. It is possible that the myth about the customary nature of alien property protection is based on unsupported claims from a few interested states. Such an inquiry would require a much more extensive archival effort than was possible within this book.

The correlation between property protection and the economic performance of various countries also needs to be investigated empirically, despite all the difficulties with measuring indices. The pressing question is whether expanding the scope of property rights and strengthening property rights are capable on their own or in combination with other circumstances to increase the prosperity of the host state. Such studies could further shed light on the current debate on investment treaties, investment arbitration, and their effects on the economies of developing states.

Bibliography

Blogs

Lavranos N, *The German Constitutional Court Judgment in the Vattenfall Case: Lessons for the ECT Vattenfall Arbitral Tribunal* (2016).

Schifferes S, *The rise and fall of globalisation: why the world's next financial meltdown could be much worse with the US on the sidelines* (2025).

Thomadakis A, *The End of an Era: What's Next After Globalisation?* (2025).

Waibel M, 'ICSID Arbitrators: The Ultimate Social Network?' EJIL:Talk!. (2014)

Books

Acemoglu D and Robinson JA, *Why Nations Fail: the Origins of Power, Prosperity, and Poverty* (Profile Books 2013).

Aldrich GH, *The Jurisprudence of the Iran-United States Claims Tribunal: An Analysis of the Decisions of the Tribunal* (Clarendon Press 1996).

Alexander GS, *Commodity and Propriety: Competing Visions of Property in American Legal Thought, 1776–1970* (University of Chicago Press 1997).

Alexander GS, *The Global Debate Over Constitutional Property: Lessons for American Takings Jurisprudence* (University of Chicago Press 2006).

Alexander GS and Peñalver EM, *An Introduction to Property Theory* (Cambridge University Press 2012).

Alexander RJ, *Agrarian Reform in Latin America* (Collier Macmillan Publishers 1974).

Allen T, *The Right to Property in Commonwealth Constitutions* (Cambridge University Press 2000).

Alschner W, *Investment Arbitration and State-Driven Reform: New Treaties, Old Outcomes* (Oxford University Press 2022).

Alterman R and Balla E, *Takings International: A Comparative Perspective on Land Use Regulations and Compensation Rights* (American Bar Association, Section of State and Local Government Law 2011).

Amerasinghe CF, *State Responsibility for Injuries to Aliens* (Clarendon Press 1967).

Amsden AH, Kochanowicz J and Taylor L, *The Market Meets its Match: Restructuring the Economies of Eastern Europe* (Harvard University Press 1994).

Anghie A, *Imperialism, Sovereignty, and the Making of International Law*, vol 37 (Cambridge University Press 2005).

Arai-Takahashi Y, *The Margin of Appreciation Doctrine and the Principle of Proportionality in the Jurisprudence of the ECHR* (Intersentia 2002).
Azuela A, *Property in the Post-post-revolution: Notes on the Crisis of the Constitutional Idea of Property in Contemporary Mexico*, vol 89 (2011).
Banning TRv, *The Human Right to Property* (Intersentia 2003).
Bar Cv, Drobnig U and Protection ECD-GfHaC, *The interaction of Contract Law and Tort and Property Law in Europe: a Comparative Study* (Sellier 2004).
Barnes M, *The Law of Compulsory Purchase and Compensation* (Hart Publishing 2014).
Baur F, Stürmer R and Baur F, *Sachenrecht* (Beck 2009).
Bederman DJ, *International Law in Antiquity* (Cambridge University Press 2001).
Bell DA, *East Meets West: Human Rights and Democracy in East Asia* (Princeton University Press 2000).
Bell J, *French Constitutional Law* (Clarendon Press 1992).
Bell J, Boyron S and Whittaker S, *Principles of French law* (Oxford University Press 2008).
Benton LA, *Law and Colonial Cultures: Legal Regimes in World History, 1400–1900* (Cambridge University Press 2002).
Bermann GA and Picard E, *Introduction to French law* (Kluwer Law International 2008).
Bevilaqua C, *Direito Das Coisas* (Freitas Bastos 1941).
Bezrukov A, *Constitutional Law of Russia* (Justicinform 2015).
Bishop RD, Crawford J and Reisman WM, *Foreign Investment Disputes Cases, Materials, and Commentary* (Kluwer Law International 2005).
Bonnitcha J, *Substantive Protection under Investment Treaties: A Legal and Economic Analysis* (Cambridge University Press 2014).
Borchard E, *The Diplomatic Protection of Citizens Abroad* (1914).
Borner S, Brunetti A and Weder B, *Political Credibility and Economic Development* (St Martin's Press 1995).
Bridge MG, *Personal Property Law* (4th edn, Oxford University Press 2015).
Brodecki Z, *Polish Business Law* (Kluwer Law International 2003).
Brownlie I, *Principles of Public International Law* (6th edn, Oxford University Press 2003).
Brownlie I, *Principles of Public International Law* (7th edn, Oxford University Press 2008).
Byers, M *Custom, Power and the Power of Rules* (Cambridge University Press 1999).
Cairns W and McKeon R, *Introduction to French law* (Cavendish Publishing Ltd 1995).
Calamita NJ and Berman A, *Investment Treaties and the Rule of Law Promise: An Examination of the Internalisation of International Commitments in Asia* (Cambridge University Press 2022).

Campos RA, *O Conflito Entre O Direito De Propriedade E O Meio Ambiente E A Questão Da Indenização Das Áreas De Preservação Florestal* (Juruá 2007).

Carmody C, *A Communitarian Theory of WTO Law* (Cambridge University Press 2023).

Chorus J, Gerver P and Hondius E, *Introduction to Dutch law* (4th rev edn, Kluwer Law International 2006).

Cohn EJ and Giles OC, *Manual of German law*, vol 2 (2nd edn, The British Institute of international and comparative law 1968–71).

Conforti B, *International Law and the Role of Domestic Legal Systems* (Martinus Nijhoff 1993).

Corfield FVS, Carnwath R and Richards D, *Compulsory Acquisition and Compensation* (Butterworths 1978).

Cotula L, *Human Rights, Natural Resource and Investment Law in a Globalised World: Shades of Grey in the Shadow of the Law* (Routledge 2012).

Crawford J and Brownlie I, *Brownlie's Principles of Public International Law* (8th edn, Oxford University Press 2012).

d'Aspremont J, *International Law as a Belief System* (Cambridge University Press 2017).

D'Aspremont J, *The Discourse on Customary International Law* (Oxford University Press 2021).

Davis DR, *The Boundaries of Hindu Law: Tradition, Custom and Politics in Medieval Kerala* (CESMEO 2004).

Davis JDR, *The Spirit of Hindu Law* (Cambridge University Press 2010).

Denyer-Green B, *Compulsory purchase and compensation* (12th edn, Routledge 2025).

de Vattel E, *Law of Nations or the Principles of Natural Law* (Fenwick CD tr, Carnegie Institution of Washington 1916).

Desierto DA, *Public Policy in International Economic Law: the ICESCR in Trade, Finance, and Investment* (1st edn, Oxford University Press 2015).

di Robilant A, *The Making of Modern Property: Reinventing Roman Law in Europe and its Peripheries 1789–1950* (Cambridge University Press 2023).

Didžiulis L, Taminskas A and Matiukas M, *Daiktinė Teisė* (Vilniaus universiteto leidykla 2025).

Dixon R and Ginsburg T, *Comparative Constitutional Law in Latin America* (1st edn, Edward Elgar MUA 2017).

Dolzer R and Schreuer C, *Principles of International Investment Law*, vol Second edition (Oxford University Press 2012).

Douglas Z, *The International Law of Investment Claims* (Cambridge University Press 2009).

Duguit L, Laski F and Laski HJ, *Law in The Modern State* (BW Huebsch 1919).

Dumberry P, *The Formation and Identification of Rules of Customary International Law in International Investment Law* (Cambridge University Press 2016).

Dupuy PM, Francioni F and Petersmann EU, *Human Rights in International Investment Law and Arbitration* (Oxford University Press 2009).

Eftekhar R, *The Role of the Domestic Law of the Host State in Determining the Jurisdiction ratione materiae of Investment Treaty Tribunals: The Partial Revival of the Localisation Theory?* (Brill | Nijhoff 2021).

Epstein RA, *Takings: Private Property and the Power of Eminent Domain* (Harvard University Press 1985).

Erades L, Fitzmaurice M and Flinterman C, *Interactions Between International and Municipal Law: A Comparative Case Law Study* (TMC Asser Instituut 1993).

Escarcena SL, *Indirect Expropriation in International Law* (Edward Elgar Publishing Limited 2014).

Fahner JH, *Judicial Deference in International Adjudication: A Comparative Analysis* (1st edn, Hart Publishing 2020).

Feldbrugge FJM, Berg GPVd and Simons WB, *Encyclopedia of Soviet Law* (M. Nijhoff 1985).

Fischel WA, *Regulatory Takings: Law, Economics, and Politics* (Harvard University Press 1995).

Fisher HD, *The German legal system and Legal System and Legal Language: A General Survey Together with Notes and German Vocabulary* (4th edn, Routledge-Cavendish 2009).

Fitzmaurice A, *Sovereignty, Property and Empire, 1500–2000* (Cambridge University Press 2014).

Frankowski S and Stephan PB, *Legal Reform in Post-Communist Europe: The View from Within* (M Nijhoff 1995).

García-Amador F, Sohn LB and Baxter R, *Recent Codification of the Law of State Responsibility for Injuries to Aliens* (A. Sijthoff 1974).

Garnsey P, *Thinking About Property: From Antiquity to the Age of Revolution* (Cambridge University Press 2007).

Garnsey P, *Thinking about property from antiquity to the age of revolution* (Cambridge University Press, 2008).

Gazzini T and De Brabandere E, *International Investment Law: The Sources of Rights and Obligations* (Nijhoff 2012).

Gill S and Cutler CA, *New Constitutionalism and World Order* (Cambridge University Press 2014).

Ginsburgs G, *The Soviet Union and International Cooperation in Legal Matters* (Nijhoff 1992).

Glendon MA, *Rights Talk: The Impoverishment of Political Discourse* (The Free Press 1991).

Glenn HP, *Legal Traditions of the World: Sustainable Diversity in Law* (5th edn, Oxford University Press 2014).

Goff of Chieveley RGB and Jones GH, *The law of Restitution* (6th edn, Sweet & Maxwell 2002).
Gordley J, *Foundations of private law: Private Law: Property, Tort, Contract, Unjust Enrichment* (Oxford University Press 2006).
Gray KJ and Gray SF, *Elements of Land law* (5th edn, Oxford University Press 2009).
Grewe WG and Byers M, *The Epochs of International Law* (Walter de Gruyter 2000).
Habdas M, *Property and Trust Law in Poland* (Kluwer Law International 2015).
Hayek FAv and Caldwell B, *The Road to Serfdom: Text and Documents*, vol 2 (Definitive edn, University of Chicago Press 2007).
Hegel GWF, *Philosophy of Right* (Dyde SW tr, Batoche Books Kitchener 2001).
Henckels C, *Proportionality and Deference in Investor-State Arbitration: Balancing Investment Protection and Regulatory Autonomy* (Cambridge University Press 2015).
Higgins R, *The Taking Of Property By The State: Recent Developments In International Law* (the Hague Academy of International Law 1982).
Ho J, *New Property in International Law* (Oxford Academic, Oxford University Press 2024).
Hobma F and Jong P, *Planning and Development Law in the Netherlands: An Introduction* ('s-Gravenhage: Instituut voor Bouwrecht 2016).
Hofmann R and Tams C, *International Investment Law and Its Others* (Nomos 2012).
Hopcroft RL, *Regions, Institutions, and Agrarian Change in European History* (University of Michigan Press 1999).
Horn N and others, *German Private and Commercial Law: An Introduction* (Clarendon Press 1982).
Hume D, *A Treatise of Human Nature* (Oxford University Press 2000).
Justen Filho M, *Curso de Direito Administrativo* (Saraiva 2006).
Justice ICo, *Barcelona Traction, Light and Power Company Case: Separate Opinion of Judge Padilla Nervo* (1970).
Kant I, *The Metaphysics of Morals* (Gregor MJ tr, Cambridge University Press 1996).
Karamanukian D, Minzhurenko A and others, *Human Rights in Russia: History, Theory and Practice* (2015).
Kennedy D and Stiglitz JE, *Law and Economics with Chinese Characteristics: Institutions for Promoting Development in the Twenty-First Century* (Oxford University Press 2013).
Keynes JM, *The Collected Writings of John Maynard Keynes: The General Theory of Employment, Interest and Money*, vol 7 (Cambridge University Press 2013).
Khan R, *The Iran-United States Claims Tribunal: Controversies, Cases, and Contribution* (M Nijhoff 1990).
Kim I, Lee H and Somin I (eds), *Eminent Domain: A Comparative Perspective* (Cambridge University Press 2017)

Kjos HE, *Applicable Law in Investor-State Arbitration the Interplay Between National andInternational Law* (Oxford University Press 2013).

Klabbers J, Peters A and Ulfstein G, *The Constitutionalization of International Law* (Oxford University Press 2009).

Koskenniemi M, *The Gentle Civilizer of Nations: The Rise and Fall of International Law 1870–1960* (Cambridge University Press 2002).

Koskenniemi M, *From Apology to Utopia: The Structure of International Legal Argument* (Cambridge University Press 2006).

Koskenniemi M, *To the Uttermost Parts of the Earth: Legal Imagination and International Power 1300–1870* (Cambridge University Press 2021).

Krygier M and Czarnota AW, *The Rule of Law After Communism: Problems and Prospects in East-Central Europe* (Ashgate 1998).

Kulick A, *Global Public Interest in International Investment Law* (Cambridge University Press 2012).

Lalive PA, *The Doctrine of Acquired Rights* (Matthew Bender 1965).

Lauterpacht HS, *Private Law Sources and Analogies of International Law: With Special Reference to International Arbitration* (Archon Books 1970).

Lawson FH and Rudden B, *The Law of Property* (3rd rev edn, Oxford University Press 2002).

Lehavi A, *Property Law in a Globalizing World* (Cambridge University Press 2019).

Leiter A, *Making the World Safe for Investment: The Protection of Foreign Property 1922–1959* (Cambridge University Press 2023).

Lillich RB, *International Law of State Responsibility for Injuries to Aliens* (University Press of Virginia 1993).

Linarelli J, Salomon ME and Sornarajah M, *The Misery of International Law: Confrontations with Injustice in the Global Economy* (Oxford University Press 2018).

Locke J, *Two Treatises of Government* (Cambridge University Press 1988).

Loenen T and Rodrigues PR, *Non-discrimination law: Comparative Perspectives* (Kluwer Law International 1999).

Lustig D, *Veiled Power: International Law and the Private Corporation 1886–1981* (Oxford University Press 2020).

Macfarlane A, *The Origins of English Individualism: the Family, Property and Social Transition* (Blackwell 1978).

Macpherson CB, *Property: Mainstream and Critical Positions* (University of Toronto Press 1978).

Mälksoo L, *Russian Approaches to International law* (Oxford University Press 2015).

McDougal MS, Lasswell HD and Miller JC, *The Interpretation of International Agreements and World Public Order: Principles of Content and Procedure*, vol 8 (M Nijhoff Publishers 1994).

McLachlan C, Shore L and Weiniger M, *International Investment Arbitration: Substantive Principles* (Oxford University Press 2007).

Michalowski S and Woods L, *German Constitutional Law: the Protection of Civil Liberties* (Ashgate/Dartmouth 1999).

Miles K, *The Origins of International Investment Law: Empire, Environment, and the Safeguarding of Capital* (Cambridge University Press 2013).

Montt S, *State Liability in Investment Treaty Arbitration: Global Constitutional and Administrative Law in the BIT Generation*, vol 26 (Hart Publishing 2009).

Moore JB, *History and Digest of the International Arbitrations to Which the United States has Been a Party*, vol 3 (Hein, Online 1898).

Mouri A, *The International Law of Expropriation as Reflected in the Work of the Iran-US Claims Tribunal*, vol 17 (M Nijhoff 1994).

Moyn S, *The Last Utopia: Human Rights in History* (Belknap Press of Harvard University Press 2010).

Moyn S, *Not Enough: Human Rights In An Unequal World* (The Belknap Press of Harvard University Press 2018).

Newcombe AP and Paradell L, *Law and Practice of Investment Treaties: Standards of Treatment* (Wolters Kluwer Law & Business 2009).

Nichols P and others, *Nichols on eminent domain* (3rd edn, LexisNexis 2012).

Nijman JE and Nollkaemper A, *New Perspectives on the Divide Between National and International Law* (4th edn, Oxford University Press 2007).

North DC, *Institutions, Institutional Change, and Economic Performance* (Cambridge University Press 1990).

Nosov S, IA A and others, *Constitutional law of Russian Federation* (Statut 2014).

Oppenheim L, *International Law: A Treatise* (8th edn, Longmans, Green 1905).

Oppenheim L, Jennings R and Watts A, *Oppenheim's International Law*: *Peace*, vol 1 (9th edn, Longman Group UK Ltd 1992).

Pahuja S, *Decolonising International Law: Development, Economic Growth and the Politics of Universality* (Cambridge University Press 2011).

Palmer NE and McKendrick E, *Interests in Goods* (Lloyd's of London Press 1993).

Parra AR, *The history of ICSID* (2017).

Peat D, *Comparative Reasoning in International Courts and Tribunals* (Cambridge University Press 2019).

Perrone NM, *Investment Treaties and the Legal Imagination: How Foreign Investors Play By Their Own Rules* (Oxford Academic, Oxford University Press 2021).

Peters A, *Beyond Human Rights: The Legal Status of the Individual in International Law* (Huston J tr, Cambridge University Press 2016).

Pierson C, *Just Property: A History in the Latin West. Volume One: Wealth, Virtue, and the Law* (Oxford University Press 2013).

Pierson C, *Just property: Enlightenment, Revolution, and History Volume two* (1st edn, Oxford University Press 2016).

Pipes R, *Property and Freedom* (1st edn, Vintage Books 2000).

Plato, *The Republic* (Jowett B tr, 360 BCE).

Port KL, *Comparative Law: Law and the Legal Process in Japan* (McAlinn GP ed, Carolina Academic Press 2003).

Pravilova E, *A Public Empire: Property and the Quest for the Common Good in Imperial Russia* (Princeton University Press 2014).

Rajput A, *Regulatory Freedom and Indirect Expropriation in Investment Arbitration* (Kluwer Law International 2018).

Reale M, *O Projeto Do novo Código Civil: Situação Após A Aprovação Pelo Senado Federal* (Saraiva 1999).

Regan J and Smith C, *Agrarian Reform and Resistance in an Age of Globalisation: The Euro-American World and Beyond, 1780–1914* (Taylor & Francis Group 2020).

Riedel EH, *Theorie der Menschenrechtsstandards: Funktion, Wirkungsweise und Begründung wirtschaftlicher und sozialer Menschenrechte mit exemplarischer Darstellung der Rechte auf Eigentum und Arbeit in verschiedenen Rechtsordnungen* (Duncker & Humblot 1986).

Roberts A and Koskenniemi M, *Is International Law International?* (Oxford Academic, Oxford University Press 2017).

Rook D, *Property Law and Human Rights* (Blackstone 2001).

Rousseau JJ, *Discourse Upon the Origin and Foundation of the Inequality Among Mankind* (R and J Dodsley 1761).

Sabahi B, *Compensation and Restitution in Investor-State Arbitration: Principles and Practice* (OUP 2011).

Sabahi B, *Compensation and Restitution in Investor-State Arbitration: Principles and Practice* (Oxford University Press 2011).

Salacuse JW, *The Law of Investment Treaties* (2nd edn, Oxford University Press 2015).

Salomon ME, *Global Responsibility for Human Rights: World Poverty and the Development of International Law* (Oxford University Press 2007).

Sasson M, *Substantive Law in Investment Treaty Arbitration: the Unsettled Relationship Between International Law and Municipal Law* (Kluwer Law International 2010).

Schill S, *International investment law and comparative public law* (Oxford University Press, 2010).

Sen P, *Tagore Law Lectures, 1909. The General Principles of Hindu Jurisprudence* (1918).

Schill S, *The Multilateralization of International Investment Law* (Cambridge University Press 2009).

Schilling-Vacaflor A and Nolte D, *New Constitutionalism in Latin America: Promises and Practices* (Routledge Ltd 2016).

Schlatter R, *Private Property: the History of An Idea* (Allen & Unwin 1951).

Schneiderman D, *Constitutionalizing Economic Globalization: Investment Rules and Democracy's Promise* (Cambridge University Press 2008).

Schneiderman D, *Investment Law's Alibis: Colonialism, Imperialism, Debt and Development* (Cambridge University Press 2022).

Schreuer CH and others, *The ICSID Convention: A Commentary* (Cambridge University Press 2009).

Shihata IFI, *The World Bank Legal Papers* (Martinus Nijhoff 2000).

Shirlow E, *Judging at the Interface: Deference to State Decision-Making Authority in International Adjudication* (Cambridge University Press 2021).

Singer JW, *Entitlement: the Paradoxes of Property* (Yale University Press 2000).

Singer JW, *Introduction to Property* (2nd edn, Aspen Publishers 2005).

Slobodian Q, *Globalists: The End of Empire and the Birth of Neoliberalism* (Harvard University Press 2018).

Sluysmans JAMA, Verbist S and Waring E, *Expropriation Law in Europe* (Wolters Kluwer 2015).

Smaliukas A, *Property and Trust Law in Lithuania* (2017).

Smith A, *Lectures on Jurisprudence (Lectures on Justice, Police, Revenue and Arms, delivered in the University of Glasgow)* (Clarendon Press 1869).

Sornarajah M, *The International Law on Foreign Investment* (Cambridge University Press, 2010).

Sornarajah M, *The Pursuit of Nationalized Property* (1986).

Sornarajah M, *The International Law on Foreign Investment* (3rd edn, Cambridge University Press 2010).

Sornarajah M, *Resistance and Change in the International Law on Foreign Investment* (Cambridge University Press 2015).

Sornarajah M, *The International Law on Foreign Investment* (5th edn, Cambridge University Press 2021).

Soto Hd, *The Mystery of Capital: Why Capitalism Triumphs in the West and Fails Everywhere Else* (Basic Books 2000).

Sprankling JG, *The International Law of Property* (Oxford University Press 2014).

St John T, *The Rise of Investor-State Arbitration: Politics, Law, and Unintended Consequences* (Oxford Academic, Oxford University Press 2018).

Stern SM, Lewinsohn-Zamir D and Demaine LJ, *The Psychology of Property Law* (NYU Press 2020).

Sukhanov Y, *Russian Civil Law* (Statut 2011).

Tams CJ, *Conclusion: The Sources of International Investment Law: Concluding Thoughts* (Brill 2012).

Taube MA and Schücking W, *Russland und Westeuropa (Russlands histor. Sonderentwicklg in d. europäischen Völkergemeinschaft)* (G Stilke 1928).

Titi A, *The Right to Regulate in International Investment Law*, vol 10 (Nomos 2014).

Todd ECE, *The Law of Expropriation and Compensation in Canada* (Carswell 1992).

Tunkin GI, *Theory of International Law: Translation with an introduction* (Butler WE tr, Allen & Unwin 1974).

Tzouvala N, *Capitalism As Civilisation: A History of International Law* (Cambridge University Press 2020).

Underkuffler LS, *The Idea of Property: its Meaning and Power* (Oxford University Press 2003).

Upham FK, *The Great Property Fallacy: Theory, Reality, and Growth in Developing Countries* (Cambridge University Press 2018).

Vadi V, *Analogies in International Investment Law and Arbitration* (Cambridge University Press 2015).

Vadi V, *Proportionality, Reasonableness and Standards of Review in International Investment Law and Arbitration* (Edward Elgar Publishing 2018).

Valeeva R, Abashidze A and others, *International and Internal Protection of Human Rights* (Statut 2011).

Van Harten G, *Investment Treaty Arbitration and Public Law* (Oxford University Press 2007).

Victoria F, *De Indis et de Ivre Belli Relectiones* (Pawley J tr, The Carnegie Institution of Washington 1917).

Wagner WG, *Marriage, Property, and Law in Late Imperial Russia* (Clarendon 1994).

Waibel M, *The Backlash Against Investment Arbitration: Perceptions and Reality* (Wolters Kluwer Law & Business 2010).

Waldron J, *The Rule of Law and the Measure of Property* (Cambridge University Press 2012).

Walt AJvd, *Property and Constitution* (Pretoria University Law Press (PULP) 2012).

Walt Avd, *Constitutional Property Clauses: A Comparative Analysis* (Juta 1999).

Walt Avd, *Property in the Margins* (Bloomsbury Publishing (UK) 2009).

Wang C, *The Constitutional Protection of Private Property in China: Historical Evolution and Comparative Research* (Cambridge University Press 2016).

Warendorf H, Thomas R and Sumner I, *The Civil Code of the Netherlands* (Kluwer Law International 2009).

Weber M, *From Max Weber: Essays in Sociology* (Routledge 2009).

Whitehead AN, *Process and Reality: an Essay in Cosmology* (The Free Press 1979).

Whiteman MM, Hackworth GH and others, *Digest of international law*, vol 1–15 (US Department of State 1963).

Zorkin V, *Russia and Constitution in 21st century* (2nd edn, Norma 2008).

Zweigert K and Kötz H, *Introduction to Comparative Law*, vol 3 (Clarendon Press 1998).

Edited books

Aisbett E, 'Bilateral Investment Treaties and Foreign Direct Investment: Correlation versus Causation' in Sauvant KPSLE (ed), *The Effect of Treaties on Foreign Direct Investment: Bilateral Investment Treaties, Double Taxation Treaties, and Investment Flows* (Oxford University Press 2009).

Allen T, 'The Right to Property' in Ginsburg T and Dixon R (eds), *Comparative Constitutional Law* (Elgar 2011).

Allen T, 'Comparative Constitutional Law in Asia' in *The Right to Property in Asia* (2014).

Allen T, 'Constitutional Law, Social Justice and the Redistribution of Land' in Xu T and Allain J (eds), *Property and Human Rights in A Global Context*, vol 20 (Hart Publishing Ltd 2015).

Alviar Garcia H, 'Looking beyond the Constitution: the Social and Ecological Function of Property' in Dixon R and Ginsburg T (eds), *Comparative Constitutional Law in Latin America* (1st edn, Edward Elgar MUA 2017).

Ambrazevičiūtė K, *Problems of applying right to property, right to economic activities and initiative, consumer rights* in Beliūnienė L (ed) Aktualiausios žmogaus teisių užtikrinimo Lietuvoje 2008–2013 m. problemos (2012).

Aspremont Jd, 'International Customary Investment Law: Story of a Paradox' in *International Investment Law* (Brill 2012).

von Bar C and others (eds), *Principles, Definitions and Model Rules of European Private Law : Draft Common Frame of Reference* (Sellier European Law Publishers 2009).

Bentsi-Enchill K, 'The Traditional Legal Systems of Africa' in Lawson FH and others (eds), *International Encyclopedia of Comparative Law: Property and Trust*, vol 6 (JCB Mohr (Paul Siebeck) 1973).

Bjorklund AK, 'Nafta Chapter 11' in Brown C (ed), *Commentaries on Selected Model Investment Treaties* (1st edn, Oxford University Press 2013).

Boast RP and Frankel S, 'Defining the Ambit of Regulatory Takings' in Frankel S and Ryder D (eds), *Recalibrating Behaviour: Smarter Regulation in a Global World* (LexisNexis NZ 2013).

Boast RP and Quigley NC, 'Regulatory Reform and Property Rights in New Zealand' in Frankel S (ed), *Learning From the Past, Adapting for The Future: Regulatory Reform in New Zealand* (LexisNexis NZ 2011).

Borrows J, 'Indigenous Diversities in International Investment and Trade' in Borrows J and Schwartz R (eds), *Indigenous Peoples and International Trade: Building Equitable and Inclusive International Trade and Investment Agreements* (Cambridge University Press 2020).

Brown C and Sheppard A, 'United Kingdom' in Brown C (ed), *Commentaries on selected model investment treaties* (Oxford University Press 2013).

Brown R, 'Possibilities and Pitfalls of Comparative Analysis of Property Rights Protections and the Canadian Regime of Legal Protection against Takings' in Frankel S (ed), *Learning from the past, adapting for the future: regulatory reform in New Zealand* (LexisNexis NZ 2011).

Cabrol E, 'Pren Nreka V. Czech Republic and the Notion of Investment under Bilateral Investment Treaties. Does "Investment" Really Mean "Every Kind of Asset"?' in Sauvant K (ed), *Yearbook on International Investment Law & Policy* (Oxford University Press 2010).

Calamita NJ, 'the Principle of Proportionality and the Problem of Indeterminacy in International Investment Treaties' in Calamita NJ, Earnest D and Burgstaller M (eds), *The Future of ICSID and The Place of Investment Treaties in International Law* (2013).

Cardenas F and d'Aspremont J, 'International Investment Law in Latin America: Universalizing Resistance' in Droubi S and Elizondo CJF (eds), *Latin America and international investment law* (Manchester University Press 2022).

Chen L, '100 Years of Chinese Property Law: Looking back and Thinking forward' in Chen L & van Rhee C (eds) Towards a Chinese civil code: comparative and historical perspectives 87 (Brill 2012).

Clarke A, 'Land Titling and Communal Property' in Barr W (ed), *Modern Studies in Property Law – Volume 8* (Bloomsbury Publishing PLC 2015).

Coleman J, Cordes KY and Johnson L, 'Human Rights Law and the Investment Treaty Regime' in Surya D and David B (eds), *Research Handbook on Human Rights and Business* (Edward Elgar Publishing 2020).

Conticelli M, 'Property Rights, Administrative Limits and Procedural Requirements in the Eu, the Echr, and the Iil' in Conticelli M and Perroud T (eds), *Procedural Requirements for Administrative Limits to Property Rights* (Oxford Academic, Oxford University Press 2022).

D'Aspremont J, 'International Legal Constitutionalism, Legal Forms, and the Need for Villains' in Lang AF and Wiener A (eds), *Handbook on Global Constitutionalism* (Edward Elgar 2017).

Davis JDR, 'a Historical Overview of Hindu Law' in Davis Jr DR, Krishnan JK and Lubin T (eds), *Hinduism and Law: An Introduction* (Cambridge University Press 2010).

De Brabandere E, Fitzmaurice M and Merkouris P, 'The Interpretation and Application of the European Convention of Human Rights: Legal and Practical Implications' in *Human Rights Considerations in International Investment Arbitration* (Brill | Nijhoff 2013).

del Guayo I, Kühne G and Roggenkamp M, 'Ownership Unbundling and Property Rights in the Eu Energy Sector' in McHarg A and others (eds), *Property and the Law in Energy and Natural Resources* (Oxford University Press 2010).

Derrett JDM, 'The Development of the Concept of Property in India C. A.D. 800–1800' in Derrett JDM (ed), *Essays in Classical and Modern Hindu Law* (Brill 1976).

Dolzer R, 'The Notion of Investment in Recent Practice' in Charnovitz S, Steger DP and Van den Bossche P (eds), *Law in the Service of Human Dignity: Essays in Honour of Florentino Feliciano* (Cambridge University Press 2005).

Dolzer R and Kim YI, 'Germany' in Brown C (ed), *Commentaries on selected model investment treaties* (1st edn, Oxford University Press 2013).

Dolzer R and others, 'History, Sources, and Nature of International Investment Law' in *Principles of International Investment Law* (Oxford University Press 2022).

Douglas Z, 'Property, Investment and the Scope of Investment Protection Obligations' in Douglas Z, Pauwelyn J and Viñuales JE (eds), *The Foundations of International Investment Law: Bringing Theory into Practice* (Oxford University Press 2014).

Esquirol JL, 'Formalizing Property in Latin America' in Graziadei M and Smith LD (eds), *Comparative Property Law: Global Perspectives* (Edward Elgar Publishing 2017).

Esser R, 'Citizenship and Immigration in 16th and Early 17th-Century England' in Ellis, Hálfdanarson and Isaacs (eds), *Citizenship in Historical Perspective* (Pisa University Press 2006).

Gaillard E, 'Identify or Define? Reflections on the Evolution of the Concept of Investment in Icsid Practice' in Binder C and Schreuer C (eds), *International investment Law for The 21st Century: Essays in Honour of Christoph Schreuer* (Oxford University Press 2009).

Gallagher N and Shan W, 'China' in Brown C (ed), *Commentaries on Selected Model Investment Treaties* (Oxford University Press 2013).

Gerencsér BS, 'the Value of Property in Central and Eastern Europe: Comparative Expropriation in Poland, Ukraine, and Hungary' in Conticelli M and Perroud T (eds), *Procedural Requirements for Administrative Limits to Property Rights* (Oxford Academic, Oxford University Press 2022).

Greenman K and others, 'International Law and Revolution: 1917 and beyond' in Saunders A and others (eds), *Revolutions in International Law: The Legacies of 1917* (Cambridge University Press 2021) .

Guernaoui E, 'Procedural Requirements for Administrative Limits to Property Rights in France' in Conticelli M and Perroud T (eds), *Procedural Requirements for Administrative Limits to Property Rights* (Oxford Academic, Oxford University Press 2022) accessed 3/27/2025.

Habdas M, 'Expropriation Law in Poland' in Sluysmans JAMA, Verbist S and Waring E (eds), *Expropriation Law in Europe* (Wolters Kluwer 2015).

Hamamoto S and Nottage L, 'Japan' in Brown C (ed), *Commentaries on Selected Model Investment Treaties* (1st edn, Oxford University Press 2013).

Ho J, 'Singapore' in Brown C (ed), *Commentaries on Selected Model Investment Treaties* (1st edn, Oxford University Press 2013).

Ho J, 'Internationalisation and State Contracts: are State Contracts the Future or the Past?' in Lim CL (ed), *Alternative Visions of the International Law on Foreign Investment: Essays in Honour of Muthucumaraswamy Sornarajah* (Cambridge University Press 2016).

Huang CY, 'Judicial Deference to Legislative Delegation and Administrative Discretion in New Democracies: Recent Evidence from Poland, Taiwan, and South Africa' in Ackerman SR and Lindseth PL (eds), *Comparative Administrative Law* (2010).

Jakab E, 'Property Rights in Ancient Rome' in Erdkamp P, Verboven K and Zuiderhoek A (eds), *Ownership and Exploitation of Land and Natural Resources in the Roman World* (Oxford University Press 2015).

Jansen N and Van Erp S, 'Comparative Property Law' in, vol 1 (Oxford University Press 2006).

Jansen N and Van Erp S, 'Comparative Property Law' in Reimann M and Zimmermann R (eds), *The Oxford Handbook of Comparative Law* (Oxford University Press 2006).

Kaeckenbeeck G, 'La Protection Internationale Des Droits Acquis (Volume 059)' in The Hague Academy of International L (ed), *Collected Courses of the Hague Academy of International Law* (Brill).

Kalus S and Habdas M, 'The Notion of Real Estate and Rights in Selected Legal Systems' in Cooke E, Dixon MMA and Hopkins N (eds), *Modern studies in property law*, vol 3 (Hart Pub 2001).

Kawka I and Kozera Ł, 'Procedural Requirements for Administrative Limits to Property Rights in Poland' in Conticelli M and Perroud T (eds), *Procedural Requirements for Administrative Limits to Property Rights* (Oxford Academic, Oxford University Press 2022) accessed 3/27/2025.

Kleinheisterkamp J, 'Development of Comparative Law in Latin America' in Reimann M and Zimmermann R (eds), *The Oxford Handbook of Comparative Law* (2006).

Koskenniemi M, 'International Law and the Emergence of Mercantile Capitalism: Grotius to Smith' in *The Roots of International Law: Liber Amicorum Peter Haggenmacher* (Martinus Nijhoff Publishers 2014).

Kotaka T, 'Japan's Land Use Law' in Kotaka T and Callies DL (eds), *Taking Land: Compulsory Purchase and Regulation in Asian-Pacific Countries* (University of Hawai'i Press 2002).

Krommendijk J and Morijn J, '"Proportional" by What Measure(S)? Balancing Investor Interests and Human Rights by Way of Applying the Proportionality Principle in Investor-State Arbitration' in Dupuy PM, Francioni F and Petersmann EU (eds), *Human Rights in International Investment Law and Arbitration* (Oxford University Press 2009).

Levesque C and Newcombe A, 'Canada' in Brown C (ed), *Commentaries on Selected Model Investment Treaties* (Oxford University Press 2013).

Mann FA, 'State Contracts and State Responsibility' in *Studies in International Law* (Oxford University Press 1973).

Martenet V, 'Comparative Perspectives on Expropriation and Other Takings: England, France, Germany, and the United States' in Conticelli M and Perroud T (eds), *Procedural Requirements for Administrative Limits to Property Rights* (Oxford Academic, Oxford University Press 2022).

Martinkute I, 'State Interference with Private Property' in Grote R, Lachenmann F and Wolfrum R (eds), *Max Planck Encyclopedia of Comparative Constitutional Law* (Oxford University Press 2020).

Merwe Cvd, Waal MJd and Miller DLC, 'South Africa' in Blanpain R and others (eds), *International Encyclopaedia of Laws: Property and Trust Law* (Kluwer Law International 2000).

Miles K, '1917: Property, Revolution and Rejection in International Law' in K. Greenman and others (eds), *Revolutions in International Law The Legacies of 1917* (Cambridge University Press 2021).

Milo MJ, 'Property and Real Rights' in Smits JM (ed), *Elgar Encyclopedia of Comparative Law* (2nd edn, Edward Elgar 2012).

Mitra MD, 'Evolution of Property Rights in India' in Pellissery S, Davy B and Jacobs HM (eds), *Land Policies in India: Promises, Practices and Challenges* (Springer Singapore 2017).

Neff SC, 'Peace and Prosperity: Commercial Aspects of Peacemaking' in Lesaffer R (ed), *Peace Treaties and International Law in European History: From the Late Middle Ages to World War One* (Cambridge University Press 2004).

Oda H, 'Property and Land Law' in *Russian Commercial Law* (Brill 2007).

Peerenboom R, 'Law and Development in China and India' in Wang J and Sornarajah M (eds), *China, India and the International Economic Order* (Cambridge University Press 2010).

Perkams M, 'the Concept of Indirect Expropriation in Comparative Public Law – Searching for Light in the Dark' in Schill SW (ed), *International Investment Law and Comparative Public Law* (2010).

Perrone NM, 'Expropriation' in Schneiderman D and Van Harten G (eds), *Rethinking Investment Law* (Oxford Academic, Oxford University Press 2023).

Perrone NsM, 'Neoliberalism and Economic Sovereignty: Property, Contracts, and Foreign Investment Relations' in Brabazon H (ed), *Neoliberal legality Understanding the Role of Law in the Neoliberal Project* (Routledge 2016).

Praduroux S, 'Objects of Property Rights: Old and New' in Graziadei M and Smith LD (eds), *Comparative Property Law: Global Perspectives* (Edward Elgar Pub 2017).

Radi Y, 'Introduction: Taking Stock of the Societal and Legal Interplay between Human Rights and Investment' in Radi Y (ed), *Research Handbook on Human Rights and Investment* (Edward Elgar Publishing Limited 2018).

Raff M and Taitslin A, 'Private Law in the Shadow of Public Law: a Legacy of 20th Century Marxism and the Soviet Legal Model' in Bustamante T and Onazi O (eds), *Human Rights, Language and Law* (Franz Steiner Verlag 2012).

Redgwell C, 'Property Law Sources and Analogies in International Law' in McHarg Aileen and others (eds), *Property and the Law in Energy and Natural Resources* (Oxford University Press 2010).

Reinisch A, 'Austria' in Brown C (ed), *Commentaries on Selected Model Investment Treaties* (1st edn, Oxford University Press 2013).

Ricquier WJM, 'Compulsory Purchase in Singapore' in Kotaka T and Callies DL (eds), *Taking Land: Compulsory Purchase and Regulation in Asian-Pacific Countries* (University of Hawai'i Press 2002).

Roberts A and others, 'Conceptualizing Comparative International Law' in *Comparative International Law* (Oxford University Press 2018).

Sabahi B and Birch N, 'Comparative Compensation for Expropriation' in Schill SW (ed), *International Investment Law and Comparative Public Law* (Oxford University Press 2010).

Schneiderman D and Van Harten G (eds), *Rethinking Investment Law* (Oxford Academic, Oxford University Press 2023).

Schäfer H-B, 'Taking Law from an Economic Perspective with Reference to German Law' in Kim I, Lee H and Somin I (eds), *Eminent Domain: A Comparative Perspective* (Cambridge University Press 2017).

Schill SWB, 'the Sixth Path: Reforming Investment Law from within' in Kalicki JE and Joubin-Bret A (eds), *Reshaping the Investor-State Dispute Settlement System: Journeys for The 21st Century* (Brill 2015).

Schrijver N and Prislan V, 'the Netherlands' in Brown C (ed), *Commentaries on Selected Model Investment Treaties* (1st edn, Oxford University Press 2013).

Shan W, 'China and International Investment Law' in Trakman LE and Ranieri NW (eds), *Regionalism in International Investment Law* (Oxford University Press 2014).

Shin HT, 'Republic of Korea' in Brown C (ed), *Commentaries on Selected Model Investment Treaties* (1st edn, Oxford University Press 2013).

Shirvani F, 'Procedural Requirements for Administrative Limits to Property Rights in Germany' in Conticelli M and Perroud T (eds), *Procedural Requirements for Administrative Limits to Property Rights* (Oxford Academic, Oxford University Press 2022).

Sirks B, 'Public Law' in Johnston D (ed), *The Cambridge Companion to Roman Law* (Cambridge University Press 2015).

Slaughter AM and Burke-White WW, 'the Future of International Law Is Domestic' in Nolkaemper A and Nijman J (eds), *New perspectives on the divide between national and international law* (Oxford University Press 2007).

Smith T, 'Mixed Jurisdictions' in Lawson FH and others (eds), *International encyclopedia of comparative law: Property and trust / Volume 6* (JCB Mohr (Paul Siebeck) 1973).

Sornarajah M, 'The Past, Present and Future of the International Law on Foreign Investment' in Wenhua S and Jinyuan S (eds), *China and International Investment Law: Twenty Years of ICSID Membership* (2014).

Starzhenetskiy V, 'Property Rights in Russia: Reconsidering the Socialist Legal Tradition' in Mälksoo L and Benedek W (eds), *Russia and the European Court of Human Rights: The Strasbourg Effect* (Cambridge University Press 2017).

Straumann B, 'Natural Rights and Just Wars' in *Roman Law in the State of Nature: The Classical Foundations of Hugo Grotius' Natural Law* (Cambridge University Press 2015).

Suh WW, 'Land Use Planning and Compensation in Korea' in Kotaka T and Callies DL (eds), *Taking Land: Compulsory Purchase and Regulation in Asian-Pacific Countries* (University of Hawai'i Press 2002).

Tavela LD and Andrade LAGd, 'Expropriation in Brazilian Law: an International Standard?' in Levy DdA, Borja AGd and Pucci AN (eds), *Investment protection in Brazil* (Wolters Kluwer, Law & Business 2014).

Trochev A, 'Russia's Constitutional Spirit: Judge-Made Principles in Theory and Practice' in Smith GB and Sharlet RS (eds), *Russia and its Constitution: Promise and Political Reality* (Nijhoff 2008).

Van Erp S, *Can European Property Law be Codified?* in Chen L and van Rhee C H (ed) *Towards a Chinese Civil Code* (Brill 2012).

Van Harten G, 'Fortifying Inequality' in *The Trouble with Foreign Investor Protection* (Oxford University Press 2020).

Vogler R, 'Due Process' in Rosenfeld M and Sajó A (eds), *The Oxford Handbook of Comparative Constitutional Law* (Oxford University Press 2012).

Walde T and Sabahi B, 'Compensation for Expropriation and Action Tantamount to Expropriation' in Muchlinski P, Ortino F and Schreuer C (eds), *The Oxford Handbook of International Investment Law* (Oxford University Press 2008).

Walt Avd and Walsh R, 'Comparative Constitutional Property Law' in Graziadei M and Smith LD (eds), *Comparative Property Law: Global Perspectives* (Edward Elgar Publishing 2017).

Wheeler F, 'Due Process' in Saunders C and Stone A (eds), *The Oxford Handbook of the Australian Constitution* (Oxford University Press 2018).

Cases

Abaclat and Others (formerlyGiovanna a Beccara and Others) v Argentine Republic (ICSID).
Abengoa, SA y COFIDES, SA v United Mexican States (ICSID).
Adapting Agriculture to the Environment (French Constitutional Council).
ADC Affiliate Limited and ADC & ADMC Management Limited v Republic of Hungary (ICSID).
AIG Capital Partners, Inc and CJSC Tema Real Estate Company v Republic of Kazakhstan (ICSID).
Alejandra Marcela Matus Acun˜a and ors v Chile Report No 90/05 (ACtHR).
Alpha Projektholding GmbH v Ukraine (ICSID).
Alps Finance & Trade AG v the Slovak Republic (UNCITRAL).
Anatolie Stati, Gabriel Stati, Ascom Group SA and Terra Raf Trans Traiding Ltd v Republic of Kazakhstan (SCC).
Anglia Auto Accessories Ltd v Czech Republic (SCC).
Application of Privatization (French Constitutional Council).
Azurix Corp v Argentine Republic (ICSID).
Bernhard von Pezold and others v Republic of Zimbabwe (ICSID).
The Brazilian electricity crisis case 13 December 2001, ADC 09, Official Gazette 23 April 2004 (Brazil Supreme Federal Tribunal).
British Medical Association v The Commonwealth (1949) 79 CLR 201.
Caquelard v Lemoine S 34 I 205 (Cour de Cassation Chambre des Requetes).
Cargill Inc v United Mexican States (ICSID).
Centre for Minority Rights Development (Kenya) and Minority Rights Group International on behalf of Endorois Welfare Council v Kenya (African Commission on Human and Peoples' Rights).
CME (Netherlands) v Czech Republic (Partial Award) (UNCITRAL).
CME Czech Republic BV v Czech Republic (UNCITRAL).
CMS Gas Transmission Co v Argentina (ICSID).
Compañía del Desarrollo de Santa Elena v Republic of Costa Rica (ICSID).
Continental Casualty Company v Argentine Republic (ICSID).
Crystallex International Corporation v Bolivarian Republic of Venezuela (ICSID)*Cultura 2000 and another v Government of the Republic of Namibia and others* 1993 (2) SA 12 (NHC).
Davis & Co v Mexican Eagle Co [1938–40] Annual Digest and Reports of Public International Law Cases 25 (No 12) (Court of Rotterdam).
Democratization of the Public Sector (French Constitutional Council).
Deposit Copy case BVerfGE 58.
Deutsche Bank AG v Democratic Socialist Republic of Sri Lanka (ICSID).

Disarmament Statute case No ADI 3112, Official Gazette 26 October 2007 (Brazil Supreme Federal Tribunal).
DR Energy Holdings Limited and Empresa Distribuidora de Electricidad del Este SA v Dominican Republic (UNCITRAL).
Dwarkadas Shrinivas v Sholapur Spinning and Weaving Co Ltd AIR 1954 SC 119.
Eiffel Tower Amendment case (French Constitutional Council).
El Paso Energy International Company v Argentine Republic (ICSID).
Emmis International Holding, BV, Emmis Radio Operating, BV and MEM Magyar Electronic Media Kereskedelmi és Szolgáltató Kft v Hungary (ICSID).
Energoalians SARL v Republic of Moldova (UNCITRAL).
Eureko BV v Republic of Poland (Ad Hoc).
Fireman's Fund Insurance Company v 111 United Mexican States (ICSID).
Five Pensioners v Peru Series C No 98 (ACtHR).
Former King of Greece and others v Greece (ECtHR).
Gavrilovic and Gavrilovic doo v Republic of Croatia (ICSID).
Generation Ukraine v Ukraine (ICSID).
Glamis Gold Ltd v The United States of America (UNCITRAL).
Granting a Private Developer to Claim Transfer of Land from Private Owner Case Decision of 26 November 2009, No 2008Hun-Ba133 (Korean Constitutional Court).
Guaracachi America, Inc and Rurelec PLC v Plurinational State of Bolivia (PCA).
Gustav FW Hamester GmbH & Co KG v Republic of Ghana (ICSID).
Hassan Awdi, Enterprise Business Consultants, Inc and Alfa El Corporation v Romania (ICSID).
Hawaii Housing Authority v Midkiff 467 US (1984).
Hubert Wachauf Case 5/88 [1989] (ECJ).
Imposition of Expenses for the Excavation of Cultural Heritage case Decision of 28 October 2010, No 2008Hun-Ba74 (Korean Constitutional Court).
Inmaris Perestroika Sailing Maritime Services GmbH and others v Ukraine (ICSID).
Ioannis Kardassopoulos v Georgia (ICSID).
Isolux Infrastructure Netherlands, BV v Kingdom of Spain (SCC).
Ivcher-Bronstein v Peru Series C No 74 (ACtHR).
James and others v The United Kingdom (ECtHR).
Jan de Nul NV and Dredging International NV v Arab Republic of Egypt (ICSID).
Jan Oostergetel and Theodora Laurentius v Slovak Republic (UNCITRAL).
Joy Mining Machinery Limited v Arab Republic of Egypt (ICSID).
Kakinada Annadana Samajam v Commissioner of Hindu Religious & Charitable Endowments, Hyderabad and Others AIR 1971 SC 891.
Kameshwar Singh v State of Bihar AIR 1951 Patna 91.
Kelo v City of New London 545 US 469 (2005).
Kopecký v Slovakia Application No 44912/98 (ECtHR).

Les Laboratoires Servier, SAS, Biofarma, SAS and Arts et Techniques du Progres SAS v Republic of Poland (UNCITRAL).

LG&E Energy Corp, LG&E Capital Corp and LG&E International Inc v Argentine Republic (ICSID)*Liselotte Hauer v Land Rheinland-Pfalz* Case 44/79 (ECJ).

Lithgow and Others v the United Kingdom (ECtHR).

Loretto v Teleprompter Manhattan CATV Corp 458 US 419 (1982).

Luigiterzo Bosca v Republic of Lithuania (PCA).

M Meerapfel Sohne AG v Central African Republic (ICSID).

Madhav Rao Scindia v Union of India AIR 1971 SC 530.

Malaysian Historical Salvors Sdn Bhd v Government of Malaysia (ICSID).

Maltzan and others v Germany Applications Nos 71916/01, 71917/01 and 10260/02 (ECtHR).

Marion Unglaube v Republic of Costa Rica (ICSID).

Masdar Solar & Wind Cooperatief UA v Kingdom of Spain (ICSID) Case No ARB/14/1, Award, 16 May 2018.

MCI Power Group, LC and New Turbine Inc v Republic of Ecuador (ICSID).

Merrill & Ring Forestry LP v Government of Canada (UNCITRAL, ICSID Administered).

Metalclad Corporation v United Mexican States (ICSID).

Middle East Cement Shipping and Handling Co SA v Arab Republic of Egypt (ICSID).

Millicom International Operations BV and Sentel GSM SA v Republic of Senegal (ICSID).

Mondev International Ltd v USA (ICSID).

Nationalizations (French Constitutional Council).

Nollan v California Coastal Commission 483 US 825 (1987).

Nordzucker AG v Republic of Poland (UNCITRAL).

Occidental Exploration and Production Company v Republic of Ecuador (LCIA).

OKO Pankki Oyj and others v Republic of Estonia (ICSID).

Palamara-Iribarne v Chile Series C No 135.

Patrick Mitchell v The Democratic Republic of Congo (ICSID).

Penn Central Transportation Company v New York City 438 US 104, 127 (1978).

Philip Morris Asia Limited v Commonwealth of Australia (PCA).

Philip Morris Brand Sàrl (Switzerland), Philip Morris Products SA (Switzerland) and Abal Hermanos SA (Uruguay) v Oriental Republic of Uruguay (ICSID).

Philip Morris Brand Sàrl, Philip Morris Products SA and Abal Hermanos SA v Oriental Republic of Uruguay (ICSID).

PL Holdings SARL v Republic of Poland (SCC).

Poštová banka, as and Istrokapital SE v Hellenic Republic (ICSID).

Privatizations (French Constitutional Council).

Quasar de Valors SICAV SA and others (formerly Renta 4 SVSA and others) v Russian Federation (SCC).

Quiborax SA and Non Metallic Minerals SA v Plurinational State of Bolivia (ICSID).

Rajasthan v Union of India AIR 1977 SC 1361.
Reinhard Hans Unglaube v Republic of Costa Rica (ICSID).
Revere Copper v OPIC 56 ILR 258, 292.
Romak SA v the Republic of Uzbekistan (UNCITRAL).
RosInvestCo UK Ltd v Russian Federation (SCC).
Rumeli Telekom AS and Telsim Mobil Telekomunikasyon Hizmetleri AS v Republic of Kazakhstan (ICSID) Case No ARB/05/16, Award, 29 July 2008.
Rusoro Mining Ltd v Bolivarian Republic of Venezuela (ICSID).
Saar Papier Vertriebs GmbH v Republic of Poland (UNCITRAL).
Saghir Ahmad v The State of Uttar Pradesh [1955] SCR 707.
Saint-Gobain Performance Plastics Europe v Bolivarian Republic of Venezuela (ICSID).
Saipem SpA v People's Republic of Bangladesh (ICSID).
Salini Costruttori SPA and Italstrade SPA v Kingdom of Morocco (ICSID).
Saluka Investments BV v Czech Republic (UNCITRAL).
Sanum Investments Limited v Lao People's Democratic Republic (PCA).
SAUR International SA v Argentine Republic (ICSID).
Scordino v Italy (No 1) (ECtHR)*SD Myers Inc v Canada* (UNCITRAL NAFTA Chapter 11 Arbitration Tribunal).
Serra do Mar State Park case case No 9 842765/1–00-Paraibuna (Braz) (São Paulo Court of Appeal).
SGS Société Générale de Surveillance SA v Republic of the Philippines (ICSID).
Slivenko and Others v Latvia Application No 48321/99 (ECtHR).
Southern Pacific Properties (Middle East) Limited v Arab Republic of Egypt (ICSID).
Sporrong and Lonnroth v Sweden (1982) 52 ECHR (Ser A) 26.
Starrett Housing Corp v Iran (1983) 4 Iran-US CTR 122.
State of West Bengal v Bela Banerjee AIR 1954 SC 170.
Structure of Agricultural Law (French Constitutional Council).
SwemBalt AB v Republic of Latvia (UNCITRAL).
Tecnicas Medioambientales Tecmed SA v The United Mexican States (ICSID).
Telenor Mobile Communications AS v Republic of Hungary (ICSID).
TGV Nord (French Constitutional Council).
Tippetts, Abbett, McCarthy, Stratton v TAMS-AFFA Consulting Engineers of Iran 6 Iran-US CTR 219.
Tobacco and Alcohol Advertising (French Constitutional Council).
Town Planning (French Constitutional Council).
Transport Law case (French Constitutional Council).
Tre Traktörer Aktiebolag v Sweden.
Tza Yap Shum v Republic of Peru (ICSID).
UP (formerly Le Chèque Déjeuner) and CD Holding Internationale v Hungary (ICSID).

Urban Planning Long-term Non-performance case Decision of 21 October 1999, No 97Hun-Ba26 (Korean Constitutional Court).

Urbaser SA and Consorcio de Aguas Bilbao Biskaia, Bilbao Biskaia Ur Partzuergoa v Argentine Republic (ICSID).

Vajravelu v Special Deputy Collector, West Madras AIR 1965 SC 1017.

Van der Mussele v Belgium Application No 8919/80 (ECtHR).

Vattenfall AB, Vattenfall Europe AG, Vattenfall Europe Generation AG & Co KG v The Federal Republic of Germany (ICSID).

Venezuela Holdings BV and others (formerly Mobil Corporation and others) v Bolivarian Republic of Venezuela (ICSID).

Vestey Group Ltd v Bolivarian Republic of Venezuela (ICSID).

Viaşu v Roumanie Requête No 75951/01 (ECtHR).

Vigotop Limited v Hungary (ICSID).

Waguih Elie George Siag & Clorinda Vecchi v Arab Republic of Egypt (ICSID).

Wena Hotels LTD v Arab Republic of Egypt (ICSID).

Yakye Axa Indigenous Community v Paraguay (ACtHR).

Yukos Universal Limited (Isle of Man) v Russian Federation (PCA).

Yukos Universal Limited v Russian Federation (PCA).

Gardner v Trustees of Village of Newburgh et al 2 Johns Ch 162 (NY).

Callender v Marsh 18 Mass (I Pick) 418.

Proprietors of Piscataqua Bridge v New-Hampshire Bridge 7 NH 35.

Knight v Knight 3 Beav 148.

Monongahela Navigation Co v Coons 6 Watts&S 101, 114 (Pa).

O'Connor v Pittsburgh 18 Pa (6 Harris) 187.

Slaughterhouse Cases 83 US (16 Wall)36.

Munn v Illinois 94 US 113.

Bowditch v Boston 101 US 16, 18–19.

Mugler v Kansas 123 US 623.

Chicago, Milwaukee & St Paul Ry v Minnesota 134 US 418.

People v Pullman's Palace-Car Co 51 NE 664, 674 (Ill).

Smyth v Ames 169 US 466.

Richards v Washington Terminal Company 233 US 546.

Hadacheck v Sebastian 239 US 394.

Reinman v Little Rock 237 US 171.

Corn Products Refining Company v Eddy 249 US 427 431–432.

Calhoun v Massie 253 US 170, 175.

Block v Hirsh 256 US 135, 155.

Norwegian shipowners claims (Norway v USA) Reports of International Arbitral Awards.

Pennsylvania Coal Company v Mahon 260 US 393.

Certain German Interests in Polish Upper Silesia (*Germany v Poland*) Series A No 7 (PCIJ).
VLFH Neer and PE Neer (*United States v Mexico*) UNRIAA 4 (US-Mexico General Claims Commission).
Shufeldt Claim (*USA v Guatemala*) 2 UN RIAA 1079.
Randall v City of Milwaukee 212 Wis 374, 249 NW 73.
Panevezys-Saldutiškis Railway case (*Estonia v Lithuania*) Ser A/B No 76 (PCIJ).
Bank of New South Wales v Commonwealth 76 CLR 1.
British Medical Association v The Commonwealth 79 CLR 201.
State of West Bengal v Subodh Gopal Bose SCR 587.
Saghir Ahmad v The State of Uttar Pradesh SCR 707.
Nunnally v United States 239 F2d 521 (4th Cir).
Belfast Corporation v OD Cars AC 490.
Belfast Corporation v OD Cars Limited AC 490.
Batten v United States 306 F2d 580 (10th Cir).
D'Aguiar v Attorney-General 4 WIR 481 (SC British Guiana).
Goldblatt v Hempstead 369 US 590.
Decision of 6 June 1963 17 Keisyu 521 (Japanese Supreme Court).
Tilkayat Shri Govindlalji v Rajasthan 1 SCR 561, AIR 1963 SC 1638.
National Provincial Bank v Ainsworth AC 1175 (HL).
Golak Nath v State of Punjab AIR 1643.
Decision of 27 November 1968 22 Keishu 12, 1402 (Japanese Supreme Court).
Hamburg Dyke Order Act case BVerfGE 24, 421.
Decision 18 October 1973 27 Minshu 9, 1210 (Japanese Supreme Court).
Kesavananda v State of Kerala 4 SCC 225.
Decision of 13 March 1975 771 Hanrei-Jiho 37 (Japanese Supreme Court).
Murphyores Inc Pty Ltd v Commonwealth HCA 20, 136 CLR 1 (14 April 1976) (High Court).
Manitoba Fisheries v The Queen 88 DLR (3d) 462.
Penn Central Transportation Company v New York City 438 US 104, 127.
Allotment decision BVerfGE 52, 1.
Co-Determination decision 50 BVerfGE 339.
Trademark decision 51 BVerfGE 193.
Egualisation of Pensions upon Dissolution of Marriage Decision BVerfGE 53, 257.
Groundwater cases 58 BVerfGE 300.
Loretto v Teleprompter Manhattan CATV Corp 458 US 419.
Commonwealth v Tasmania 158 CLR 1.
Decision of 18 February 1983 37 Minshu 1, 59 (Japanese Supreme Court).
Guerin v The Queen 13 DLR (4th) 321.
Hawaii Housing Authority v Midkiff 467 US.

The Union of Campement Sites Owners and Lessees v The Government of Mauritius MR 100.

Attorney-General v Lawrence LRC (Const) 921 (the Court of Appeal of St Christopher and Nevis).

The Queen v Tener 1 SCR 533.

The Queen v Oakes 26 DLR (4th) 200, 227.

Amoco v Iran Award 27 International Legal Materials 301 (1988).

Boxberg decision BVerfGE 74, 264.

Nollan v California Coastal Commission 483 US 825.

Ackerman v Nova Scotia 47 DLR (4th).

Mobil Oil v Iran 86 International Law Reports 231 (1988).

Commissioner of Taxes v CW (Pvt) Ltd 3 ZLR 361 (Zimbabwean Supreme Court).

Elettronica Sicula SpA (ELSI) case (United States v Italy) ICJ Rep (ICJ).

Phillips Petroleum v Iran 21 Iran-US CTR 81.

Basco Enterprises Pte Ltd v Soh Siang Wai 1 MLJ 193.

Decision No K2/90 OTK ZU 1/1990 poz 3 (Polish Constitutional Tribunal).

Decision No K 1/90 OTK ZU 1990, poz 2 (Polish Constitutional Tribunal).

R v Sparrow 70 DLR (4th) 385.

Casamiro Resource Corp v British Columbia (Attorney-General) 80 DLR (4th) 1 (BCCA).

The Right of Pre-Emption case BVerfGE 83, 201.

Sanders v British Columbia (Milk Board) 77 DLR (4th) 603.

Government of Mauritius v Union Flacq Sugar Estates Co Ltd 1 WLR 903 (PC Mauritius).

Lucas v South Carolina Coastal Council 505 US 1003.

Cream Silver Mines Ltd v British Columbia 99 DLR (4th) 199, 208.

Decision on the repayment of a loan contract in case 4/94 (Lithuanian Constitutional Court).

Diepsloot Resident's and Landowners's Association v Administrator, Transvaal 3 SA 336 (A).

Georgiadis v Australian and Overseas Telecommunications Corporation 179 CLR 297.

Decision on the restoration of the ownership rights of citizens to land in case No 2/95 (Lithuanian Constitutional Court).

Davies and others v the Minister of Land, Agriculture and Water Development (1) BCLR 83 (Zimbabwean High Cout).

Decision of 17 December 1996 No 20-P (Russian Constitutional Court).

Decision on Privatisation of Dwellings Act and etc in case No 3-4-1-2-96 (Estonian Supreme Court).

Nyambirai v National Social Security Authority and another 1 LRC 64 (Zimbabwean Supreme Court).

Re (First) Certification of the Constitution of the Republic of South Africa case (10) BLCR 1253 (South African Constitutional Court).
Waverley Borough v Flether QB 334, 345 (CA).
Alleyne-Forte v Att-Gen and Another LRC 338 (PC TT).
Decision of 20 May 1997 in case No 4-P (Russian Constitutional Court).
Decision of 20 May 1997 in case No 8-P (Russian Constitutional Court).
Decision on the administrative penalty of property confiscation in case No 12/96–5/97 (Lithuanian Constitutional Court).
Delmaguukw v British Columbia 153 DLR (4th) 193.
Commonwealth v WMC Resources 194 CLR 1.
Decision of 11 March 1998 in case No 8-P (Russian Constitutional Court).
Decision on the manufacture, storage, transporting, sale and realisation of alcohol in case No 10/97–3/98–10/98 (Lithuanian Constitutional Court).
Decision on the methods for establishing the nominal price of land purchased by the state in cases No 11/96, 27/01–5/02–01/03 (Lithuanian Constitutional Court).
Decision on the restoration of the ownership rights of citizens to land and residential houses, case No 15/97 (Lithuanian Constitutional Court).
Harksen v Lane CCT 9/97, 2 LRC 171 (CC SA).
Decision No P 2/98 OTK ZU No 1/1999 (Polish Constitutional Tribunal).
Decision on the Procedure for the Repayment in Cash to Persons who were Granted Vouchers for the Former Landed Property in Rural Areas in case No 04–01 (99) (Latvian Constitutional Court).
Decision No K 8/98 OTK ZU 3/2000, poz 87 (Polish Constitutional Tribunal).
Decision No K 14/99 OTK ZU 2/2000, poz 61 (Polish Constitutional Tribunal).
Decision of 16 May 2000 in case No 8-P (Russian Constitutional Court).
Decision on membership in the associations of apartment house owners in case No 8/99 (Lithuanian Constitutional Court).
Decision on the reorganisation of the joint-stock companies 'Būtingės nafta', 'Mažeikių nafta', and 'Naftotiekis' in case No 29/98–16/99–3/2000 (Lithuanian Constitutional Court).
Decision on the Saeima Election Law and the Law on Electing City Council and County Council in case No 2000–03-01 (Latvian Constitutional Court).
Pope & Talbot Inc v Government of Canada (UNCITRAL).
Decision of 3 July 2001 in case No 10-P (Russian Constitutional Court).
Decision of 13 December 2001 in case No 16-P (Russian Constitutional Court).
Decision on the restoration of the ownership rights of citizens to land in case No 18/99 (Lithuanian Constitutional Court).
Genin v Estonia 6 ICSID Rep 241.
Decision of 24 February 2002 in case No 3-P (Russian Constitutional Court).

Decision on Amendments to the Cabinet of Ministers Regulation 'On Keeping Dogs and Cats' in case No 2002–01-03 (Latvian Constitutional Court).

Decision on Principles of Ownership Reform Act in case No 3–4-1–5-02 (Estonian Supreme Court).

Tahoe-Sierra Preservation Council, Inc v Tahoe Regional Planning Agency 122 S Ct 1465, 1483.

Decision No K20/02 OTK ZU 7A/2003 poz 76 (Polish Constitution Tribunal).

Decision of 6 November 2003 in case No 387-O (Russian Constitutional Court).

Decision of 10 April 2003 in case No 5-P (Russian Constitutional Court).

Decision on the state pensions of officials and servicemen in a cases No 46/2001–48/2001–50/2001–2/2002–6/2002–18/2002 (Lithuanian Constitutional Court).

Decision of 24 February 2004 in case No 3-P (Russian Constitutional Court)*Decision of 30 April 2004 in case No 3–4-1–3-04* (Estonian Supreme Court).

Decision K 9/04 OTK ZU 3A/2005, poz 24 (Polish Constitutional Tribunal).

Decision No P 25/02 OTK ZU No 6/A/2005 (Polish Constitutional Tribunal).

Decision of 10 March 2005 in case No 97-O (Russian Constitutional Court).

Decision of 15 February 2005 in case No 59-O (Russian Constitutional Court)*Decision of 18 March 2005 in case No 3–2-1–59-04* (Estonian Supreme Court).

Decision of 31 May 2005 in case No 6-P (Russian Constitutional Court).

Decision on Amendments to Law 'On Coercive Expropriation of Real Estate for State or Public Needs' in case No 2005–12-0103 (Latvian Constitutional Court).

Canadian Pacific Railway Co v Vancouver (City) SCC 5, 1 SCR 227.

Decision of 8 March 2006 in case No 2005–16-01 (Latvian Constitutional Court).

Decision on the invalidation of the Tallinn City decision for Return of and Compensation for Unlawfully Expropriated Property in case No 3–3-1–63-05 (Estonian Supreme Court) *Du Toit v Minister of Transport* 1 SA 297 (Constitutional Court of South Africa).

Decision of 3 July 2007 in case No 714-O-P (Russian Constitutional Court).

Decision on the Spatial Plan of Limbaži in case No 2006–38-03 (Latvian Constitutional Court).

Decision on the Tax on Pensions in case No 2007–01-01 (Latvian Constitutional Court).

Siemens AG v Argentine Republic ((ICSID) Case No ARB/02/8).

Teng Fuh Holdings Pte Ltd v Collector of Land Revenue 2 SLR 568.

Decision of the of 16 July 2008 in case No 9-P (Russian Constitutional Court).

Cases Nos 293142/HA ZA 07–2538, 296094/HA ZA 07–3089 and 306147/HA ZA 08–756 (Rechtbank's Gravenhage) *Decision in case No AS-143–92-09* (Lithuanian Supreme Administrative Court).

Decision of 16 April 2009 in case No 495-O-O (Russian Constitutional Court).

Decision of 23 June 2009 in case No 662-O-O (Russian Constitutional Court).

Decision on certain provisions of the Criminal Code regulating criminal liability of legal persons in cases No 34/2008–36/2008–40/2008–1/2009–4/2009–5/2009–6/2009–7/2009–9/2009–12/2009–13/2009–14/2009–17/2009–18/2009–19/2009–20/2009–22/2009 (Lithuanian Constitutional Court).

Decision on territorial planning in case No 16/07–17/07–20/08 (Lithuanian Constitutional Court).

Decision on the Expropriation of Immoveable Property (The Border Checkpoint Terehova) in case No 2009–01-01 (Latvian Constitutional Court).

Decision regarding changes to territorial planning in case No 2008–38-03 (Latvian Constitutional Court).

Decision regarding forced leased agreements in case No 2008–34-01 (Latvian Constitutional Court).

Decision regarding the requirements for companies to re-register in case No 2009–113-0106 (Latvian Constitutional Court).

Eng Foong Ho & Ors v Attorney-General 2 SLR 542.

ICM Agriculture Pty Ltd & Ors v The Commonwealth of Australia 240 CLR 140 *Private Taking decision of 24 September 2009* case No 2007Hun-Ba114 (Korean Constitutional Court).

Decision in case No 3K-3–143/2010 (Lithuanian Supreme Court).

Decision on Compulsory Social Insurance in Respect of Accidents at Work and Occupational Diseases in case No 2010–17-01 (Latvian Constitutional Court).

Decision on Regulations on Financial Assistance Quotas for Biofuel in case No 2010–12-03 (Latvian Constitutional Court).

Decision on State Funded Pensions in case No 2010–21-01 (Latvian Constitutional Court).

Decision on termination of proceedings in case No 2009–100-03 (Latvian Constitutional Court).

Decision regarding bio-fuel subsidies and others in case No 2010–12-03 (Latvian Constitutional Court).

Decision regarding the taxation of dividends in case No 2010–25-01 (Latvian Constitutional Court).

Merrill & Ring Forestry LP v Government of Canada (UNCITRAL, ICSID Administrated).

Total SA v Argentine Republic (ICSID).

Decision of 12 May 2011 in case No 7-P (Russian Constitutional Court).

Decision of 22 April 2011 in case No 5-P (Russian Constitutional Court).

Decision on Compliance of the Binding Regulation 'On Spatial Plans of Rucava County' in the Part of Establishing Wind Energy Zone in the Territory of Dunika Parish in case No 2010–48-03 (Latvian Constitutional Court).

Decision on Increasing the State's Participation in a Credit Institution in case No 2010–71-01 (Latvian Constitutional Court).

Decision on Public Procurement Law in case No 2011–05-01 (Latvian Constitutional Court)*Decision in case No K 4/10* OTK ZU 9A/ 2012 poz 106 (Polish Constitutional Tribunal).

Decision No P 12/11 OTK ZU No 135/11/A/2012 (Polish Constitutional Tribunal).

Decision of 11 May 2012 in case No 758-O (Russian Constitutional Court).

Decision of 17 April 2012 in case No 3–4-1–25-11 (Estonian Supreme Court).

Decision of 24 December 2012 in case No 2353-O (Russian Constitutional Court).

Agri South Africa v Minister for Minerals and Energy ZACC 9.

Decision on compensation for urban land subject to purchase by the state in case No 5/ 2012 (Lithuanian Constitutional Court).

Decision on Credit Institutions Law in case No 2012–07-01 (Latvian Constitutional Court).

Decision on the restoration of ownership rights to leased land case No 28/2010 (Lithuanian Constitutional Court).

Decision of 7 October 2014 in case No 2026-O (Russian Constitutional Court).

Decision of 10 December 2014 No 31-P (Russian Constitutional Court).

Decision of 25 September 2014 in case No 2295-O (Russian Constitutional Court).

Decision on Binding Regulation on the Use of and Construction in the Territory of Culture and Recreation Park 'Mežaparks' in case No 2014–04-03 (Latvian Constitutional Court).

Decision on Compensation for Damages Caused by Animals under Special Protection in case No 2013–13-01 (Latvian Constitutional Court).

Decision of 4 June 2015 No 13-P (Russian Constitutional Court) *Decision of 14 August 2015 in case No 303-es15–5520* (Russian Supreme Court).

Decision on Control of Aid for Commercial Activity in case No 2014–36-01 (Latvian Constitutional Court).

Decision on Subsidized Electricity Tax Law in case No 2014–12-01 (Latvian Constitutional Court).

Decision on the Natural Resources Tax for Small Hydroelectric Power Stations in case No 2014–11-0103 (Latvian Constitutional Court).

Oxus Gold plc v Republic of Uzbekistan (UNCITRAL).

Tidewater Investment SRL and Tidewater Caribe, CA v Bolivarian Republic of Venezuela (ICSID).

Decision of 9 December 2016 in case No 2016–08-01 (Latvian Constitutional Court).

Decision of 12 April 2016 in case No 10-P (Russian Constitutional Court).

Decision of 13 December 2016 in case No 28-P (Russian Constitutional Court).

Decision on the Municipal Fee for the Maintenance and Development of the Municipality Infrastructure in Riga in case No 2015–13-03 (Latvian Constitutional Court).

Decision on Transitional Provisions of the Law 'On State Pensions' in case No 2016–03-01 (Latvian Constitutional Court).
Decisions of 10 November 2016 in case No 23-P (Russian Constitutional Court).
Decisions of 29 September 2016 in case No 1984-O (Russian Constitutional Court).
Bear Creek Mining Corporation v Republic of Peru (ICSID).
Decision of 19 January 2017 in case No 1-P (Russian Constitutional Court).
Casinos Austria International GmbH and Casinos Austria Aktiengesellschaft v. Argentine Republic (ICSID) Case No ARB/14/32, Decision on Jurisdiction 29 June 2018.
R (Mott) v Environment Agency UKSC 10.
UAB DMD Investment v BVI Visagino statybininkai and UAB Sėlių investicijos in case No e3K-3–399-219/2018 (Lithuanian Supreme Court).
European Commission v Hungary Case C 235/17 (ECJ (Grand Chamber)).
Magyar Farming and others v Hungary (ICSID) Case No ARB/17/27.
Decision on land use rights in case No 2022–02-01 (Latvian Constitutional Court).
Decision on confiscation of property obtained through criminal means in case No 2022–32-01 (Latvian Constitutional Court).

Papers and reports

Australian Law Reform Commission *Traditional Rights and Freedoms – Encroachments by Commonwealth Laws* (2015).
Behn D, Berge TL and Langford M, 'Poor states or poor governance? Testing claims of systemic bias in investment treaty arbitration' University of Oslo Faculty of Law Research Paper No 2016–08.
Borchard E, 'Minimum Standard of the Treatment of Aliens' Faculty Scholarship Series.
Ducrocq MI, 'The Debate on Property during the First English Revolution 1647–1659: A Historical Perspective' Miranda.
Grgic A and others, 'The right to property under the European Convention on Human Rights: a guide to the implementation of the European Convention on Human Rights and its protocols' (Council of Europe 2007).
International Chamber of Commerce, *Fair Treatment for Foreign Investment. International Code* (1949).
Muchlinski P, *Scope and Definition* (UNCTAD Series on Issues in International Investment Agreements II, 2011).
Späth J, 'The End of an Era: The Decline of Neoliberalism and the Emerging Interregnum' Trend Report.

UNCTAD, 'International investment agreements trends: The increasing dichotomy between new and old treaties' IIA Issues Note No 2.

UNCTAD series on issues in international investment agreements II (2012).

World Bank, *Involuntary Resettlement in Brazil: A Review of Policies and Practices* (2011).

Yannaca-Small C and OECD, *'Indirect Expropriation' and the 'Right to Regulate' in International Investment Law* (2004).

Encyclopedias

Irani PK, *India, International Encyclopedia of Comparative Law* (Mohr Siebeck 1973).

Khaitan T, *Discrimination*, Max Planck Encyclopedia of Comparative Constitutional Law (2017).

Merwe Cvd, Pienaar JM and Waal MJd, *South Africa, International Encyclopaedia of Laws: Property and Trust Law* (Kluwer Law International 2015).

Articles

Aaviksoo B, 'Judicial Activism in Constitutional Review Decisions of the Supreme Court of Estonia' XIII Juridica International.

A. B M, 'Expropriation of Alien Property' 109 University of Pennsylvania Law Review 245.

Adeleke F, 'Human rights and international investment arbitration' [Routledge] 32 South African Journal on Human Rights 48.

Alexander GS, 'Property as a fundamental constitutional right?: the German example' 88 Cornell Law Review 733.

Alexander GS, 'The Sporting Life: Democratic Culture and the Historical Origins of the Scottish Right to Roam' [University of Illinois Press] 2016 University of Illinois Law Review 321.

Alexandre dos Santos C, 'The Social Function of Property in Brazilian Law' 80 Fordham Law Review.

Almutawa A, 'The Arab Court of Human Rights and the Enforcement of the Arab Charter on Human Rights' 21 Human Rights Law Review 506.

Alvarez JE, 'The Human Right of Property' 72 University of Miami Law Review.

Amunategui Perello CF, 'The Definition of Property in Andrés Bello's Code and the Limits of Use against the Rights of Others' [Osaka University] 57 Osaka University Law Review.

Antinori MR, 'Does Lochner Live in Luxembourg: An Analysis of the Property Rights Jurisprudence of the European Court of Justice Note' 18 Fordham International Law Journal 1778.

Antinori MR, 'Does Lochner Live in Luxembourg? An Analysis of the Property Rights Jurisprudence of the European Court of Justice' 18 Fordham International Law Journal 1778.

Arato J, 'The Private Law Critique of International Investment Law' 113 American Journal of International Law 1.

Atuahene B, 'Property Rights & the Demands of Transformation' 31 Michigan Journal of International Law 765.

Baetens F, 'Judicial Review of International Adjudicatory Decisions: A Cross-Regime Comparison of Annulment and Appellate Mechanisms' 8 Journal of International Dispute Settlement 432.

Baltag C, Joshi R and Duggal K, 'Recent Trends in Investment Arbitration on the Right to Regulate, Environment, Health and Corporate Social Responsibility: Too Much or Too Little?' 38 ICSID Review – Foreign Investment Law Journal 381.

Barrera EB, 'Property Rights as Human Rights in International Investment Arbitration: A Critical Approach' 59 Boston College Law Review.

Batselé F, 'Foreign Investors of the World, Unite! The International Association for the Promotion and Protection of Private Foreign Investments (APPI) 1958–1968' 34 European Journal of International Law 415.

Bauman RW, 'Property Rights in the Canadian Constitutional Context' 8 South African Journal on Human Rights 344.

Baxter Richard R, 'Multilateral Treaties as Evidence of Customary International Law' 44 British Yearbook of International Law 275.

Been V and Beauvais JC, 'The Global Fifth Amendment? NAFTA's Investment Protections and the Misguided Quest for an International "Regulatory Takings" Doctrine' 78 New York University Law Review.

Bílková V, 'Sovereignty, Property and the Russian Revolution' 19 Journal of the History of International Law 147.

Bjørnskov C, 'Constitutional property rights protection and economic growth: evidence from the post-communist transition' 26 Constitutional Political Economy 247.

Boas TC and Gans-Morse J, 'Neoliberalism: From New Liberal Philosophy to Anti-Liberal Slogan' 44 Studies in Comparative International Development.

Boyce B, 'Property as a Natural Right and as a Conventional Right in Constitutional Law"29 Loyola of Los Angeles International and Comparative Law Review.

Bray HL, 'The Neer Rumour' 25 Hague Yearbook of International Law.

Brenninkmeijer M and Gélinas F, 'Counterclaims in Investment Arbitration: Towards an Integrated Approach' 38 ICSID Review – Foreign Investment Law Journal 567.

Broek PVD, 'The protection of property rights under the European Convention on Human Rights' Legal Issues of European Integration 52.

Brower CN, 'Current Developments in the Law of Expropriation and Compensation: a Preliminary Survey of Awards of the Iran-United States Claims Tribunal' 21 The International Lawyer.

Chatterjee C, 'Bias in Arbitrators and Bias against Arbitrators?' (Netherland) [BRILL] 3 The Journal of World Investment & Trade 369.

Chew B and others, 'Compulsory Acquisition of Land in Singapore: A Fair Regime?' 22 Singapore Academy of Law Journal 166.

Baltag C, Joshi R and Duggal K, 'Recent Trends in Investment Arbitration on the Right to Regulate, Environment, Health and Corporate Social Responsibility: Too Much or Too Little?' 38 ICSID Review – Foreign Investment Law Journal 381.

Barrera EB, 'Property Rights as Human Rights in International Investment Arbitration: A Critical Approach' 59 Boston College Law Review.

Batselé F, 'Foreign Investors of the World, Unite! The International Association for the Promotion and Protection of Private Foreign Investments (APPI) 1958–1968' 34 European Journal of International Law 415.

Bauman RW, 'Property Rights in the Canadian Constitutional Context' 8 South African Journal on Human Rights 344.

Baxter Richard R, 'Multilateral Treaties as Evidence of Customary International Law' 44 British Yearbook of International Law 275.

Been V and Beauvais JC, 'The Global Fifth Amendment? NAFTA's Investment Protections and the Misguided Quest for an International "Regulatory Takings" Doctrine' 78 New York University Law Review.

Bílková V, 'Sovereignty, Property and the Russian Revolution' 19 Journal of the History of International Law 147.

Bjørnskov C, 'Constitutional property rights protection and economic growth: evidence from the post-communist transition' 26 Constitutional Political Economy 247.

Boas TC and Gans-Morse J, 'Neoliberalism: From New Liberal Philosophy to Anti-Liberal Slogan' 44 Studies in Comparative International Development.

Boyce B, 'Property as a Natural Right and as a Conventional Right in Constitutional Law''29 Loyola of Los Angeles International and Comparative Law Review.

Bray HL, 'The Neer Rumour' 25 Hague Yearbook of International Law.

Brenninkmeijer M and Gélinas F, 'Counterclaims in Investment Arbitration: Towards an Integrated Approach' 38 ICSID Review – Foreign Investment Law Journal 567.

Broek PVD, 'The protection of property rights under the European Convention on Human Rights' Legal issues of European integration 52.

Brower CN, 'Current Developments in the Law of Expropriation and Compensation: a Preliminary Survey of Awards of the Iran-United States Claims Tribunal' 21 The International Lawyer.

Chatterjee C, 'Bias in Arbitrators and Bias against Arbitrators?' (Netherland) [BRILL] 3 The Journal of World Investment & Trade 369.

Chew B and others, 'Compulsory Acquisition of Land in Singapore: A Fair Regime?' 22 Singapore Academy of Law Journal 166.

Christie G, 'What Constitutes a Taking of Property under International Law?' British Yearbook of International Law 307.

Clark JA, 'Eminent Domain and Expropriation: A Comparison between Fifth Amendment Precedent and Latin American Land Redistribution' 28 Regent University Law Review.

Clover Alcolea L, 'The importance of property in international investment law' 16 Journal of International Dispute Settlement.

Cohen MR, 'Property and sovereignty' 13 Cornell Law Review.

Colly F, 'Le Conseil constitutionnel et le droit de propriete' (Paris) [Librairie Générale de Droit et de Jurisprudence] Revue Du Droit Public et De La Science Politique en France et À l'étranger.

Cotula L, 'Property in a shrinking planet: fault lines in international human rights and investment law' (Cambridge, UK) [Cambridge University Press] 11 International Journal of Law in Context 113.

De Brabandere E, 'The 2019 Dutch Model Bilateral Investment Treaty: Navigating the Turbulent Ocean of Investment Treaty Reform' 36 ICSID Review – Foreign Investment Law Journal 319.

Demsetz H, 'Toward a Theory of Property Rights' [American Economic Association] 57 The American Economic Review 347.

Diebold NF, 'Standards of Non-discrimination in International Economic Law' (Oxford) [Cambridge University Press] 60 International and Comparative Law Quarterly 831.

Dolzer R, 'New Foundations of the Law of Expropriation of Alien Property' [Cambridge University Press] 75 American Journal of International Law.

Dolzer R, 'Indirect Expropriation of Alien Property' 1 ICSID Review 41.

Doman NR, 'Postwar Nationalization of Foreign Property in Europe' [Columbia Law Review Association, Inc.] 48 Columbia Law Review 1125.

Doman NR, 'Compensation for Nationalised Property in Post-War Europe' 3 International Law Quarterly 323.

Donaubauer J, Neumayer E and Nunnenkamp P, 'Winning or losing in investor-to-state dispute resolution: The role of arbitrator bias and experience' (Oxford) [Blackwell Publishing Ltd] 26 Review of International Economics 892.

Douglas Z, 'The hybrid foundations of investment treaty arbitration' 74 British Yearbook of International Law 151.

Dumberry P, 'Are BITs Representing the 'New' Customary International Law in International Investment Law' 28 Penn State International Law Review.

Ederington LB, 'Property as a Natural Institution: The Separation of Property from Sovereignty in International Law' 13 American University International Law Review 263.

Fachiri AP, 'International Law and the Property of Aliens' 10 British Yearbook of International Law.

Fischer Williams J, 'International Law and the Property of Aliens' 9 British Yearbook of International Law.

Fortier LY and Drymer SL, 'Indirect Expropriation in the Law of International Investment: I Know It When I See It, or Caveat Investor' 19 ICSID Review 293.

Foster SR and Bonilla D, 'Introduction' 80 Fordham Law Review.

Franck SD, 'The Legitimacy Crisis in Investment Treaty Arbitration: Privatizing Public International Law Through Inconsistent Decisions' 73 Fordham Law Review.

Fry JD, 'International Human Rights Law in Investment Arbitration: Evidence of International Law's Unity' 18 Duke Journal of Comparative & International Law 77.

Gann PB, 'The US Bilateral Investment Treaty Program' 21 Stanford Journal of International Law.

Gans-Morse J, 'Threats to Property Rights in Russia: From Private Coercion to State Aggression' (Columbia) [V.H. Winston & Son, Inc] 28 Post-Soviet Affairs 263.

Gazzini T, 'The Role of Customary International Law in the Protection of Foreign Investment' 8 Journal of World Investment and Trade.

Ginsburg T, 'Confucian Constitutionalism? The Emergence of Constitutional Review in Korea and Taiwan' [Cambridge University Press] 27 Law & Social Inquiry 763.

Ginsburg T, 'Pitfalls of Measuring the Rule of Law' 3 Hague Journal on the Rule of Law 269.

Goldsmith AA, 'Democracy, property rights and economic growth' [Routledge] 32 The Journal of Development Studies 157.

Gray K, 'Property in Thin Air' 50 The Cambridge Law Journal.

Guha Roy SN, 'Is the Law of Responsibility of States for Injuries to Aliens a Part of Universal International Law?' 55 American Journal of International Law.

Guzman AT, 'Why LDCs sign treaties that hurt them: explaining the popularity of bilateral investment treaties' 38(4) Virginia Journal of International Law.

Haggard S, MacIntyre A and Tiede L, 'The Rule of Law and Economic Development' 11 Annual Review of Political Science 205.

Herman S, 'War Damage and Nationalization in Eastern Europe' [Duke University School of Law] 16 Law and Contemporary Problems 498.

Ho NP, 'A Confucian Theory of Property' 9 Tsinghua China Law Review 1.

Home R, "Culturally Unsuited to Property Rights?': Colonial Land Laws and African Societies' [Blackwell Publishing Ltd] 40 Journal of Law and Society 403.
Hutchinson MR, 'The margin of appreciation doctrine in the European Court of Human Rights' 48 International and Comparative Law Quarterly 638.
Hwang M and Fong Lee Cheng J, 'Definition of "Investment": a Voice from the Eye of the Storm' 1 The Asian Journal of International Law.
Jann EC, 'Private International Law in the Soviet Union and Eastern Europe' [Library of Congress] 22 The Quarterly Journal of the Library of Congress 347.
Johnson L and Volkov O, 'Investor-state contracts, host-state "commitments" and the myth of stability in international law' [Juris Publishing, Inc] 24 American Review of International Arbitration 361.
Joost P, 'The Rule of Law without the Rule of Lawyers? Why Investment Arbitrators are from Mars, Trade Adjudicators from Venus' [American Society of International Law, Cambridge University Press] 109 The American Journal of International Law 761.
Kaeckenbeeck G, 'The Character and Work of the Arbitral Tribunal of Upper Silesia' [Cambridge University Press] 21 Transactions of the Grotius Society 27.
Kaeckenbeeck G, 'The Protection of Vested Rights in International Law' 17 British Year Book of International Law.
Kainen JL, 'The Historical Framework for Reviving Constitutional Protection for Property and Contract Rights' 79 Cornell Law Review 87.
Kazimierz G, 'Reform of Civil Law in Hungary, Poland, and the Soviet Union' [American Society of Comparative Law] 10 The American Journal of Comparative Law 253.
Kishoiyian B, 'The utility of bilateral investment treaties in the formulation of customary international law' (Chicago) [Northwestern University, School of Law] 14 Northwestern Journal of International Law & Business 327.
Knack S and Keefer P, 'Institutions and economic performance: Cross-country tests using alternative institutional measures' (Oxford, UK) [Blackwell Publishing Ltd] 7 Economics & Politics 207.
Koskenniemi M, 'The politics of international law' 112 European Journal of International Law 4.
Koskenniemi M, 'The Advantage of Treaties: International Law in the Enlightenment' 13 The Edinburgh Law Review 27.
Koskenniemi M, 'Empire and International Law: The Real Spanish Contribution' 61 University of Toronto Law Journal University of Toronto Law Journal 1.
Koskenniemi M, 'Sovereignty, Property and Empire: Early Modern English Contexts' (Tel Aviv) [De Gruyter] 18 Theoretical Inquiries in Law 355.
Koskenniemi M and Leino P, 'Fragmentation of International Law? Postmodern Anxieties' [Cambridge University Press] 15 Leiden Journal of International Law 553.

Kriebaum U, 'Regulatory Takings: Balancing the Interests of the Investor and the State' 8 The Journal of World Investment & Trade 717.

Kriebaum U, 'The Right to Water Before Investment Tribunals' 1 Brill Open Law 16.

Kryvoi Y, 'Counterclaims in Investor-State Arbitration' Minnesota Journal of International Law 216.

Lametti D, 'General Concepts of Private Law Relating to Private Property in the Civil Code of the Russian Federation and in the Civil Code of Quebec' 30 Review of Central and East European Law 7.

Lametti D, 'Objects of Private Property in the Civil Code of the Russian Federation and in the Civil Code of Quebec' 30 Review of Central & East European Law 19.

Lametti D, 'Rights of Private Property in the Civil Code of the Russian Federation and in the Civil Code of Quebec' 30 Review of Central and East European Law 29.

Langford M and others, 'Special Issue: UNCITRAL and Investment Arbitration Reform: Matching Concerns and Solutions: An Introduction' 21 The Journal of World Investment & Trade 167.

Lauterpacht E, 'International Law and Private Foreign Investment' [Indiana University School of Law] 4 Indiana Journal of Global Legal Studies 259.

Leblang DA, 'Property Rights, Democracy and Economic Growth' 49 Political Research Quarterly 5.

Leiter A, 'Protecting concessionary rights: General principles and the making of international investment law' [Cambridge University Press] 35 Leiden Journal of International Law 55.

Levashova Y, 'The Right of Access to Water in the Context of Investment Disputes in Argentina: Urbaser and Beyond' 16 Utrecht Law Review 110.

Lin L and Allison JR, 'An Analysis of Expropriation and Nationalization Risk in China' 19 Yale Journal of International Law 135.

Long Q, 'Reinterpreting Chinese Property Law' 19 The Southern California Interdisciplinary Law Journal 55.

Lowe V, 'Regulation or Expropriation?' 55 Current Legal Problems 447.

Maggs PB, 'The Security of Individually-Owned Property under Soviet Law' Duke Law Journal 525.

Mälksoo L, 'The History of International Legal Theory in Russia: a Civilizational Dialogue with Europe' 19 European Journal of International Law.

Manji A, 'Land reform in the shadow of the state: The implementation of new land laws in Sub-Saharan Africa' (London) [Taylor & Francis Group] 22 Third World Quarterly 327.

Mann FA, 'Outlines of a History of Expropriation' (London) [Stevens and Sons] 75 Law Quarterly Review 188.

Martin A, 'Private Property, Rights and Interests in the Paris Peace Treaties' 24 British Year Book of International Law.

Martinkute I, 'The delimitation of contractual rights and property in international investment law' 1 European Investment Law and Arbitration Review 3.

McConnell MW, 'Contract Rights and Property Rights: A Case Study in the Relationship between Individual Liberties and Constitutional Structure' [California Law Review, Inc] 76 California Law Review 267.

McLachlan C, 'Investment Treaties and General International Law' 57 International and Comparative Law Quarterly.

McNulty WD, 'The Power of "Compulsory Purchase" under the Law of England' [The Yale Law Journal Company, Inc] 21 The Yale Law Journal 639.

Meijer GA and Meijer SYT, 'Influence of the Code Civil in the Netherlands' (Boston) [Kluwer Academic Publishers] 14 European Journal of Law and Economics 227.

Menon PK, 'The Traditional Hindu Law in India – Transformation from Customary to Codified Law' 16 Korean Journal of Comparative Law 105.

Merino R, 'The Land of Nations: Indigenous Struggles for Property and Territory in International Law' [Cambridge University Press] 115 AJIL Unbound 129.

Mirow MC, 'Borrowing private law in Latin American: Andrés Bello's use of the Code Napoléon in drafting the Chilean civil code' 61 Louisiana Law Review.

Mistelis LA, 'Award as an Investment: The Value of an Arbitral Award or the Cost of Non-Enforcement' 28 ICSID Review – Foreign Investment Law Journal 64.

Mountfield H, 'Regulatory Expropriations in Europe: the Approach of the European Court of Human Rights' [New York University School of Law] 11 New York University Environmental Law Journal 136.

Nafziger S, 'Communal property rights and land redistributions in Late Tsarist Russia' (Oxford) [Wiley Subscription Services, Inc] 69 The Economic History Review 773.

Naldi GJ, 'Limitation of rights under the African Charter on Human and Peoples' Rights: the contribution of the African Commission on Human and Peoples' Rights' 17 South African Journal on Human Rights 109.

Ortino F, 'The Social Dimension of International Investment Agreements: Drafting a New BIT/MIT Model?' 7 International Law Forum Du Droit International 243.

Ortino F, 'Investment Treaties, Sustainable Development and Reasonableness Review: A Case Against Strict Proportionality Balancing' (Cambridge) [Cambridge University Press] 30 Leiden Journal of International Law 71.

Paparinskis M, *'The International Minimum Standard and Fair and Equitable Treatment'* (OUP 2013).

Parvanov PP and Kantor M, 'Comparing U.S. law and recent U.S. investment agreements: Much more similar than you might expect' 2010–2011 Yearbook on International Investment Law and Policy.

Paulsson J and Petrochilos G, 'Neer-ly Misled?' 22 ICSID Review.

Perrone NM, 'The Emerging Global Right to Investment: Understanding the Reasoning behind Foreign Investor Rights' 8 Journal of International Dispute Settlement 673.

Peukert W, 'Protection of Ownership under Article I of the First Protocol to the European Convention on Human Rights' (Kehl am Rhein [West Germany]) [N.P. Engel] 2 Human Rights Law Journal.

Plotkin MA and Biske R, 'Legal status of foreigners in the USSR' (Moscow) [USSR chamber of commerce].

Porterfield M, 'State Practice and the (Purported) Obligation under Customary International Law to Provide Compensation for Regulatory Expropriations' 37 North Carolina Journal of International Law and Commercial Regulation 159.

Potestà M, 'Legitimate Expectations in Investment Treaty Law: Understanding the Roots and the Limits of a Controversial Concept' 28 ICSID Review – Foreign Investment Law Journal 88.

Puig S, 'Social Capital in the Arbitration Market' 25 European Journal of International Law 387.

Radin MJ, 'The Liberal Conception of Property: Cross Currents in the Jurisprudence of Takings' (New York, N. Y) [Columbia University School of Law] 88 Columbia Law Review 1667.

Raff M and Taitslin A, 'A Comparative Perspective on the Concept of Ownership in Russian Law: From the Svod Zakonov to the 1994 Civil Code' 41 Review of Central and East European Law.

Rajput A, 'Problems with the Jurisprudence of the Iran–US Claims Tribunal on Indirect Expropriation' 30 ICSID Review 589.

Ratner SR, 'Regulatory Takings in Institutional Context: Beyond the Fear of Fragmented International Law' [American Society of International Law] 102 The American Journal of International Law 475.

Ratner SR, 'International Investment Law and Domestic Investment Rules: Tracing the Upstream and Downstream Flows' 21 The Journal of World Investment & Trade 7.

Rattigan W, 'Customary Law in India' 10 Law Magazine and Law Review 1.

Rehm GM and Julius H, 'The New Chinese Property Rights Law: An Evaluation from a Continental Perspective' 22 Columbia Journal of Asian Law 177.

Reisman WM, 'The Regime for Lacunae in the ICSID Choice of Law Provision and the Question of Its Threshold' 15 ICSID Review 362.

Riffel C, 'International Investment Law, Rule of Law, and Democracy: When the Solution Is Part of the Problem' [Cambridge University Press] 26 German Law Journal 613.

Root E, 'The Basis of Protection to Citizens Residing Abroad' [American Society of International Law] 4 The American Journal of International Law.

Rose CM, 'Property as the Keystone Right?' 71 Notre Dame Law Review 329.

Rose CM, 'Property and Exporpriation: Themes and Variations in American Law' 1 Utah Law Review.

Rozenfelds J, 'Latvian Property and Collateral Law and Protection of Foreign Investments' 6 Juridica International 108.

Salgado RA, 'Protection of nationals' rights to property under the European Convention on Human Rights: Lithgow v. United Kingdom' 27 Virginia journal of international law – 865.

Sax J, 'Takings and the Police Power' 74 Yale Law Journal.

Schneiderman D, 'Property rights and regulatory innovation: Comparing constitutional cultures' [Oxford University Press] 4 International Journal of Constitutional Law 371.

Schneiderman D, "Writing the rules of the global economy': how America defines the contours of international investment law' 6 London Review of International Law 255.

Schuster EJ, 'The Peace Treaty in Its Effects on Private Property' 1 British Year Book of International Law.

Schwebel SM, 'The Influence of Bilateral Investment Treaties on Customary International Law' 98 American Society of International Law Proceedings.

Shevtsov VS, 'The legal status of foreigners in the USSR' 5 Denver Journal of International Law and Policy 273.

Shihata IFI and Parra AR, 'Applicable Substantive Law in Disputes Between States and Private Foreign Parties: The Case of Arbitration under the ICSID Convention' 9 ICSID Review 183.

Simma B, 'Foreign Investment Arbitration: a Place for Human Rights?' [Cambridge University Press] 60 The International and Comparative Law Quarterly 573.

Skaaning SE, 'Measuring the Rule of Law' 63 Political Research Quarterly 449.

Spears SA, 'The Quest for Policy Space in a New Generation of International Investment Agreements' 13 Journal of International Economic Law 1037.

Stern B, 'The Contours of the Notion of Protected Investment' 24 ICSID Review 534.

Stoebuck WB, 'A General Theory of Eminent Domain' 47 Washington Law Review 553.

Sukhanov Y, 'The Concept of Ownership in Current Russian Law' 6 Juridica International 102.

Summers LM, 'The Calvo Clause' [Virginia Law Review Association] 19 Virginia law review 459.

Svilpaite E, 'Constitution and the possibilities of limiting property rights' 30 Jurisprudencija.

Takatsuji M, 'Study on Property Right' 38 Jichi-Kenkyu.

Tamanaha B, 'The Dark Side of the Relationship between the Rule of Law and Liberalism' 3 New York University Journal of Law & Liberty 516.

Tushnet M, 'The Possibilities of Comparative Constitutional Law' (New Haven, Conn) [The Yale Law Journal Company] 108 The Yale Law Journal 1225.

Underkuffler-Freund LS, 'Takings and the Nature of Property' 9 Canadian Journal of Law and Jurisprudence.

Vadi VS, 'Through the Looking-Glass: International Investment Law through the Lens of a Property Theory' 8 Manchester Journal of International Economic Law 22.

van Aaken A, 'Fragmentation of International Law: The Case of International Investment Protection' 17 Finnish Yearbook of International Law 91.

Vandevelde KJ, 'The Bilateral Investment Treaty Program of the United States' 21 Cornell International Law Journal.

Vandevelde KJ, 'U.S. Bilateral Investment Treaties: The Second Wave' 14 Michigan Journal of International Law.

Vandevelde KJ, 'Sustainable liberalism and the international investment regime' [University of Michigan Law School] 19 Michigan Journal of International Law 373.

Varul P, 'Legal Policy Decisions and Choices in the Creation of New Private Law in Estonia' 5 Juridica International 104.

Vaskela G, 'The Land Reform of 1919–1940: Lithuania and the Countries of Eastern and Central Europe' 1 Lithuanian Historical Studies 116.

von Bernstorff J, 'The Use of Force in International Law before World War I: On Imperial Ordering and the Ontology of the Nation-State' 29 European Journal of International Law 233.

Walt Avd, ' Towards the Development of Post-apartheid Land Law: An Exploratory Survey' 23 De Jure.

Washburn VJ, 'Regular takings or regulatory takings? Land expropriation in rural China' (Seattle, WA) [Students of the University of Washington School of Law] Pacific Rim Law & Policy Journal 124.

Weiler JHH, 'Eurocracy and distrust: some questions concerning the role of the European Court of Justice in the protection of fundamental human rights within the legal order of the European Communities' (Seattle) [Washington Law Review Association] 61 Washington Law Review 1103.

Zarbiyev F, ''These are my principles. If you don't like them I have others.' On justifications of foreign investment protection under international law' 26 Journal of International Economic Law 525.

Zhang M, 'From public to private: The newly enacted Chinese property law and the protection of property rights in China' 5 Berkeley Business Law Journal 317.

Zhang T, 'Social Hierarchies and the Formation of Customary Property Law in Pre-industrial China and England' [American Journal of Comparative Law] 62 American Journal of Comparative Law 171.

Malleret C, 'Controversial Brazil Law Curbing Indigenous Rights Comes into Force' *The Guardian* (28 December 2023).

Legislation and Treaties

Declaration of the Rights of Man and of the Citizen 1789 (France).
The Fifth Amendment of the United States Constitution 1791 (the USA).
Civil Code 1804 (France).
Lands Clauses Consolidation Act 1845 (the UK).
Expropriation Act 1851 (Netherlands).
BGB 1900 (Germany).
Commonwealth of Australia Constitution Act 1900 (Australia).
Constitution of the Republic of Latvia 1922 (Latvia).
Government of India Act 1935 (India).
Civil Law Act 1937 (Latvia).
Federal Decree-law on Expropriation for Public Purposes No 3.365 1941 (Brazil).
Constitution of Japan 1946 (Japan).
Constitution of the Republic of Korea 1948 (S Korea).
Universal Declaration of Human Rights 1948.
Basic Law for the Federal Republic of Germany 1949 (Germany).
Constitution of India 1949 (India).
European Convention on Human Rights 1950.
Convention relating to the Status of Refugees 1951.
Land Expropriation Law No 219 1951 (Japan).
Convention relating to the Status of Stateless Persons 1954.
Constitution of France 1958.
Bill of Rights 1960 (Canada).
Land Compensation Act 1961 (the UK).
Law of Special Measure for Land Acquisition No 150 1961 (Japan).
Cabinet decisions on the Guideline of Standard for Compensation for Loss Caused by Acquisition of Land for Public Use 1962 (Japan).
Federal Law on Expropriation for Social Interest No 4,132 1962 (Brazil).
Compulsory Purchase Act 1965 (the UK).
International Convention on the Elimination of All Forms of Racial Discrimination 1965.
International Covenant on Civil and Political Rights the International Covenant on Economic, Social, and Cultural Rights 1966.

Land Acquisition Act No 41 1966 (Singapore).
The Guideline of Standard for Compensation for Public Loss Caused by Execution of Public Project 1967 (Japan).
American Convention on Human Rights 1969.
Expropriation for Public Interest code 1977 (France).
International Convention on the Elimination of All Forms of Discrimination against Women 1979.
Constitution of the People's Republic of China 1982 (China).
Expropriation Act (RSC, c E-21) 1985 (Canada).
Housing Act 1985 (the UK).
Treaty between the United States of America and the Republic of Turkey concerning the Reciprocal Encouragement and Protection of Investments 1985.
General Principles of the Civil Law 1986 (China).
Law on the Administration of Land 1986 (China).
Constitution of the Federal Republic of Brazil 1988 (Brazil).
International Labour Organization Convention No 169 concerning Indigenous and Tribal Peoples 1989.
Lands Acquisition Act 1989 (Australia).
Constitution of the Republic of Namibia 1990 (Namibia).
International Convention on the Protection of the Rights of All Migrant Workers and Members of Their Families 1990.
Provisional Regulation on Transfer and Surrender of Rights of Use to Urban State-owned Land in China No 55 1990 (China).
Town and Country Planning Act 1990 (the UK).
Treaty Between the United States of America and the Republic of Poland Concerning Business and Economic Relations 1990.
Planning and Compensation Act 1991 (the UK).
Constitution of the Republic of Estonia 1992 (Estonia).
Constitution of the Republic of Lithuania 1992 (Lithiania).
Law on Environmental Protection No I-2223 1992 (Lithuania).
Constitution of the Russian Federation 1993 (Russia).
Land law No I-446 1994 (Lithuania).
Constitution of the Republic of South Africa 1996 (S Africa).
Constitution of Poland 1997 (Poland).
Constitution of the Federal Republic of Nigeria 1999 (Nigeria).
Foreign Investment Law 1999 (Russia).
Land Code No 136-F3 2001 (Russia).
Law on Forests No IX-240 2001 (Lithuania).
Act on Acquisition of and Compensation for Land for Public Works Projects 2002 (S Korea).

Disarmament Statute No 10.826 2003 (Brazil).
Land Planning Act 2003 (Poland).
Arab Charter on Human Rights 2004.
Law on Protection of Immovable Cultural Heritage No IX-2452 2004 (Lithuania).
Planning and Compulsory Purchase Act 2004 (the UK).
Convention on the Rights of Persons with Disabilities 2006.
Property Laws 2007 (China).
Constitution of the Kingdom of the Netherlands 1983 (Netherlands).
Law on Protection of Movable Cultural Valuables No X-1682 2008 (Lithuania).
Charter of Fundamental Rights of the European Union 2009.
Law on Expropriation of Real Estate Necessary for Public Purposes 2010 (Latvia).
Law on taking a land in the interest of society for special projects of state importance No XI-1307 2011 (Lithuania).
Constitution of Zimbabwe Amendment (No 20) Act 2013 (Zimbabwe).
Law on Zoning and Planning of Territories No XII-407 2013 (Lithuania).
The Right to Fair Compensation and Transparency in Land Acquisition, Rehabilitation and Resettlement Act 2013 (India).
Environment and Planning Act (Omgevingswet) 2016 (Netherlands).
EU-Canada Comprehensive Economic and Trade Agreement 2016.
Law on Construction No XII-2573 2016 (Lithuania).
EU – Singapore Investment Protection Agreement 2018.
Immovables Expropriation Act No 274 2018 (Estonia).
The EU-Vietnam Investment Protection Agreement 2019.
Land Law No XIV-1311 2022 (Lithuania).
The Act on Security Screening of Investments, Mergers and Acquisitions (Wet veiligheidstoets investeringen, fusies en overnames) 2023 (Netherlands).
Law on Protected Territories No XIV-2350 2023 (Lithuania).
Expropriation Act No 13 2024 (S Africa).

Theses

Munhoz L, 'The environmental limitations to property rights in Brazil and the United States of America' (Pace University 2014).

Nissel TA, 'A History of State Responsibility: The Struggle for International Standards (1870–1960)' (Doctoral Dissertation, University of Helsinki 2016).

Roth AH, 'The minimum standard of international law applied to aliens' (Leiden AW Sijthoff 1949).

Sijde Evd, 'Reconsidering the relationship between property and regulation: A systemic constitutional approach' (Doctor of Laws, Stellenbosch University 2015).

Index